Chevrolet Sprint & Geo Metro Automotive Repair Manual

**by Larry Warren
and John H Haynes**
Member of the Guild of Motoring Writers

Models covered:
Chevrolet Sprint – 1985 through 1988
Geo Metro – 1989 through 1991

ABCDE
FGHIJ
KLMNO
PQRST

Haynes Publishing Group
Sparkford Nr Yeovil
Somerset BA22 7JJ England

Haynes Publications, Inc
861 Lawrence Drive
Newbury Park
California 91320 USA

Acknowledgements

We are grateful for the help and cooperation of Chevrolet Motor Division of General Motors Corporation for assistance with tecnical information, certain illustrations and vehicle photos. The Champion Spark Plug Company supplied the illustrations of various spark plug conditions. Technical writers who contributed to this project include Mike Stubblefield, Ken Freund, Robert Maddox and Brian Styve.

A book in the **Haynes Automotive Repair Manual Series**

Printed in the USA

ISBN 1 85010 727 0

Library of Congress Catalog Card Number 91-71158

Contents

1990 Geo Metro

About this manual

Its purpose

The purpose of this manual is to help you get the best value from your vehicle. It can do so in several ways. It can help you decide what work must be done, even if you choose to have it done by a dealer service department or a repair shop; it provides information and procedures for routine maintenance and servicing; and it offers diagnostic and repair procedures to follow when trouble occurs.

We hope you use the manual to tackle the work yourself. For many simpler jobs, doing it yourself may be quicker than arranging an appointment to get the vehicle into a shop and making the trips to leave it and pick it up. More importantly, a lot of money can be saved by avoiding the expense the shop must pass on to you to cover its labor and overhead costs. An added benefit is the sense of satisfaction and accomplishment that you feel after doing the job yourself.

Using the manual

The manual is divided into Chapters. Each Chapter is divided into numbered Sections, which are headed in bold type between horizontal lines. Each Section consists of consecutively numbered paragraphs.

At the beginning of each numbered Section you will be referred to any illustrations which apply to the procedures in that Section. The reference numbers used in illustration captions pinpoint the pertinent Section and the Step within that Section. That is, illustration 3.2 means the illustration refers to Section 3 and Step (or paragraph) 2 within that Section.

Procedures, once described in the text, are not normally repeated. When it's necessary to refer to another Chapter, the reference will be given as Chapter and Section number. Cross references given without use of the word "Chapter" apply to Sections and/or paragraphs in the same Chapter. For example, "see Section 8" means in the same Chapter.

References to the left or right side of the vehicle assume you are sitting in the driver's seat, facing forward.

Even though we have prepared this manual with extreme care, neither the publisher nor the author can accept responsibility for any errors in, or omissions from, the information given.

NOTE

A **Note** provides information necessary to properly complete a procedure or information which will make the procedure easier to understand.

CAUTION

A **Caution** provides a special procedure or special steps which must be taken while completing the procedure where the **Caution** is found. Not heeding a **Caution** can result in damage to the assembly being worked on.

WARNING

A **Warning** provides a special procedure or special steps which must be taken while completing the procedure where the **Warning** is found. Not heeding a **Warning** can result in personal injury.

Introduction to the Chevrolet Sprint/Geo Metro

These models are available in two and four-door hatchback body styles.

The transversely-mounted inline three-cylinder engines used in these models are equipped with either a carburetor or fuel injection.

The engine drives the front wheels through a manual or automatic transaxle via independent driveaxles.

Independent suspension, featuring coil springs and struts, is used at the front wheels. At the rear, a beam axle with leaf or coil springs and shock absorbers is used on Sprint models, while Geo models have independent suspension with struts. The rack and pinion steering unit is mounted behind the engine.

The brakes on most models are disc at the front and drums at the rear, with power assist standard.

Vehicle identification numbers

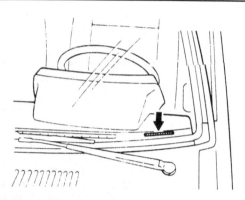

The Vehicle Identification Number (VIN) is visible from outside the vehicle through the driver's side of the windshield

Modifications are a continuing and unpublicized process in vehicle manufacturing. Since spare parts lists are compiled on a numerical basis, the individual vehicle numbers are essential to correctly identify the component required.

Vehicle Identification Number (VIN)

This very important identification number is stamped on a plate attached to the left side of the dashboard, just inside the windshield on the driver's side of the vehicle (see illustration). The VIN also appears on the Vehicle Certificate of Title and Registration. It contains information such as the vehicle model, engine type and when it was manufactured.

Engine identification number

The engine identification number is stamped into the front side of the block at the rear (transaxle) end (see illustration). It tells what type of engine it is, its displacement and when it was produced. This number is often required when ordering parts.

Transaxle identification number

On manual transaxles, the ID number is stamped into the case near the transaxle-to-engine mating surface and clutch release lever (see illustration).

Service parts identification label

This label is located on the glove compartment door, the spare tire cover or the load floor at the rear of the vehicle. It lists the VIN, model designation, paint information and production operations and special equipment. Refer to this label when ordering parts and do not remove it from the vehicle for any reason.

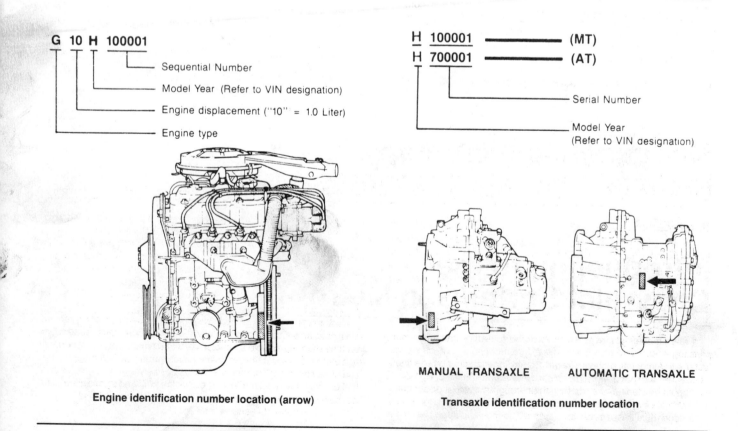

```
G  10  H  100001
                └─── Sequential Number
          └─────── Model Year (Refer to VIN designation)
      └─────────── Engine displacement ("10" = 1.0 Liter)
   └────────────── Engine type
```

```
H  100001 ──────── (MT)
H  700001 ──────── (AT)
          └──────── Serial Number
   └─────────────── Model Year
                    (Refer to VIN designation)
```

Engine identification number location (arrow)

MANUAL TRANSAXLE   AUTOMATIC TRANSAXLE

Transaxle identification number location

Buying parts

Replacement parts are available from many sources, which generally fall into one of two categories – authorized dealer parts departments and independent retail auto parts stores. Our advice concerning these parts is as follows:

Retail auto parts stores: Good auto parts stores will stock frequently needed components which wear out relatively fast, such as clutch components, exhaust systems, brake parts, tune-up parts, etc. These stores often supply new or reconditioned parts on an exchange basis, which can save a considerable amount of money. Discount auto parts stores are often very good places to buy materials and parts needed for general vehicle maintenance such as oil, grease, filters, spark plugs, belts, touch-up paint, bulbs, etc. They also usually sell tools and general accessories, have con-

venient hours, charge lower prices and can often be found not far from home.

Authorized dealer parts department: This is the best source for parts which are unique to the vehicle and not generally available elsewhere (such as major engine parts, transmission parts, trim pieces, etc.).

Warranty information: If the vehicle is still covered under warranty, be sure that any replacement parts purchased – regardless of the source – do not invalidate the warranty!

To be sure of obtaining the correct parts, have engine and chassis numbers available and, if possible, take the old parts along for positive identification.

Maintenance techniques, tools and working facilities

Maintenance techniques

There are a number of techniques involved in maintenance and repair that will be referred to throughout this manual. Application of these techniques will enable the home mechanic to be more efficient, better organized and capable of performing the various tasks properly, which will ensure that the repair job is thorough and complete.

Fasteners

Fasteners are nuts, bolts, studs and screws used to hold two or more parts together. There are a few things to keep in mind when working with fasteners. Almost all of them use a locking device of some type, either a lockwasher, locknut, locking tab or thread adhesive. All threaded fasteners should be clean and straight, with undamaged threads and undamaged corners on the hex head where the wrench fits. Develop the habit of replacing all damaged nuts and bolts with new ones. Special locknuts

with nylon or fiber inserts can only be used once. If they are removed, they lose their locking ability and must be replaced with new ones.

Rusted nuts and bolts should be treated with a penetrating fluid to ease removal and prevent breakage. Some mechanics use turpentine in a spout-type oil can, which works quite well. After applying the rust penetrant, let it work for a few minutes before trying to loosen the nut or bolt. Badly rusted fasteners may have to be chiseled or sawed off or removed with a special nut breaker, available at tool stores.

If a bolt or stud breaks off in an assembly, it can be drilled and removed with a special tool commonly available for this purpose. Most automotive machine shops can perform this task, as well as other repair procedures, such as the repair of threaded holes that have been stripped out.

Flat washers and lockwashers, when removed from an assembly, should always be replaced exactly as removed. Replace any damaged washers with new ones. Never use a lockwasher on any soft metal surface (such as aluminum), thin sheet metal or plastic.

Fastener sizes

For a number of reasons, automobile manufacturers are making wider and wider use of metric fasteners. Therefore, it is important to be able to tell the difference between standard (sometimes called U.S. or SAE) and metric hardware, since they cannot be interchanged.

All bolts, whether standard or metric, are sized according to diameter, thread pitch and length. For example, a standard 1/2 – 13 x 1 bolt is 1/2 inch in diameter, has 13 threads per inch and is 1 inch long. An M12 – 1.75 x 25 metric bolt is 12 mm in diameter, has a thread pitch of 1.75 mm (the distance between threads) and is 25 mm long. The two bolts are nearly identical, and easily confused, but they are not interchangeable.

In addition to the differences in diameter, thread pitch and length, metric and standard bolts can also be distinguished by examining the bolt heads. To begin with, the distance across the flats on a standard bolt head is measured in inches, while the same dimension on a metric bolt is sized in millimeters (the same is true for nuts). As a result, a standard wrench should not be used on a metric bolt and a metric wrench should not be used on a standard bolt. Also, most standard bolts have slashes radiating out from the center of the head to denote the grade or strength of the bolt, which is an indication of the amount of torque that can be applied to it. The greater the number of slashes, the greater the strength of the bolt. Grades 0 through 5 are commonly used on automobiles. Metric bolts have a property class (grade) number, rather than a slash, molded into their heads to indicate bolt strength. In this case, the higher the number, the stronger the bolt. Property class numbers 8.8, 9.8 and 10.9 are commonly used on automobiles.

Strength markings can also be used to distinguish standard hex nuts from metric hex nuts. Many standard nuts have dots stamped into one side, while metric nuts are marked with a number. The greater the number of dots, or the higher the number, the greater the strength of the nut.

Metric studs are also marked on their ends according to property class (grade). Larger studs are numbered (the same as metric bolts), while smaller studs carry a geometric code to denote grade.

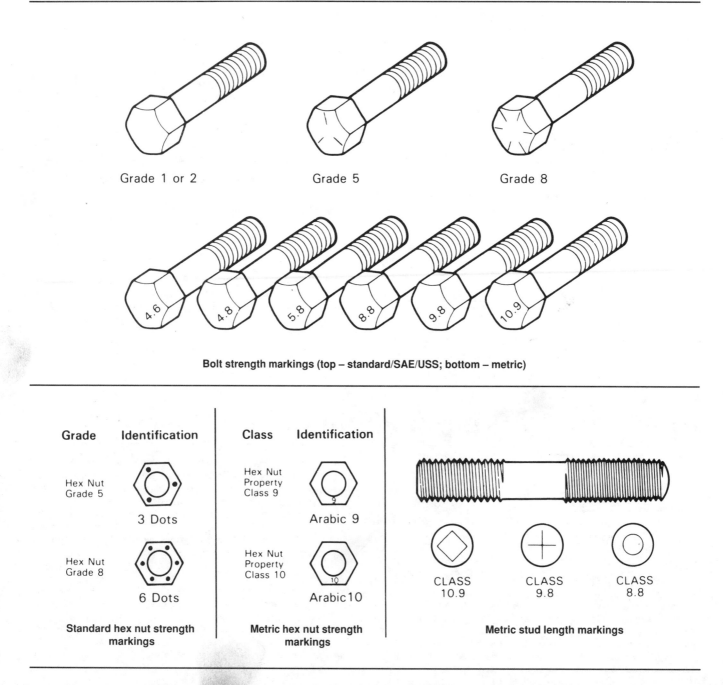

Bolt strength markings (top – standard/SAE/USS; bottom – metric)

Standard hex nut strength markings

Metric hex nut strength markings

Metric stud length markings

It should be noted that many fasteners, especially Grades 0 through 2, have no distinguishing marks on them. When such is the case, the only way to determine whether it is standard or metric is to measure the thread pitch or compare it to a known fastener of the same size.

Standard fasteners are often referred to as SAE, as opposed to metric. However, it should be noted that SAE technically refers to a non-metric *fine thread* fastener only. Coarse thread non-metric fasteners are referred to as USS sizes.

Since fasteners of the same size (both standard and metric) may have different strength ratings, be sure to reinstall any bolts, studs or nuts removed from your vehicle in their original locations. Also, when replacing a fastener with a new one, make sure that the new one has a strength rating equal to or greater than the original.

Tightening sequences and procedures

Most threaded fasteners should be tightened to a specific torque value (torque is the twisting force applied to a threaded component such as a nut or bolt). Overtightening the fastener can weaken it and cause it to break, while undertightening can cause it to eventually come loose. Bolts, screws and studs, depending on the material they are made of and their thread diameters, have specific torque values, many of which are noted in the Specifications at the beginning of each Chapter. Be sure to follow the torque recommendations closely. For fasteners not assigned a specific torque, a general torque value chart is presented here as a guide. These torque values are for dry (unlubricated) fasteners threaded into steel or cast iron (not aluminum). As was previously mentioned, the size and grade of a fastener determine the amount of torque that can safely be

Metric thread sizes	Ft-lbs	Nm
M-6	6 to 9	9 to 12
M-8	14 to 21	19 to 28
M-10	28 to 40	38 to 54
M-12	50 to 71	68 to 96
M-14	80 to 140	109 to 154

Pipe thread sizes		
1/8	5 to 8	7 to 10
1/4	12 to 18	17 to 24
3/8	22 to 33	30 to 44
1/2	25 to 35	34 to 47

U.S. thread sizes		
1/4 – 20	6 to 9	9 to 12
5/16 – 18	12 to 18	17 to 24
5/16 – 24	14 to 20	19 to 27
3/8 – 16	22 to 32	30 to 43
3/8 – 24	27 to 38	37 to 51
7/16 – 14	40 to 55	55 to 74
7/16 – 20	40 to 60	55 to 81
1/2 – 13	55 to 80	75 to 108

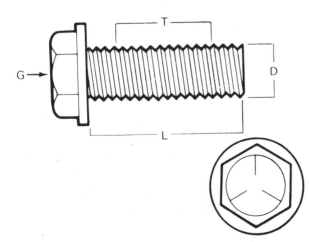

Standard (SAE and USS) bolt dimensions/grade marks

G   Grade marks (bolt length)
L   Length (in inches)
T   Thread pitch (number of threads per inch)
D   Nominal diameter (in inches)

Metric bolt dimensions/grade marks

P   Property class (bolt strength)
L   Length (in millimeters)
T   Thread pitch (distance between threads in millimeters)
D   Diameter

applied to it. The figures listed here are approximate for Grade 2 and Grade 3 fasteners. Higher grades can tolerate higher torque values.

Fasteners laid out in a pattern, such as cylinder head bolts, oil pan bolts, differential cover bolts, etc., must be loosened or tightened in sequence to avoid warping the component. This sequence will normally be shown in the appropriate Chapter. If a specific pattern is not given, the following procedures can be used to prevent warping.

Initially, the bolts or nuts should be assembled finger-tight only. Next, they should be tightened one full turn each, in a criss-cross or diagonal pattern. After each one has been tightened one full turn, return to the first one and tighten them all one-half turn, following the same pattern. Finally, tighten each of them one-quarter turn at a time until each fastener has been tightened to the proper torque. To loosen and remove the fasteners, the procedure would be reversed.

Component disassembly

Component disassembly should be done with care and purpose to help ensure that the parts go back together properly. Always keep track of the sequence in which parts are removed. Make note of special characteristics or marks on parts that can be installed more than one way, such as a grooved thrust washer on a shaft. It is a good idea to lay the disassembled parts out on a clean surface in the order that they were removed. It may also be helpful to make sketches or take instant photos of components before removal.

When removing fasteners from a component, keep track of their locations. Sometimes threading a bolt back in a part, or putting the washers and nut back on a stud, can prevent mix-ups later. If nuts and bolts cannot be returned to their original locations, they should be kept in a compartmented box or a series of small boxes. A cupcake or muffin tin is ideal for this purpose, since each cavity can hold the bolts and nuts from a particular area (i.e. oil pan bolts, valve cover bolts, engine mount bolts, etc.). A pan of this type is especially helpful when working on assemblies with very small parts, such as the carburetor, alternator, valve train or interior dash and trim pieces. The cavities can be marked with paint or tape to identify the contents.

Whenever wiring looms, harnesses or connectors are separated, it is a good idea to identify the two halves with numbered pieces of masking tape so they can be easily reconnected.

Gasket sealing surfaces

Throughout any vehicle, gaskets are used to seal the mating surfaces between two parts and keep lubricants, fluids, vacuum or pressure contained in an assembly.

Many times these gaskets are coated with a liquid or paste-type gasket sealing compound before assembly. Age, heat and pressure can sometimes cause the two parts to stick together so tightly that they are very difficult to separate. Often, the assembly can be loosened by striking it with a soft-face hammer near the mating surfaces. A regular hammer can be used if a block of wood is placed between the hammer and the part. Do not hammer on cast parts or parts that could be easily damaged. With any particularly stubborn part, always recheck to make sure that every fastener has been removed.

Avoid using a screwdriver or bar to pry apart an assembly, as they can easily mar the gasket sealing surfaces of the parts, which must remain smooth. If prying is absolutely necessary, use an old broom handle, but keep in mind that extra clean up will be necessary if the wood splinters.

After the parts are separated, the old gasket must be carefully scraped off and the gasket surfaces cleaned. Stubborn gasket material can be soaked with rust penetrant or treated with a special chemical to soften it so it can be easily scraped off. A scraper can be fashioned from a piece of copper tubing by flattening and sharpening one end. Copper is recommended because it is usually softer than the surfaces to be scraped, which reduces the chance of gouging the part. Some gaskets can be removed with a wire brush, but regardless of the method used, the mating surfaces must be left clean and smooth. If for some reason the gasket surface is gouged, then a gasket sealer thick enough to fill scratches will have to be used during reassembly of the components. For most applications, a non-drying (or semi-drying) gasket sealer should be used.

Hose removal tips

Warning: *If the vehicle is equipped with air conditioning, do not disconnect any of the A/C hoses without first having the system depressurized by a dealer service department or a service station.*

Hose removal precautions closely parallel gasket removal precautions. Avoid scratching or gouging the surface that the hose mates against or the connection may leak. This is especially true for radiator hoses. Because of various chemical reactions, the rubber in hoses can bond itself to the metal spigot that the hose fits over. To remove a hose, first loosen the hose clamps that secure it to the spigot. Then, with slip-joint pliers, grab the hose at the clamp and rotate it around the spigot. Work it back and forth until it is completely free, then pull it off. Silicone or other lubricants will ease removal if they can be applied between the hose and the outside of the spigot. Apply the same lubricant to the inside of the hose and the outside of the spigot to simplify installation.

As a last resort (and if the hose is to be replaced with a new one anyway), the rubber can be slit with a knife and the hose peeled from the spigot. If this must be done, be careful that the metal connection is not damaged.

If a hose clamp is broken or damaged, do not reuse it. Wire-type clamps usually weaken with age, so it is a good idea to replace them with screw-type clamps whenever a hose is removed.

Tools

A selection of good tools is a basic requirement for anyone who plans to maintain and repair his or her own vehicle. For the owner who has few tools, the initial investment might seem high, but when compared to the spiraling costs of professional auto maintenance and repair, it is a wise one.

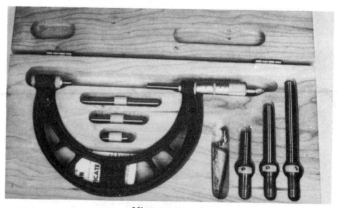

Micrometer set

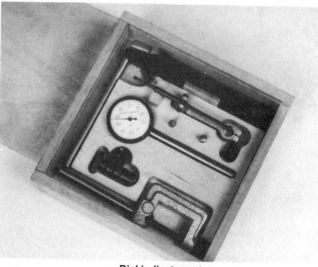

Dial indicator set

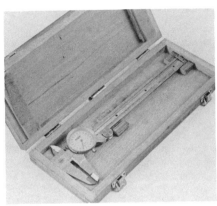

Dial caliper

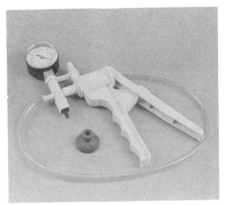

Hand-operated vacuum pump

Timing light

Compression gauge with spark plug hole adapter

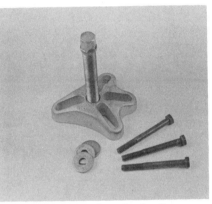

Damper/steering wheel puller

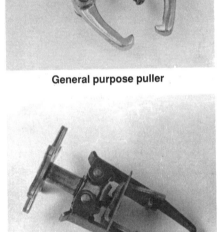

General purpose puller

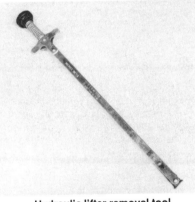

Hydraulic lifter removal tool

Valve spring compressor

Valve spring compressor

Ridge reamer

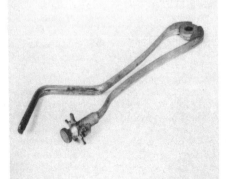

Piston ring groove cleaning tool

Ring removal/installation tool

Ring compressor

Cylinder hone

Brake hold-down spring tool

Brake cylinder hone

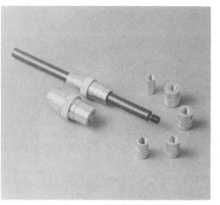

Clutch plate alignment tool

Tap and die set

To help the owner decide which tools are needed to perform the tasks detailed in this manual, the following tool lists are offered: *Maintenance and minor repair, Repair/overhaul* and *Special*.

The newcomer to practical mechanics should start off with the maintenance and minor repair tool kit, which is adequate for the simpler jobs performed on a vehicle. Then, as confidence and experience grow, the owner can tackle more difficult tasks, buying additional tools as they are needed. Eventually the basic kit will be expanded into the repair and overhaul tool set. Over a period of time, the experienced do-it-yourselfer will assemble a tool set complete enough for most repair and overhaul procedures and will add tools from the special category when it is felt that the expense is justified by the frequency of use.

Maintenance and minor repair tool kit

The tools in this list should be considered the minimum required for performance of routine maintenance, servicing and minor repair work. We recommend the purchase of combination wrenches (box-end and open-end combined in one wrench). While more expensive than open end wrenches, they offer the advantages of both types of wrench.

Combination wrench set (1/4-inch to 1 inch or 6 mm to 19 mm)
Adjustable wrench, 8 inch
Spark plug wrench with rubber insert
Spark plug gap adjusting tool
Feeler gauge set
Brake bleeder wrench
Standard screwdriver (5/16-inch x 6 inch)
Phillips screwdriver (No. 2 x 6 inch)
Combination pliers – 6 inch
Hacksaw and assortment of blades
Tire pressure gauge
Grease gun
Oil can
Fine emery cloth
Wire brush

Battery post and cable cleaning tool
Oil filter wrench
Funnel (medium size)
Safety goggles
Jackstands(2)
Drain pan

Note: *If basic tune-ups are going to be part of routine maintenance, it will be necessary to purchase a good quality stroboscopic timing light and combination tachometer/dwell meter. Although they are included in the list of special tools, it is mentioned here because they are absolutely necessary for tuning most vehicles properly.*

Repair and overhaul tool set

These tools are essential for anyone who plans to perform major repairs and are in addition to those in the maintenance and minor repair tool kit. Included is a comprehensive set of sockets which, though expensive, are invaluable because of their versatility, especially when various extensions and drives are available. We recommend the 1/2-inch drive over the 3/8-inch drive. Although the larger drive is bulky and more expensive, it has the capacity of accepting a very wide range of large sockets. Ideally, however, the mechanic should have a 3/8-inch drive set and a 1/2-inch drive set.

Socket set(s)
Reversible ratchet
Extension – 10 inch
Universal joint
Torque wrench (same size drive as sockets)
Ball peen hammer – 8 ounce
Soft-face hammer (plastic/rubber)
Standard screwdriver (1/4-inch x 6 inch)
Standard screwdriver (stubby – 5/16-inch)
Phillips screwdriver (No. 3 x 8 inch)
Phillips screwdriver (stubby – No. 2)

Pliers – vise grip
Pliers – lineman's
Pliers – needle nose
Pliers – snap-ring (internal and external)
Cold chisel – 1/2-inch
Scribe
Scraper (made from flattened copper tubing)
Centerpunch
Pin punches (1/16, 1/8, 3/16-inch)
Steel rule/straightedge – 12 inch
Allen wrench set (1/8 to 3/8-inch or 4 mm to 10 mm)
A selection of files
Wire brush (large)
Jackstands (second set)
Jack (scissor or hydraulic type)

Note: *Another tool which is often useful is an electric drill with a chuck capacity of 3/8-inch and a set of good quality drill bits.*

Special tools

The tools in this list include those which are not used regularly, are expensive to buy, or which need to be used in accordance with their manufacturer's instructions. Unless these tools will be used frequently, it is not very economical to purchase many of them. A consideration would be to split the cost and use between yourself and a friend or friends. In addition, most of these tools can be obtained from a tool rental shop on a temporary basis.

This list primarily contains only those tools and instruments widely available to the public, and not those special tools produced by the vehicle manufacturer for distribution to dealer service departments. Occasionally, references to the manufacturer's special tools are included in the text of this manual. Generally, an alternative method of doing the job without the special tool is offered. However, sometimes there is no alternative to their use. Where this is the case, and the tool cannot be purchased or borrowed, the work should be turned over to the dealer service department or an automotive repair shop.

Valve spring compressor
Piston ring groove cleaning tool
Piston ring compressor
Piston ring installation tool
Cylinder compression gauge
Cylinder ridge reamer
Cylinder surfacing hone
Cylinder bore gauge
Micrometers and/or dial calipers
Hydraulic lifter removal tool
Balljoint separator
Universal-type puller
Impact screwdriver
Dial indicator set
Stroboscopic timing light (inductive pick-up)
Hand operated vacuum/pressure pump
Tachometer/dwell meter
Universal electrical multimeter
Cable hoist
Brake spring removal and installation tools
Floor jack

Buying tools

For the do-it-yourselfer who is just starting to get involved in vehicle maintenance and repair, there are a number of options available when purchasing tools. If maintenance and minor repair is the extent of the work to be done, the purchase of individual tools is satisfactory. If, on the other hand, extensive work is planned, it would be a good idea to purchase a modest tool set from one of the large retail chain stores. A set can usually be bought at a substantial savings over the individual tool prices, and they often come with a tool box. As additional tools are needed, add–on sets, individual tools and a larger tool box can be purchased to expand the tool selection. Building a tool set gradually allows the cost of the tools to be spread over a longer period of time and gives the mechanic the freedom to choose only those tools that will actually be used.

Tool stores will often be the only source of some of the special tools that are needed, but regardless of where tools are bought, try to avoid cheap ones, especially when buying screwdrivers and sockets, because they won't last very long. The expense involved in replacing cheap tools will eventually be greater than the initial cost of quality tools.

Care and maintenance of tools

Good tools are expensive, so it makes sense to treat them with respect. Keep them clean and in usable condition and store them properly when not in use. Always wipe off any dirt, grease or metal chips before putting them away. Never leave tools lying around in the work area. Upon completion of a job, always check closely under the hood for tools that may have been left there so they won't get lost during a test drive.

Some tools, such as screwdrivers, pliers, wrenches and sockets, can be hung on a panel mounted on the garage or workshop wall, while others should be kept in a tool box or tray. Measuring instruments, gauges, meters, etc. must be carefully stored where they cannot be damaged by weather or impact from other tools.

When tools are used with care and stored properly, they will last a very long time. Even with the best of care, though, tools will wear out if used frequently. When a tool is damaged or worn out, replace it. Subsequent jobs will be safer and more enjoyable if you do.

Working facilities

Not to be overlooked when discussing tools is the workshop. If anything more than routine maintenance is to be carried out, some sort of suitable work area is essential.

It is understood, and appreciated, that many home mechanics do not have a good workshop or garage available, and end up removing an engine or doing major repairs outside. It is recommended, however, that the overhaul or repair be completed under the cover of a roof.

A clean, flat workbench or table of comfortable working height is an absolute necessity. The workbench should be equipped with a vise that has a jaw opening of at least four inches.

As mentioned previously, some clean, dry storage space is also required for tools, as well as the lubricants, fluids, cleaning solvents, etc. which soon become necessary.

Sometimes waste oil and fluids, drained from the engine or cooling system during normal maintenance or repairs, present a disposal problem. To avoid pouring them on the ground or into a sewage system, pour the used fluids into large containers, seal them with caps and take them to an authorized disposal site or recycling center. Plastic jugs, such as old antifreeze containers, are ideal for this purpose.

Always keep a supply of old newspapers and clean rags available. Old towels are excellent for mopping up spills. Many mechanics use rolls of paper towels for most work because they are readily available and disposable. To help keep the area under the vehicle clean, a large cardboard box can be cut open and flattened to protect the garage or shop floor.

Whenever working over a painted surface, such as when leaning over a fender to service something under the hood, always cover it with an old blanket or bedspread to protect the finish. Vinyl covered pads, made especially for this purpose, are available at auto parts stores.

Booster battery (jump) starting

Observe these precautions when using a booster battery to start a vehicle:

a) Before connecting the booster battery, make sure the ignition switch is in the Off position.

b) Turn off the lights, heater and other electrical loads.

c) Your eyes should be shielded. Safety goggles are a good idea.

d) Make sure the booster battery is the same voltage as the dead one in the vehicle.

e) The two vehicles MUST NOT TOUCH each other!

f) Make sure the transmission is in Neutral (manual) or Park (automatic).

g) If the booster battery is not a maintenance-free type, remove the vent caps and lay a cloth over the vent holes.

Connect the red jumper cable to the positive (+) terminals of each battery.

Connect one end of the black jumper cable to the negative (−) terminal of the booster battery. The other end of this cable should be connected to a good ground on the vehicle to be started, such as a bolt or bracket on the engine block **(see illustration)**. Make sure the cable will not come into contact with the fan, drivebelts or other moving parts of the engine.

Start the engine using the booster battery, then, with the engine running at idle speed, disconnect the jumper cables in the reverse order of connection.

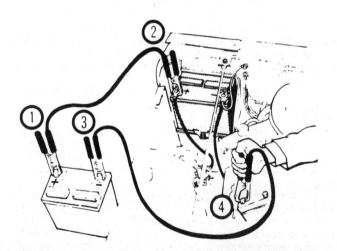

Make the booster battery cable connections in the numerical order shown (note that the negative cable of the booster battery is NOT attached to the negative terminal of the dead battery)

Jacking and towing

Jacking

Warning: *The jack supplied with the vehicle should only be used for raising the vehicle when changing a tire or placing jackstands under the frame. Never work under the vehicle or start the engine while the jack is being used as the only means of support.*

The vehicle must be on a level surface with the wheels blocked and the transaxle in Park (automatic) or Reverse (manual). Apply the parking brake if the front of the vehicle must be raised. Make sure no one is in the vehicle as it's being raised with the jack.

Remove the jack, lug nut wrench and spare tire (if needed) from the vehicle. If a tire is being replaced, use the lug wrench to remove the wheel cover. The plastic wheel covers are easy to break, so pry carefully. **Warning:** *Wheel covers may have sharp edges – be very careful not to cut yourself.* Loosen the lug nuts one-half turn, but leave them in place until the tire is raised off the ground.

Position the jack under the vehicle at the indicated jacking point. There's a front and rear jacking point on each side of the vehicle (**see illustration**).

Turn the jack handle clockwise until the tire clears the ground. Remove the lug nuts, pull the tire off and replace it with the spare. Replace the lug nuts with the beveled edges facing in and tighten them snugly. Don't attempt to tighten them completely until the vehicle is lowered or it could slip off the jack.

Turn the jack handle counterclockwise to lower the vehicle. Remove the jack and tighten the lug nuts in a criss-cross pattern. If possible, tighten the nuts with a torque wrench (see Chapter 1 for the torque figures). If you don't have access to a torque wrench, have the nuts checked by a service station or repair shop as soon as possible. **Caution:** *The compact spare included with these vehicles is intended for temporary use only. Have the tire repaired and reinstall it on the vehicle at the earliest opportunity and don't exceed 50 mph with the spare tire on the car.*

Stow the tire, jack and wrench and unblock the wheels.

Towing

Do not tow the vehicle with all four wheels on the ground – transaxle damage may occur if you do. Use a towing dolly to keep the front wheels off the road. Make sure the parking brake is released and the ignition switch is in the ACC position. Safety is a major consideration when towing and all applicable state and local laws must be obeyed.

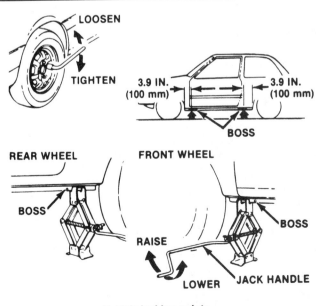

Vehicle jacking points

Automotive chemicals and lubricants

A number of automotive chemicals and lubricants are available for use during vehicle maintenance and repair. They include a wide variety of products ranging from cleaning solvents and degreasers to lubricants and protective sprays for rubber, plastic and vinyl.

Cleaners

Carburetor cleaner and choke cleaner is a strong solvent for gum, varnish and carbon. Most carburetor cleaners leave a dry-type lubricant film which will not harden or gum up. Because of this film it is not recommended for use on electrical components.

Brake system cleaner is used to remove grease and brake fluid from the brake system, where clean surfaces are absolutely necessary. It leaves no residue and often eliminates brake squeal caused by contaminants.

Electrical cleaner removes oxidation, corrosion and carbon deposits from electrical contacts, restoring full current flow. It can also be used to clean spark plugs, carburetor jets, voltage regulators and other parts where an oil-free surface is desired.

Demoisturants remove water and moisture from electrical components such as alternators, voltage regulators, electrical connectors and fuse blocks. They are non-conductive, non-corrosive and non-flammable.

Degreasers are heavy-duty solvents used to remove grease from the outside of the engine and from chassis components. They can be sprayed or brushed on and, depending on the type, are rinsed off either with water or solvent.

Lubricants

Motor oil is the lubricant formulated for use in engines. It normally contains a wide variety of additives to prevent corrosion and reduce foaming and wear. Motor oil comes in various weights (viscosity ratings) from 5 to 80. The recommended weight of the oil depends on the season, temperature and the demands on the engine. Light oil is used in cold climates and under light load conditions. Heavy oil is used in hot climates and where high loads are encountered. Multi-viscosity oils are designed to have characteristics of both light and heavy oils and are available in a number of weights from 5W-20 to 20W-50.

Gear oil is designed to be used in differentials, manual transmissions and other areas where high-temperature lubrication is required.

Chassis and wheel bearing grease is a heavy grease used where increased loads and friction are encountered, such as for wheel bearings, balljoints, tie-rod ends and universal joints.

High-temperature wheel bearing grease is designed to withstand the extreme temperatures encountered by wheel bearings in disc brake equipped vehicles. It usually contains molybdenum disulfide (moly), which is a dry-type lubricant.

White grease is a heavy grease for metal-to-metal applications where water is a problem. White grease stays soft under both low and high temperatures (usually from −100 to +190-degrees F), and will not wash off or dilute in the presence of water.

Assembly lube is a special extreme pressure lubricant, usually containing moly, used to lubricate high-load parts (such as main and rod bearings and cam lobes) for initial start-up of a new engine. The assembly lube lubricates the parts without being squeezed out or washed away until the engine oiling system begins to function.

Silicone lubricants are used to protect rubber, plastic, vinyl and nylon parts.

Graphite lubricants are used where oils cannot be used due to contamination problems, such as in locks. The dry graphite will lubricate metal parts while remaining uncontaminated by dirt, water, oil or acids. It is electrically conductive and will not foul electrical contacts in locks such as the ignition switch.

Moly penetrants loosen and lubricate frozen, rusted and corroded fasteners and prevent future rusting or freezing.

Heat-sink grease is a special electrically non-conductive grease that is used for mounting electronic ignition modules where it is essential that heat is transferred away from the module.

Sealants

RTV sealant is one of the most widely used gasket compounds. Made from silicone, RTV is air curing, it seals, bonds, waterproofs, fills surface irregularities, remains flexible, doesn't shrink, is relatively easy to remove, and is used as a supplementary sealer with almost all low and medium temperature gaskets.

Anaerobic sealant is much like RTV in that it can be used either to seal gaskets or to form gaskets by itself. It remains flexible, is solvent resistant and fills surface imperfections. The difference between an anaerobic sealant and an RTV-type sealant is in the curing. RTV cures when exposed to air, while an anaerobic sealant cures only in the absence of air. This means that an anaerobic sealant cures only after the assembly of parts, sealing them together.

Thread and pipe sealant is used for sealing hydraulic and pneumatic fittings and vacuum lines. It is usually made from a Teflon compound, and comes in a spray, a paint-on liquid and as a wrap-around tape.

Chemicals

Anti-seize compound prevents seizing, galling, cold welding, rust and corrosion in fasteners. High-temperature anti-seize, usually made with copper and graphite lubricants, is used for exhaust system and exhaust manifold bolts.

Anaerobic locking compounds are used to keep fasteners from vibrating or working loose and cure only after installation, in the absence of air. Medium strength locking compound is used for small nuts, bolts and screws that may be removed later. High-strength locking compound is for large nuts, bolts and studs which aren't removed on a regular basis.

Oil additives range from viscosity index improvers to chemical treatments that claim to reduce internal engine friction. It should be noted that most oil manufacturers caution against using additives with their oils.

Gas additives perform several functions, depending on their chemical makeup. They usually contain solvents that help dissolve gum and varnish that build up on carburetor, fuel injection and intake parts. They also serve to break down carbon deposits that form on the inside surfaces of the combustion chambers. Some additives contain upper cylinder lubricants for valves and piston rings, and others contain chemicals to remove condensation from the gas tank.

Miscellaneous

Brake fluid is specially formulated hydraulic fluid that can withstand the heat and pressure encountered in brake systems. Care must be taken so this fluid does not come in contact with painted surfaces or plastics. An opened container should always be resealed to prevent contamination by water or dirt.

Weatherstrip adhesive is used to bond weatherstripping around doors, windows and trunk lids. It is sometimes used to attach trim pieces.

Undercoating is a petroleum-based, tar-like substance that is designed to protect metal surfaces on the underside of the vehicle from corrosion. It also acts as a sound-deadening agent by insulating the bottom of the vehicle.

Waxes and polishes are used to help protect painted and plated surfaces from the weather. Different types of paint may require the use of different types of wax and polish. Some polishes utilize a chemical or abrasive cleaner to help remove the top layer of oxidized (dull) paint on older vehicles. In recent years many non-wax polishes that contain a wide variety of chemicals such as polymers and silicones have been introduced. These non-wax polishes are usually easier to apply and last longer than conventional waxes and polishes.

Safety first!

Regardless of how enthusiastic you may be about getting on with the job at hand, take the time to ensure that your safety is not jeopardized. A moment's lack of attention can result in an accident, as can failure to observe certain simple safety precautions. The possibility of an accident will always exist, and the following points should not be considered a comprehensive list of all dangers. Rather, they are intended to make you aware of the risks and to encourage a safety conscious approach to all work you carry out on your vehicle.

Essential DOs and DON'Ts

DON'T rely on a jack when working under the vehicle. Always use approved jackstands to support the weight of the vehicle and place them under the recommended lift or support points.

DON'T attempt to loosen extremely tight fasteners (i.e. wheel lug nuts) while the vehicle is on a jack – it may fall.

DON'T start the engine without first making sure that the transmission is in Neutral (or Park where applicable) and the parking brake is set.

DON'T remove the radiator cap from a hot cooling system – let it cool or cover it with a cloth and release the pressure gradually.

DON'T attempt to drain the engine oil until you are sure it has cooled to the point that it will not burn you.

DON'T touch any part of the engine or exhaust system until it has cooled sufficiently to avoid burns.

DON'T siphon toxic liquids such as gasoline, antifreeze and brake fluid by mouth, or allow them to remain on your skin.

DON'T inhale brake lining dust – it is potentially hazardous (see *Asbestos* below)

DON'T allow spilled oil or grease to remain on the floor – wipe it up before someone slips on it.

DON'T use loose fitting wrenches or other tools which may slip and cause injury.

DON'T push on wrenches when loosening or tightening nuts or bolts. Always try to pull the wrench toward you. If the situation calls for pushing the wrench away, push with an open hand to avoid scraped knuckles if the wrench should slip.

DON'T attempt to lift a heavy component alone – get someone to help you.

DON'T rush or take unsafe shortcuts to finish a job.

DON'T allow children or animals in or around the vehicle while you are working on it.

DO wear eye protection when using power tools such as a drill, sander, bench grinder, etc. and when working under a vehicle.

DO keep loose clothing and long hair well out of the way of moving parts.

DO make sure that any hoist used has a safe working load rating adequate for the job.

DO get someone to check on you periodically when working alone on a vehicle.

DO carry out work in a logical sequence and make sure that everything is correctly assembled and tightened.

DO keep chemicals and fluids tightly capped and out of the reach of children and pets.

DO remember that your vehicle's safety affects that of yourself and others. If in doubt on any point, get professional advice.

Asbestos

Certain friction, insulating, sealing, and other products – such as brake linings, brake bands, clutch linings, torque converters, gaskets, etc. – contain asbestos. *Extreme care must be taken to avoid inhalation of dust from such products, since it is hazardous to health.* If in doubt, assume that they *do* contain asbestos.

Fire

Remember at all times that gasoline is highly flammable. Never smoke or have any kind of open flame around when working on a vehicle. But the risk does not end there. A spark caused by an electrical short circuit, by two metal surfaces contacting each other, or even by static electricity built up in your body under certain conditions, can ignite gasoline vapors, which in a confined space are highly explosive. Do not, under any circumstances, use gasoline for cleaning parts. Use an approved safety solvent.

Always disconnect the battery ground (–) cable *at the battery* before working on any part of the fuel system or electrical system. Never risk spilling fuel on a hot engine or exhaust component.

It is strongly recommended that a fire extinguisher suitable for use on fuel and electrical fires be kept handy in the garage or workshop at all times. Never try to extinguish a fuel or electrical fire with water.

Fumes

Certain fumes are highly toxic and can quickly cause unconsciousness and even death if inhaled to any extent. Gasoline vapor falls into this category, as do the vapors from some cleaning solvents. Any draining or pouring of such volatile fluids should be done in a well ventilated area.

When using cleaning fluids and solvents, read the instructions on the container carefully. Never use materials from unmarked containers.

Never run the engine in an enclosed space, such as a garage. Exhaust fumes contain carbon monoxide, which is extremely poisonous. If you need to run the engine, always do so in the open air, or at least have the rear of the vehicle outside the work area.

If you are fortunate enough to have the use of an inspection pit, never drain or pour gasoline and never run the engine while the vehicle is over the pit. The fumes, being heavier than air, will concentrate in the pit with possibly lethal results.

The battery

Never create a spark or allow a bare light bulb near a battery. They normally give off a certain amount of hydrogen gas, which is highly explosive.

Always disconnect the battery ground (–) cable *at the battery* before working on the fuel or electrical systems.

If possible, loosen the filler caps or cover when charging the battery from an external source (this does not apply to sealed or maintenance-free batteries). Do not charge at an excessive rate or the battery may burst.

Take care when adding water to a non maintenance–free battery and when carrying a battery. The electrolyte, even when diluted, is very corrosive and should not be allowed to contact clothing or skin.

Always wear eye protection when cleaning the battery to prevent the caustic deposits from entering your eyes.

Household current

When using an electric power tool, inspection light, etc., which operates on household current, always make sure that the tool is correctly connected to its plug and that, where necessary, it is properly grounded. Do not use such items in damp conditions and, again, do not create a spark or apply excessive heat in the vicinity of fuel or fuel vapor.

Secondary ignition system voltage

A severe electric shock can result from touching certain parts of the ignition system (such as the spark plug wires) when the engine is running or being cranked, particularly if components are damp or the insulation is defective. In the case of an electronic ignition system, the secondary system voltage is much higher and could prove fatal.

Conversion factors

Length (distance)

Inches (in)	X	25.4	= Millimetres (mm)	X 0.0394	= Inches (in)
Feet (ft)	X	0.305	= Metres (m)	X 3.281	= Feet (ft)
Miles	X	1.609	= Kilometres (km)	X 0.621	= Miles

Volume (capacity)

Cubic inches (cu in; in^3)	X	16.387	= Cubic centimetres (cc; cm^3)	X 0.061	= Cubic inches (cu in; in^3)
Imperial pints (Imp pt)	X	0.568	= Litres (l)	X 1.76	= Imperial pints (Imp pt)
Imperial quarts (Imp qt)	X	1.137	= Litres (l)	X 0.88	= Imperial quarts (Imp qt)
Imperial quarts (Imp qt)	X	1.201	= US quarts (US qt)	X 0.833	= Imperial quarts (Imp qt)
US quarts (US qt)	X	0.946	= Litres (l)	X 1.057	= US quarts (US qt)
Imperial gallons (Imp gal)	X	4.546	= Litres (l)	X 0.22	= Imperial gallons (Imp gal)
Imperial gallons (Imp gal)	X	1.201	= US gallons (US gal)	X 0.833	= Imperial gallons (Imp gal)
US gallons (US gal)	X	3.785	= Litres (l)	X 0.264	= US gallons (US gal)

Mass (weight)

Ounces (oz)	X	28.35	= Grams (g)	X 0.035	= Ounces (oz)
Pounds (lb)	X	0.454	= Kilograms (kg)	X 2.205	= Pounds (lb)

Force

Ounces-force (ozf; oz)	X	0.278	= Newtons (N)	X 3.6	= Ounces-force (ozf; oz)
Pounds-force (lbf; lb)	X	4.448	= Newtons (N)	X 0.225	= Pounds-force (lbf; lb)
Newtons (N)	X	0.1	= Kilograms-force (kgf; kg)	X 9.81	= Newtons (N)

Pressure

Pounds-force per square inch (psi; lbf/in^2; lb/in^2)	X	0.070	= Kilograms-force per square centimetre (kgf/cm^2; kg/cm^2)	X 14.223	= Pounds-force per square inch (psi; lbf/in^2; lb/in^2)
Pounds-force per square inch (psi; lbf/in^2; lb/in^2)	X	0.068	= Atmospheres (atm)	X 14.696	= Pounds-force per square inch (psi; lbf/in^2; lb/in^2)
Pounds-force per square inch (psi; lbf/in^2; lb/in^2)	X	0.069	= Bars	X 14.5	= Pounds-force per square inch (psi; lbf/in^2; lb/in^2)
Pounds-force per square inch (psi; lbf/in^2; lb/in^2)	X	6.895	= Kilopascals (kPa)	X 0.145	= Pounds-force per square inch (psi; lbf/in^2; lb/in^2)
Kilopascals (kPa)	X	0.01	= Kilograms-force per square centimetre (kgf/cm^2; kg/cm^2)	X 98.1	= Kilopascals (kPa)

Torque (moment of force)

Pounds-force inches (lbf in; lb in)	X	1.152	= Kilograms-force centimetre (kgf cm; kg cm)	X 0.868	= Pounds-force inches (lbf in; lb in)
Pounds-force inches (lbf in; lb in)	X	0.113	= Newton metres (Nm)	X 8.85	= Pounds-force inches (lbf in; lb in)
Pounds-force inches (lbf in; lb in)	X	0.083	= Pounds-force feet (lbf ft; lb ft)	X 12	= Pounds-force inches (lbf in; lb in)
Pounds-force feet (lbf ft; lb ft)	X	0.138	= Kilograms-force metres (kgf m; kg m)	X 7.233	= Pounds-force feet (lbf ft; lb ft)
Pounds-force feet (lbf ft; lb ft)	X	1.356	= Newton metres (Nm)	X 0.738	= Pounds-force feet (lbf ft; lb ft)
Newton metres (Nm)	X	0.102	= Kilograms-force metres (kgf m; kg m)	X 9.804	= Newton metres (Nm)

Power

Horsepower (hp)	X	745.7	= Watts (W)	X 0.0013	= Horsepower (hp)

Velocity (speed)

Miles per hour (miles/hr; mph)	X	1.609	= Kilometres per hour (km/hr; kph)	X 0.621	= Miles per hour (miles/hr; mph)

Fuel consumption*

Miles per gallon, Imperial (mpg)	X	0.354	= Kilometres per litre (km/l)	X 2.825	= Miles per gallon, Imperial (mpg)
Miles per gallon, US (mpg)	X	0.425	= Kilometres per litre (km/l)	X 2.352	= Miles per gallon, US (mpg)

Temperature

Degrees Fahrenheit = (°C x 1.8) + 32

Degrees Celsius (Degrees Centigrade; °C) = (°F - 32) x 0.56

*It is common practice to convert from miles per gallon (mpg) to litres/100 kilometres (l/100km), where mpg (Imperial) x l/100 km = 282 and mpg (US) x l/100 km = 235

Troubleshooting

Contents

This section provides an easy reference guide to the more common problems which may occur during the operation of your vehicle. These problems and possible causes are grouped under various components or systems; i.e. Engine, Cooling System, etc., and also refer to the Chapter and/or Section which deals with the problem.

Remember that successful troubleshooting is not a mysterious black art practiced only by professional mechanics. It's simply the result of a bit of knowledge combined with an intelligent, systematic approach to the problem. Always work by a process of elimination, starting with the simplest solution and working through to the most complex – and never overlook the obvious. Anyone can forget to fill the gas tank or leave the lights on overnight, so don't assume that you are above such oversights.

Finally, always get clear in your mind why a problem has occurred and take steps to ensure that it doesn't happen again. If the electrical system fails because of a poor connection, check all other connections in the system to make sure that they don't fail as well. If a particular fuse continues to blow, find out why – don't just go on replacing fuses. Remember, failure of a small component can often be indicative of potential failure or incorrect functioning of a more important component or system.

Engine and performance

1 Engine will not rotate when attempting to start

1   Battery terminal connections loose or corroded. Check the cable terminals at the battery. Tighten the cable or remove corrosion as necessary.
2   Battery discharged or faulty. If the cable connections are clean and tight on the battery posts, turn the key to the On position and switch on the headlights and/or windshield wipers. If they fail to function normally, the battery may be discharged.
3   Automatic transaxle not completely engaged in Park or Neutral or clutch pedal not completely depressed.
4   Broken, loose or disconnected wiring in the starting circuit.
Inspect all wiring and connectors at the battery, starter solenoid, starter safety switch and ignition switch.
5   Starter motor pinion jammed in flywheel ring gear. If manual transaxle, place transaxle in gear and rock the vehicle to manually turn the engine. Remove starter and inspect pinion and flywheel at earliest convenience (see Chapter 5).
6   Starter solenoid faulty (see Chapter 5).
7   Starter motor faulty (see Chapter 5).
8   Ignition switch faulty (see Chapter 12).
9   Neutral start switch (automatic transaxle – see Chapter 7B) or clutch interlock switch (see Chapter 8) faulty.

2 Engine rotates but will not start

1   Fuel tank empty or ice in fuel line.
2   Fault in the carburetor or fuel injection system (see Chapter 4).
3   Battery discharged (engine rotates slowly). Check the operation of electrical components as described in the previous Section.
4   Battery terminal connections loose or corroded (see previous Section).
5   Fuel pump faulty (see Chapter 4).
6   Excessive moisture on, or damage to, ignition components (see Chapter 5).
7   Worn, faulty or incorrectly gapped spark plugs (see Chapter 1).

8   Broken, loose or disconnected wiring in the starting circuit (see previous Section).
9   Distributor loose, causing ignition timing to change. Turn the distributor as necessary to start the engine, then set the ignition timing as soon as possible (see Chapter 1).
10   Broken, loose or disconnected wires at the ignition coil or faulty coil (see Chapter 5).

3 Starter motor operates without rotating engine

1   Starter pinion sticking. Remove the starter (see Chapter 5) and inspect.
2   Starter pinion or flywheel teeth worn or broken. Remove the flywheel/driveplate access cover and inspect.
3   Starter bolts loose.

4 Engine hard to start or runs poorly when cold

1   Battery discharged or low. Check as described in Section 1.
2   Fault in the fuel or electrical systems (see Chapters 4 and 5).
3   Carburetor in need of overhaul (see Chapter 4).
4   Distributor rotor carbon tracked and/or damaged (see Chapters 1 and 5).
5   Choke control stuck or inoperative (carbureted models) (see Chapters 1 and 4).
6   Heater air intake inoperative.
7   Coolant thermostat stuck open.

5 Engine hard to start or runs poorly when hot

1   Air filter clogged (see Chapter 1).
2   Fault in the fuel or igition systems (see Chapters 4 and 5).
3   Fuel not reaching the carburetor (carburetor-equipped models) (see Section 2).
4   Choke stuck shut.
5   Excessively rich fuel mixture.
6   Vapor lock.

6 Starter motor noisy or excessively rough in engagement

1   Pinion or flywheel gear teeth worn or broken. Remove the cover at the bellhousing and inspect.
2   Starter motor mounting bolts loose or missing.
3   Faulty starter motor.

7 Engine starts but stops immediately

1   Loose or faulty electrical connections at distributor, coil or alternator.
2   Fault in the fuel or electrical systems (see Chapters 4 and 5).
3   Insufficient fuel reaching the carburetor (carburetor-equipped models). Check the fuel pump and filter (see Chapter 4).
4   Vacuum leak at the gasket surfaces of the intake manifold, or carburetor/throttle body. Make sure all mounting bolts/nuts are tightened securely and all vacuum hoses connected to the carburetor and manifold are positioned properly and in good condition.

8 Engine lopes while idling or idles erratically

1 Vacuum leakage. Check the mounting bolts/nuts at the carburetor/throttle body and intake manifold for tightness. Make sure all vacuum hoses are connected and in good condition. Use a stethoscope or a length of fuel hose held against your ear to listen for vacuum leaks while the engine is running. A hissing sound will be heard. A soapy water solution will also detect leaks.
2 Fault in the fuel or electrical systems (see Chapters 4 and 5).
3 Leaking EGR valve or plugged PCV valve (see Chapters 1 and 6).
4 Air filter clogged or incorrect air filter type (see Chapter 1).
5 Fuel pump not delivering sufficient fuel (see Chapter 4).
6 Fuel mixture out of adjustment (see Chapter 4).
7 Leaking head gasket. Perform a compression check (see Chapter 2).
8 Camshaft lobes worn (see Chapter 2).

9 Engine misses at idle speed

1 Spark plugs worn or not gapped properly (see Chapter 1).
2 Fault in the fuel or electrical systems (see Chapters 4 and 5).
3 Faulty spark plug wires or distributor cap (see Chapter 1).
4 Vacuum leaks.
5 Incorrect fuel mixture.

10 Engine misses throughout driving speed range

1 Fuel filter clogged and/or impurities in the fuel system (see Chapter 1).
2 Faulty or incorrectly gapped spark plugs (see Chapter 1).
3 Fault in the fuel or electrical systems (see Chapters 4 and 5).
4 Incorrect ignition timing (see Chapter 1).
5 Check for cracked distributor cap, disconnected distributor wires and damaged distributor components (see Chapter 1).
6 Defective spark plug wires (see Chapter 1).
7 Faulty emissions system components (see Chapter 6).
8 Low or uneven cylinder compression pressures. Remove the spark plugs and test the compression with a gauge (see Chapter 2).
9 Weak or faulty ignition system (see Chapter 5).
10 Vacuum leaks at the carburetor/throttle body, intake manifold or vacuum hoses (see Section 8).

11 Engine stalls

1 Idle speed incorrect. Refer to the VECI label and Chapter 1.
2 Fuel filter clogged and/or water and impurities in the fuel system (see Chapter 1).
3 Distributor components damp or damaged (see Chapter 5).
4 Fault in the fuel system or sensors (see Chapters 4 and 6).
5 Faulty emissions system components (see Chapter 6).
6 Faulty or incorrectly gapped spark plugs (see Chapter 1). Also check the spark plug wires (see Chapter 1).
7 Vacuum leak at the carburetor/throttle body, intake manifold or vacuum hoses. Check as described in Section 8.

12 Engine lacks power

1 Incorrect ignition timing (see Chapter 1).

2 Fault in the fuel or electrical systems (see Chapters 4 and 5).
3 Excessive play in the distributor shaft. At the same time, check for a damaged rotor, faulty distributor cap, wires, etc. (see Chapters 1 and 5).
4 Faulty or incorrectly gapped spark plugs (see Chapter 1).
5 Carburetor not adjusted properly or excessively worn (carbureted models) (see Chapter 4).
6 Faulty coil (see Chapter 5).
7 Brakes binding (see Chapter 1).
8 Automatic transaxle fluid level incorrect (see Chapter 1).
9 Clutch slipping (see Chapter 8).
10 Fuel filter clogged and/or impurities in the fuel system (see Chapter 1).
11 Emissions control system not functioning properly (see Chapter 6).
12 Use of substandard fuel. Fill the tank with the proper octane fuel.
13 Low or uneven cylinder compression pressures. Test with a compression tester, which will detect leaking valves and/or a blown head gasket (see Chapter 2).

13 Engine backfires

1 Emissions system not functioning properly (see Chapter 6).
2 Fault in the fuel or electrical systems (see Chapters 4 and 5).
3 Ignition timing incorrect (see Chapter 1).
4 Faulty secondary ignition system (cracked spark plug insulator, faulty plug wires, distributor cap and/or rotor) (see Chapters 1 and 5).
5 Carburetor or fuel injection system in need of adjustment or worn excessively (see Chapter 4).
6 Vacuum leak at the carburetor/throttle body, intake manifold or vacuum hoses. Check as described in Section 8.
7 Valves burned or sticking (see Chapter 2).
8 Plug wires installed in wrong firing order.

14 Pinging or knocking engine sounds during acceleration or uphill

1 Incorrect grade of fuel. Fill the tank with fuel of the proper octane rating.
2 Fault in the fuel or electrical systems (see Chapters 4 and 5).
3 Ignition timing incorrect (see Chapter 1).
4 Fuel mixture in need of adjustment (see Chapter 4).
5 Improper spark plugs. Check the plug type against the VECI label located in the engine compartment. Also check the plugs and wires for damage (see Chapter 1).
6 Worn or damaged distributor components (see Chapter 5).
7 EGR valve stuck shut. (see Chapter 6).
8 Vacuum leak. Check as described in Section 9.

15 Engine diesels (continues to run) after switching off

1 Idle speed too high. Refer to Chapter 1.
2 Fault in the fuel or electrical systems (see Chapters 4 and 5).
3 Ignition timing incorrectly adjusted (see Chapter 1).
4 Heated Air Intake (HAI) air cleaner system not operating properly (see Chapters 1 and 6).
5 Excessive engine operating temperature. Probable causes of this are a malfunctioning thermostat, clogged radiator, faulty water pump (see Chapter 3).
6 Low octane fuel.
7 Carbon deposits in combustion chambers.

Engine electrical system

16   Battery will not hold a charge

1   Alternator drivebelt defective or not adjusted properly (see Chapter 1).
2   Electrolyte level low or battery discharged (see Chapter 1).
3   Battery terminals loose or corroded (see Chapter 1).
4   Alternator not charging properly (see Chapter 5).
5   Loose, broken or faulty wiring in the charging circuit (see Chapter 5).
6   Short in the vehicle wiring causing a continual drain on battery (refer to Chapter 12 and the Wiring Diagrams).
7   Battery defective internally.

17   Ignition light fails to go out

1   Fault in the alternator or charging circuit (see Chapter 5).
2   Alternator drivebelt defective or not properly adjusted (see Chapter 1).

18   Ignition light fails to come on when key is turned on

1   Instrument cluster warning light bulb defective (see Chapter 12).
2   Alternator faulty (see Chapter 5).
3   Fault in the instrument cluster printed circuit, dashboard wiring or bulb holder (see Chapter 12).

Fuel system

19   Excessive fuel consumption

1   Dirty or clogged air filter element (see Chapter 1).
2   Incorrectly set ignition timing (see Chapter 1).
3   Choke sticking or improperly adjusted (carbureted models) (see Chapter 1).
4   Emissions system not functioning properly (see Chapter 6).
5   Fault in the fuel or electrical systems (see Chapters 4 and 5).
6   Carburetor or fuel injection system internal parts excessively worn or damaged (see Chapter 4).
7   Low tire pressure or incorrect tire size (see Chapter 1).

20   Fuel leakage and/or fuel odor

1   Leak in a fuel feed or vent line (see Chapter 4).
2   Tank overfilled. Fill only to automatic shut-off.
3   Evaporative emissions system canister clogged (see Chapters 1 or 6).
4   Vapor leaks from system lines (see Chapter 4).
5   Carburetor or fuel injection system internal parts excessively worn or out of adjustment (see Chapter 4).

Cooling system

21   Overheating

1   Insufficient coolant in the system (see Chapter 1).
2   Water pump drivebelt defective or not adjusted properly (see Chapter 1).
3   Radiator core blocked or radiator grille dirty and restricted (see Chapter 3).
4   Thermostat faulty (see Chapter 3).
5   Fan blades broken or cracked (see Chapter 3).
6   Radiator cap not maintaining proper pressure. Have the cap pressure tested by gas station or repair shop.
7   Ignition timing incorrect (see Chapter 1).
8   Electric engine cooling fan malfunctioning (see Chapter 3).

22   Overcooling

1   Thermostat faulty (see Chapter 3).
2   Emgine cooling fan stuck on (see Chapter 3).

23   External coolant leakage

1   Deteriorated or damaged hoses or loose clamps. Replace hoses and/or tighten the clamps at the hose connections (see Chapter 1).
2   Water pump seals defective. If this is the case, water may drip from the weep hole in the water pump body (see Chapter 3).
3   Leakage from radiator core or header tank. This will require the radiator to be professionally repaired (see Chapter 3 for removal procedures).
4   Engine drain plug leaking (see Chapter 1) or water jacket core plugs leaking (see Chapter 2).
5   Faulty cylinder head gasket (see Chapter 2).

24   Internal coolant leakage

Note: *Internal coolant leaks can usually be detected by examining the oil. Check the dipstick and inside of the valve cover for water deposits and an oil consistency like that of a milkshake.*
1   Leaking cylinder head gasket. Have the cooling system pressure tested.
2   Cracked cylinder bore or cylinder head. Dismantle the engine and inspect (see Chapter 2).

25   Coolant loss

1   Too much coolant in the system (see Chapter 1).
2   Coolant boiling away due to overheating (see Section 15).
3   External or internal leakage (see Sections 23 and 24).
4   Faulty radiator cap. Have the cap pressure tested.

26   Poor coolant circulation

1   Inoperative water pump. A quick test is to pinch the top radiator hose closed with your hand while the engine is idling, then let it loose. You should feel the surge of coolant if the pump is working properly (see Chapter 1).

2 Restriction in the cooling system. Drain, flush and refill the system (see Chapter 1). If necessary, remove the radiator (see Chapter 3) and have it reverse flushed.
3 Water pump drivebelt defective or not adjusted properly (see Chapter 1).
4 Thermostat sticking (see Chapter 3).

Clutch

27 Fails to release (pedal pressed to the floor – shift lever does not move freely in and out of Reverse)

1 Clutch plate warped or damaged (see Chapter 8).
2 Worn or dry clutch release shaft bushing (see Chapter 8).
3 Worn, broken or improperly adjusted cable (see Chapters 1 and 8).

28 Clutch slips (engine speed increases with no increase in vehicle speed)

1 Linkage out of adjustment (see Chapter 8).
2 Clutch plate oil soaked or lining worn. Remove clutch (see Chapter 8) and inspect.
3 Clutch plate not seated. It may take 30 or 40 normal starts for a new one to seat.

29 Grabbing (chattering) as clutch is engaged

1 Oil on clutch plate lining. Remove (see Chapter 8) and inspect. Correct any leakage source.
2 Worn or loose engine or transaxle mounts. These units move slightly when the clutch is released. Inspect the mounts and bolts (see Chapter 2).
3 Worn splines on clutch plate hub. Remove the clutch components (see Chapter 8) and inspect.
4 Warped pressure plate or flywheel. Remove the clutch components and inspect.

30 Squeal or rumble with clutch fully disengaged (pedal depressed)

1 Worn, defective or broken release bearing (see Chapter 8).
2 Worn or broken pressure plate springs (or diaphragm fingers) (see Chapter 8).

31 Clutch pedal stays on floor when disengaged

Linkage or release bearing binding. Inspect the linkage or remove the clutch components as necessary.

Manual transaxle

32 Noisy in Neutral with engine running

1 Input shaft bearing worn.
2 Damaged main drive gear bearing.
3 Worn countershaft bearings.
4 Worn or damaged countershaft endplay shims.

33 Noisy in all gears

1 Any of the above causes, and/or:
2 Insufficient lubricant (see the checking procedures in Chapter 1).

34 Noisy in one particular gear

1 Worn, damaged or chipped gear teeth for that particular gear.
2 Worn or damaged synchronizer for that particular gear.

35 Slips out of high gear

1 Transaxle loose on clutch housing (see Chapter 7).
2 Shift rods interfering with the engine mounts or clutch lever (see Chapter 7).
3 Shift rods not working freely (see Chapter 7).
4 Dirt between the transaxle case and engine or misalignment of the transaxle (see Chapter 7).
5 Worn or improperly adjusted linkage (see Chapter 7).

36 Difficulty in engaging gears

1 Clutch not releasing completely (see clutch adjustment in Chapter 1).
2 Loose, damaged or out-of-adjustment shift linkage. Make a thorough inspection, replacing parts as necessary (see Chapter 7).

37 Oil leakage

1 Excessive amount of lubricant in the transaxle (see Chapter 1 for correct checking procedures). Drain lubricant as required.
2 Defective driveaxle oil seal or speedometer oil seal (see Chapter 7).

Automatic transaxle

Note: *Due to the complexity of the automatic transaxle, it's difficult for the home mechanic to properly diagnose and service this component. For problems other than the following, the vehicle should be taken to a dealer service department or a transmission shop.*

38 General shift mechanism problems

1 Chapter 7 deals with checking and adjusting the shift linkage on automatic transaxles. Common problems which may be attributed to poorly

adjusted linkage are:

Engine starting in gears other than Park or Neutral.
Indicator on shifter pointing to a gear other than the one actually being selected.
Vehicle moves when in Park.

2   Refer to Chapter 7 to adjust the linkage.

39   Transaxle will not downshift with accelerator pedal pressed to the floor

Chapter 7 deals with adjusting the throttle cable to enable the transaxle to downshift properly.

40   Transaxle slips, shifts rough, is noisy or has no drive in forward or reverse gears

1   There are many probable causes for the above problems, but the home mechanic should be concerned with only one possibility – fluid level.
2   Before taking the vehicle to a repair shop, check the level and condition of the fluid as described in Chapter 1. Correct fluid level as necessary or change the fluid and filter if needed. If the problem persists, have a professional diagnose the probable cause.

41   Fluid leakage

1   Automatic transaxle fluid is a deep red color. Fluid leaks should not be confused with engine oil, which can easily be blown by air flow to the transaxle.
2   To pinpoint a leak, first remove all built-up dirt and grime from around the transaxle. Degreasing agents and/or steam cleaning will achieve this. With the underside clean, drive the vehicle at low speeds so air flow will not blow the leak far from its source. Raise the vehicle and determine where the leak is coming from. Common areas of leakage are:
   a) **Pan:** Tighten the mounting bolts and/or replace the pan gasket as necessary (see Chapter 7).
   b) **Filler pipe:** Replace the rubber seal where the pipe enters the transaxle case.
   c) **Transaxle oil lines:** Tighten the connectors where the lines enter the transaxle case and/or replace the lines.
   d) **Vent pipe:** Transaxle overfilled and/or water in fluid (see checking procedures, Chapter 1).
   e) **Speedometer connector:** Replace the O-ring where the speedometer cable enters the transaxle case (see Chapter 7).

Driveaxles

42   Clicking noise in turns

Worn or damaged outer joint. Check for cut or damaged seals. Repair as necessary (see Chapter 8).

43   Knock or clunk when accelerating after coasting

Worn or damaged inner joint. Check for cut or damaged seals. Repair as necessary (see Chapter 8).

44   Shudder or vibration during acceleration

1   Excessive joint angle. Have checked and correct as necessary (see Chapter 8).
2   Worn or damaged CV joints. Repair or replace as necessary (see Chapter 8).
3   Sticking CV joint assembly. Correct or replace as necessary (see Chapter 8).

Rear axle

45   Noise

1   Road noise. No corrective procedures available.
2   Tire noise. Inspect tires and check tire pressures (see Chapter 1).
3   Rear wheel bearings loose, worn or damaged (see Chapter 1).

Brakes

Note: *Before assuming that a brake problem exists, make sure the tires are in good condition and inflated properly (see Chapter 1), the front end alignment is correct and the vehicle is not loaded with weight in an unequal manner.*

46   Vehicle pulls to one side during braking

1   Defective, damaged or oil contaminated disc brake pads on one side. Inspect as described in Chapter 9.
2   Excessive wear of brake pad material or disc on one side. Inspect and correct as necessary.
3   Loose or disconnected front suspension components. Inspect and tighten all bolts to the specified torque (see Chapter 10).
4   Defective caliper assembly. Remove the caliper and inspect for a stuck piston or other damage (see Chapter 9).

47   Noise (high-pitched squeal with the brakes applied)

Disc brake pads worn out. The noise comes from the pad backing plate rubbing against the disc. Replace the pads with new ones immediately (see Chapter 9). If the pad material has worn completely away, the brake discs should be inspected for damage as described in Chapter 9.

48   Excessive brake pedal travel

1   Partial brake system failure. Inspect the entire system (see Chapter 9) and correct as required.
2   Insufficient fluid in the master cylinder. Check (see Chapter 1), add fluid and bleed the system if necessary (see Chapter 9).

3   Rear brakes not adjusting properly. Make a series of starts and stops while the vehicle is in Reverse. If this does not correct the situation, inspect the self-adjusting mechanism (see Chapter 9).

49   Brake pedal feels spongy when depressed

1   Air in the hydraulic lines. Bleed the brake system (see Chapter 9).
2   Faulty flexible hoses. Inspect all system hoses and lines. Replace parts as necessary.
3   Master cylinder mounting bolts/nuts loose.
4   Master cylinder defective (see Chapter 9).

50   Excessive effort required to stop vehicle

1   Power brake booster not operating properly (see Chapter 9).
2   Excessively worn linings or pads. Inspect and replace if necessary (see Chapter 9).
3   One or more caliper pistons or wheel cylinders seized or sticking. Inspect and rebuild as required (see Chapter 9).
4   Brake linings or pads contaminated with oil or grease. Inspect and replace as required (see Chapter 9).
5   New pads or shoes installed and not yet seated. It will take a while for the new material to seat against the drum (or rotor).

51   Pedal travels to the floor with little resistance

   Little or no fluid in the master cylinder reservoir caused by leaking wheel cylinder(s), leaking caliper piston(s), loose, damaged or disconnected brake lines. Inspect the entire system and correct as necessary.

52   Brake pedal pulsates during brake application

1   Caliper improperly installed. Remove and inspect (see Chapter 9).
2   Disc or drum defective. Remove (see Chapter 9) and check for excessive lateral runout and parallelism. Have the disc or drum resurfaced or replace it with a new one.

Suspension and steering systems

53   Vehicle pulls to one side

1   Tire pressures uneven (see Chapter 1).
2   Defective tire (see Chapter 1).
3   Excessive wear in suspension or steering components (see Chapter 10).
4   Front end in need of alignment.
5   Front brakes dragging. Inspect the brakes as described in Chapter 9.

54   Shimmy, shake or vibration

1   Tire or wheel out-of-balance or out-of-round. Have professionally balanced.
2   Loose, worn or out-of-adjustment rear wheel bearings (see Chapter 1).
3   Shock absorbers and/or suspension components worn or damaged (see Chapter 10).

55   Excessive pitching and/or rolling around corners or during braking

1   Defective shock absorbers. Replace as a set (see Chapter 10).
2   Broken or weak springs and/or suspension components. Inspect as described in Chapter 10.

56   Excessively stiff steering

1   Lack of fluid in power steering fluid reservoir (see Chapter 1).
2   Incorrect tire pressures (see Chapter 1).
3   Front end out of alignment.

57   Excessive play in steering

1   Excessive wear in suspension or steering components (see Chapter 10).
2   Steering gear damaged (see Chapter 10).

58   Lack of power assistance

1   Steering pump drivebelt faulty or not adjusted properly (see Chapter 1).
2   Fluid level low (see Chapter 1).
3   Hoses or lines restricted. Inspect and replace parts as necessary.
4   Air in power steering system. Bleed the system (see Chapter 10).

59   Excessive tire wear (not specific to one area)

1   Incorrect tire pressures (see Chapter 1).
2   Tires out-of-balance. Have professionally balanced.
3   Wheels damaged. Inspect and replace as necessary.
4   Suspension or steering components excessively worn (see Chapter 10).

60   Excessive tire wear on outside edge

1   Inflation pressures incorrect (see Chapter 1).
2   Excessive speed in turns.
3   Front end alignment incorrect (excessive toe-in). Have professionally aligned.
4   Suspension arm bent or twisted (see Chapter 10).

61   Excessive tire wear on inside edge

1   Inflation pressures incorrect (see Chapter 1).
2   Front end alignment incorrect. Have professionally aligned.
3   Loose or damaged steering components (see Chapter 10).

62   Tire tread worn in one place

1   Tires out-of-balance.
2   Damaged or buckled wheel. Inspect and replace if necessary.
3   Defective tire (see Chapter 1).

Chapter 1   Tune-up and routine maintenance

Contents

1

Specifications

Recommended lubricants and fluids

Engine oil
    Type . . . .   API grade SG or SG/CD multigrade and fuel efficient oil
    Viscosity . . . .   See accompanying chart
Fuel . . . .   Unleaded gasoline, 87 octane or higher
Automatic transaxle fluid . . . .   Dexron II ATF
Manual transaxle lubricant . . . .   API GL-5 SAE 75W90 or 80W90 gear oil
Brake fluid . . . .   DOT 3 brake fluid

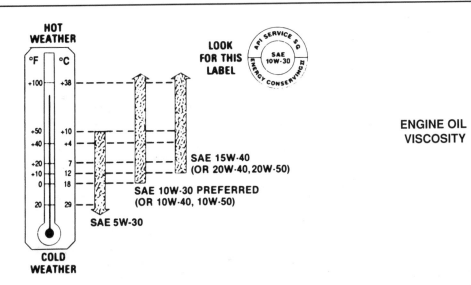

ENGINE OIL VISCOSITY

Capacities

Engine oil (including filter)	3.7 qts (3.5 liters)
Cooling system	4.0 qts
Automatic transaxle	3.16 qts (3.5 liters
Manual transaxle	2.5 qts (3.9 liters)

Ignition system

Spark plug
Type	AC R43CSLX or NGK BPR6ES-11
Gap	0.039 to 0.043 in (1.0 to 1.1 mm)
Ignition timing	Refer to the Vehicle Emission Control Information label in the engine compartment
Firing order	1-3-2
Cylinder numbers (drivebelt end-to-transaxle end)	1-2-3

Filters

Air filter	AC A893C
PCV Valve	AC 9601849
Engine oil filter	AC PF53

Clutch

Clutch pedal freeplay	9/16 to 13/16 in (15 to 20 mm)
Clutch release arm freeplay	3/16 to 19/32 in (2 to 4 mm)
Brake pad/shoe lining thickness (minimum)	3/64 in (1 mm)
Radiator cap pressure	13 psi
Engine drivebelt deflection	1/4 to 9/32-in (6 to 9 mm)

Valve clearances

Intake valve
Engine hot	0.010 in (0.27 mm)
Engine cold	0.006 in (0.17 mm)

Exhaust valve
Engine hot	0.012 in (0.32 mm)
Engine cold	0.008 in (0.22 mm)

Torque specifications   **Ft-lbs** (unless otherwise indicated)

Automatic transaxle
Pan bolts	48 in-lbs
Filter bolts	36 to 48 in-lbs
Drain plug	18 to 23
Carburetor/TBI nuts/bolts	14 to 18
Throttle body nuts/bolts	15 to 17
Manual transaxle drain and fill plugs	29
Spark plugs	21
Wheel lug nuts	45
Valve rocker arm locknut	13 to 17

---

1   Introduction

This Chapter is designed to help home mechanics maintain their vehicles with the goals of maximum performance, economy, safety and reliability in mind.

Included is a master maintenance schedule, followed by procedures dealing specifically with each item on the schedule. Visual checks, adjustments, component replacement and other helpful items are included. Refer to the accompanying illustrations of the engine compartment and the underside of the vehicle for the locations of various components.

Adhering to the mileage/time maintenance schedule and following the step-by-step procedures, which is simply a preventive maintenance program, will result in maximum reliability and vehicle service life. Keep in mind that it's a comprehensive program – maintaining some items but not others at the specified intervals will not produce the same results.

As you service the vehicle, you'll discover many of the procedures can – and should – be grouped together because of the nature of the particular procedure you're performing or because of the close proximity of two otherwise unrelated components to one another.

For example, if the vehicle is raised for a transaxle fluid and filter change, you should inspect the exhaust, suspension, steering and fuel systems while you're under the vehicle. When you're rotating the tires, it makes good sense to check the brakes, since the wheels are already removed. Finally, let's suppose you have to borrow or rent a torque wrench. Even if you only need it to tighten the spark plugs, you might as well check the torque of as many critical fasteners as time allows.

The first step in this maintenance program is to prepare yourself before the actual work begins. Read through all the procedures you're planning to do, then gather up all the parts and tools needed. If it looks like you might run into problems during a particular job, seek advice from a mechanic or an experienced do-it-yourselfer.

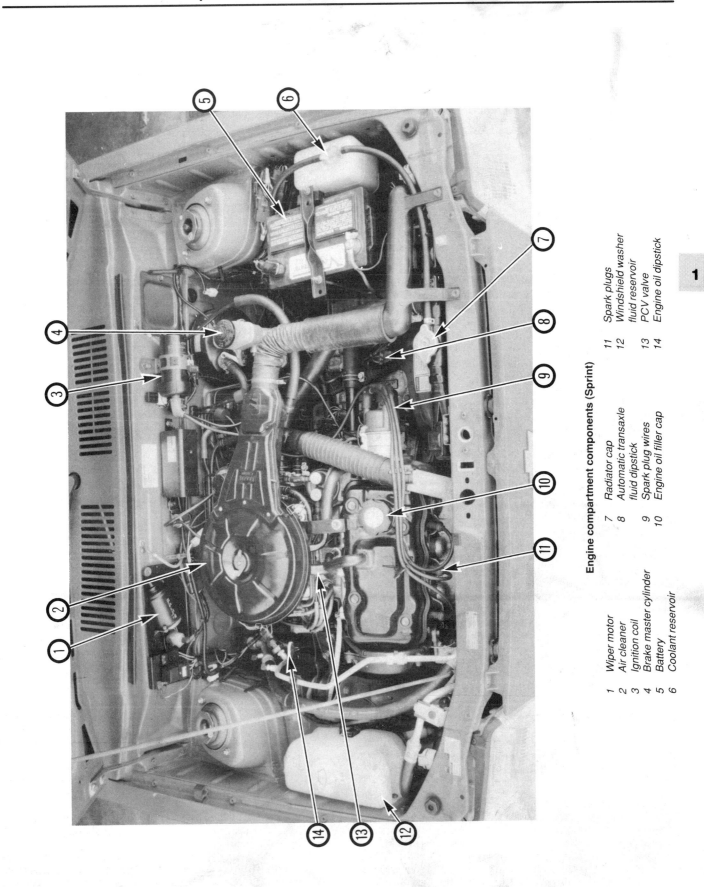

Engine compartment components (Sprint)

1 Wiper motor
2 Air cleaner
3 Ignition coil
4 Brake master cylinder
5 Battery
6 Coolant reservoir

7   Radiator cap
8   Automatic transaxle
    fluid dipstick
9   Spark plug wires
10 Engine oil filler cap

11 Spark plugs
12 Windshield washer
    fluid reservoir
13 PCV valve
14 Engine oil dipstick

1

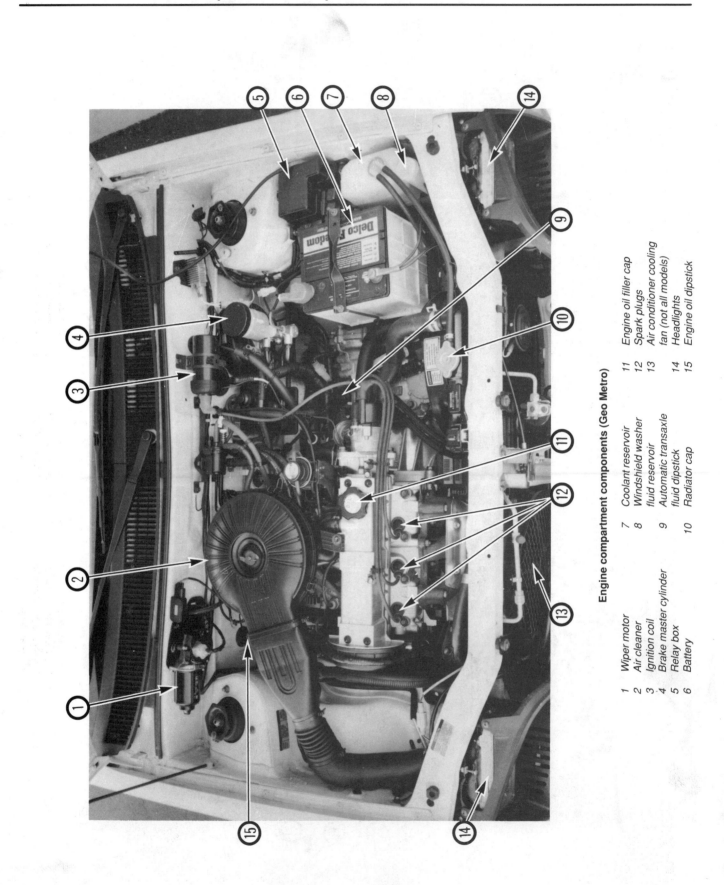

Engine compartment components (Geo Metro)

1	Wiper motor	7	Coolant reservoir	11	Engine oil filler cap
2	Air cleaner	8	Windshield washer	12	Spark plugs
3	Ignition coil		fluid reservoir	13	Air conditioner cooling
4	Brake master cylinder	9	Automatic transaxle		fan (not all models)
5	Relay box		fluid dipstick	14	Headlights
6	Battery	10	Radiator cap	15	Engine oil dipstick

1

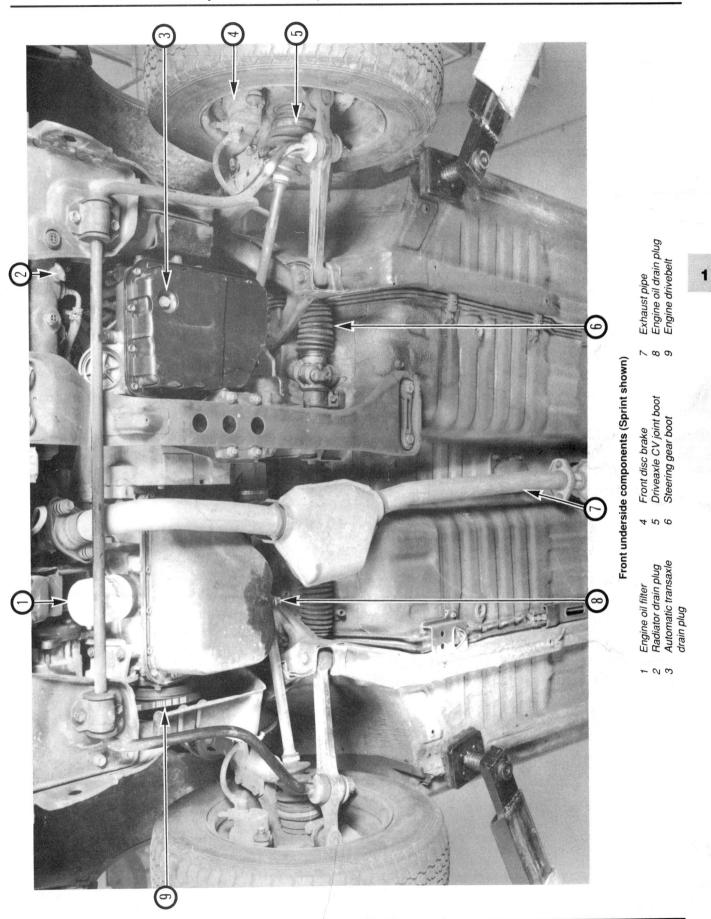

Front underside components (Sprint shown)

1   Engine oil filter
2   Radiator drain plug
3   Automatic transaxle
     drain plug

4   Front disc brake
5   Driveaxle CV joint boot
6   Steering gear boot

7   Exhaust pipe
8   Engine oil drain plug
9   Engine drivebelt

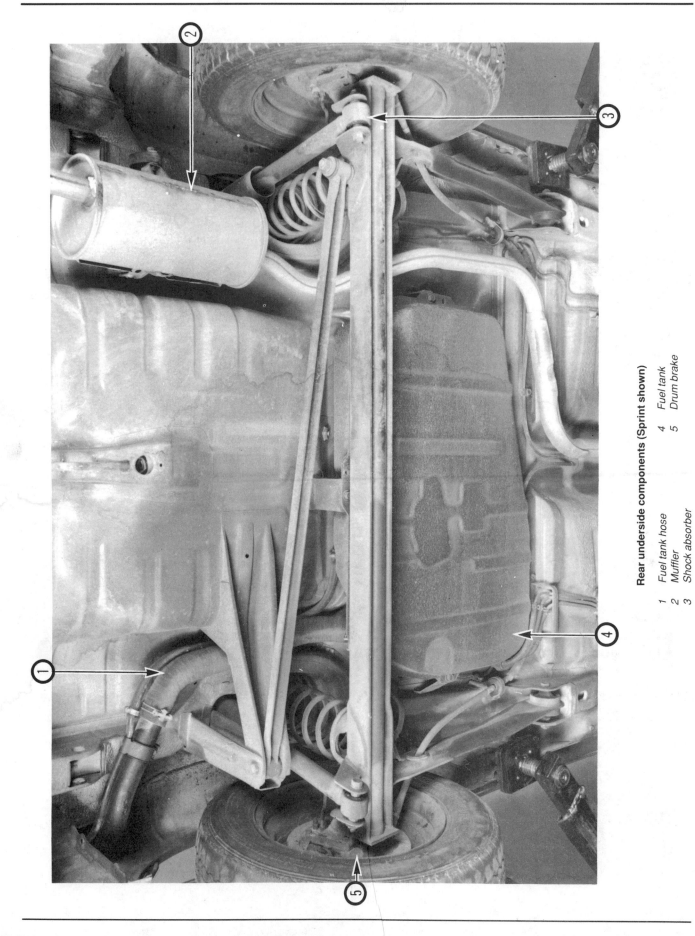

Rear underside components (Sprint shown)

1   Fuel tank hose
2   Muffler
3   Shock absorber
4   Fuel tank
5   Drum brake

2 Chevrolet Sprint and Geo Metro Maintenance Schedule

The following maintenance intervals are based on the assumption that the vehicle owner will be doing the maintenance or service work, as opposed to having a dealer service department do the work. Although the time/mileage intervals are loosely based on factory recommendations, most have been shortened to ensure, for example, that such items as filters, lubricants and fluids are checked/changed at intervals that promote maximum engine/driveline service life. Also, subject to the preference of the individual owner interested in keeping his or her vehicle in peak condi-

tion at all times, and with the vehicle's ultimate resale in mind, many of the maintenance procedures may be performed more often than recommended in the following schedule. We encourage such owner initiative.

When the vehicle is new it should be serviced initially by a factory authorized dealer service department to protect the factory warranty. In many cases the initial maintenance check is done at no cost to the owner (check with your dealer service department for more information).

Every 250 miles or weekly, whichever comes first

Check the engine oil level (Section 4)
Check the engine coolant level (Section 4)
Check the windshield washer fluid level (Section 4)
Check the brake fluid level (Section 4)
Check the tires and tire pressures (Section 5)

Every 3500 miles or 3 months, whichever comes first

All items listed above, plus:
Check the automatic transaxle fluid level (Section 6)
Change the engine oil and filter (Section 7)

Every 7500 miles or 6 months, whichever comes first

Inspect/replace the windshield wiper blades (Section 8)
Check/adjust the clutch pedal freeplay (Section 9)
Check and service the battery (Section 10)
Check/adjust the engine drivebelts (Section 11)
Inspect/replace all underhood hoses (Section 12)
Check the cooling system (Section 13)
Rotate the tires (Section 14)
Inspect the brakes (Section 15)
Check the manual transaxle lubricant level (Section 16)

Every 15,000 miles or 12 months, whichever comes first

All items listed above, plus:
Check the carburetor/TBI mounting bolt/nut torque (Section 17)
Check the starter safety switch operation (Section 18)
Check the seatbelt operation (Section 19)
Inspect the fuel system (Section 20)
Inspect the steering and suspension components (Section 21)*
Check the driveaxle boots (Section 22)*
Inspect the exhaust system (Section 23)
Check/adjust the valve clearances (Section 24)
If the vehicle is equipped with a manual transaxle, drain it and refill with new lubricant (Section 25)

Every 30,000 miles or 24 months, whichever comes first

Inspect the timing belt (Chapter 2, Part A)
Check/replace the air filter (Section 26)
Replace the fuel filter (Section 27)
Check/replace the spark plugs (Section 28)
Inspect/replace the spark plug wires, distributor cap and rotor (Section 29)*
Check the carburetor choke (Section 30)
Check the thermostatically controlled air cleaner (carbureted models only) (Section 31)
Drain, flush and refill the cooling system (Section 32)
Check/adjust the engine idle speed (Section 33)
If the vehicle is equipped with an automatic transaxle, change the fluid and filter (Section 34)**
Check the Pulse Air System operation (carbureted models only) (Section 35)
Check the fuel cutoff system (carbureted models only) (Section 36)
Check and reset the oxygen sensor system light (Section 37)
Inspect the evaporative emissions control system (Section 38)
Check/replace the PCV valve (Section 39)

Every 50,000 miles or 40 months, whichever comes first

Check/adjust the ignition timing (Chapter 5)

This item is affected by "severe" operating conditions as described below. If the vehicle in question is operated under "severe" conditions, perform all maintenance indicated with an asterisk (*) at 7500 mile/6 month intervals. Consider the conditions "severe" if most driving is done . . .

In dusty areas
When towing a trailer
At low speeds or with extended periods of engine idling
When outside temperatures remain below freezing and most trips are less than four miles

** *If most driving is done under one or more of the following conditions, change the automatic transaxle fluid every 15,000 miles:*

In heavy city traffic where the outside temperature regularly reaches 90-degrees F (32-degrees C) or higher
In hilly or mountainous terrain
Frequent trailer pulling

1

4.2   The engine oil dipstick is located on the passenger side of the engine

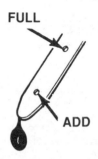

4.4   The oil level should be between the Full and Add holes in the dipstick – if it isn't, add enough oil to bring the level up to or near the Full hole (it takes one quart to raise the level from the Add to Full hole)

3   Tune-up general information

The term tune-up is used in this manual to represent a combination of individual operations rather than one specific procedure.

If, from the time the vehicle is new, the routine maintenance schedule is followed closely and frequent checks are made of fluid levels and high wear items, as suggested throughout this manual, the engine will be kept in relatively good running condition and the need for additional work will be minimized.

More likely than not, however, there will be times when the engine is running poorly due to lack of regular maintenance. This is even more likely if a used vehicle, which has not received regular and frequent maintenance checks, is purchased. In such cases, an engine tune-up will be needed outside of the regular routine maintenance intervals.

The first step in any tune-up or diagnostic procedure to help correct a poor running engine is a cylinder compression check (see Chapter 2). This check will help determine the condition of internal engine components and should be used as a guide for tune-up and repair procedures. For instance, if a compression check indicates serious internal engine wear, a conventional tune-up will not improve the performance of the engine and would be a waste of time and money. Because of its importance, the compression check should be done by someone with the right equipment and the knowledge to use it properly.

The following procedures are those most often needed to bring a generally poor running engine back into a proper state of tune.

Minor tune-up

Check all engine related fluids (Section 4)
Check the air filter (Section 26)
Clean, inspect and test the battery (Section 10)
Check and adjust the drivebelts (Section 11)
Check all underhood hoses (Section 12)
Check the cooling system (Section 13)
Replace the spark plugs (Section 28)
Inspect the spark plug wires, distributor cap and rotor (Section 29)
Check and adjust the idle speed (Section 33)
Check the PCV valve (Section 39)

Major tune-up

All items listed under Minor tune-up, plus . . .
Check the EGR system (Chapter 6)
Check the ignition system (Chapter 5)
Check the charging system (Chapter 5)
Check the fuel system (Chapter 4)
Replace the air filter (Section 26)
Replace the distributor cap and rotor (Section 29)
Replace the spark plug wires (Section 29)

4.6   Turn the oil filler cap counterclockwise to remove it – always make sure the area around the opening is clean before unscrewing the cap (to prevent dirt from contaminating the engine)

4   Fluid level checks

Warning: *The electric cooling fan can activate at any time, even when the ignition is in the Off position. Disconnect the fan motor or negative battery cable when working in the vicinity of the fan.*
Note: *The following fluid level checks should be done on a 250 mile or weekly basis. Additional fluid level checks can be found in specific maintenance procedures which follow. Regardless of intervals, be alert for fluid leaks under the vehicle which would indicate a leak that should be fixed immediately.*

1   Fluids are an essential part of the lubrication, cooling, brake and windshield washer systems. Because the fluids are gradually depleted and/or contaminated during normal operation of the vehicle, they must be periodically replenished. See *Recommended lubricants and fluids* at the beginning of this Chapter before adding fluid to any of the following components.
Note: *The vehicle must be on level ground when fluid levels are checked.*

Engine oil

Refer to illustrations 4.2, 4.4 and 4.6

2   The engine oil level is checked with a dipstick located at the drivebelt end of the engine **(see illustration)**. It extends through a tube and into the oil pan at the bottom of the engine.

3   The oil level should be checked before the vehicle has been started, or about 15 minutes after the engine has been shut off. If the oil is checked immediately after driving the vehicle, some of the oil will remain in the upper part of the engine, resulting in an inaccurate reading on the dipstick.

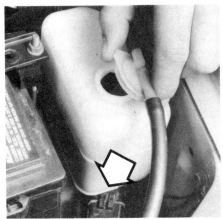

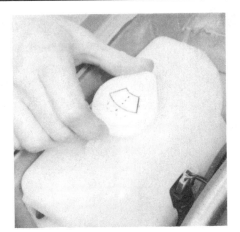

4.8 Make sure the coolant level in the reservoir is above the LOW mark (arrow) – if it's below the mark, add more antifreeze/water mixture

4.14 The windshield washer reservoir is located on the passenger side of the engine compartment on Sprint models

14.17 Remove the cell caps to check the water level in the battery – if the level is low, add distilled water only

1

4   Pull the dipstick out and wipe all the oil off the end with a clean rag or paper towel. Insert the clean dipstick all the way back into the tube, then pull it out again. Note the oil at the end of the dipstick. Add oil as necessary to keep the level between the marks on the dipstick **(see illustration)**.

5   Don't overfill the engine by adding too much oil, since it may result in oil fouled spark plugs, oil leaks or oil seal failures.

6   Oil is added to the engine after removing the cap from the valve cover **(see illustration)**.

7   Checking the oil level is an important preventive maintenance step. A consistently low oil level indicates oil leakage through damaged seals, defective gaskets or past worn rings or valve guides. If the oil looks milky or has water droplets in it, the cylinder head gasket may be blown or the head or block may be cracked. The engine should be checked immediately. The condition of the oil should also be noted. Whenever you check the oil level, slide your thumb and index finger up the dipstick before wiping off the oil. If you see small dirt or metal particles clinging to the dipstick, the oil should be changed (see Section 7).

Engine coolant

Refer to illustration 4.8

Warning: *Do not allow antifreeze to come in contact with your skin or painted surfaces of the vehicle. Flush contaminated areas immediately with plenty of water. Don't store new coolant or leave old coolant lying around where it's accessible to children or pets – they're attracted by its sweet smell. Ingestion of even a small amount of coolant can be fatal! Wipe up garage floor and drip pan coolant spills immediately. Keep antifreeze containers covered and repair leaks in the cooling system as soon as they are noted.*

8   All vehicles covered by this manual are equipped with a pressurized coolant recovery system. A white plastic coolant reservoir located near the battery (Geo) or on the passenger's side (Sprint) in the engine compartment is connected by a hose to the radiator filler neck **(see illustration)**. If the engine overheats, coolant escapes through a valve in the radiator cap and travels through the hose into the reservoir. As the engine cools, the coolant is automatically drawn back into the cooling system to maintain the correct level.

9   The coolant level in the reservoir should be checked regularly. **Warning:** *Do not remove the radiator cap to check the coolant level when the engine is warm. The level in the reservoir varies with the temperature of the engine. When the engine is cold, the coolant level should be at or slightly above the LOW mark on the reservoir* **(see illustration 4.8).** Once the engine has warmed up, the level should be above the LOW mark but below the top of the reservoir. If it isn't, allow the engine to cool, then remove the cap from the reservoir and add a 50/50 mixture of ethylene glycol-based antifreeze and water.

10   Drive the vehicle and recheck the coolant level. If only a small amount of coolant is required to bring the system up to the proper level, water can be used. However, repeated additions of water will dilute the antifreeze and water solution. In order to maintain the proper ratio of antifreeze and water, always top up the coolant level with the correct mixture. A clean empty plastic milk jug or bleach bottle makes an excellent container for mixing coolant. Do not use rust inhibitors or additives.

11   If the coolant level drops consistently, there may be a leak in the system. Inspect the radiator, hoses, filler cap, drain plugs and water pump (see Section 13). If no leaks are noted, have the radiator cap pressure tested by a service station.

12   If you have to remove the radiator cap, wait until the engine has cooled, then wrap a thick cloth around the cap and turn it to the first stop. If coolant or steam escapes, let the engine cool down longer, then remove the cap.

13   Check the condition of the coolant as well. It should be relatively clear. If it's brown or rust colored, the system should be drained, flushed and refilled. Even if the coolant appears to be normal, the corrosion inhibitors wear out, so it must be replaced at the specified intervals.

Windshield washer fluid

Refer to illustration 4.14

14   Fluid for the windshield washer system is located in a plastic reservoir in the engine compartment **(see illustration)**.

15   In milder climates, plain water can be used in the reservoir, but it should be kept no more than 2/3 full to allow for expansion if the water freezes. In colder climates, use windshield washer system antifreeze, available at any auto parts store, to lower the freezing point of the fluid. Mix the antifreeze with water in accordance with the manufacturer's directions on the container. **Caution:** *Don't use cooling system antifreeze – it will damage the vehicle's paint.*

16   To help prevent icing in cold weather, warm the windshield with the defroster before using the washer.

Battery electrolyte

Refer to illustration 4.17

17   All vehicles with which this manual is concerned are equipped with a battery which is permanently sealed (except for vent holes) and has no filler caps. Water doesn't have to be added to these batteries at any time. If an aftermarket maintenance-type battery is installed, the caps on top of the battery should be removed periodically to check for a low water level **(see illustration)**. This check is most critical during the warm summer months.

Brake fluid

Refer to illustration 4.19

18   The brake master cylinder is mounted on the front of the power booster unit in the engine compartment.

4.19   Brake fluid level

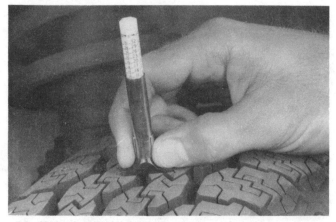

5.2   Use a tire tread depth indicator to monitor tire wear – they are available at auto parts stores and service stations and cost very little

19   The fluid inside the reservoir is readily visible. The level should be between the MIN and MAX marks on the reservoir **(see illustration)**. If a low level is indicated, be sure to wipe the top of the reservoir cover with a clean rag to prevent contamination of the system before removing the cover.

20   When adding fluid, pour it carefully into the reservoir to avoid spilling on surrounding painted surfaces. Be sure the specified fluid is used, since mixing different types of brake fluid can cause damage to the system. See *Recommended lubricants and fluids* at the front of this Chapter or your owner's manual. **Warning:** *Brake fluid can harm your eyes and damage painted surfaces, so use extreme caution when handling or pouring it. Do not use brake fluid that has been standing open or is more than one year old. Brake fluid absorbs moisture from the air. Excess moisture can cause a dangerous loss of braking effectiveness.*

21   At this time the fluid and master cylinder can be inspected for contamination. The system should be drained, refilled and bled if deposits or dirt particles are seen in the fluid (see Chapter 9).

22   After filling the reservoir to the proper level, make sure the cover is on tight to prevent fluid leakage.

23   The brake fluid level in the master cylinder will drop slightly as the pads and the brake shoes at each wheel wear down during normal operation. If the master cylinder requires repeated additions to keep it at the proper level, it's an indication of leakage in the system, which should be corrected immediately. Check all brake lines and connections (see Section 15 for more information).

24   If, upon checking the master cylinder fluid level, you discover the reservoir empty or nearly empty, the hydraulic system should be inspected for leaks and the system should be bled (see Chapter 9).

5   Tire and tire pressure checks

Refer to illustrations 5.2, 5.3, 5.4a, 5.4b and 5.8

1   Periodic inspection of the tires may spare you the inconvenience of being stranded with a flat tire. It can also provide you with vital information regarding possible problems in the steering and suspension systems before major damage occurs.

Condition	Probable cause	Corrective action	Condition	Probable cause	Corrective action
Shoulder wear	• Underinflation (both sides wear) • Incorrect wheel camber (one side wear) • Hard cornering • Lack of rotation	• Measure and adjust pressure. • Repair or replace axle and suspension parts. • Reduce speed. • Rotate tires.	Feathered edge Toe wear	• Incorrect toe	• Adjust toe-in.
Center wear	• Overinflation • Lack of rotation	• Measure and adjust pressure. • Rotate tires.	Uneven wear	• Incorrect camber or caster • Malfunctioning suspension • Unbalanced wheel • Out-of-round brake drum • Lack of rotation	• Repair or replace axle and suspension parts. • Repair or replace suspension parts. • Balance or replace. • Turn or replace. • Rotate tires.

5.3   This chart will help you determine the condition of the tires, the probable cause(s) of abnormal wear and the corrective action necessary

5.4a If a tire loses air on a steady basis, check the valve core first to make sure it's snug (special inexpensive wrenches are commonly available at auto parts stores)

5.4b If the valve core is tight, raise the corner of the vehicle with the low tire and spray a soapy water solution onto the tread as the tire is turned slowly – leaks will cause small bubbles to appear

5.8 To extend the life of the tires, check the air pressure at least once a week with an accurate gauge (don't forget the spare!)

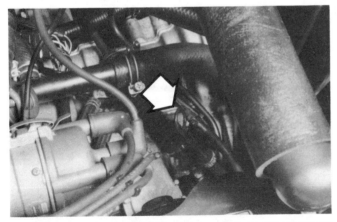

6.4 The automatic transaxle dipstick (arrow) is on the passenger side of the engine compartment

2   The original tires on this vehicle are equipped with 1/2-inch side bands that will appear when tread depth reaches 1/16-inch, but they don't appear until the tires are worn out. Tread wear can be monitored with a simple, inexpensive device known as a tread depth indicator **(see illustration)**.

3   Note any abnormal tread wear **(see illustration)**. Tread pattern irregularities such as cupping, flat spots and more wear on one side than the other are indications of front end alignment and/or balance problems. If any of these conditions are noted, take the vehicle to a tire shop or service station to correct the problem.

4   Look closely for cuts, punctures and embedded nails or tacks. Sometimes a tire will hold air pressure for a short time or leak down very slowly

after a nail has embedded itself in the tread. If a slow leak persists, check the valve stem core to make sure it's tight **(see illustration)**. Examine the tread for an object that may have embedded itself in the tire or for a "plug" that may have begun to leak (radial tire punctures are sometimes repaired with a plug that's installed in a puncture). If a puncture is suspected, it can be easily verified by spraying a solution of soapy water onto the suspected area **(see illustration)**. The soapy solution will bubble if there's a leak. Unless the puncture is unusually large, a tire shop or service station can usually repair the tire.

5   Carefully inspect the inner sidewall of each tire for brake fluid. If you see any, inspect the brakes immediately.

6   Correct air pressure adds miles to the lifespan of the tires, improves mileage and enhances overall ride quality. Tire pressure cannot be accurately estimated by looking at a tire, especially if it's a radial. A tire pressure gauge is essential. Keep an accurate gauge in the vehicle. The pressure gauges attached to the nozzles of air hoses at gas stations are often inaccurate.

7   Always check tire pressure when the tires are cold. Cold, in this case, means the vehicle has not been driven over a mile in the three hours preceding a tire pressure check. A pressure rise of four to eight pounds is not uncommon once the tires are warm.

8   Unscrew the valve cap protruding from the wheel or hubcap and push the gauge firmly onto the valve stem **(see illustration)**. Note the reading on the gauge and compare the figure to the recommended tire pressure shown on the label attached to the inside of the glove compartment door. Be sure to reinstall the valve cap to keep dirt and moisture out of the valve stem mechanism. Check all four tires and, if necessary, add enough air to bring them up to the recommended pressure.

9   Don't forget to keep the spare tire inflated to the specified pressure (refer to your owner's manual or the tire sidewall).

---

6   Automatic transaxle fluid level check

Refer to illustrations 6.4 and 6.6

Warning: *The electric cooling fan can activate at any time. Disconnect the fan motor or negative battery cable when working in the vicinity of the fan.*

1   The level of the automatic transaxle fluid should be carefully maintained. Low fluid level can lead to slipping or loss of drive, while overfilling can cause foaming, loss of fluid and transaxle damage.

2   The transaxle fluid level should be checked when the engine is at normal operating temperature. **Caution:** *If the vehicle has just been driven for a long time at high speed or in city traffic in hot weather, or if it has been pulling a trailer, an accurate fluid level reading cannot be obtained. Allow the fluid to cool for about 30 minutes.*

3   Park on level ground, apply the parking brake and start the engine. While the engine is idling, depress the brake pedal and move the selector lever through all the gear ranges, beginning and ending in Park.

4   With the engine still idling, remove the dipstick **(see illustration)**.

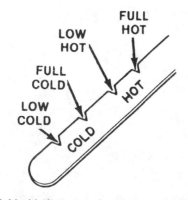

6.6 Check the fluid with the transaxle at normal operating temperature – the level should be kept in the Hot range (between the two notches)

5   Wipe the fluid off the dipstick with a clean rag and reinsert it until the cap seats.
6   Pull the dipstick out again. The fluid level should be in the HOT range (**see illustration**). If the level is at the low side of the range, add the specified automatic transmission fluid through the dipstick tube with a funnel.
7   Add the fluid a little at a time and keep checking the level until it's correct.
8   The condition of the fluid should also be checked along with the level. If the fluid at the end of the dipstick is black or a dark reddish-brown color, or if it smells burned, the fluid should be changed (see Section 34). If you're in doubt about the condition of the fluid, purchase some new fluid and compare the two for color and odor.

7   Engine oil and filter change

Refer to illustrations 7.3, 7.9, 7.14 and 7.18

1   Frequent oil changes are the most important preventive maintenance procedures that can be done by the home mechanic. As engine oil ages, it becomes diluted and contaminated, which leads to premature engine wear.
2   Although some sources recommend oil filter changes every other oil change, a new filter should be installed every time the oil is changed.
3   Gather up all necessary tools and materials before beginning this procedure (**see illustration**).
4   You should have plenty of clean rags and newspapers handy to mop up any spills. Access to the underside of the vehicle is greatly improved if it can be lifted on a hoist, driven onto ramps or supported by jackstands. **Warning:** *Do not work under a vehicle that's supported only by a bumper, hydraulic or scissors-type jack.*
5   If this is your first oil change, get under the vehicle and familiarize yourself with the locations of the oil drain plug and the oil filter. The engine and exhaust components will be warm during the actual work, so note how they're situated to avoid touching them when working under the vehicle.
6   Run the engine until it's at normal operating temperature. If the new oil or any tools are needed, use this warm-up time to gather everything necessary for the job. Refer to *Recommended lubricants and fluids* at the beginning of this Chapter for the type of oil required.
7   With the engine oil warm (warm engine oil will drain better and more built-up sludge will be removed with it), raise and support the vehicle. Make sure it's safely supported!
8   Move all necessary tools, rags and newspapers under the vehicle. Set the drain pan under the drain plug. Keep in mind that the oil will initially flow out with some force; position the pan accordingly.
9   Being careful not to touch any of the hot exhaust components, use a wrench to remove the drain plug near the bottom of the oil pan (**see illustration**). Depending on how hot the oil is, you may want to wear gloves while unscrewing the plug the final few turns.
10   Allow the old oil to drain into the pan. It may be necessary to move the pan as the oil flow slows to a trickle.

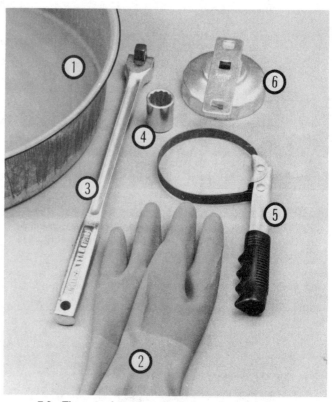

7.3   These tools are required when changing the engine oil and filter

1   ***Drain pan*** *– It should be fairly shallow in depth, but wide to prevent spills*
2   ***Rubber gloves*** *– When removing the drain plug and filter, you will get oil on your hands (the gloves will prevent burns)*
3   ***Breaker bar*** *– Sometimes the oil drain plug is tight and a long breaker bar is needed to loosen it*
4   ***Socket*** *– To be used with the breaker bar or a ratchet (must be the correct size to fit the drain plug – six-point preferred)*
5   ***Filter wrench*** *– This is a metal band-type wrench, which requires clearance around the filter to be effective*
6   ***Filter wrench*** *– This type fits on the bottom of the filter and can be turned with a ratchet or breaker bar (different size wrenches are available for different types of filters)*

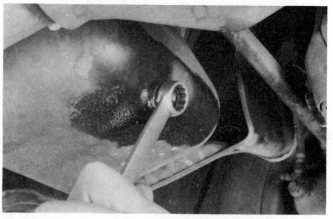

7.9   To avoid rounding off the hex on the drain plug, use a box-end wrench (a six-point wrench or socket is preferred)

11   After all the oil has drained, wipe off the drain plug with a clean rag. Small metal particles may cling to the plug and would immediately contaminate the new oil.

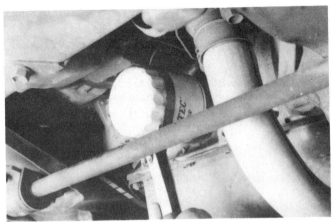

7.14   The oil filter is usually on very tight and will require a special wrench for removal – DO NOT use the filter wrench to tighten the filter

7.18   Lubricate the oil filter gasket with clean engine oil before installing the filter on the engine

1

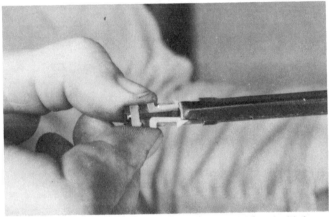

8.5   On Sprint models, squeeze the retaining clip and withdraw the blade element from the frame

12   Clean the area around the drain plug opening and reinstall the plug. Tighten it securely with the wrench. If a torque wrench is available, use it to tighten the plug.

13   Move the drain pan into position under the oil filter.

14   Use the filter wrench to loosen the oil filter (**see illustration**). Chain or metal band filter wrenches may distort the filter canister, but it doesn't matter since the filter will be discarded anyway.

15   Completely unscrew the old filter. Be careful; it's full of oil. Empty the oil inside the filter into the drain pan.

16   Compare the old filter with the new one to make sure they're the same type.

17   Use a clean rag to remove all oil, dirt and sludge from the area where the oil filter mounts to the engine.

18   Apply a light coat of clean oil to the rubber gasket on the new oil filter (**see illustration**).

19   Attach the new filter to the engine, following the tightening directions printed on the filter canister or packing box. Most filter manufacturers recommend against using a wrench due to the possibility of overtightening the filter and damaging the seal.

20   Remove all tools, rags, etc. from under the vehicle, being careful not to spill the oil in the drain pan, then lower the vehicle.

21   Move to the engine compartment and locate the oil filler cap.

22   Pour the fresh oil through the filler opening into the engine. A funnel should be used to prevent spills.

23   Pour four quarts of fresh oil into the engine. Wait a few minutes to allow the oil to drain into the pan, then check the level on the oil dipstick (see Section 4 if necessary). If the oil level is above the lower mark, start the engine and allow the new oil to circulate.

24   Run the engine for only about a minute and then shut it off. Immediate-

ly look under the vehicle and check for leaks at the oil pan drain plug and around the oil filter. If either is leaking, tighten with a bit more force.

25   With the new oil circulated and the filter now completely full, recheck the level on the dipstick and add more oil as necessary.

26   During the first few trips after an oil change, make it a point to check frequently for leaks and proper oil level.

27   The old oil drained from the engine cannot be reused in its present state and should be disposed of. Oil reclamation centers, auto repair shops and gas stations will normally accept the oil, which can be refined and used again. After the oil has cooled it can be drained into a container (capped plastic jugs, topped bottles, milk cartons, etc.) for transport to a disposal site.

---

8   Windshield wiper blade inspection and replacement

Refer to illustration 8.5

1   The windshield wiper and blade assembly should be inspected periodically for damage, loose components and cracked or worn blade elements.

2   Road film can build up on the wiper blades and affect their efficiency, so they should be washed regularly with a mild detergent solution.

3   The action of the wiping mechanism can loosen bolts, nuts and fasteners, so they should be checked and tightened, as necessary, at the same time the wiper blades are checked.

4   If the wiper blade elements are cracked, worn or warped, or no longer clean adequately, they should be replaced with new ones.

Sprint

5   Lift the arm assembly away from the glass for clearance, squeeze the release clip and slide the element out of the blade frame (**see illustration**).

6   Installation is the reverse of removal.

Metro

7   Pull the wiper blade/arm away from the glass, depress the retaining tab and slide the assembly out of the hook in the arm.

8   Bend the end of the element out of the way and use needle-nose pliers to pull the two metal support rods out of the rubber element. With the rods removed, slide the element out of the wiper frame.

9   Slide the new element into place in the frame, then insert the rods to lock it in place.

---

9   Clutch pedal height and freeplay check and adjustment

Refer to illustrations 9.1, 9.3 and 9.4

1   The clutch pedal must be at the same height as the brake pedal. If the pedal is more than 5/16-inch higher or lower than the brake pedal, loosen

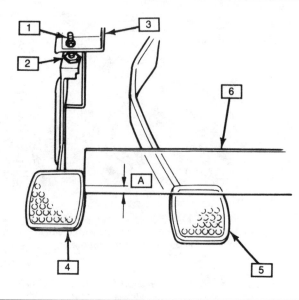

9.1 Use a ruler to determine if the clutch pedal is the same height as the brake pedal – adjust the bolt on the pedal bracket if necessary

A	Height difference (no more than 5/16-inch)
1	Adjusting bolt
2	Locknut
3	Pedal bracket
4	Clutch pedal
5	Brake pedal
6	Ruler

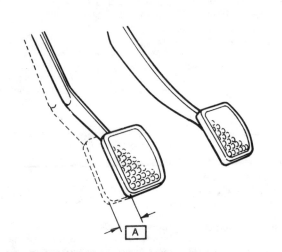

9.3 Freeplay (A) is the distance the clutch pedal moves without resistance

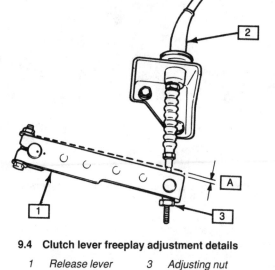

9.4 Clutch lever freeplay adjustment details

| 1 | Release lever | 3 | Adjusting nut |
| 2 | Clutch cable | A | Freeplay |

the locknut and turn the adjusting bolt until the height is correct (see illustration).

2   Tighten the locknut and recheck the pedal height.

3   Push down on the clutch pedal and use a ruler to measure the distance that it moves freely before resistance is felt (see illustration). The freeplay should be within the limits listed in this Chapter's specifications. If it isn't, it must be adjusted.

4   Turn the adjusting nut at the end of the clutch cable in the engine compartment until the release lever freeplay is within the limits listed in this Chapter's specifications (see illustration).

10   Battery check, maintenance and charging

Refer to illustrations 10.1, 10.6, 10.7a, 10.7b and 10.7c

Warning: *Certain precautions must be followed when checking and servicing the battery. Hydrogen gas, which is highly flammable, is always present in the battery cells, so keep lighted tobacco and all other open flames and sparks away from it. The electrolyte inside the battery is actually dilute sulfuric acid, which will cause injury if splashed on your skin or in your eyes. It will also ruin clothes and painted surfaces. When removing the battery cables, always detach the negative cable first and reconnect it last!*

Check and maintenance

1   Battery maintenance is an important procedure which will help ensure you aren't stranded because of a dead battery. Several tools are required for this procedure (see illustration).

2   When checking/servicing the battery, always turn the engine and all accessories off.

3   A sealed (sometimes called maintenance-free), battery is standard equipment on these vehicles. The cell caps cannot be removed, no electrolyte checks are required and water cannot be added to the cells. However, if a standard aftermarket battery has been installed, the following maintenance procedure can be used.

4   Remove the caps and check the electrolyte level in each of the battery cells (see Section 4). It must be above the plates. There's usually a splitring indicator in each cell to indicate the correct level. If the level is low, add distilled water only, then reinstall the cell caps. **Caution:** *Overfilling the cells may cause electrolyte to spill over during periods of heavy charging, causing corrosion and damage to nearby components.*

5   The external condition of the battery should be checked periodically. Look for damage such as a cracked case.

6   Check the tightness of the battery cable bolts (see illustration) to ensure good electrical connections. Inspect the entire length of each cable, looking for cracked or abraded insulation and frayed conductors.

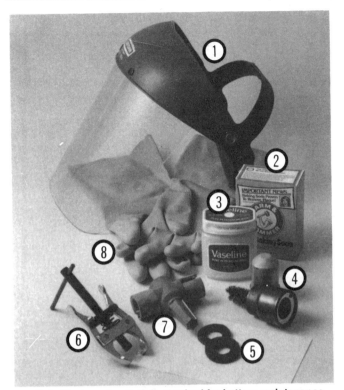

10.1   Tools and materials required for battery maintenance

1   *Face shield/safety goggles* – *When removing corrosion with a brush, the acidic particles can easily fly up into your eyes*

2   *Baking soda* – *A solution of baking soda and water can be used to neutralize corrosion*

3   *Petroleum jelly* – *A layer of this on the battery posts will help prevent corrosion*

4   *Battery post/cable cleaner* – *This wire brush cleaning tool will remove all traces of corrosion from the battery posts and cable clamps*

5   *Treated felt washers* – *Placing one of these on each post, directly under the cable clamps, will help prevent corrosion*

6   *Puller* – *Sometimes the cable clamps are very difficult to pull off the posts, even after the nut/bolt has been completely loosened. This tool pulls the clamp straight up and off the post without damage.*

7   *Battery post/cable cleaner* – *Here is another cleaning tool which is a slightly different version of number 4 above, but it does the same thing*

8   *Rubber gloves* – *Another safety item to consider when servicing the battery; remember that's acid inside the battery!*

7   If corrosion (visible as white, fluffy deposits) **(see illustration)** is evident, remove the cables from the terminals, clean them with a battery brush and reinstall them **(see illustrations)**. Corrosion can be kept to a minimum by applying a layer of petroleum jelly or grease to the terminals.

8   Make sure the battery carrier is in good condition and the hold-down clamp is tight. If the battery is removed (see Chapter 5 for the removal and installation procedure), make sure no parts remain in the bottom of the carrier when it's reinstalled. When reinstalling the hold-down clamp, don't overtighten the nuts.

9   Corrosion on the carrier, battery case and surrounding areas can be removed with a solution of water and baking soda. Apply the mixture with a small brush, let it work, then rinse it off with plenty of clean water.

10   Any metal parts of the vehicle damaged by corrosion should be coated with a zinc-based primer, then painted.

11   Additional information on the battery, charging and jump starting can be found in the front of this manual and in Chapter 5.

12   Always replace the battery with one of similar type and size.

10.6   Removing the cable from a battery post with a wrench – sometimes a special battery pliers is required for this procedure if corrosion has caused deterioration of the nut hex (always remove the ground cable first and hook it up last!)

1

10.7a   Battery terminal corrosion usually appears as light, fluffy powder

10.7b   When cleaning the cable clamps, all corrosion must be removed (the inside of the clamp is tapered to match the taper on the post, so don't remove too much material)

Charging

Warning: *When a battery is being charged, hydrogen gas, which is very explosive and flammable, is produced. Do not smoke or allow open flames near a charging or recently charged battery. Wear eye protection when near the battery during charging. Also, make sure the charger is unplugged before connecting or disconnecting the battery from the charger.*

13   Slow-rate charging is the best way to restore a battery that's discharged to the point where it will not start the engine. It's also a good way to maintain the battery charge in a vehicle that's only driven a few miles between starts. Maintaining the battery charge is particularly important in the

10.7c   Regardless of the type of tool used on the battery posts, a clean, shiny surface should be the result

winter when the battery must work harder to start the engine and electrical accessories that drain the battery are in greater use.

14   It's best to use a one or two-amp battery charger (sometimes called a "trickle" charger). They're the safest and put the least strain on the battery. They are also the least expensive. For a faster charge, you can use a higher amperage charger, but don't use one rated more than 1/10th the amp/hour rating of the battery. Rapid boost charges that claim to restore the power of the battery in one to two hours are hardest on the battery and can damage batteries not in good condition. This type of charging should only be used in emergency situations.

15   The average time necessary to charge a battery should be listed in the instructions that come with the charger. As a general rule, a trickle charger will charge a battery in 12 to 16 hours.

16   Remove all of the cell caps (if equipped) and cover the holes with a clean cloth to prevent spattering electrolyte. Disconnect the negative battery cable and hook the battery charger leads to the battery posts (positive to positive, negative to negative), then plug in the charger. Make sure it's set at 12-volts if it has a selector switch.

17   If you're using a charger with a rate higher than two amps, check the battery regularly during charging to make sure it doesn't overheat. If you're using a trickle charger, you can safely let the battery charge overnight after you've checked it regularly for the first couple of hours.

18   If the battery has removeable cell caps, measure the specific gravity with a hydrometer every hour during the last few hours of the charging cycle. Inexpensive hydrometers are available from auto parts stores – follow the instructions that come with the hydrometer. Consider the battery charged when there's no change in the specific gravity reading for two hours and the electrolyte in the cells is gassing (bubbling) freely. The spe-

cific gravity reading from each cell should be very close to the others. If not, the battery probably has a bad cell or cells.

19   Some batteries with sealed tops have built-in hydrometers on the top that indicate the state of charge by the color displayed in the hydrometer window. Normally, a bright-colored hydrometer indicates a full charge and a dark hydrometer indicates the battery still needs charging. Check the battery manufacturer's instructions to be sure you know what the colors mean.

20   If the battery has a sealed top and no built-in hydrometer, you can hook up a digital voltmeter across the battery terminals to check the charge. A fully charged battery should read 12.6-volts or higher.

---

11   Drivebelt check, adjustment and replacement

Refer to illustrations 11.3, 11.4 and 11.6
Warning: *The electric cooling fan can activate at any time. Disconnect the fan motor or negative battery cable when working in the vicinity of the fan.*

Check

1   The alternator and air conditioning compressor drivebelts, also referred to simply as "fanbelts", are located at the right (passenger's) side of the engine compartment. The condition and proper adjustment of the drivebelts is critical to the operation of the engine. Since they stretch and deteriorate as they get older, they must be inspected periodically.

2   The number of belts used on a particular vehicle depends on the accessories installed. One belt transmits power from the crankshaft to the alternator and water pump. If the vehicle is equipped with air conditioning, the compressor is driven by a separate belt.

3   With the engine off, open the hood and locate the drivebelts on the end of the engine. With a flashlight, check each belt for separation, cracks, hardness and other damage **(see illustration)**. Also check for fraying and glazing, which gives the belt a shiny appearance. Both sides of the belt should be inspected, which means you'll have to twist the belt to check the underside. Use your fingers to feel the belt where you can't see it. If any of the above conditions are evident, replace the belt (go to Step 7).

4   The tension of each V-belt is checked by pushing firmly on it with your thumb at a distance halfway between the pulleys and noting how far the belt can be moved (deflected). Measure the deflection with a ruler **(see illustration)**. Compare this measurement with the specifications at the beginning of this Chapter.

Adjustment

5   If the alternator belt must be adjusted, loosen the adjustment bolt that secures the alternator to the slotted bracket and pivot the alternator or

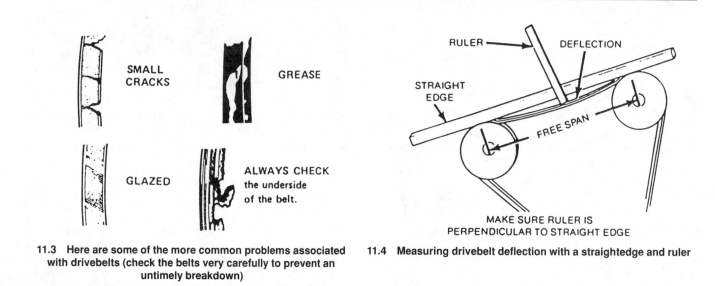

11.3   Here are some of the more common problems associated with drivebelts (check the belts very carefully to prevent an untimely breakdown)

11.4   Measuring drivebelt deflection with a straightedge and ruler

11.6   On air conditioned models, turn the idler pulley bolt (arrow) to adjust the drivebelt tension

power steering pump (away from the engine block to tighten the belt, toward the block to loosen the belt). It's helpful to lever the alternator with a large pry bar when adjusting the belt because the pry bar enables you to precisely position the component until the adjuster bolt is tightened. Be very careful not to damage the aluminum housing of the alternator or power steering pump. Recheck the belt tension using one of the above methods. Repeat this Step until the alternator drivebelt tension is correct.

6   If the air conditioner compressor drivebelt must be adjusted, locate the idler pulley on the front corner of the block and turn the idler pulley adjuster bolt **(see illustration)**. Measure the belt tension. Repeat this step until the air conditioning compressor drivebelt is adjusted.

Replacement

7   To replace a belt, follow the above procedures for drivebelt adjustment but slip the belt off the pulleys to remove it. If you're replacing the power steering belt or air conditioning compressor belt, you'll have to remove the alternator belt first because of the way they're arranged on the pulleys. Because of this and because belts tend to wear out more or less together, it's a good idea to replace both belts at the same time. Mark each belt and its appropriate pulley groove so the replacement belts can be installed in the proper positions.

8   Take the old belts to the parts store to make a direct comparison for length, width and design.

9   Adjust the belt(s) as described above.

---

12   Underhood hose check and replacement

Caution: *Replacement of air conditioning hoses should be left to a dealer service department or air conditioning shop that has the equipment to depressurize the system safely. Never remove air conditioning components or hoses until the system has been depressurized.*

General

1   High temperatures in the engine compartment can cause the deterioration of the rubber and plastic hoses used for engine, accessory and emission systems operation. Periodic inspection should be made for cracks, loose clamps, material hardening and leaks.

2   Information specific to the cooling system hoses can be found in Section 13.

3   Some, but not all, hoses are secured to the fittings with clamps. Where clamps are used, check to be sure they haven't lost their tension, allowing the hose to leak. If clamps aren't used, make sure the hose has not expanded and/or hardened where it slips over the fitting, allowing it to leak.

Vacuum hoses

4   It's quite common for vacuum hoses, especially those in the emissions system, to be color coded or identified by colored stripes molded into

them. Various systems require hoses with different wall thicknesses, collapse resistance and temperature resistance. When replacing hoses, be sure the new ones are made of the same material.

5   Often the only effective way to check a hose is to remove it completely from the vehicle. If more than one hose is removed, be sure to label the hoses and fittings to ensure correct installation.

6   When checking vacuum hoses, be sure to include any plastic T-fittings in the check. Inspect the fittings for cracks and the hose where it fits over the fitting for distortion, which could cause leakage.

7   A small piece of vacuum hose (1/4-inch inside diameter) can be used as a stethoscope to detect vacuum leaks. Hold one end of the hose to your ear and probe around vacuum hoses and fittings, listening for the "hissing" sound characteristic of a vacuum leak. **Warning:** *When probing with the vacuum hose stethoscope, be very careful not to come into contact with moving engine components such as the drivebelts, cooling fan, etc.*

Fuel hose

Warning: *There are certain precautions which must be taken when inspecting or servicing fuel system components. Work in a well ventilated area and do not allow open flames (cigarettes, appliance pilot lights, etc.) or bare light bulbs near the work area. Mop up any spills immediately and do not store fuel soaked rags where they could ignite.*

8   Check all rubber fuel lines for deterioration and chafing. Check especially for cracks in areas where the hose bends and just before fittings, such as where a hose attaches to the fuel filter.

9   High quality fuel line, usually identified by the word Fluroelastomer printed on the hose, should be used for fuel line replacement. Never, under any circumstances, use unreinforced vacuum line, clear plastic tubing or water hose for fuel lines.

10   Spring-type clamps are commonly used on fuel lines. These clamps often lose their tension over a period of time, and can be "sprung" during removal. Replace all spring-type clamps with screw clamps whenever a hose is replaced.

Metal lines

11   Sections of metal line are often used for fuel line between the fuel pump and carburetor or fuel injection. Check carefully to be sure the line has not been bent or crimped and that cracks haven't started in the line.

12   If a section of metal fuel line must be replaced, only seamless steel tubing should be used, since copper and aluminum tubing don't have the strength necessary to withstand normal engine vibration.

13   Check the metal brake lines where they enter the master cylinder and brake proportioning unit (if used) for cracks in the lines or loose fittings. Any sign of brake fluid leakage calls for an immediate thorough inspection of the brake system.

---

13   Cooling system check

Refer to illustration 13.4

1   Many major engine failures can be attributed to a faulty cooling system. If the vehicle is equipped with an automatic transaxle, the cooling system also cools the transmission fluid and thus plays an important role in prolonging transmission life.

2   The cooling system should be checked with the engine cold. Do this before the vehicle is driven for the day or after the engine has been shut off for at least three hours.

3   Remove the radiator cap by turning it to the left until it reaches a stop. If you hear a hissing sound (indicating there is still pressure in the system), wait until it stops. Now press down on the cap with the palm of your hand and continue turning to the left until the cap can be removed. Thoroughly clean the cap, inside and out, with clean water. Also clean the filler neck on the radiator. All traces of corrosion should be removed. The coolant inside the radiator should be relatively transparent. If it's rust colored, the system should be drained and refilled (see Section 32). If the coolant level isn't up to the top, add additional antifreeze/coolant mixture (see Section 4).

4   Carefully check the large upper and lower radiator hoses along with the smaller diameter heater hoses which run from the engine to the firewall. Inspect each hose along its entire length – replace any that are cracked, swollen or otherwise deteriorated. Cracks may show up better if

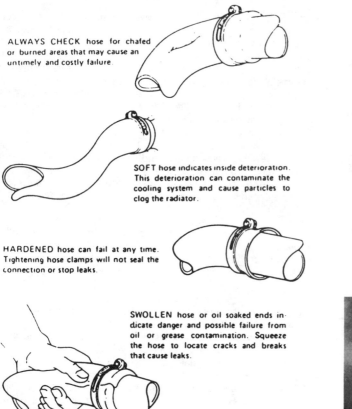

ALWAYS CHECK hose for chafed or burned areas that may cause an untimely and costly failure.

SOFT hose indicates inside deterioration. This deterioration can contaminate the cooling system and cause particles to clog the radiator.

HARDENED hose can fail at any time. Tightening hose clamps will not seal the connection or stop leaks.

SWOLLEN hose or oil soaked ends indicate danger and possible failure from oil or grease contamination. Squeeze the hose to locate cracks and breaks that cause leaks.

13.4   Hoses, like drivebelts, have a habit of failing at the worst possible time – to prevent the inconvenience of a blown radiator or heater hose, inspect them carefully as shown here

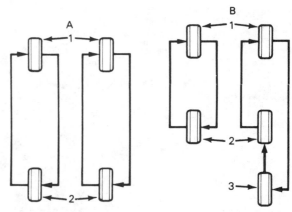

14.2   The recommended tire rotation pattern for these models

A   When spare tire is used   2   Rear tires
B   When spare tire is not used   3   Spare tire
1   Front tires

15.6   You'll find an inspection hole in each caliper – placing a ruler across the hole should enable you to determine the thickness of the remaining pad material for both the inner and outer pads

the hose is squeezed **(see illustration)**. Regardless of condition, it's a good idea to replace hoses with new ones every two years.
5   Make sure all hose connections are tight. A leak in the cooling system will usually show up as white or rust colored deposits on the areas adjoining the leak. If wire-type clamps are used at the ends of the hoses, it may be a good idea to replace them with more secure screw-type clamps.
6   Use a garden hose or a soft brush to remove bugs, leaves, etc. from the front of the radiator or air conditioning condenser. Be careful not to damage the delicate cooling fins or cut yourself on them.
7   Every other inspection, or at the first indication of cooling system problems, have the cap and system pressure tested. If you don't have a pressure tester, most gas stations and repair shops will do this for a minimal charge.

14   Tire rotation

Refer to illustration 14.2
1   The tires should be rotated at the specified intervals and whenever uneven wear is noticed. Since the vehicle will be raised and the tires removed anyway, check the brakes (see Section 15) at this time.
2   Radial tires must be rotated in a specific pattern **(see illustration)**.
3   Refer to the information in *Jacking and towing* at the front of this manual for the proper procedures to follow when raising the vehicle and changing a tire. If the brakes must be checked, do not apply the parking brake as stated. Make sure the tires are blocked to prevent the vehicle from rolling.
4   Preferably, the entire vehicle should be raised at the same time. This can be done on a hoist or by jacking up each corner and then lowering the vehicle onto jackstands placed under the frame rails. Always use four jackstands and make sure the vehicle is securely supported.
5   After rotation, check and adjust the tire pressures as necessary and

be sure to check the lug nut tightness.
6   For more information on the wheels and tires, refer to Chapter 10.

15   Brake check

Note: *For detailed illustrations of the brake system, refer to Chapter 9.*
1   In addition to the specified intervals, the brakes should be inspected every time the wheels are removed or whenever a problem is suspected. Any of the following symptoms could indicate a potential brake system defect: The vehicle pulls to one side when the brake pedal is depressed; the brakes make squealing or dragging noises when applied; brake pedal travel is excessive; the pedal pulsates; brake fluid leaks, usually onto the inside of the tire or wheel.
2   Loosen the wheel lug nuts.
3   Raise the vehicle and place it securely on jackstands.
4   Remove the wheels (see *Jacking and towing* at the front of this book, or your owner's manual, if necessary).

Disc brakes

Refer to illustration 15.6
5   The disc brake pads have built-in wear indicators which make a high-pitched squealing or cricket-like warning sound when the pads are worn.
6   There are two pads – an outer and an inner – in each caliper. The pads are visible through small inspection holes in each caliper **(see illustration)**.

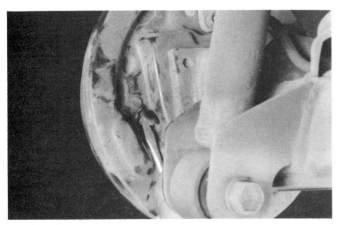

15.12a   On Sprint models you can check the thickness of the remaining brake shoe lining material by first removing the rubber plug in the backing plate with a screwdriver, . . .

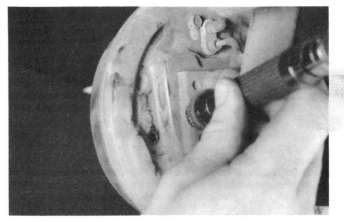

15.12b   . . . then using a small flashlight to inspect the lining

7   Check the pad thickness by looking at each end of the caliper and through the inspection hole in the caliper body. If the lining material is less than the specified thickness, replace the pads. **Note:** *Keep in mind that the lining material is riveted or bonded to a metal backing plate and the metal portion is not included in this measurement.*
8   If it's difficult to determine the exact thickness of the remaining pad material by the above method, or if you're at all concerned about the condition of the pads, remove the caliper(s), then remove the pads from the calipers for further inspection (refer to Chapter 9).
9   Once the pads are removed from the calipers, clean them with brake cleaner and remeasure them with a ruler or a vernier caliper.
10   Check the disc. Look for score marks, deep scratches and burned spots. If these conditions exist, the hub/disc assembly will have to be removed (see Chapter 9).
11   Before installing the wheels, check all brake lines and hoses for damage, wear, deformation, cracks, corrosion and leakage, particularly in the vicinity of the rubber hoses at the calipers. Check the clamps for tightness and the connections for leakage. Make sure all hoses and lines are clear of sharp edges, moving parts and the exhaust system. If any of the above conditions are noted, repair, reroute or replace the lines and/or fittings as necessary (refer to Chapter 9).

Rear drum brakes

Refer to illustrations 15.12a, 15.12b and 15.14

12   On Sprint models, the rear brake lining can be checked without removing the brake drum. Remove the rubber plugs in the backing plates with a small screwdriver and use a flashlight to check the lining thickness **(see illustrations)**.
13   On Geo Metro models, or for more complete brake inspection on Sprint models, refer to Chapter 9 and remove the rear brake drums. **Warning:** *Brake dust produced by lining wear and deposited on brake components may contain asbestos, which is hazardous to your health. DO NOT blow it out with compressed air and DO NOT inhale it! DO NOT use gasoline or solvents to remove the dust. Brake system cleaner should be used to flush the dust into a drain pan. After the brake components are wiped clean with a damp rag, dispose of the contaminated rag(s) and solvent in a covered and labelled container. Try to use non-asbestos replacement parts whenever possible.*
14   Note the thickness of the lining material on the rear brake shoes **(see illustration)** and look for signs of contamination by brake fluid and grease. If the lining material is within 3/64-inch of the recessed rivets or metal shoes, replace the brake shoes with new ones. The shoes should also be replaced if they are cracked, glazed (shiny lining surfaces) or contaminated with brake fluid or grease. See Chapter 9 for the replacement procedure.
15   Check the shoe return and hold-down springs and the adjusting mechanism to make sure they're installed correctly and in good condition.

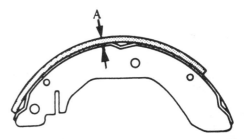

15.14   The rear brake shoe lining thickness is measured from the outer surface of the lining to the metal shoe (arrows)

Deteriorated or distorted springs, if not replaced, could allow the linings to drag and wear prematurely.
16   Check the wheel cylinders for leakage by carefully peeling back the rubber boots. If brake fluid is noted behind the boots, the wheel cylinders must be replaced (see Chapter 9).
17   Check the drums for cracks, score marks, deep scratches and hard spots, which will appear as small discolored areas. If imperfections cannot be removed with emery cloth, the drums must be resurfaced by an automotive machine shop (see Chapter 9 for more detailed information).
18   Refer to Chapter 9 and install the brake drums.
19   Install the wheels and tighten the wheel lug nuts finger-tight.
20   Remove the jackstands and lower the vehicle.
21   Tighten the wheel lug nuts to the torque listed in this Chapter's specifications.

Parking brake

22   A simple method of checking the parking brake is to park the vehicle on a steep hill with the parking brake set and the transmission in Neutral. If the parking brake cannot prevent the vehicle from rolling, adjust it (see Chapter 9).

16   Manual transaxle lubricant level check

Sprint

Refer to illustration 16.2

1   A dipstick is used for checking the lubricant level in the manual transaxle used on these models.

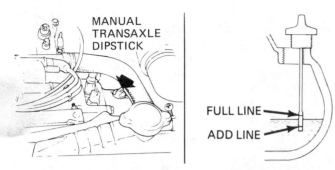

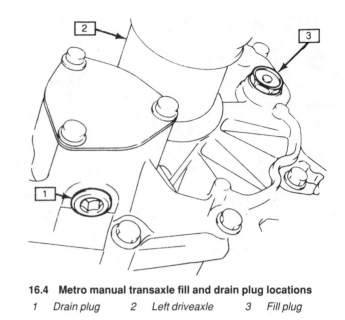

16.2   On Sprint models, the manual transaxle dipstick is located adjacent to the distributor – the lubricant level should be kept between the Full and Add lines

2   With the transaxle cold (cool to the touch) and the vehicle parked on a level surface, remove the dipstick located at the left rear side of the engine compartment **(see illustration)**. The level must be between the two marks on the dipstick.
3   If the level is low, add the specified lubricant through the dipstick hole (use a funnel).

Metro

Refer to illustration 16.4
4   The manual transaxle on these models doesn't have a dipstick. To check the lubricant level, raise the vehicle and support it securely on jackstands. On the left side of the transaxle housing you'll see a plug **(see illustration)**. Remove it. If the lubricant level is correct, it should be up to the lower edge of the hole. Use your finger as a dipstick to check the level.
5   If the transaxle needs more lubricant (if the level is not up to the hole), use a syringe to add more. Stop filling the transaxle when the lubricant begins to run out the hole.
6   Install the plug and tighten it securely. Drive the vehicle a short distance, then check for leaks.

---

17   Carburetor/TBI mounting nut/bolt torque check

---

1   The carburetor or Throttle Body Injection (TBI) body is attached to the top of the intake manifold by several bolts or nuts. These fasteners can sometimes work loose from vibration and temperature changes during normal engine operation and cause a vacuum leak.
2   If you suspect a vacuum leak exists at the bottom of the carburetor or throttle body, obtain a length of hose. Start the engine and place one end of the hose next to your ear as you probe around the base with the other end. You'll hear a hissing sound if a leak exists (be careful of hot or moving engine components).
3   Remove the air cleaner assembly (see Chapter 4), tagging each hose to be disconnected with a piece of numbered tape to make reassembly easier.
4   Locate the mounting bolts at the base of the carburetor or top of the throttle body. Decide what special tools or adapters will be necessary, if any, to tighten the fasteners.
5   Tighten the bolts or nuts to the torque listed in this Chapter's specifications. Don't overtighten them as the threads could strip.
6   If, after the bolts are properly tightened, a vacuum leak still exists, the carburetor or throttle body must be removed and a new gasket installed. See Chapter 4 for more information.
7   After tightening the fasteners, reinstall the air cleaner and return all hoses to their original positions.

---

18   Starter safety switch check

Warning: *During the following checks there's a chance the vehicle could lunge forward, possibly causing damage or injuries. Allow plenty of room*

16.4   Metro manual transaxle fill and drain plug locations
1   Drain plug   2   Left driveaxle   3   Fill plug

---

around the vehicle, apply the parking brake and hold down the regular brake pedal during the checks.
1   On automatic transaxle equipped vehicles, try to start the engine in each gear. The engine should crank only in Park or Neutral.
2   If equipped with a manual transaxle, place the shift lever in Neutral and push the clutch pedal down about half way. The engine should crank only with the clutch pedal fully depressed.
3   Make sure the steering column lock allows the key to go into the Lock position only when the shift lever is in Park (automatic transaxle) or Reverse (manual transaxle).
4   The ignition key should come out only in the Lock position.

---

19   Seatbelt check

Seatbelts

1   Check the seatbelts, buckles, latch plates and guide loops for any obvious damage or signs of wear.
2   Make sure the seatbelt reminder light comes on when the key is turned to the On or Start positions. A chime should also sound.
3   The seatbelts are designed to lock up during a sudden stop or impact, yet allow free movement during normal driving. Make sure the retractors return the belt against your chest while driving and rewind the belt completely when the buckle is unlatched.
4   If any of the above checks reveal problems with the seatbelts, replace parts as necessary.

Automatic shoulder harnesses

5   Many late model vehicles are equipped with automatic front seat shoulder harnesses. They're termed automatic because you don't have to buckle them – the shoulder harness automatically positions itself when the door is closed and the key is turned on. An emergency release lever allows the harness to be manually removed for exit in an emergency. **Warning:** *Be sure to fasten the manual seatbelt as well. The automatic shoulder harness will not work properly unless the seatbelt is fastened.*
6   Most systems have a warning light and buzzer that indicate the emergency release lever has been pulled up, releasing the shoulder harness. Make sure the release lever is down and the light/buzzer are off to ensure proper operation of the automatic shoulder harness. Also, if you disconnect any wires or remove any automatic shoulder harness components when performing repair procedures on other vehicle components, be sure to reinstall everything and check the harness for proper operation when the repairs are complete.

22.2 Push on the driveaxle boot to check for cracks and lubricant leaks

7   Since the automatic shoulder harness is operated by several electrical switches and is computer controlled, diagnosis and repair must be done by a dealer service department. Do not jeopardize the safety of front seat occupants – if the automatic shoulder harness malfunctions, or you have questions regarding the proper use or operation of the system, contact a dealer service department.

___

20 Fuel system check

___

Warning: *Certain precautions should be observed when inspecting or servicing the fuel system components. Work in a well ventilated area and do not allow open flames (cigarettes, appliance pilot lights, etc.) near the work area. Mop up spills immediately and do not store fuel soaked rags where they could ignite. It's a good idea to keep a dry chemical (Class B) fire extinguisher near the work area any time the fuel system is being serviced.*

1   If you smell gasoline while driving or after the vehicle has been sitting in the sun, inspect the fuel system immediately.
2   Remove the gas filler cap and inspect if for damage and corrosion. The gasket should have an unbroken sealing imprint.
3   Inspect the fuel feed and return lines for cracks. Check the metal fuel line connections to make sure they're tight.
4   Since some components of the fuel system – the fuel tank and part of the fuel feed and return lines, for example – are underneath the vehicle, they can be inspected more easily with the vehicle raised on a hoist. If that's not possible, raise the vehicle and secure it on jackstands.
5   With the vehicle raised and safely supported, inspect the gas tank and filler neck for punctures, cracks and other damage. The connection between the filler neck and the tank is particularly critical. Sometimes a rubber filler neck will leak because of loose clamps or deteriorated rubber. These are problems a home mechanic can usually rectify. **Warning:** *Do not, under any circumstances, try to repair a fuel tank (except rubber components). A welding torch or any open flame can easily cause fuel vapors inside the tank to explode.*
6   Carefully check all rubber hoses and metal lines leading away from the fuel tank. Check for loose connections, deteriorated hoses, crimped lines and other damage. Carefully inspect the lines from the tank to the engine. Repair or replace damaged sections as necessary.

___

21 Steering and suspension check

___

Note: *For detailed illustrations of the steering and suspension components, refer to Chapter 10.*

With the wheels on the ground

1   With the vehicle stopped and the front wheels pointed straight ahead, rock the steering wheel gently back-and-forth. If free play is excessive, a

front wheel bearing, main shaft yoke, intermediate shaft yoke, control arm balljoint or steering system joint is worn or the steering gear is out of adjustment or broken. Refer to Chapter 10 for the appropriate repair procedure.
2   Other symptoms, such as excessive vehicle body movement over rough roads, swaying (leaning) around corners and binding as the steering wheel is turned, may indicate faulty steering and/or suspension components.
3   Check the shock absorbers by pushing down and releasing the vehicle several times at each corner. If the vehicle doesn't come back to a level position within one or two bounces, the shocks/struts are worn and must be replaced. When bouncing the vehicle up-and-down, listen for squeaks and noises from the suspension components. Additional information on suspension components can be found in Chapter 10.

With the vehicle raised

4   Raise the vehicle and support it securely on jackstands. See Jacking and towing at the front of this book for the proper jacking points.
5   Check the tires for irregular wear patterns and proper inflation. See Section 5 in this Chapter for information regarding tire wear and Chapter 10 for the wheel bearing servicing procedures.
6   Inspect the universal joint between the steering shaft and the steering gear housing. Check the steering gear housing for leaks. Make sure the dust seals and boots are undamaged and the boot clamps are tight. Check the steering linkage for play and damage. Check the tie-rod ends for excessive play. Look for loose bolts, broken or disconnected parts and deteriorated rubber bushings on all suspension and steering components. While an assistant turns the steering wheel from side-to-side, check the steering components for free movement, chafing and binding. If the steering components do not seem to be responding to movement of the steering wheel, try to determine where the slack is located.
7   Inspect the balljoint boots for damage and leaking grease.

___

22 Driveaxle boot check

___

Refer to illustration 22.2

1   The driveaxle boots are very important because they prevent dirt, water and foreign material from entering and damaging the constant velocity (CV) joints. The boot material can deteriorate prematurely, so it's a good idea to occasionally wash the boots with soap and water.
2   Inspect the boots for tears and cracks as well as loose clamps **(see illustration)**. If there is any evidence of cracks or leaking lubricant, they must be replaced as described in Chapter 8.

___

23 Exhaust system check

___

1   With the engine cold (at least three hours after the vehicle has been driven), check the complete exhaust system from its starting point at the engine to the end of the tailpipe. This should be done on a hoist where unrestricted access is available.
2   Check the pipes and connections for evidence of leaks, severe corrosion or damage. Make sure all brackets and hangers are in good condition and tight.
3   At the same time, inspect the underside of the body for holes, corrosion, open seams, etc. which may allow exhaust gases to enter the passenger compartment. Seal all body openings with silicone or body putty.
4   Rattles and other noises can often be traced to the exhaust system, especially the mounts and hangers. Try to move the pipes, muffler and catalytic converter. If the components can come in contact with the body or suspension parts, secure the exhaust system with new mounts.
5   Check the running condition of the engine by inspecting inside the end of the tailpipe. The exhaust deposits here are an indication of engine condition. If the pipe is wet with oil or coated with white deposits, the engine is in need of service, including a compression test, a thorough fuel system inspection and adjustment.

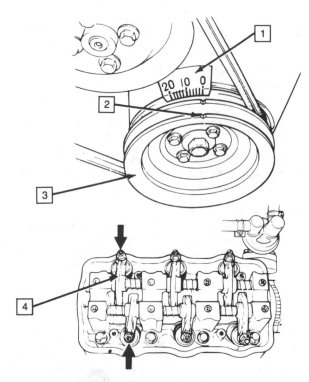

24.4   Position the number one piston at TDC on the compression stroke and adjust the valves indicated by arrows

1	*Timing tag*
2	*Pulley notch*
3	*Crankshaft pulley*

4	*Number one cylinder rocker*
	arms (arrows)

24   Valve clearance check and adjustment (Sprint only)

Refer to illustrations 24.4, 24.6, 24.7, 24.8 and 24.10

Warning: *The electric cooling fan can activate at any time. Disconnect the fan motor or negative battery cable when working in the vicinity of the fan.*

1   The valve clearances are checked and adjusted with the engine at normal operating temperature.

2   Remove the air cleaner assembly.

3   Remove the valve cover (see Chapter 2, Part A).

4   Place the number one piston at Top Dead Center (TDC) on the compression stroke (see Chapter 2, Part A). The number one cylinder rocker arms (closest to the timing belt end of the engine) should be loose (able to move up-and-down slightly) and the notch in the crankshaft pulley should line up with the 0 on the timing tag **(see illustration)**. If they aren't, the number one piston is not at TDC on the compression stroke.

5   Check/adjust only the valves indicated by arrows in illustration 24.4. The valve clearances can be found in the Specifications at the beginning of this Chapter.

6   The clearance is measured by inserting the specified size feeler gauge between the end of the valve stem and the adjusting screw. You should feel a slight amount of drag when the feeler gauge is moved back-and-forth **(see illustration)**.

7   If the gap is too large or too small, loosen the locknut and turn the adjusting screw to obtain the correct gap **(see illustration)**. Recheck the clearance to make sure it hasn't changed.

8   Rotate the crankshaft 240-degrees until the number three piston is at TDC on the compression stroke. The number three cylinder rocker arms (closest to the transaxle end of the engine) should be loose and notch in the crankshaft pulley should be lined up with the timing cover bolt at the lower left corner of the engine **(see illustration)**.

9   Adjust the valves indicated by arrows in illustration 24.8 as described in Steps 6 and 7.

24.6   You should feel a slight amount of drag when the feeler gauge is moved back-and-forth

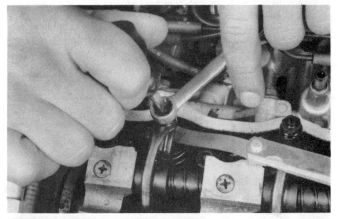

24.7   To adjust the valve clearance, use a box-end wrench to loosen the locknut slightly and a screwdriver to turn the adjusting screw

10   Rotate the crankshaft an additional 240-degrees until the number two piston is at TDC on the compression stroke. The number two rocker arms should be loose and the crankshaft pulley notch should line up with the lower right timing cover bolt **(see illustration)**.

11   Adjust the valves indicated by arrows in illustration 24.10.

12   Install the valve cover and air cleaner assembly.

25   Manual transaxle lubricant change

1   Remove the drain plug from the bottom of the transaxle and allow all lubricant to drain into a pan.

2   Reinstall the drain plug and tighten it to the specified torque.

3   On sprint models, add the specified amount of lubricant through the dipstick hole and check the level with the dipstick (Section 16).

4   On Metro models, add new lubricant until it begins to run out of the filler hole (see Section 16). See *Recommended lubricants and fluids* for the specified lubricant type.

5   Reinstall and tighten the fill plug (Metro).

6   Drive the vehicle and check for leaks at the drain plug after the engine reaches normal operating tremperature.

26   Air filter replacement

Refer to illustrations 26.2 and 26.3

Warning: *The electric cooling fan can activate at any time. Disconnect the fan motor or negative battery cable when working in the vicinity of the fan.*

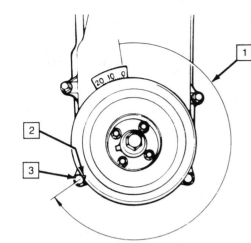

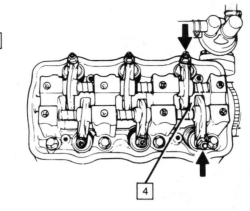

24.8   Number three cylinder valve adjustment details

1   Rotate the crankshaft 240-degrees
2   Crankshaft pulley notch
3   Lower left timing belt cover bolt
4   Number three cylinder rocker arms (arrows)

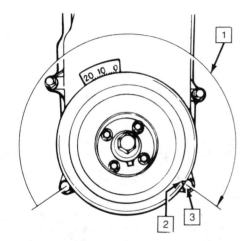

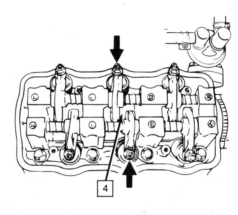

24.10   Number two cylinder valve adjustment details

1   Rotate the crankshaft 240-degrees
2   Crankshaft pulley notch
3   Lower right timing belt cover bolt
4   Number two cylinder rocker arms (arrows)

26.2   Release the clips around the edge, unscrew the wing nut in the center, then lift the top of the filter housing off

26.3   Hold the top up out of the way and lift out the air filter element, then wipe out the inside of the housing with a clean rag

1   The air filter should be replaced with a new one at the specified intervals. The engine air cleaner also supplies filtered air to the PCV system.
2   The filter is located on top of the carburetor or throttle body and is replaced by unscrewing the wing nut, detaching the clips from the top of the filter housing and lifting off the cover **(see illustration)**.
3   Lift the filter element out **(see illustration)** and wipe out the inside of the housing with a clean rag.
4   Place the new filter in the housing. Make sure it seats properly in the bottom of the housing.

5   Install the top plate and any hoses which were disconnected. Don't overtighten the wing nut.

27   Fuel filter replacement

Warning: *Gasoline is extremely flammable, so extra precautions must be taken when working on any part of the fuel system. Do not smoke or allow open flames or bare light bulbs in or near the work area. Also, don't work in a garage if a natural gas-type appliance with a pilot light is present.*

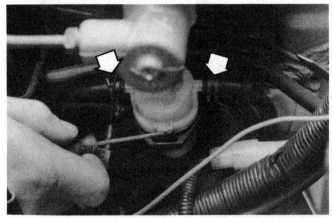

27.4   Loosen the clamps (arrows), detach the hoses, then use a screwdriver to disconnect the filter from the bracket

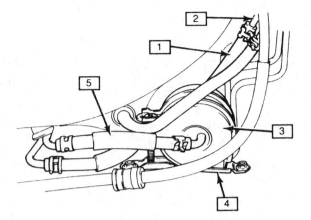

27.12   Fuel-injected model fuel filter

1	Outlet hose	3	Fuel filter	5	Inlet hose
2	Fuel feed line	4	Mounting bracket		

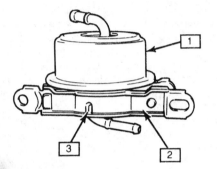

27.13   Make sure the match marks on the filter and the bracket line up

1	Fuel filter	2	Bracket	3	Match marks

Carburetor-equipped engines

Refer to illustration 27.4

1   Remove the fuel filler cap to eliminate the residual pressure from the fuel system, then reinstall it .

2   The fuel filter is located on the firewall, below the brake master cylinder.

3   Release the hose clamps at the filter fittings and slide them back up the hoses.

4   Detach the filter from the bracket and disconnect the hoses **(see illustration)**. Now would be a good time to replace the hoses if they're deteriorated.

5   Push the hoses onto the new filter and position the clamps approximately 1/4-inch back from the ends.

6   Push the filter back into the bracket. Check to make sure it's held securely and the hoses aren't kinked.

7   Start the engine and check for fuel leaks at the filter.

Fuel-injected engines

Refer to illustrations 27.12 and 27.13

Warning: *Before removing the fuel filter, the fuel system pressure must be relieved – refer to Chapter 4 for the procedure. Wear eye protection.*

8   The fuel filter is located under the rear of the vehicle at the left front corner of the fuel tank.

9   Disconnect the negative battery cable, raise the vehicle and support it securely on jackstands.

10   Place a metal drain pan under the filter.

11   Slide back the hose clamps, then disconnect the fuel filter inlet and outlet hoses.

12   Remove the bolts and detach the filter from the vehicle **(see illustration)**. Remove the bracket and transfer it to the new filter.

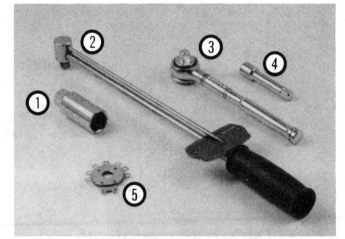

28.1   Tools required for changing spark plugs

1   **Spark plug socket** – *This will have special padding inside to protect the spark plug's porcelain insulator*

2   **Torque wrench** – *Although not mandatory, using this tool is the best way to ensure the plugs are tightened properly*

3   **Ratchet** – *Standard hand tool to fit the spark plug socket*

4   **Extension** – *Depending on model and accessories, you may need special extensions and universal joints to reach one or more of the plugs*

5   **Spark plug gap gauge** – *This gauge for checking the gap comes in a variety of styles. Make sure the gap for your engine is included.*

13   Attach the bracket to the new filter; be sure to line up the match marks **(see illustration)**.

14   Install the fuel filter and bracket assembly. Tighten the bolts securely.

15   Connect the inlet and outlet hoses.

16   Start the engine and check for fuel leaks at the filter.

---

28   Spark plug replacement

Refer to illustrations 28.1, 28.4a, 28.4b, 28.6, 28.8 and 28.10

1   Spark plug replacement requires a spark plug socket which fits onto a ratchet. This socket is lined with rubber to protect the porcelain insulator of the spark plug and to hold the plug while you insert it into the spark plug hole. You'll also need a wire-type feeler gauge to check and adjust the spark plug gap and a torque wrench to tighten the new plugs to the specified torque **(see illustration)**.

CARBON DEPOSITS

Symptoms: Dry sooty deposits indicate a rich mixture or weak ignition. Causes misfiring, hard starting and hesitation.

Recommendation: Check for a clogged air cleaner, high float level, sticky choke and worn ignition points. Use a spark plug with a longer core nose for greater anti-fouling protection.

OIL DEPOSITS

Symptoms: Oily coating caused by poor oil control. Oil is leaking past worn valve guides or piston rings into the combustion chamber. Causes hard starting, misfiring and hesition.

Recommendation: Correct the mechanical condition with necessary repairs and install new plugs.

TOO HOT

Symptoms: Blistered, white insulator, eroded electrode and absence of deposits. Results in shortened plug life.

Recommendation: Check for the correct plug heat range, over-advanced ignition timing, lean fuel mixture, intake manifold vacuum leaks and sticking valves. Check the coolant level and make sure the radiator is not clogged.

PREIGNITION

Symptoms: Melted electrodes. Insulators are white, but may be dirty due to misfiring or flying debris in the combustion chamber. Can lead to engine damage.

Recommendation: Check for the correct plug heat range, over-advanced ignition timing, lean fuel mixture, clogged cooling system and lack of lubrication.

HIGH SPEED GLAZING

Symptoms: Insulator has yellowish, glazed appearance. Indicates that combustion chamber temperatures have risen suddenly during hard acceleration. Normal deposits melt to form a conductive coating. Causes misfiring at high speeds.

Recommendation: Install new plugs. Consider using a colder plug if driving habits warrant.

GAP BRIDGING

Symptoms: Combustion deposits lodge between the electrodes. Heavy deposits accumulate and bridge the electrode gap. The plug ceases to fire, resulting in a dead cylinder.

Recommendation: Locate the faulty plug and remove the deposits from between the electrodes.

NORMAL

Symptoms: Brown to grayish-tan color and slight electrode wear. Correct heat range for engine and operating conditions.

Recommendation: When new spark plugs are installed, replace with plugs of the same heat range.

ASH DEPOSITS

Symptoms: Light brown deposits encrusted on the side or center electrodes or both. Derived from oil and/or fuel additives. Excessive amounts may mask the spark, causing misfiring and hesitation during acceleration.

Recommendation: If excessive deposits accumulate over a short time or low mileage, install new valve guide seals to prevent seepage of oil into the combustion chambers. Also try changing gasoline brands.

WORN

Symptoms: Rounded electrodes with a small amount of deposits on the firing end. Normal color. Causes hard starting in damp or cold weather and poor fuel economy.

Recommendation: Replace with new plugs of the same heat range.

DETONATION

Symptoms: Insulators may be cracked or chipped. Improper gap setting techniques can also result in a fractured insulator tip. Can lead to piston damage.

Recommendation: Make sure the fuel anti-knock values meet engine requirements. Use care when setting the gaps on new plugs. Avoid lugging the engine.

SPLASHED DEPOSITS

Symptoms: After long periods of misfiring, deposits can loosen when normal combustion temperature is restored by an overdue tune-up. At high speeds, deposits flake off the piston and are thrown against the hot insulator, causing misfiring.

Recommendation: Replace the plugs with new ones or clean and reinstall the originals.

MECHANICAL DAMAGE

Symptoms: May be caused by a foreign object in the combustion chamber or the piston striking an incorrect reach (too long) plug. Causes a dead cylinder and could result in piston damage.

Recommendation: Remove the foreign object from the engine and/or install the correct reach plug.

28.4a Spark plug manufacturers recommend using a wire type gauge when checking the gap – if the wire does not slide between the electrodes with a slight drag, adjustment is required

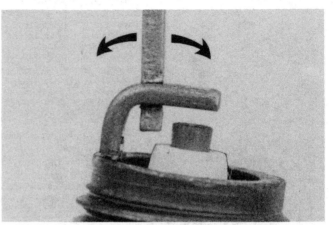

28.4b To change the gap, bend the *side* electrode only, as indicated by the arrows, and be very careful not to crack or chip the porcelain insulator surrounding the center electrode

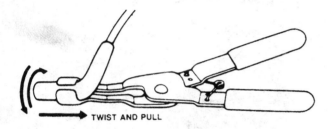

TWIST AND PULL

28.6 When removing the spark plug wires, pull only on the boot and twist it back-and-forth

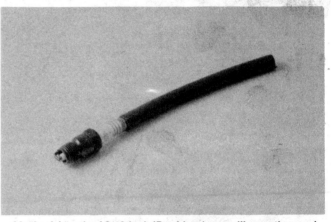

28.10 A length of 3/16-inch ID rubber hose will save time and prevent damaged threads when installing the spark plugs

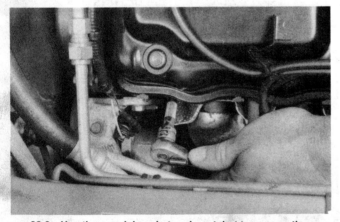

28.8 Use the special socket and a ratchet to remove the spark plugs

2   When replacing plugs, purchase new ones in advance, adjust the gap and then replace each plug one at a time. **Note:** *When buying new spark plugs, it's essential that you obtain the correct plugs for your specific vehicle. This information can be found in this Chapter's specifications, on the Vehicle Emissions Control Information (VECI) label located on the underside of the hood or in the owner's manual. If these sources specify different plugs, purchase the type specified on the VECI label because that information is provided specifically for your engine.*

3   Inspect each of the new plugs for defects. If there are any cracks in the porcelain insulator of a plug, don't use it.

4   Check the gaps on the new plugs by inserting a wire gauge of the proper thickness between the electrodes **(see illustration)**. The gap between the electrodes should be as specified on the VECI label. If the gap is incorrect, use the notched adjuster on the feeler gauge body to bend the curved side electrode slightly **(see illustration)**.

5   If the side electrode is not exactly over the center electrode, use the notched adjuster to align them.

6   To prevent the possibility of mixing up spark plug wires, work on one spark plug at a time. Remove the wire and boot from one spark plug. Grasp the boot – not the cable – as shown, give it a half twist and pull it off **(see illustration)**.

7   If compressed air is available, blow any dirt or foreign material away from the spark plug area before proceeding (a bicycle tire pump will also work).

8   Remove the spark plug **(see illustration)**.

9   Compare each old spark plug with those shown in the accompanying color photos to determine the overall running condition of the engine.

10   It's often difficult to insert spark plugs into their holes without cross-threading them. To avoid this possibility, fit a short piece of 3/16-inch ID rubber hose over the end of the spark plug **(see illustration)**. The flexible hose acts as a universal joint to help align the plug with the plug hole. If the plug begins to cross-thread, the hose will slip on the spark plug, preventing thread damage. Tighten the plug securely.

11   Attach the plug wire to the new spark plug, again using a twisting motion on the boot until it's firmly seated on the end of the spark plug.

12   Follow the above procedure for the remaining spark plugs, replacing them one at a time to prevent mixing up the spark plug wires.

---

29   Spark plug wire, distributor cap and rotor check and replacement

---

Refer to illustrations 29.11a, 29.11b and 29.12

1   The spark plug wires should be checked whenever new spark plugs are installed.

29.11a   After detaching the clips, the distributor cap can be lifted off

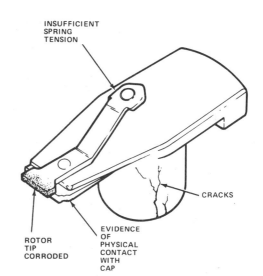

29.12   The ignition rotor should be checked for wear and corrosion as indicated here (if in doubt about its condition, buy a new one)

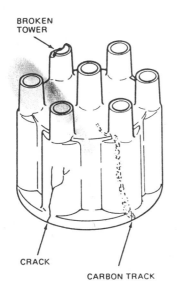

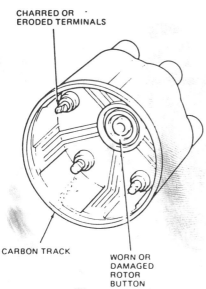

29.11b   Shown here are some of the common defects to look for when inspecting the distributor cap (if in doubt about its condition, install a new one)

2   Begin this procedure by making a visual check of the spark plug wires while the engine is running. In a darkened garage (make sure there's ventilation) start the engine and watch each plug wire. Be careful not to come into contact with any moving engine parts. If there's a break in the wire, you'll see arcing or a small spark at the damaged area. If arcing is noticed, make a note to obtain new wires, then allow the engine to cool and check the distributor cap and rotor.

3   The spark plug wires should be inspected one at a time to prevent mixing up the order, which is essential for proper engine operation. Each original plug wire should be numbered to help identify its location. If the number is illegible, a piece of tape can be marked with the correct number and wrapped around the plug wire.

4   Disconnect the plug wire from the spark plug. A removal tool can be used for this purpose or you can grasp the rubber boot, twist it and pull it off. Do not pull on the wire itself.

5   Check inside the boot for corrosion, which will look like a white crusty powder.

6   Push the wire and boot back onto the end of the spark plug. It should fit tightly. If it doesn't, remove the wire and use pliers to carefully crimp the metal connector inside the wire boot until the fit is snug.

7   Using a clean rag, wipe the entire length of the wire to remove built-up dirt and grease. Once the wire is clean, check for burns, cracks and other damage. Don't bend the wire sharply, because the conductor might break.

8   Disconnect the wire from the distributor. Again, pull only on the rubber boot. Check for corrosion and a tight fit. Press the wire back into the distributor.

9   Inspect the remaining spark plug wires, making sure each one is securely fastened at the distributor and spark plug when the check is complete.

10   If new spark plug wires are required, purchase a set for your specific engine model. Pre-cut wire sets with the boots already installed are available. Remove and replace the wires one at a time to avoid mix-ups in the firing order.

11   Remove the distributor cap by detaching the clips (**see illustration**). Look inside it for cracks, carbon tracks and worn, burned or loose contacts (**see illustration**).

12   Pull the rotor off the distributor shaft and examine it for cracks and carbon tracks (**see illustration**). Replace the cap and rotor if any damage or defects are noted.

13   It's common practice to install a new cap and rotor whenever new spark plug wires are installed, but if you reuse the old cap, clean the terminals first.

14   When installing a new cap, remove the wires from the old cap one at a time and attach them to the new cap in the exact same location – do not

30.3   With the air cleaner removed, the choke plate is visible in the carburetor throat

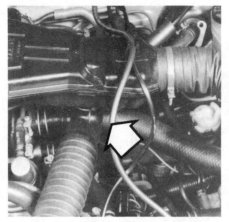

31.3   The air control valve is located in the air cleaner snorkel (arrow)

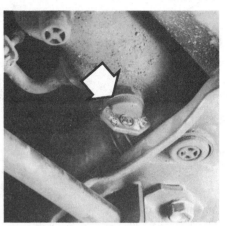

32.4   The radiator drain (arrow) is mounted in the bottom tank

simultaneously remove all the wires from the old cap or firing order mix-ups may occur.

30   Carburetor choke check

Refer to illustration 30.3

Warning: *The electric cooling fan can activate at any time. Disconnect the fan motor or negative battery cable when working in the vicinity of the fan.*

1   The choke operates only when the engine is cold, so this check should be performed before the engine has been started for the day.

2   Take off the top plate of the air cleaner assembly. It's held in place by a wing nut at the top and clips on the side. If any vacuum hoses must be disconnected, make sure you tag the hoses for reinstallation in their original positions. Place the top plate and wing nut aside, out of the way of moving engine components.

3   Look at the center of the air cleaner housing. You'll notice a flat plate at the carburetor opening **(see illustration)**.

4   Press the accelerator pedal to the floor. The plate should close completely. Start the engine while you watch the plate at the carburetor. Don't position your face near the carburetor, as the engine could backfire, causing serious burns. When the engine starts, the choke plate should open slightly.

5   Allow the engine to continue running at an idle speed. As the engine warms up to operating temperature, the plate should slowly open, allowing more air to enter through the top of the carburetor.

6   After a few minutes, the choke plate should be fully open to the vertical position. Blip the throttle to make sure the fast idle cam disengages.

7   You'll notice that engine speed corresponds with the plate opening. With the plate nearly closed, the engine should run at a fast idle speed. As the plate opens and the throttle is moved to disengage the fast idle cam, the engine speed will decrease.

8   Refer to Chapter 4 for specific information on adjusting and servicing the choke components.

31   Thermostatically controlled air cleaner check (carburetor-equipped models only)

Refer to illustration 31.3

Warning: *The electric cooling fan can activate at any time. Disconnect the fan motor or negative battery cable when working in the vicinity of the fan.*

1   Carburetor-equipped engines have a thermostatically controlled air cleaner which draws air from different locations, depending on engine temperature.

2   This is a visual check, requiring use of a small mirror.

3   When the engine is cold, locate the air control valve inside the air cleaner assembly. It's inside the snorkel of the air cleaner housing **(see illustration)**.

4   There's a flexible air duct attached to the end of the snorkel, disconnect it at the snorkel. This will enable you to look through the end of the snorkel and see the air control valve inside.

5   Start the engine and look through the snorkel at the valve, which should move up to block off the air cleaner snorkel. With the valve closed, air cannot enter through the end of the snorkel, but instead enters the air cleaner through the flexible duct attached to the exhaust manifold and the heat stove passage.

6   As the engine warms up to operating temperature, the valve should move down to allow air to be drawn through the snorkel end. Depending on outside temperature, this may take 10-to-15 minutes. To speed up this check you can reconnect the snorkel air duct, drive the vehicle, then check to see if the valve is completely open.

7   If the thermostatically controlled air cleaner isn't operating properly, see Chapter 6 for more information.

32   Cooling system servicing (draining, flushing and refilling)

Refer to illustration 32.4

Warning: *Antifreeze is a corrosive and poisonous solution, so be careful not to spill any of the coolant mixture on the vehicle's paint or your skin. If this happens, rinse immediately with plenty of clean water. Consult local authorities regarding proper disposal procedures for antifreeze before draining the cooling system. In many areas, reclamation centers have been established to collect used oil and coolant mixtures. The electric cooling fan can activate at any time, even when the ignition is in the Off position. Disconnect the fan motor or negative battery cable when working in the vicinity of the fan.*

1   The cooling system should periodically be drained, flushed and re-filled to replenish the antifreeze mixture and prevent formation of rust and corrosion, which can impair the performance of the cooling system and cause engine damage. When the cooling system is serviced, all hoses and the radiator cap should be checked and replaced if necessary.

Draining

2   Apply the parking brake and block the wheels. If the vehicle has just been driven, wait several hours to allow the engine to cool before beginning this procedure.

3   Once the engine is completely cool, remove the radiator cap.

4   Remove the splash panel located beneath the radiator (if equipped), then move a large container under the radiator drain to catch the coolant. Open the drain fitting **(see illustration)**.

5   After the coolant stops flowing out of the radiator, move the container under the engine block drain plug (if equipped). Loosen the plug and allow the coolant in the block to drain.

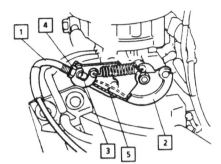

33.3 Before checking the idle speed, check the accelerator cable to make sure it isn't too tight (it should have about 1/8-inch play)

1   Accelerator cable   3   Cable adjusting nut   5   Cable play
2   Throttle lever   4   Locknut

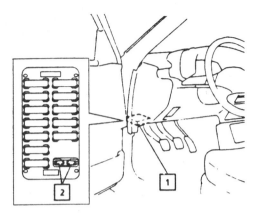

33.4 On Metro models, remove the spare fuse (1) and place it in the diagnosis terminal (2) before checking the idle speed

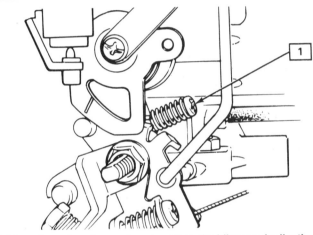

33.9a On carburetor-equipped models, the idle speed adjusting screw (1) is located at the rear of the carburetor

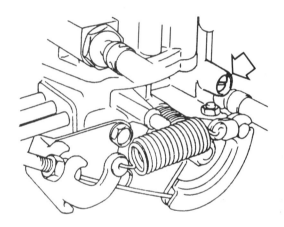

33.9b Idle speed adjusting screw location (fuel-injected models)

6   While the coolant is draining, check the condition of the radiator hoses, heater hoses and clamps (refer to Section 13 if necessary).
7   Replace any damaged clamps or hoses (refer to Chapter 3 for detailed replacement procedures).

Flushing

8   Once the system is completely drained, flush the radiator with fresh water from a garden hose until water runs clear at the drain. The flushing action of the water will remove sediments from the radiator but will not remove rust and scale from the engine and cooling tube surfaces.
9   These deposits can be removed by the chemical action of a cleaner. Follow the procedure outlined in the manufacturer's instructions. If the radiator is severely corroded, damaged or leaking, it should be removed (see Chapter 3) and taken to a radiator repair shop.
10   Remove the overflow hose from the coolant recovery reservoir. Drain the reservoir and flush it with clean water, then reconnect the hose.

Refilling

11   Close the radiator drain. Install and tighten the block drain plug.
12   Place the heater temperature control in the maximum heat position.
13   Slowly add new coolant (a 50/50 mixture of water and antifreeze) to the radiator until it's full. Add coolant to the reservoir up to the lower mark.
14   Leave the radiator cap off and run the engine in a well-ventilated area until the thermostat opens (coolant will begin flowing through the radiator and the upper radiator hose will get hot).
15   Turn the engine off and let it cool. Add more coolant mixture to bring the level back up to the lip on the radiator filler neck.

16   Squeeze the upper radiator hose to expel air, then add more coolant mixture if necessary. Replace the radiator cap.
17   Start the engine, allow it to reach normal operating temperature and check for leaks.

33   Idle speed check and adjustment

Refer to illustrations 33.3, 33.4, 33.9a and 33.9b

1   Engine idle speed is the speed at which the engine operates when no accelerator pedal pressure is applied, as when stopped at a traffic light. This speed is critical to the performance of the engine itself, as well as many engine subsystems.
2   Set the parking brake and block the wheels to prevent the vehicle from rolling. Put the transaxle in Neutral (manual) or Park (automatic).
3   Make sure the accelerator cable is not too tight. If necessary, turn the adjusting nut so there is approximately 1/8-inch play in the cable where it connects to the throttle lever **(see illustration)**.
4   On Metro models, remove the spare fuse from the fuse block and install it in the diagnosis terminal **(see illustration)**.
5   Connect a hand-held tachometer.
6   Start the engine and allow it to reach normal operating temperature.
7   Check, and adjust if necessary, the ignition timing (see Chapter 5).
8   Check the engine idle speed on the tachometer and compare it to the Vehicle Emission Control Information label in the engine compartment.
9   If the idle speed is too low or too high, turn the idle speed adjusting screw **(see illustrations)** until the specified idle speed is obtained.

34.7   The automatic transaxle drain plug is located in a recess in the bottom of the pan (arrow) – use a socket wrench to avoid rounding off the hex

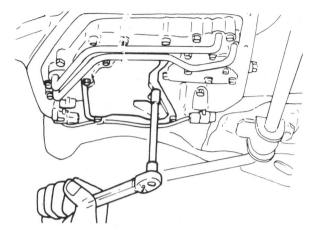

34.9   Remove the filter bolts and detach the filter

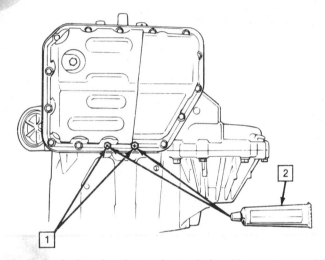

34.12   Apply thread sealant to the two bolts with cross grooved heads before installing them

1   Cross grooved head bolts   2   Thread sealant

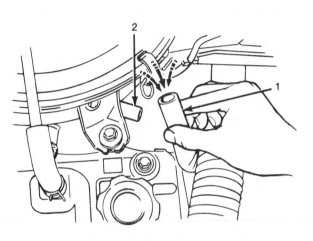

35.2   With the engine cold and the second air hose (1) disconnected from the air cleaner housing (2), a bubbling sound should be heard as air is drawn in

34   Automatic transaxle fluid and filter change

Refer to illustrations 34.7, 34.9 and 34.12

1   At the specified time intervals, the automatic transaxle fluid should be drained and replaced.

2   Before beginning work, purchase the specified transmission fluid (see *Recommended lubricants and fluids* at the front of this Chapter).

3   Other tools necessary for this job include jackstands to support the vehicle in a raised position, a drain pan capable of holding several quarts, newspapers and clean rags.

4   The fluid should be drained immediately after the vehicle has been driven. Hot fluid is more effective than cold fluid at removing built up sediment. **Warning:** *Fluid temperature can exceed 350-degrees in a hot transaxle. Wear protective gloves.*

5   After the vehicle has been driven to warm up the fluid, raise it and place it on jackstands for access to the transaxle drain plug. On some models it may be necessary to remove bolts from the engine torque rod and suspension sway bar for access.

6   Move the necessary equipment under the vehicle, being careful not to touch any of the hot exhaust components.

7   Place the drain pan under the drain plug in the transaxle pan. Remove the drain plug **(see illustration)**. Be sure the drain pan is positioned cor-

rectly, as fluid will come out with some force. Once the fluid is drained, reinstall the drain plug securely.

8   Remove the transaxle pan bolts, carefully pry the pan loose with a screwdriver and remove it.

9   Remove the filter retaining bolts and detach the filter from the transaxle **(see illustration)**. Be careful when lowering the filter as it contains residual fluid.

10   Place the new filter in position and install the bolts. Tighten them to the torque listed in this Chapter's Specifications.

11   Carefully clean the gasket surfaces of the pan, removing all traces of old gasket material. Clean the pan with solvent and dry it with compressed air. Be sure to clean and reinstall any magnet(s).

12   Install a new gasket, place the pan in position and install the bolts. Apply sealant to the threads of the two bolts with cross grooved heads before installing them **(see illustration)**. Tighten the bolts to the specified torque.

13   With the engine off, add new fluid to the transaxle through the dipstick tube (see *Recommended lubricants and fluids* for the recommended fluid type and capacity). Use a funnel to prevent spills. It's best to add a little fluid at a time, continually checking the level with the dipstick (see Section 6). Allow the fluid time to drain into the pan.

14   Start the engine and shift through all positions from Park through Low, then shift into Park and apply the parking brake.

15   With the engine idling, check the fluid level. Add fluid up to the HOT level on the dipstick.

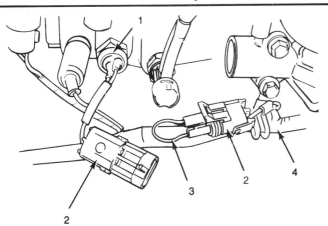

35.4a   On 1985 and 1986 models, short the connector with a jumper wire

1	Coolant temperature sender	3	Jumper wire
2	Disconnected plug	4	Wiring harness

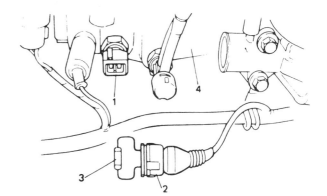

35.4b   1987 and 1988 model Pulse Air system check details

1   Coolant temperature sensor
2   Disconnected plug
3   Jumper incorporating a 10,000 ohm resistor
4   Intake manifold

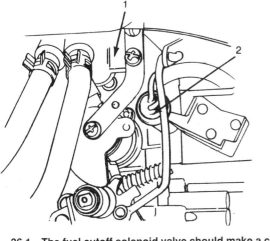

36.1   The fuel cutoff solenoid valve should make a clicking sound when the ignition switch is turned on

1   Carburetor   2   Fuel cutoff solenoid valve

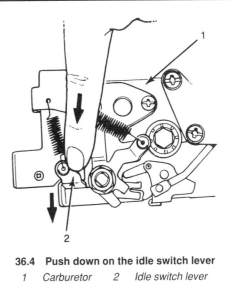

36.4   Push down on the idle switch lever

1   Carburetor   2   Idle switch lever

---

35   Pulse Air System check (carburetor-equipped models only)

Refer to illustrations 35.2, 35.4a and 35.4b

1   Inspect the Pulse Air System hoses, pipe and electrical connector connected to the air cleaner housing for damage and loose connections.

2   With the engine cold, disconnect the second air hose from the air cleaner housing, start the engine, allow it to idle, then make sure air can be heard being drawn into the hose (listen for a bubbling sound) **(see illustration)**.

3   Allow the engine to warm up to normal operating temperature. Air should no longer be drawn into the hose. Increase the engine speed to around 3000 rpm, then release the throttle. Air should be now be drawn into the hose as the engine speed drops.

4   Unplug the coolant temperature sensor electrical connector. Install a jumper in the wiring harness side of the connector (1985 and 1986 models) or a jumper incorporating a 10 thousand ohm resistance (1987 and 1988 models). Shorting the connector in this manner will cause air to again be drawn into the hose **(see illustrations)**.

5   Refer to Chapter 6 for more information on the Pulse Air System.

36   Fuel cutoff system check (carburetor-equipped models only)

Refer to illustrations 36.1 and 36.4

1   Turn the ignition switch on and off several times and listen for a clicking sound from the fuel cutoff solenoid valve (located on the carburetor) indicating that it's operating **(see illustration)**.

2   Start the engine and allow it to idle and warm up to normal operating temperature.

3   On manual transaxle models, make sure the clutch is engaged (transaxle in Neutral).

4   Have an assistant push down on the accelerator and hold the engine at a fast idle speed (between 3000 and 4000 rpm), then push down on the idle switch lever on the carburetor and make sure the engine speed changes **(see illustration)**.

5   On manual transaxle models, repeat this check with the clutch pedal depressed (clutch disengaged). The engine speed should not change when the idle switch lever is pushed.

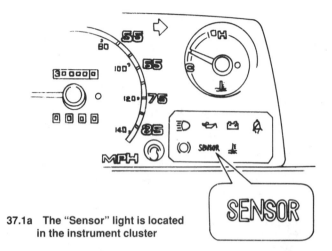

37.1a The "Sensor" light is located in the instrument cluster

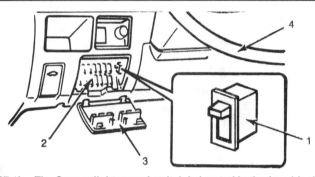

37.1b The Sensor light cancel switch is located in the fuse block

1   Cancel switch   2   Fuses   3   Cover   4   Steering wheel

37 Oxygen sensor system light check and resetting (1985 and 1986 models only)

Refer to illustrations 37.1a and 37.1b

1   At the specified intervals the "Sensor" light in the instrument cluster will flash when the engine reaches normal operating temperature, indicating the oxygen sensor and feedback carburetor system is in good condition. If this is the case, remove the fuse block cover and turn the Cancel switch off to reset the light **(see illustrations)**.

2   If the light doesn't flash at the specified intervals, remove the instru-

ment cluster (Chapter 12), make sure the wiring is in good condition and the bulb isn't burned out.

3   If the wiring and bulb are in good condition, push the cancel switch to the On position. Turn the ignition switch on (don't start the engine) and make sure the "Sensor" light goes on but doesn't flash.

4   Start the engine and allow it to warm up to normal operating temperature.

5   Increase the engine speed to between 1500 and 2000 rpm. The Sensor light should now flash.

6   If it does, turn off the engine and reset the Cancel switch.

7   If it doesn't, there is a fault in the carburetor feedback and/or oxygen sensor systems. Refer to Chapters 4 and 6.

38 Evaporative emissions control system check and canister replacement

Refer to illustration 38.2

1   The function of the evaporative emissions control system is to draw fuel vapors from the gas tank and fuel system, store them in a charcoal canister and route them to the intake manifold during normal engine operation.

2   The most common symptom of a fault in the evaporative emissions system is a strong fuel odor in the engine compartment. If a fuel odor is detected, inspect the charcoal canister, located in the engine compartment below the master cylinder **(see illustration)**. Check the canister and all hoses for damage and deterioration.

3   The evaporative emissions control system is explained in more detail in Chapter 6.

39 Positive Crankcase Ventilation (PCV) valve check and replacement

Refer to illustrations 39.3 and 39.4

1   The PCV valve is located in the intake manifold.

2   Disconnect the hose from the PCV valve.

3   With the engine idling at normal operating temperature, place your finger over the valve opening **(see illustration)**. If there's no vacuum at the valve, check for a plugged hose or valve. Replace any plugged or deteriorated hoses.

4   Turn off the engine. Connect a piece of hose to the PCV valve. Blow through the valve from the valve cover end **(see illustration)**. If the valve is operating properly, air should pass through the valve with some difficulty. If no air passes through the valve or it passes easily, install a new one.

5   When purchasing a replacement PCV valve, make sure it's for your particular vehicle and engine. Compare the new valve to the old one to make sure they're the same.

38.2 The charcoal canister (arrow) is located in the engine compartment on the driver's side firewall

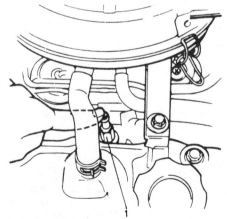

39.3 Place your finger over the PCV valve (1) and make sure suction can be felt – if there is no suction, the valve is faulty

39.4 Connect a piece of hose to the PCV valve and blow through it – air should pass through the valve into the intake manifold only with some difficulty

Chapter 2 Part A Engine

Contents

Specifications

General

Firing order 1-3-2
Cylinder numbers (drivebelt end-to-transaxle end) 1–2–3

Camshaft

Cam lobe height
  Sprint (intake and exhaust)
    Standard .... 1.5012 in (38.132 mm)
    Wear limit .... 1.4973 in (38.032 mm)
  Metro (intake and exhaust)
    Standard .... 1.5601 to 1.5664 in (39.638 to 39.788 mm)
    Wear limit .... 1.5562 in (39.528 mm)
Camshaft bearing oil clearance
  Standard .... 0.002 to 0.0035 in (0.05 to 0.09 mm)
  Service limit .... 0.006 in (0.15 mm)

Camshaft (continued)

Camshaft journal diameter (front-to-rear)

Sprint

1	1.7372 to 1.7381 in (44.125 to 44.150 mm)
2	1.7451 to 1.7460 in (44.325 to 44.350 mm)
3	1.7530 to 1.7539 in (44.525 to 44.550 mm)
4	1.7609 to 1.7618 in (44.725 to 44.750 mm)

Metro

1	1.0220 to 1.0228 in (25.959 to 25.980 mm)
2 and 3	1.1795 to 1.1803 in (29.959 to 29.980 mm)

Camshaft journal bore (inside) diameter

Sprint

1	1.7402 to 1.7407 in (44.200 to 44.216 mm)
2	1.7480 to 1.7486 in (44.400 to 44.416 mm)
3	1.7560 to 1.7565 in (44.600 to 44.616 mm)
4	1.7638 to 1.7644 in (44.800 to 44.816 mm)

Metro

1	1.0236 to 1.0244 in (26.000 to 26.021 mm)
2 and 3	1.1811 to 1.1819 in (30.000 to 30.021 mm)

Valves and related components

Sprint

Rocker arm shaft diameter	0.628 to 0.629 in (15.973 to 15.988 mm)
Rocker arm inside diameter	0.629 to 0.630 in (16.000 to 16.018 mm)
Shaft-to-rocker arm clearance	
Standard	0.0005 to 0.0017 in (0.012 to 0.045 mm)
Service limit	0.0035 in (0.09 mm)

Metro

Valve lifter outside diameter	1.2188 to 1.2194 in (30.959 to 30.975 mm)
Valve lifter bore inside diameter	1.2205 to 1.2214 in (31.000 to 31.025 mm)
Valve lifter-to-bore clearance	
Standard	0.0010 to 0.0025 in (0.025 to 0.066 mm)
Wear limit	0.0059 in (0.15 mm)

Oil pump clearances

Outer gear-to-oil pump housing (service limit)	0.0122 in (0.310 mm)
Gear endplay limit	0.0059 in (0.15 mm)

Torque specifications

	Ft-lbs (unless otherwise indicated)
Camshaft bearing cap bolts (Metro)	96 in-lbs
Camshaft sprocket bolt	44
Cylinder head bolts	
Sprint	48
Metro	54
Crankshaft pulley bolts (4)	96 in-lbs
Crankshaft pulley center bolt	
Sprint	52
Metro	81
Distributor gear case	96 in-lbs
Exhaust manifold	17
Intake manifold	17
Flywheel bolts	45
Driveplate bolts	14
Oil pump cover bolts	96 in-lbs
Oil pump-to-block bolts	96 in-lbs
Oil pan bolts/nuts	96 in-lbs
Crankshaft rear oil seal retainer	96 in-lbs
Rocker arm shaft retaining screws (Sprint)	96 in-lbs
Timing belt cover	96 in-lbs
Timing belt tensioner	
Bolt	20
Nut	96 in-lbs
Valve cover bolts/nuts	96 in-lbs

3.6 Mark the distributor housing adjacent to the number one terminal on the cap

3.8 Turn the crankshaft until the notch in the pulley is aligned with the "O" on the timing belt cover (arrows)

1 General information

This Part of Chapter 2 is devoted to in-vehicle repair procedures for the engine. All information concerning engine removal and installation and engine block and cylinder head overhaul can be found in Part B of this Chapter.

The following repair procedures are based on the assumption the engine is installed in the vehicle. If the engine has been removed from the vehicle and mounted on a stand, many of the steps outlined in this Part of Chapter 2 will not apply.

The Specifications included in this Part of Chapter 2 apply only to the procedures contained in this Part. Part B of Chapter 2 contains the Specifications necessary for cylinder head and engine block rebuilding.

2 Repair operations possible with the engine in the vehicle

Many major repair operations can be accomplished without removing the engine from the vehicle.

Clean the engine compartment and the exterior of the engine with some type of degreaser before any work is done. It'll make the job easier and help keep dirt out of the internal areas of the engine.

Depending on the components involved, it may be helpful to remove the hood to improve access to the engine as repairs are performed (see Chapter 11, if necessary). Cover the fenders to prevent damage to the paint. Special pads are available, but an old bedspread or blanket will also work.

If vacuum, exhaust, oil or coolant leaks develop, indicating a need for gasket or seal replacement, the repairs can generally be made with the engine in the vehicle. The intake and exhaust manifold gaskets, oil pan gasket, crankshaft oil seals and cylinder head gasket are all accessible with the engine in place.

Exterior engine components, such as the intake and exhaust manifolds, the oil pan, the oil pump, the water pump, the starter motor, the alternator, the distributor and the fuel system components can be removed for repair with the engine in place.

Since the cylinder head can be removed without pulling the engine, valve component servicing can also be accomplished with the engine in the vehicle. Replacement of the camshaft, timing belt and sprockets is also possible with the engine in the vehicle.

In extreme cases caused by a lack of necessary equipment, repair or replacement of piston rings, pistons, connecting rods and rod bearings is possible with the engine in the vehicle. However, this practice is not recommended because of the cleaning and preparation work that must be done to the components involved.

3 Top Dead Center (TDC) for number one piston – locating

Refer to illustrations 3.6, 3.8 and 3.9

Note: *The following procedure is based on the assumption the spark plug wires and distributor are correctly installed. If you're trying to locate TDC to install the distributor correctly, piston position must be determined by feeling for compression at the number one spark plug hole, then aligning the ignition timing marks as described in Step 8.*

1 Top Dead Center (TDC) is the highest point in the cylinder each piston reaches as it travels up-and-down when the crankshaft turns. Each piston reaches TDC on the compression stroke and again on the exhaust stroke, but TDC generally refers to piston position on the compression stroke.

2 Positioning the piston(s) at TDC is an essential part of many procedures such as rocker arm removal, camshaft and timing belt/ sprocket replacement and distributor removal.

3 Before beginning this procedure, be sure to place the transaxle in Neutral (or Park on automatics), apply the parking brake and block the rear wheels. Also, disable the ignition system by detaching the coil wire from the center terminal of the distributor cap and grounding it on the block with a jumper wire. Remove the spark plugs (see Chapter 1).

4 In order to bring any piston to TDC, the crankshaft must be turned using one of the methods outlined below. When looking at the front of the engine, normal crankshaft rotation is clockwise.

   a) The preferred method is to turn the crankshaft with a socket and ratchet attached to the bolt threaded into the front of the crankshaft.

   b) A remote starter switch, which may save some time, can also be used. Follow the instructions included with the switch. Once the piston is close to TDC, use a socket and ratchet as described in the previous paragraph.

   c) If an assistant is available to turn the ignition switch to the Start position in short bursts, you can get the piston close to TDC without a remote starter switch. Make sure your assistant is out of the vehicle, away from the ignition switch, then use a socket and ratchet as described in Paragraph a) to complete the procedure.

5 Note the position of the terminal for the number one spark plug wire on the distributor cap. If the wire isn't marked, follow the plug wire from the number one cylinder spark plug to the cap.

6 Use a felt-tip pen or chalk to make a mark on the distributor body directly under the terminal **(see illustration)**.

7 Detach the cap from the distributor and set it aside (see Chapter 1 if necessary).

8 Turn the crankshaft clockwise (see Step 3 above) until the notch in the crankshaft pulley is aligned with the 0 on the timing plate (located at the front of the engine) **(see illustration)**.

9 Look at the distributor rotor – it should be pointing directly at the mark

3.9   When the number one piston is at Top Dead Center on the compression stroke, the rotor should point toward the mark you made on the distributor

4.4   Disconnect the breather hose (arrow) – Sprint

you made on the distributor body **(see illustration)**. If it is, go to Step 12.
10   If the rotor is 180-degrees off, the number one piston is at TDC on the exhaust stroke. Go to Step 11.

4.5a   Sprint engine valve cover bolt locations (arrows)

11   If the rotor is 180-degrees off, turn the crankshaft one complete turn (360-degrees) clockwise. The rotor should now be pointing at the mark on the distributor. When the rotor is pointing at the number one spark plug wire terminal in the distributor cap and the ignition timing marks are aligned, the number one piston is at TDC on the compression stroke.
12   After the number one piston has been positioned at TDC on the compression stroke, TDC for any of the remaining pistons can be located by turning the crankshaft 240-degrees and following the firing order. Mark the remaining spark plug wire terminal locations on the distributor body just like you did for the number one terminal, then number the marks to correspond with the cylinder numbers. As you turn the crankshaft, the rotor will also turn. When it's pointing directly at one of the marks on the distributor, the piston for that particular cylinder is at TDC on the compression stroke.

---

4   Valve cover – removal and installation

Refer to illustrations 4.4, 4.5a, 4.5b and 4.5c
1   Disconnect the negative cable from the battery.
2   Remove the air cleaner assembly.
3   Detach the spark plug wires from the plugs, unclip the wire loom from the cover, then set the wires aside, leaving them attached to the loom.

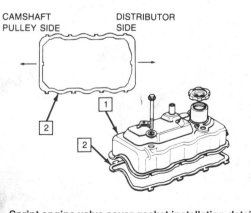

4.5b   Sprint engine valve cover gasket installation details

1	*Valve cover*	2	*Gasket*

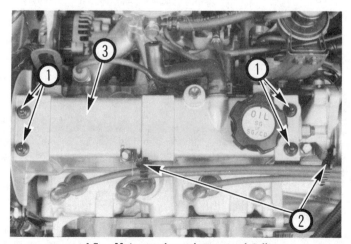

4.5c   Metro engine valve cover details

1	*Nut/sealing washer locations*	2	*Spark plug wire holders*
		3	*Valve cover*

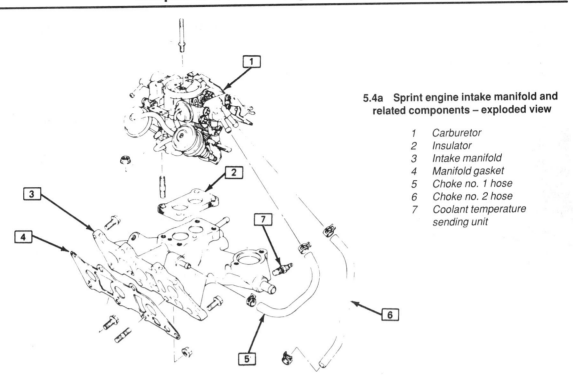

5.4a   Sprint engine intake manifold and related components – exploded view

1   Carburetor
2   Insulator
3   Intake manifold
4   Manifold gasket
5   Choke no. 1 hose
6   Choke no. 2 hose
7   Coolant temperature sending unit

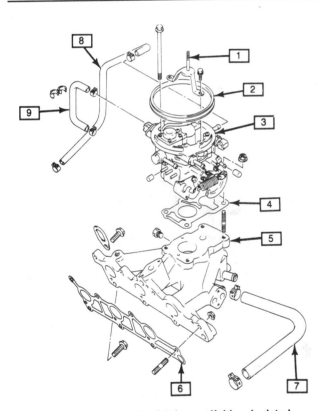

5.4b   Metro engine intake manifold and related components – exploded view

1	Stud	6 Gasket
2	Seal	7 Intake manifold inlet hose
3	Throttle body	8 Throttle body outlet hose
4	Gasket	9 Throttle body inlet hose
5	Intake manifold	

4   Disconnect the breather hose from the cover, if equipped (**see illustration**).
5   Remove the valve cover nuts/bolts and lift the cover off (**see illustrations**). If the cover sticks to the cylinder head, tap on it with a soft-face hammer or place a block of wood against the cover and tap on the wood with a hammer.
6   Thoroughly clean the valve cover and remove all traces of old gasket material with a scraper.
7   Install a new gasket on the cover, using RTV sealant to hold it in place. Place new grommets in the holes in the cover, position the cover, then install the nuts/bolts.
8   Working from the center out, tighten the nuts/bolts to the torque listed in this Chapter's Specifications.
9   The remaining steps are the reverse of removal. When finished, run the engine and check for oil leaks.

5   Intake manifold – removal and installation

Refer to illustrations 5.4a, 5.4b, 5.8 and 5.9

Removal

1   On Metro models, relieve the fuel pressure as described in Chapter 4, then disconnect the negative cable from the battery.
2   Drain the cooling system (see Chapter 1).
3   Remove the air cleaner (see Chapter 4).
4   Clearly label, then disconnect all hoses, wires, brackets and emission lines that run to the carburetor/throttle body and intake manifold (**see illustrations**).
5   Disconnect the fuel lines from the carburetor/throttle body and cap the fittings to prevent leakage (see Chapter 4).
6   Disconnect the throttle cable from the carburetor/throttle body (see Chapter 4).
7   Detach the cable that runs from the carburetor/throttle body to the transaxle (automatic transaxle only).
8   Unscrew the bolts and nuts and remove the intake manifold from the

5.8 Remove the nuts/bolts (arrows) – Sprint shown

5.9 Remove all traces of old gasket material

engine **(see illustration)**. If it sticks, tap the manifold with a soft-face hammer. **Caution:** *Do not pry between the gasket sealing surfaces or tap on the carburetor/throttle body.*

9 Thoroughly clean the manifold and cylinder head mating surfaces, removing all traces of gasket material **(see illustration)**.

Installation

10 Install the manifold and a new gasket and tighten the bolts and nuts in several steps, working from the center out, until you reach the torque listed this Chapter's Specifications.

11 Reinstall the remaining parts in the reverse order of removal.

12 Add coolant, run the engine and check for leaks and proper operation.

6 Exhaust manifold – removal and installation

Refer to illustrations 6.5, 6.6, 6.7, 6.8 and 6.12

Warning: *Allow the engine to cool completely before following this procedure.*

Removal

1 Disconnect the negative cable from the battery.

2 Set the parking brake and block the rear wheels. Raise the front of the vehicle and support it securely on jackstands.

3 Working from under the vehicle, remove the nuts that secure the exhaust system to the bottom of the exhaust manifold. Apply penetrating oil to the threads to make removal easier.

4 On air conditioned models, detach the compressor drivebelt and lower adjusting brace, if necessary.

5 Unplug the oxygen sensor wire **(see illustration)**.

6 Remove the fasteners that secure the heat shield to the exhaust manifold **(see illustration)**, then detach the heat shield.

7 Disconnect the air injection tube, if equipped **(see illustration)**.

8 Apply penetrating oil to the threads, then remove the exhaust manifold mounting nuts/bolts **(see illustration)**.

9 Separate the manifold from the cylinder head.

10 Clean and inspect all threaded fasteners.

11 Remove all traces of gasket material from the mating surfaces and inspect them for cracks and other damage.

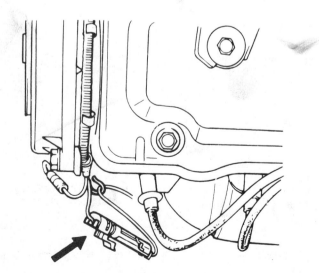

6.5 Unplug the oxygen sensor at the connector (arrow)

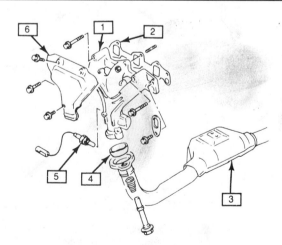

6.6 Exhaust manifold and related components – exploded view (Metro shown – Sprint similar)

1	Exhaust manifold	4 Pipe seal
2	Gasket	5 Oxygen sensor
3	Exhaust system	6 Heat shield

6.7 Disconnect the air injection tube (arrow)

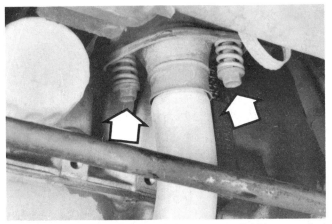

6.8 Disconnect the exhaust pipe from the manifold by removing the two bolts

Installation

12 Position a new gasket on the cylinder head (see illustration), install the manifold and tighten the fasteners in several steps, working from the center out, to the torque listed in this Chapter's Specifications.

13 Reinstall the remaining parts in the reverse order of removal. Be sure to use a new exhaust pipe seal and gasket.

14 Run the engine and check for exhaust leaks.

7 Timing belt and sprockets – removal, inspection and installation

Removal

Refer to illustrations 7.4, 7.8a, 7.8b, 7.9a, 7.9b, 7.10, 7.11, 7.14, 7.15a, 7.15b and 7.15c

Warning: *The air conditioning system is under high pressure. Do not loosen any fittings or disconnect any components until after the system has been discharged by an air conditioning technician. Always wear eye protection when disconnecting refrigerant fittings.*

Caution: *Do not try to turn the crankshaft with the camshaft sprocket bolt and do not rotate the crankshaft counterclockwise.*

1 Disconnect the negative cable from the battery.

2 Position the number one piston at Top Dead Center (see Section 3).

3 Remove the valve cover (see Section 4).

4 On Sprint models, loosen the locknuts and back off the valve adjustment screws until they're no longer in contact with the valves (see illustration).

5 Set the parking brake and block the rear wheels. Raise the front of the vehicle and support it securely on jackstands.

6.12 Place a new gasket on the cylinder head and make sure the openings line up correctly

6 Loosen the four water pump pulley nuts, then remove the drivebelts (see Chapter 1).

7 Remove the rubber plug from the right inner fender.

8 Remove the crankshaft and water pump drivebelt pulleys (see illustration). **Note:** *If you're only replacing the timing belt, it's not necessary to*

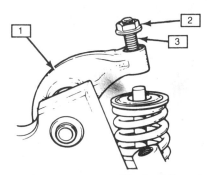

7.4 Loosen the locknuts and back off the valve adjustment screws

| 1 | Rocker arm | 2 | Locknut | 3 | Adjustment screw |

7.8a Sprint engine crankshaft pulley mounting details

| 1 | Crankshaft pulley bolts | 2 | Indexing notch |
| 3 | Center bolt | | |

7.8b   **Wrap duct tape or a rag around the pulley and grip it with a chain wrench**

remove the crankshaft center bolt; however, if you will be removing the crankshaft sprocket to replace the oil pump or oil seal, you must remove the center bolt. Do this before you remove the pulley bolts. The center bolt is very tight; to break it loose, remove the splash pan from beneath the front of the engine, wrap a rag or duct tape around the pulley and attach a chain wrench to immobilize the pulley **(see illustration)**. Use a breaker bar and socket to loosen the bolt.

9   Remove the bolts that secure the timing belt cover and detach the cover **(see illustrations)**.

10   If you plan to reuse the timing belt, and it doesn't already have arrows painted on it, paint one on to indicate the direction of rotation (clockwise) **(see illustration)**.

11   Loosen the adjusting nut and pulley bolt. Move the tensioner pulley towards the water pump as far as possible **(see illustration)**.

12   Temporarily secure the tensioner pulley by tightening the adjusting nut.

13   Slip the timing belt off the sprockets and set it aside.

14   If you intend to replace the oil pump or crankshaft front oil seal, slide off the crankshaft sprocket and the belt guide located behind it **(see illustration)**. When removing the guide, note how it's installed (the chamfered side faces out).

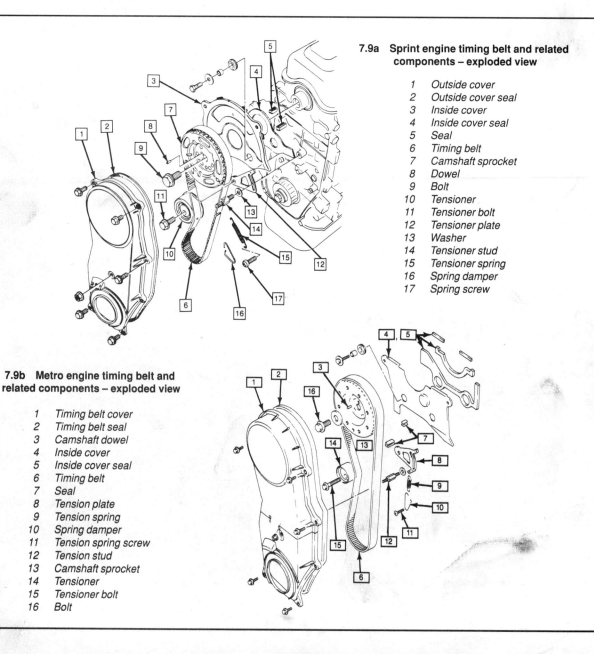

7.9a   **Sprint engine timing belt and related components – exploded view**

1   Outside cover
2   Outside cover seal
3   Inside cover
4   Inside cover seal
5   Seal
6   Timing belt
7   Camshaft sprocket
8   Dowel
9   Bolt
10   Tensioner
11   Tensioner bolt
12   Tensioner plate
13   Washer
14   Tensioner stud
15   Tensioner spring
16   Spring damper
17   Spring screw

7.9b   **Metro engine timing belt and related components – exploded view**

1   Timing belt cover
2   Timing belt seal
3   Camshaft dowel
4   Inside cover
5   Inside cover seal
6   Timing belt
7   Seal
8   Tension plate
9   Tension spring
10   Spring damper
11   Tension spring screw
12   Tension stud
13   Camshaft sprocket
14   Tensioner
15   Tensioner bolt
16   Bolt

7.10   If the timing belt doesn't have arrows like these to indicate direction of rotation, make one with chalk

7.11   Loosen the adjusting nut and pulley bolt and move the tensioner pulley as far as possible towards the water pump

A   *Adjusting nut*   B   *Pulley bolt*   C   *Tensioner pulley*

7.14   The belt guide has a notch which allows it to fit over the crankshaft key (arrows)

7.15a   Keep the camshaft sprocket from turning with a large screwdriver

15   If you intend to replace the camshaft or oil seal, unscrew the camshaft sprocket bolt and slide the sprocket off – a large screwdriver inserted through a hole in the sprocket will keep it from turning while you remove the bolt **(see illustration)**. Note: *On Metro models, the camshaft can be kept from turning by inserting a 10 mm metal rod through the hole* **(see illustration)**. Unbolt the cover **(see illustration)** to access the seal.

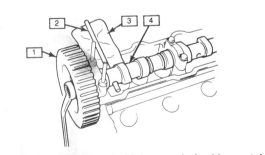

7.15b   On Metro engines, hold the camshaft with a metal rod

1	*Camshaft sprocket*	*3*	*Shop cloth*
2	*Rod*	*4*	*Camshaft*

7.15c   To get to the camshaft seal, remove the two mounting bolts and detach the cover (arrows)

7.16   Check the tensioner pulley for roughness and excess play

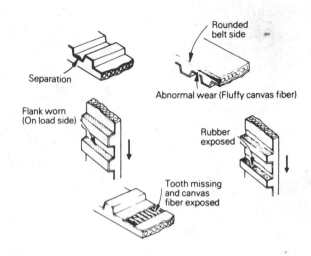

7.17   Carefully inspect the timing belt for the conditions shown here

7.18a   The camshaft sprocket is indexed by a dowel (arrow)

7.18b   The crankshaft sprocket has a slot (keyway) which must align with the key in the crankshaft

Inspection

Refer to illustrations 7.16 and 7.17

16   Rotate the tensioner pulley by hand and move it from side-to-side to detect roughness and excess play **(see illustration)**. Visually inspect the sprockets for damage and wear. Replace parts as necessary.

17   Check the timing belt for cracks, ply separation, wear, missing teeth and oil contamination. Replace the belt if it's worn or damaged **(see illustration)**. **Note:** *Unless the engine has very low mileage, it's common practice to replace the timing belt with a new one every time it's removed. Don't reinstall the original belt unless it's in like-new condition. Never reuse a belt in questionable condition.*

Installation

Refer to illustrations 7.18a, 7.18b, 7.19a and 7.19b

18   Reinstall the camshaft seal cover and timing belt sprockets, if they were removed. Note that the camshaft sprocket is indexed by a dowel **(see illustration)**. Slip the belt guide onto the crankshaft before installing the crankshaft sprocket – the chamfered side of the guide faces away from the belt. The crankshaft sprocket has a keyway which matches the key in the crankshaft **(see illustration)**.

19   Align the valve timing marks located on the crankshaft and camshaft sprockets **(see illustrations)**.

20   Slip the timing belt onto the crankshaft sprocket. While maintaining tension on the side of the belt opposite the tensioner, slip the belt onto the camshaft sprocket.

21   Release the tensioner adjusting nut to allow spring tension to apply pressure against the belt. Rotate the crankshaft clockwise two complete revolutions (720-degrees). Retighten the nut.

22   Temporarily install the crankshaft pulley, taking care to align the notch in the pulley with the raised area on the sprocket. Install the crankshaft pulley bolts and the center bolt, if removed. Tighten the center bolt to the torque listed in this Chapter's Specifications. When tightening the bolts, immobilize the crankshaft as discussed in Step 8. Remove the pulley, leaving the center bolt in place.

23   Using the bolt in the center of the crankshaft sprocket, turn the crankshaft clockwise through two complete revolutions (720-degrees). Recheck the alignment of the valve timing marks. If the marks do not align properly, loosen the tensioner, slip the belt off the camshaft sprocket, align the marks, reinstall the belt, and check the alignment again.

24   Tighten the tensioner bolt and nut to the torque listed in this Chapter's Specifications. Start with the nut, then tighten the bolt.

7.19a   The mark on the lower timing belt sprocket must align with the mark on the engine front cover (arrows)

7.19b   The timing mark on the camshaft sprocket must align with the V mark on the camshaft seal cover (arrows)

8.2   Carefully pry the seal out with a small screwdriver – wrap the tip with tape to prevent damage to the seal bore and crankshaft sealing surface

8.4   Install the new seal by gently tapping it into place with a socket and hammer

9.2   Carefully pry the camshaft oil seal out with a small screwdriver – wrap the tip with tape to prevent damage to the seal bore and camshaft sealing surface

25   Reinstall the remaining parts in the reverse order of removal.

26   Start the engine, set the ignition timing (see Chapter 1) and road test the vehicle.

8   Crankshaft front oil seal – replacement

Refer to illustrations 8.2 and 8.4

1   Remove the timing belt, crankshaft sprocket and inner belt guide (see Section 7).

2   Wrap the tip of a small screwdriver with tape. Working from below, use the screwdriver to pry the seal out of the bore **(see illustration)**. Be careful not to damage the crankshaft or the seal bore.

3   Clean and inspect the seal bore and the seal contact surface on the crankshaft. Minor imperfections can be removed with emery cloth. If there's a groove worn in the crankshaft seal surface (from contact with the seal), installing a new seal will probably not stop the leak. Try installing a repair sleeve which fits over the crankshaft sealing surface. These are normally available at larger auto parts stores.

4   Lubricate the outer edge of the new seal with multi-purpose grease or

engine oil. Also lubricate the seal lip. Drive the seal into place with a hammer and socket **(see illustration)**.

5   Reinstall the timing belt and related components as described in Section 7.

6   Run the engine and check for oil leaks.

9   Camshaft oil seal – replacement

Refer to illustrations 9.2 and 9.4

1   Remove the timing belt, camshaft sprocket and camshaft seal cover (see Section 7).

2   Note how far the seal is seated in the bore, then carefully pry it out with a small screwdriver **(see illustration)**. Wrap the tip of the screwdriver with tape so you don't scratch the bore or damage the camshaft in the process (if the camshaft is damaged, the new seal will end up leaking).

3   Clean the bore and coat the outer edge of the new seal with engine oil or multi-purpose grease. Also lubricate the seal lip.

4   Using a socket with an outside diameter slightly smaller than the outside diameter of the seal, carefully drive the new seal into place with a

9.4   Gently tap the new oil seal into place with a socket and hammer

10.4   Remove the eight rocker arm shaft retaining screws (arrows)

hammer **(see illustration).** Make sure it's installed squarely and driven in to the same depth as the original. If a socket isn't available, a short section of pipe will also work.

5   Reinstall the seal cover, camshaft sprocket and timing belt (see Section 7).

6   Run the engine and check for oil leaks at the camshaft seal.

---

10   Camshaft, rocker arms and shafts – removal, inspection and installation (Sprint only)

Removal

Rocker arms and shafts

Refer to illustrations 10.4, 10.6 and 10.7

1   Disconnect the negative cable from the battery.

2   Set the number one piston at top dead center and remove the valve cover (see Sections 3 and 4).

3   Loosen the locknuts and back off the valve adjustment screws until they're no longer in contact with the valves **(see illustration 7.4).**

4   Remove the rocker arm shaft retaining screws **(see illustration).** They can be very tight and may require an impact driver.

5   Number the rocker arms with a scribe. Start with number one at the

timing belt end and work your way toward the rear of the engine in a criss-cross pattern until all of them are marked. When you're done, the rocker arms on the intake manifold side should be numbered 1, 3 and 5, and the ones on the exhaust manifold side should be marked 2, 4, and 6.

6   Push on the rear of one rocker arm shaft until it protrudes enough at the front to grasp it with pliers **(see illustration).**

7   Slowly pull each rocker arm shaft out the front of the engine **(see illustration).** Lift the rocker arms and springs out of the head as they are released from the shaft.

Camshaft

Refer to illustrations 10.10 and 10.11

8   Remove the timing belt, cam sprocket and inner timing belt cover (see Section 7).

9   Remove the distributor and fuel pump (see Chapters 4 and 5).

10   Remove the air injection tube and unbolt the distributor case **(see illustration).**

11   Carefully guide the camshaft out of the cylinder head **(see illustration).** Don't nick the bearing surfaces in the head with the cam lobes.

Inspection

Refer to illustrations 10.13, 10.14a, 10.14b, 10.15 and 10.16

12   Thoroughly clean the parts in solvent and wipe them off with a lint-free cloth.

10.6   Push on the rear of the rocker arm shaft until it protrudes enough at the front to grip it – if necessary, use an Allen-head driver to turn the shaft as shown here

10.7   Pull the shaft out the front of the cylinder head – wrap it with a rag and twist it out with locking pliers

10.10 Remove the distributor case bolts (arrows)

10.11 Carefully guide the camshaft out of the cylinder head to avoid nicking the bearing surfaces

13 Measure the inside diameter of each rocker arm and the outside diameter of the shaft where the rocker arm rides (**see illustration**). Compare the measurements to this Chapter's Specifications. Subtract the rocker arm shaft diameter from the rocker arm inside diameter to calculate the shaft-to-arm clearance.

14 Visually inspect the camshaft, rocker arms and springs for wear and damage (**see illustrations**). Replace any components that are damaged or excessively worn.

15 Using a micrometer or accurate caliper, measure the cam lobe height (**see illustration**) and compare it to this Chapter's Specifications. If the lobe height is less than the minimum allowable, the camshaft is worn and must be replaced.

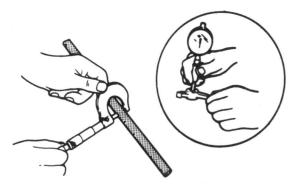

10.13 Measure the inside diameter of the rocker arms and the outside diameter of the rocker arm shafts

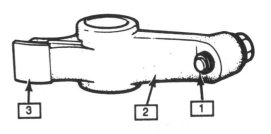

10.14a Inspect the tips of the valve adjusting screws and the cam-riding faces

1 Valve adjusting screw
2 Rocker arm
3 Cam-riding face

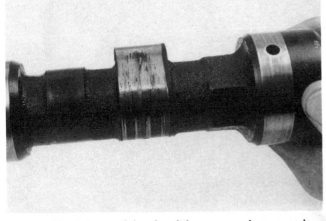

10.14b Check the cam lobes for pitting, wear and score marks – if scoring is excessive, as is the case here, install a new camshaft

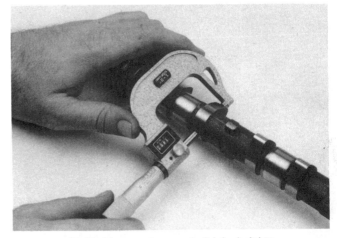

10.15 Measure the camshaft lobe heights

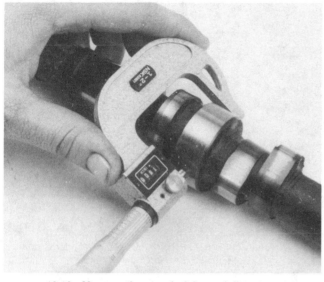

10.16   Measure the camshaft journal diameters

16   Using a micrometer or accurate caliper, measure the diameter of each bearing journal **(see illustration)** and compare it to this Chapter's specifications. If the journals are worn or damaged, replace the camshaft.
17   Using a bore gauge, measure the inside diameter of the camshaft bearing bores and record the results. Subtract the camshaft bearing journal outside diameter readings from the bore diameters to determine the bearing clearance. Do this for each bearing and compare the results to the clearances in this Chapter's Specifications. If the oil clearance is excessive, a new cylinder head may be needed (especially if the bearing journals aren't worn excessively).

Installation

Refer to illustration 10.19

18   Lubricate the camshaft bearing journals and lobes with engine assembly lube or moly-base grease, then reinstall the camshaft in the head.

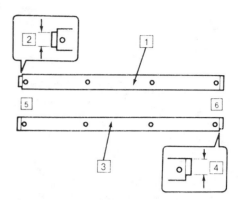

10.19   The shaft on the intake manifold side must be installed with the stepped side toward the camshaft sprocket – the shaft on the exhaust side must be installed with the stepped side toward the distributor

1	Intake rocker arm shaft	4	0.59-inch (15mm)
2	0.55-inch (14mm)	5	Camshaft sprocket side
3	Exhaust rocker arm shaft	6	Distributor side

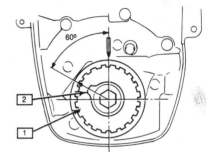

11.2   Position the crankshaft as shown here

   1   Crankshaft sprocket   2   Key

11.3   Metro engine camshaft and related components – exploded view

1   Valve cover
2   Gasket
3   Cylinder head
4   Cam bearing no. 1
5   Cam bearing no. 2
6   Cam bearing no. 3
7   Camshaft
8   Oil seal
9   Valve lifters
10   Distributor case

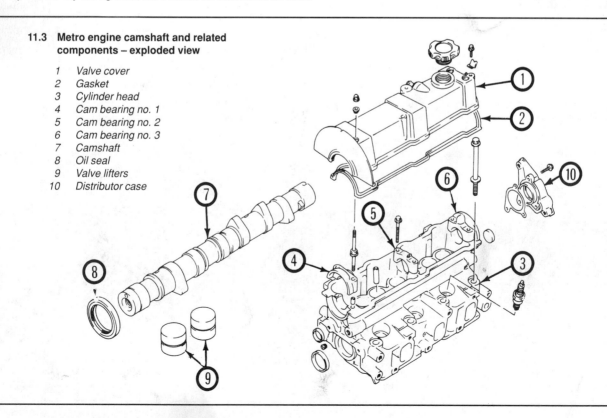

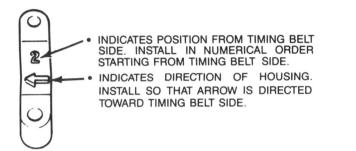

- INDICATES POSITION FROM TIMING BELT SIDE. INSTALL IN NUMERICAL ORDER STARTING FROM TIMING BELT SIDE.
- INDICATES DIRECTION OF HOUSING. INSTALL SO THAT ARROW IS DIRECTED TOWARD TIMING BELT SIDE.

11.4 Camshaft bearing cap marks

11.7 Store the lifters in a pan

1 Pan　　　　　　　*2 Lifter*

19 Apply the same lubricant to the rocker arm bores, then slowly push a rocker arm shaft into the cylinder head while guiding it into the rocker arms and springs. Note the rocker arm numbers and be sure to install them in the same positions they were in originally. Also note that the shafts are different and must be installed with the stepped sides facing the correct direction **(see illustration)**.

20 When all the rocker arm components are positioned correctly, install the retaining screws and tighten them to the torque listed in this Chapter's Specifications. You may have to rotate the shafts to get the bolt holes to line up.

21 Install the remaining components in the reverse order of removal.

22 Adjust the valves as described in Chapter 1.

---

11 Camshaft and lifters – removal, inspection and installation (Metro only)

Note: *If the valvetrain is making noise, and you suspect the lifters are causing it, before removing them for inspection, make sure the engine oil level is correct and allow some time after a cold start for them to quiet down. Hydraulic lifters are not adjustable or repairable – if they're defective, they must be discarded and new ones must be installed.*

Removal

Refer to illustrations 11.2, 11.3, 11.4 and 11.7

1 Remove the valve cover (see Section 4).

2 Remove the timing belt cover, timing belt and camshaft sprocket (see Section 7). Temporarily turn the crankshaft 60-degrees counterclockwise **(see illustration)**.

3 Remove the distributor (see Chapter 5) and case **(see illustration)** from the cylinder head.

4 The camshaft rides in three bearings. Each bearing cap is held by two bolts. The caps are marked with numbers that indicate their position and arrows that point to the timing belt end of the engine **(see illustration)**.

5 Loosen each of the cap bolts 1/4-turn at a time to relieve valve spring tension evenly until the caps are loose. If any of the caps stick, gently tap them with a soft-face hammer. **Caution:** *Failure to follow this procedure could tilt the camshaft in the bearings, which could damage the bearings or the camshaft.*

6 Lift out the camshaft, wipe it off with a clean shop towel and set it aside.

7 Remove the lifters, wipe each one off with a clean shop towel and number it with a felt-tip pen. Set them aside in a pan as shown to keep the oil from running out of them **(see illustration)**.

Inspection

Camshaft

8 Refer to Section 10 for the camshaft inspection procedures (they are the same for the Sprint and Metro).

Lifters

Refer to illustrations 11.9a, 11.9b, 11.10, 11.11 and 11.13

9 Inspect the lifters for wear, galling and signs of seizure **(see illustrations)**. If aluminum from the cylinder head is adhering to them, replace them. If any of the lifter bores are rough, scored or worn, replace the cylinder head.

10 Using a telescoping gauge and outside micrometer or a dial bore gauge, measure each lifter bore inside diameter and record the results **(see illustration)**.

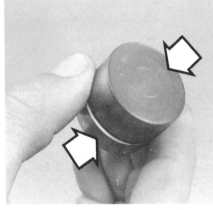

11.9a Check the lobe contact surfaces and the bore surfaces (arrows) of the lifters for wear

11.9b Check the valve side of the lifters too

11.10 Measure each lifter bore inside diameter with a bore gauge, . . .

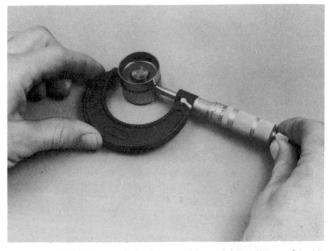

11.11   . . . then measure the lifters with a micrometer – subtract each lifter diameter from the corresponding bore diameter to obtain the lifter-to-bore clearances

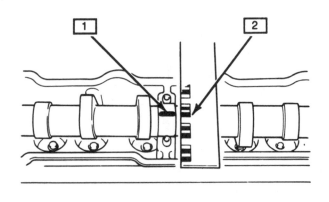

11.13   Compare the width of the crushed Plastigage to the scale on the envelope

1   Gaging plastic   2   Scale

11   Measure each lifter outside diameter and record the results **(see illustration)**.

12   Subtract the lifter outside diameter from the corresponding bore inside diameter to determine the clearance. Compare the results to this Chapter's Specifications and replace parts as necessary.

13   Check the oil clearance for each camshaft journal as follows:
   a) Clean the bearing caps and the camshaft journals with lacquer thinner or acetone.
   b) Carefully lay the camshaft in the head. Don't install the lifters and don't use any lubrication.
   c) Lay a strip of Plastigage on each journal.
   d) Install the bearing caps in their original locations.
   e) Tighten the bolts to the torque listed in this Chapter's specifications in 1/4-turn increments. **Caution:** *Don't turn the camshaft while the Plastigage is in place.*
   f) Remove the bolts and detach the caps.
   g) Compare the width of the crushed Plastigage (at its widest point) to the scale on the Plastigage envelope **(see illustration)**.
   h) If the clearance is greater than specified, replace the camshaft and/or cylinder head.
   i) Scrape off the Plastigage with your fingernail or the edge of a credit card – don't scratch or nick the journals or bearing caps.

14   If any of the conditions described above are noted, the cylinder head is probably getting insufficient lubrication or dirty oil, so make sure you track down the cause of this problem (low oil level, low oil pump capacity, clogged oil passage, etc.) before installing a new head, camshaft or lifters.

Installation

Refer to illustrations 11.18, 11.19, 11.20 and 11.22

Note: *The engine must be allowed to sit without starting it for at least 30 minutes after reassembly so the lifters can seat.*

15   Clean the camshaft, the bearing surfaces in the head and the lifters. Remove all sludge and dirt. Wipe off all components with a clean, lint-free cloth.

16   Lightly lubricate the lifters and bores with assembly lube or moly-base grease. Refer to the numbers marked on them and install the lifters in the head.

17   Lubricate the camshaft bearing surfaces in the head and the bearing journals and lobes on the camshaft with assembly lube or moly-base grease.

18   Slide a new oil seal onto the front of the camshaft, then carefully lower the camshaft into position with the dowel at the five o'clock position **(see illustration)**. **Caution:** *Failure to adequately lubricate the camshaft and related components can cause serious damage to bearing and friction surfaces during the first few seconds after engine start-up.*

19   Apply a thin coat of sealant to the mating surfaces of the number one and three bearing caps **(see illustration)**.

20   Apply a thin coat of assembly lube or moly-base grease to the bearing surfaces of the camshaft bearing caps and install the caps in their original locations **(see illustration)**.

21   Install the bolts for the bearing caps. Gradually tighten all fasteners – 1/4-turn at a time – until the camshaft is drawn down and seated in the

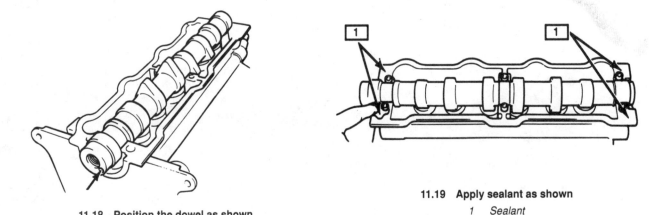

11.18   Position the dowel as shown

11.19   Apply sealant as shown

1   Sealant

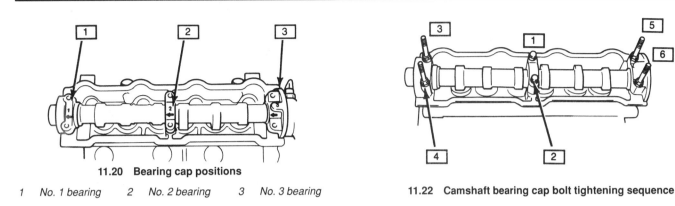

11.20 Bearing cap positions

1 No. 1 bearing   2 No. 2 bearing   3 No. 3 bearing

11.22 Camshaft bearing cap bolt tightening sequence

bearing saddles. Don't tighten the fasteners completely at this time.

22 Following the recommended sequence **(see illustration)**, tighten the fasteners for the bearing caps to the torque listed in this Chapter's Specifications.

23 Install the camshaft sprocket, timing belt, timing belt cover and related components (see Section 7).

24 Remove the spark plugs and carefully rotate the crankshaft clockwise with a socket and breaker bar to make sure the valve timing is correct. After two revolutions, the timing marks on the sprockets should still be aligned. If they're not, re-index the timing belt to the sprockets (see Section 7). **Note:** *If you feel resistance while rotating the crankshaft, stop immediately and check the valve timing.*

12 Valve spring, retainer and seal – replacement

Refer to illustrations 12.4, 12.8 and 12.16

Note: *Broken valve springs and defective valve stem seals can be replaced without removing the cylinder head. Two special tools and a compressed air source are normally required to perform this operation, so read through this Section carefully and rent or buy the tools before beginning the job. If compressed air isn't available, a length of nylon rope can be used to keep the valves from falling into the cylinder during this procedure.*

1 If you're working on a Sprint, refer to Section 10 and remove the rocker arms and shafts from the cylinder head. If you're working on a Metro, refer to Section 11 and remove the camshaft and lifters.

2 Remove the spark plug from the cylinder which has the defective component. If all of the valve stem seals are being replaced, all of the spark plugs should be removed.

3 If you're replacing all of the valve stem seals, begin with cylinder number one and work on the valves for one cylinder at a time.

4 Thread an adapter into the spark plug hole **(see illustration)** and connect an air hose from a compressed air source to it. Most auto parts stores can supply the air hose adapter. **Note:** *Many cylinder compression gauges utilize a screw-in fitting that may work with your air hose quick-disconnect fitting.*

5 Apply compressed air to the cylinder. **Warning:** *The piston may be forced down by compressed air, causing the crankshaft to turn suddenly.* If a wrench is still attached to the bolt in the crankshaft nose, it could cause damage or injury when the crankshaft moves. Keep your hands clear of the drivebelts and rotating engine components.

6 The valves should be held in place by the air pressure. If the valve faces or seats are in poor condition, leaks may prevent air pressure from retaining the valves – refer to the alternative procedure below.

7 If you don't have access to compressed air, an alternative method can be used. Position the piston at a point just before Top Dead Center, then feed a long piece of nylon rope through the spark plug hole until it fills the combustion chamber. Be sure to leave the end of the rope hanging out of the engine so it can be removed easily. Use a large ratchet and socket to rotate the crankshaft in the normal direction of rotation (clockwise) until slight resistance is felt.

8 Stuff shop rags into the cylinder head holes above and below the valves to prevent parts and tools from falling into the engine, then use a valve spring compressor to compress the spring **(see illustration)**. Remove the keepers with a small needle-nose pliers or a magnet. **Note:** *A couple of different types of tools are available for compressing the valve springs with the head in place. One type, shown here, grips the lower spring coils and presses on the retainer as the handle is turned, while another type utilizes the rocker arm shaft for leverage.*

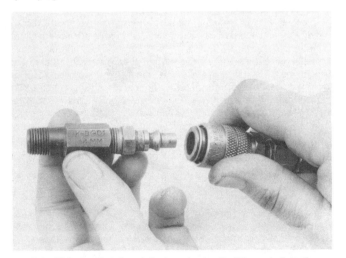

12.4 This is what the air hose adapter that threads into the spark plug hole looks like – they're commonly available from auto parts stores

12.8 Compress the spring enough to release the keepers (arrows)

12.16   Apply a small dab of grease to each keeper before installation to hold them in place on the valve stem until the spring is released

9   Remove the spring retainer and valve spring, then remove the guide seal. **Note:** *If air pressure fails to hold the valve in the closed position during this operation, the valve face and/or seat is probably damaged. If so, the cylinder head will have to be removed for additional repair operations.*
10   Wrap a rubber band or tape around the top of the valve stem so the valve won't fall into the combustion chamber, then release the air pressure. **Note:** *If a rope was used instead of air pressure, turn the crankshaft slightly in the direction opposite normal rotation.*
11   Inspect the valve stem for damage. Rotate the valve in the guide and check the end for eccentric movement, which would indicate the valve is bent.
12   Move the valve up-and-down in the guide and make sure it doesn't bind. If the valve stem binds, either the valve is bent or the guide is damaged. In either case, the head will have to be removed for repair.
13   Reapply air pressure to the cylinder to retain the valve in the closed position, then remove the tape or rubber band from the valve stem. If a rope was used instead of air pressure, rotate the crankshaft clockwise until slight resistance is felt.
14   Lubricate the valve stem with engine oil and install a new guide seal.
15   Install the spring in position over the valve.
16   Install the valve spring retainer. Compress the valve spring and carefully position the keepers in the groove. Apply a small dab of grease to the inside of each keeper to hold it in place if necessary **(see illustration)**.
17   Remove the pressure from the spring tool and make sure the keepers are seated.
18   Disconnect the air hose and remove the adapter from the spark plug hole. If a rope was used in place of air pressure, pull it out of the cylinder.
19   Refer to Section 10 and install the rocker arms and shafts or Section 11 and install the lifters and camshaft.
20   Install the spark plugs(s) and connect the wire(s).
21   Refer to Section 4 and install the valve cover.
22   Start and run the engine, then check for oil leaks and unusual sounds coming from the valve cover area.

---

13   Cylinder head – removal and installation

Caution: *Allow the engine to cool completely before following this procedure.*

Removal

Refer to illustrations 13.10 and 13.11

1   Position the number one piston at Top Dead Center (see Section 3).
2   Disconnect the negative cable from the battery.
3   Drain the cooling system and remove the spark plugs (see Chapter 1).
4   Remove the intake manifold (see Section 5).
5   Remove the exhaust manifold (see Section 6).
6   Remove the distributor (see Chapter 5) and unbolt the distributor

13.10   Cylinder head bolt loosening sequence (Sprint engine shown, Metro engine same sequence)

A   Timing belt end   B   Distributor end

13.11   Use casting protrusions to pry against – don't pry between the gasket surfaces

case from the cylinder head.
7   On carbureted models, remove the fuel pump and pushrod (see Chapter 4).
8   Remove the timing belt (see Section 7).
9   Remove the valve cover (see Section 4).
10   Loosen the cylinder head bolts, 1/4-turn at a time, in the recommended sequence **(see illustration)** until they can be removed by hand.
11   Carefully detach the cylinder head from the block and place it on wooden blocks to prevent damage to the sealing surfaces. If the head sticks to the engine block, dislodge it by prying against a protrusion on the head casting **(see illustration)**. **Note:** *Cylinder head disassembly and inspection procedures are covered in Sections 10 and 11 and in Chapter 2, Part B. It's a good idea to inspect the camshaft and have the head checked for warpage and cracks, even if you're just replacing the gasket.*

Installation

Refer to illustrations 13.12, 13.14, 13.15 and 13.16

12   The mating surfaces of the cylinder head and block must be perfectly clean when the head is installed. Use a gasket scraper to remove all traces of carbon and old gasket material **(see illustration)**, then clean the mating surfaces with lacquer thinner or acetone. If there's oil on the mating surfaces when the head is installed, the gasket may not seal correctly and leaks may develop. When working on the block, stuff the cylinders with clean shop rags to keep out debris. Use a vacuum cleaner to remove material that falls into the cylinders. Since the head is made of aluminum, aggressive scraping can cause damage. Be extra careful not to nick or gouge the mating surfaces with the scraper.

13.12   Remove all traces of old gasket material

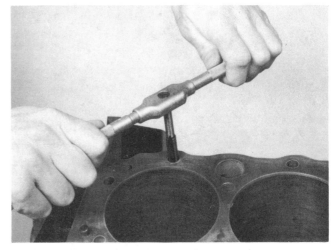

13.14   A tap should be used to remove sealant and corrosion from the head bolt holes

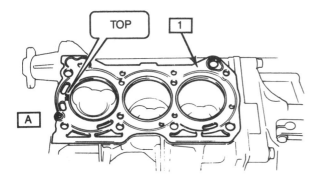

13.15   Position a new gasket with the "top" mark facing up

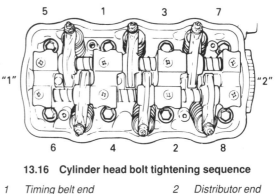

13.16   Cylinder head bolt tightening sequence

1   Timing belt end   2   Distributor end

13   Check the block and head mating surfaces for nicks, deep scratches and other damage. If damage is slight, it can be removed with a file; if it's excessive, machining may be the only alternative.

14   Use a tap of the correct size to chase the threads in the head bolt holes **(see illustration)**. Mount each bolt in a vise and run a die down the threads to remove corrosion and restore the threads. Dirt, corrosion, sealant and damaged threads will affect torque readings.

15   Place a new gasket on the block with the side marked TOP facing up **(see illustration)**. Make sure the openings in the gasket and block are lined up, then set the cylinder head in position.

16   Tighten the cylinder head bolts in three equal steps following the proper sequence **(see illustration)** until they're all at the torque listed in this Chapter's Specifications.

17   Reinstall the timing belt (see Section 7).

18   Reinstall the remaining parts in the reverse order of removal.

19   Be sure to refill the cooling system and check all fluid levels. Rotate the crankshaft clockwise slowly by hand through two complete revolutions. Recheck the camshaft timing marks (see Section 7).

20   Start the engine and set the ignition timing (see Chapter 1). Run the engine until normal operating temperature is reached. Check for leaks and proper operation. Shut off the engine, remove the valve cover and retorque the cylinder head bolts, unlesss the gasket manufacturer states otherwise. Recheck the valve adjustment.

---

14   Oil pan – removal and installation

Refer to illustrations 14.6a, 14.6b, 14.7, 14.10 and 14.11

1   Disconnect the negative cable from the battery. Raise the front of the vehicle and support it securely on jackstands.

2   Drain the engine oil (see Chapter 1).

3   Remove the splash shield from under the engine, if equipped.

4   Disconnect the front exhaust pipe from the manifold and lower it for access to the oil pan.

5   If it's in the way, remove the bellhousing lower plate.

6   Remove the bolts/nuts and detach the oil pan **(see illustration)**. Don't pry between the block and pan or damage to the sealing surfaces may result and oil leaks could develop. Use a soft-face hammer to dis-

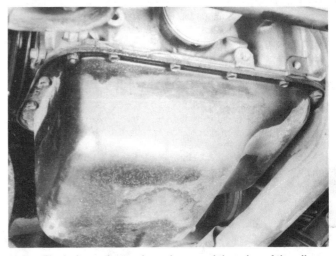

14.6a   The bolts are spaced evenly around the edge of the oil pan

14.6b   Use a soft-face hammer to dislodge the oil pan

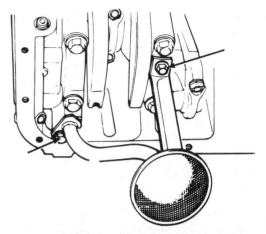

14.7   Remove the oil pickup tube bolts (arrows)

14.10   Oil pan and pickup mounting details

1	Oil pan		
2	Oil pickup tube	4	Drain plug gasket
3	Seal	5	Drain plug

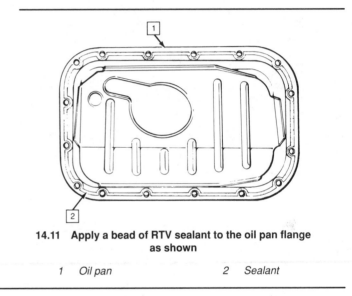

**14.11   Apply a bead of RTV sealant to the oil pan flange
as shown**

1	Oil pan	2	Sealant

lodge the pan if it's stuck **(see illustration)**.
7   The oil pickup tube can now be removed if necessary **(see illustration)**.
8   Use a scraper to remove all traces of old gasket material and sealant from the block and oil pan. Clean the gasket sealing surfaces with lacquer thinner or acetone and make sure the bolt holes in the block are clean.
9   Check the oil pan flange for distortion, particularly around the bolt holes. If necessary, place the pan on a block of wood and use a hammer to flatten and restore the gasket surface.
10   If it was removed, install the oil pickup tube with a new seal **(see illustration)**.
11   Before installing the oil pan, apply a thin coat of RTV sealant to the flange **(see illustration)**. Attach the new gasket to the pan (make sure the bolt holes are aligned).
12   Position the oil pan against the engine block and install the mounting bolts/nuts. Tighten them in a criss-cross pattern to the torque listed in this Chapter's Specifications.
13   Wait at least 30 minutes before filling the engine with oil, then start the engine and check the pan for leaks.

---

15   Oil pump – removal, inspection and installation

Removal

Refer to illustrations 15.3, 15.4a, 15.4b, 15.5 and 15.7

1   Remove the timing belt, tensioner, crankshaft sprocket and belt guide (see Section 7).
2   Remove the oil pan and oil pickup tube (see Section 14).
3   Remove the alternator (see Chapter 5) and bracket **(see illustration)**. Unbolt the dipstick tube and pull the tube out of the engine front case.
4   Remove the front cover-to-block bolts and carefully separate the cover from the engine **(see illustrations)**.
5   Remove the screws, detach the cover from the rear of the case and remove the inner and outer oil pump gears **(see illustration)**.
6   Remove the crankshaft oil seal from the front of the case (see Section 8).
7   Remove the pressure relief valve retainer, spring and plunger **(see illustration)**.

Inspection

Refer to illustrations 15.9a, 15.9b and 15.9c

8   Clean all parts thoroughly and remove all traces of old gasket material from the sealing surfaces. Visually inspect all parts for wear, cracks and other damage. Replace parts as necessary.
9   Install the oil pump outer and inner gears and measure the clearances **(see illustrations)**. Compare the clearances to this Chapter's Specifications. Replace parts as necessary. Pack the pump cavity with petroleum jelly and install the cover. Tighten the cover screws to the torque listed in this Chapter's Specifications.

15.3   Oil pump mounting details

1   *Alternator bracket nut*
2   *Dipstick tube mounting bolt*

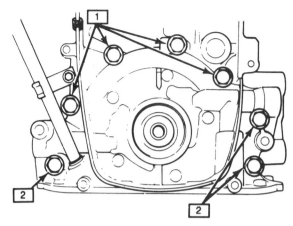

15.4a   Remove the front cover-to-block bolts – note that they come in different lengths

1   *Short bolts*   2   *Long bolts*

15.4b   Carefully separate the front cover from the engine with a prybar (arrow)

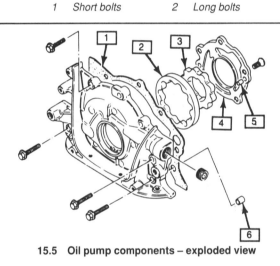

15.5   Oil pump components – exploded view

1 *Oil pump gasket*	4 *Cover*
2 *Oil pump outer gear*	5 *Pin*
3 *Oil pump inner gear*	6 *Dowel pin*

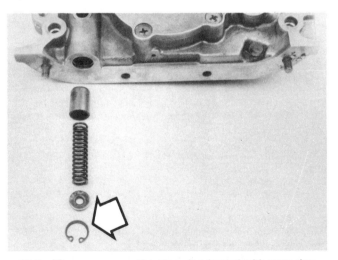

15.7   After you remove the snap-ring (arrow) with snap-ring pliers, the retainer, spring and plunger can be removed – if the plunger sticks in the bore, tap the front cover on a block of wood to dislodge it

15.9a   Install the outer gear with the dot (arrow) visible – the inner gear will only fit one way: with the raised center collar facing out

15.9b   Measure the outer gear-to-oil pump housing clearance with a feeler gauge

15.9c   Measure the gear end play with a precision straightedge and feeler gauge

15.12a   The oil pump has two tangs (arrows) . . .

15.12b   . . . which must be aligned with the flats on the crankshaft (arrows)

Installation

Refer to illustrations 15.12a and 15.12b

10   Install a new crankshaft front oil seal (see Section 8).
11   Install the pressure relief valve components.
12   Using a new gasket, position the front cover on the engine **(see illustrations)**. Install the bolts and tighten them to the torque listed in this Chapter's Specifications.
13   Reinstall the remaining parts in the reverse order of removal.
14   Add oil, start the engine and check for oil pressure and leaks.

---

16   Flywheel/driveplate – removal and installation

Refer to illustrations 16.4, 16.8a and 16.8b

1   Raise the vehicle and support it securely on jackstands, then refer to Chapter 7 and remove the transaxle. If it's leaking, now would be a very good time to replace the front pump seal/O-ring (automatic transaxle only).
2   Remove the pressure plate and clutch disc (see Chapter 8) (manual transaxle equipped models). Now is a good time to check/replace the clutch components and pilot bearing.
3   On automatic transaxle models, mark the relationship between the

driveplate and crankshaft to ensure correct alignment during reinstallation.
4   Remove the bolts that secure the flywheel/driveplate to the crankshaft. If the crankshaft turns, immobilize it by jamming a heavy screwdriver into the ring gear teeth **(see illustration)**.
5   Remove the flywheel/driveplate from the crankshaft. Since the flywheel is fairly heavy, be sure to support it while removing the last bolt.
6   Clean the flywheel to remove grease and oil. Inspect the surface for cracks, rivet grooves, burned areas and score marks. Light scoring can be removed with emery cloth. Check for cracked and broken ring gear teeth. Lay the flywheel on a flat surface and use a straightedge to check for warpage.
7   Clean and inspect the mating surfaces of the flywheel/driveplate and the crankshaft. If the crankshaft oil seal is leaking, replace it before reinstalling the flywheel/driveplate (see Section 17).
8   Position the flywheel/driveplate against the crankshaft. On manual transaxle models, be sure to align the hole in the flywheel with the aligment dowel in the crankshaft **(see illustrations)**. On automatic transaxle models, align the marks you made during removal. Before installing the bolts, apply thread locking compound to the threads.
9   Tighten the bolts to the torque listed in this Chapter's Specifications. Keep the crankshaft from turning as described above.
10   The remainder of installation is the reverse of the removal procedure.

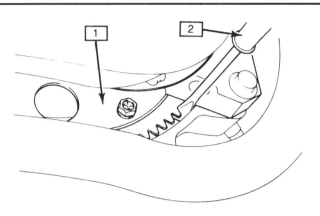

1   DRIVE PLATE
2   SLOTTED SCREWDRIVER

16.4   Jam a screwdriver into the ring gear teeth shown here
to keep the crankshaft from turning

16.8a   The alignment dowel (arrow) . . .

16.8b   . . . must be aligned with the dowel hole in the flywheel
(arrow) (they ensure the flywheel can only be installed one way)

17.2a   Gently pry out the old seal with a screwdriver – wrap the
tip with tape to prevent damage to the seal bore and crankshaft
sealing surface

17   Crankshaft rear oil seal – replacement

Refer to illustrations 17.2a, 17.2b, 17.5 and 17.6

1   The transaxle must be removed from the vehicle for this procedure
(see Chapter 7).

2   The seal can be replaced without removing the oil pan or the seal
housing. However, this method is not recommended because the lip of the
seal is quite stiff and it's possible to cock the seal in the housing bore or
damage it during installation. If you want to take the chance, pry out the old
seal **(see illustration)**. Apply multi-purpose grease to the crankshaft seal
journal and the lip of the new seal and carefully tap the new seal into place
(see illustration). The lip is stiff so carefully work it onto the seal journal of
the crankshaft with a smooth object like the end of an extension as you tap
the seal into place. Don't rush it or you may damage the seal.

3   The following method is recommended but requires removal of the oil
pan (see Section 14) and the seal housing.

4   After the oil pan has been removed, remove the bolts, detach the seal
housing and peel off all the old gasket material.

5   Position the seal and housing assembly on a couple of wood blocks
on a workbench and drive the old seal out from the back side with a punch

17.2b   Gently tap the new seal into place with a large socket
and hammer

17.5   After removing the housing from the engine, support it on wood blocks and drive out the old seal with a punch and hammer

17.6   Drive the new seal into the housing with a block of wood or a section of pipe, if you have one large enough – DO NOT cock the seal in the bore

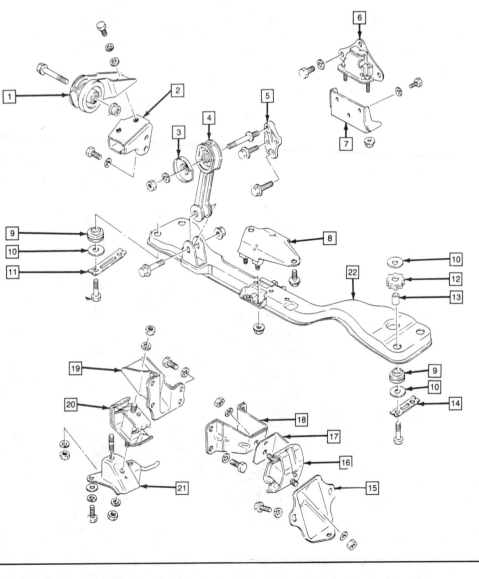

18.8a   Engine mounts – exploded view (automatic transaxle models)

1   Side mount
2   Side mount bracket
3   Stopper plate
4   Torque rod
5   Torque rod bracket
6   Transaxle mount
7   Bracket
8   Transaxle mount
9   Lower cushion
10 Washer
11 Rear lock washer
12 Upper cushion
13 Spacer
14 Front lock washer
15 Front mount body bracket
16 Front mount
17 Insulator
18 Front mount bracket
19 Rear mount bracket
20 Rear mount
21 Rear body bracket
22 Transaxle crossmember

and hammer **(see illustration)**.

6   Drive the new seal into the housing with a block of wood **(see illustration)** or a section of pipe slightly smaller in diameter than the outside diameter of the seal.

7   Lubricate the crankshaft seal journal and the lip of the new seal with multi-purpose grease. Position a new gasket on the engine block.

8   Slowly and carefully push the seal onto the crankshaft. The seal lip is stiff, so work it onto the crankshaft with a smooth object such as the end of an extension as you push the housing against the block.

9   Install and tighten the housing bolts to the torque listed in this Chapter's Specifications.

10   The remaining steps are the reverse of removal.

11   Run the engine and check for oil leaks.

18   Engine mounts – check and replacement

Refer to illustrations 18.8a and 18.8b

1   Engine mounts seldom require attention, but broken or deteriorated mounts should be replaced immediately or the added strain placed on the driveline components may cause damage or wear.

Check

2   During the check, the engine must be raised slightly to remove the weight from the mounts.

3   Raise the vehicle and support it securely on jackstands, then position a jack under the engine oil pan. Place a large block of wood between the

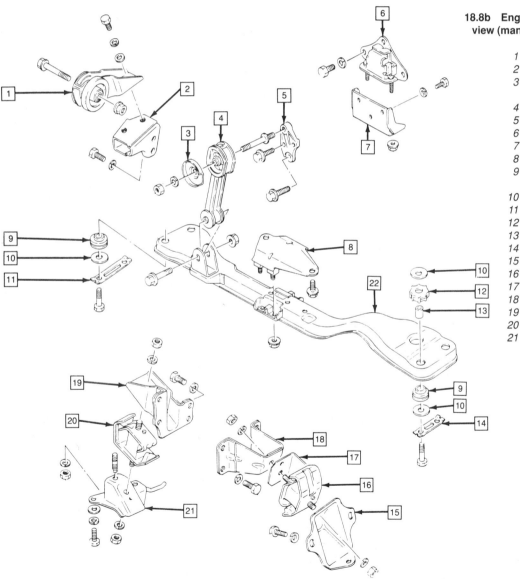

18.8b   Engine mounts – exploded view (manual transaxle models)

1	Side mount bushing
2	Side mount bracket
3	Rear torque rod bracket
4	Rear torque rod
5	Rear stopper plate
6	Front torque rod
7	Front stopper plate
8	Transaxle mount
9	Transaxle mount member
10	Washer
11	Upper cushion
12	Spacer
13	Lower cushion
14	Lock washer
15	Front body bracket
16	Front mounting
17	Heat insulator
18	Front mount bracket
19	Rear mount bracket
20	Rear mount
21	Rear body bracket

2A

jack head and the oil pan, then carefully raise the engine just enough to take the weight off the mounts. **Warning:** *DO NOT place any part of your body under the engine when it's supported only by a jack!*

4   Check the mounts to see if the rubber is cracked, hardened or separated from the metal plates. Sometimes the rubber will split right down the center.

5   Check for relative movement between the mount plates and the engine or frame (use a large screwdriver or pry bar to attempt to move the mounts). If play is noted, lower the engine and tighten the mount fasteners.

6   Rubber preservative should be applied to the mounts to slow deterioration.

Replacement

7   Disconnect the negative battery cable from the battery, then raise the vehicle and support it securely on jackstands (if not already done).

8   Raise the engine slightly with a jack or hoist. Remove the mount-to-bracket fasteners **(see illustrations)** and detach the mount.

9   Installation is the reverse of removal. Use thread locking compound on the mount bolts and nuts and be sure to tighten them securely.

Chapter 2 Part B
General engine overhaul procedures

Contents

Specifications

General

Cylinder compression pressure (at 400 rpm)
  Standard .... 199 psi
  Minimum .... 156 psi
  Maximum allowable variation between cylinders .... 14.2 psi
Oil pressure (engine warm) .... 42 to 54 psi at 3000 rpm

Cylinder head

Warpage limits
  Head gasket surface .... 0.002 in (0.05 mm)
  Manifold surfaces .... 0.004 in (0.10 mm)

Valves and related components

Valve margin width – all models . . . .   0.0512 to 0.0590 in (1.3 to 1.5 mm)
Valve stem diameter
  Sprint
    Intake . . . .   0.2742 to 0.2748 in (6.965 to 6.980 mm)
    Exhaust . . . .   0.2737 to 0.2742 in (6.950 to 6.965 mm)
  Metro
    Intake . . . .   0.2148 to 0.2157 in (5.457 to 5.480 mm)
    Exhaust . . . .   0.2146 to 0.2151 in (5.450 to 5.465 mm)
Valve stem-to-guide clearance
  Sprint
    Intake
      Standard . . . .   0.0008 to 0.0019 in (0.02 to 0.05 mm)
      Service limit . . . .   0.0027 in (0.07 mm)
    Exhaust
      Standard . . . .   0.0014 to 0.0025 in (0.035 to 0.65 mm)
      Service limit . . . .   0.0035 in (0.09 mm)
  Metro
    Intake
      Standard . . . .   0.0008 to 0.0021 in (0.020 to 0.055 mm)
      Service limit . . . .   0.0027 in (0.07 mm)
    Exhaust
      Standard . . . .   0.0014 to 0.0024 in (0.035 to 0.62 mm)
      Service limit . . . .   0.0035 in (0.09 mm)
Valve spring
  Out-of-square limit – all models . . . .   0.079 in (2.0 mm)
  Installed height
    Sprint . . . .   1.63 in (41.5 mm)
    Metro . . . .   1.28 in (32.6 mm)
  Free length
    Sprint
      Standard . . . .   1.9409 in (49.3 mm)
      Service limit . . . .   1.8937 in (48.1 mm)
    Metro
      Standard . . . .   1.6035 in (40.73 mm)
      Service limit . . . .   1.5551 in (39.5 mm)
  Pressure
    Sprint
      Standard . . . .   54.7 to 64.3 lbs at 1.63 in (24.8 to 29.2 Kg at 41.5 mm)
      Service limit . . . .   50.2 lbs at 1.63 in (22.8 Kg at 41.5 mm)
    Metro
      Standard . . . .   41.0 to 47.2 lbs at 1.28 in (18.6 to 21.4 Kg at 32.6 mm)
      Service limit . . . .   36.6 lbs at 1.28 in (16.6 Kg at 32.6 mm)

Crankshaft and connecting rods

Crankshaft endplay – all models
  Standard . . . .   0.0044 to 0.0122 in (0.11 to 0.31 mm)
  Service limit . . . .   0.0149 in (0.38 mm)
Crankshaft runout limit (at center) . . . .   0.0023 in (0.06 mm)
Connecting rod journal
  Diameter – all models . . . .   1.6529 to 1.6535 in (41.982 to 42.00 mm)
  Out-of-round/taper limits – all models . . . .   0.0004 in (0.01 mm)
  Bearing oil clearance – all models
    Standard . . . .   0.0012 to 0.0019 in (0.03 to 0.05mm)
    Service limit . . . .   0.0031 in (0.08 mm)
Connecting rod endplay (side clearance) – all models
  Standard . . . .   0.0039 to 0.0078 in (0.10 to 0.20 mm)
  Service limit . . . .   0.0137 in (0.35mm)
Main bearing journal
  Diameters (numbers stamped on crankshaft webs at no. 1 bearing)
    No. 1 . . . .   1.7714 to 1.7716 in (44.994 to 45.000 mm)
    No. 2 . . . .   1.7712 to 1.7714 in (44.988 to 44.994 mm)
    No. 3 . . . .   1.7710 to 1.7712 in (44.982 to 44.988 mm)
  Out-of-round/taper limits . . . .   0.0004 in (0.01 mm)
  Bearing oil clearance
    Standard . . . .   0.0008 to 0.0015 in (0.020 to 0.040 mm)
    Service limit . . . .   0.0023 in (0.06 mm)

Main bearing thicknesses (standard size bearing color codes)
    Green .... 0.0786 to 0.0787 in (1.996 to 2.000 mm)
    Black .... 0.0787 to 0.0788 in (1.999 to 2.003 mm)
    Colorless .... 0.0788 to 0.0789 in (2.002 to 2.006 mm)
    Yellow .... 0.0789 to 0.0790 in (2.005 to 2.009 mm)
    Blue .... 0.0790 to 0.0791 in (2.008 to 2.012 mm)
Main bearing bore sizes (marks stamped on oil pan mating surface)
    Mark "A" .... 1.9292 to 1.9294 in (49.000 to 49.006 mm)
    Mark "B" .... 1.9294 to 1.9296 in (49.006 to 49.012 mm)
    Mark "C" .... 1.9296 to 1.9298 in (49.012 to 49.018 mm)

Cylinder bore

Diameter
    Sprint (wear limit) .... 2.9193 in (74.15 mm)
    Metro
        Mark "1" .... 2.9138 to 2.9142 in (74.01 to 74.02 mm)
        Mark "2" .... 2.9134 to 2.9138 in (74.01 to 74.02 mm)
Out-of-round/taper limits .... 0.0039 in (0.10 mm)

Pistons and rings

Cylinder bore diameter
    Mark "1" .... 2.9126 to 2.9130 in (73.98 to 73.99 mm)
    Mark "2" .... 2.9122 to 2.9126 in (73.97 to 73.98 mm)
Piston-to-bore clearance .... 0.0008 to 0.0015 in (0.02 to 0.04 mm)
Piston ring end gap
    Sprint
        Compression rings
            Top "R" standard .... 0.008 to 0.013 in (0.20 to 0.33 mm)
            Top "R" service limit .... 0.0275 in (0.7 mm)
            Top "S" standard .... 0.008 to 0.016 in (0.20 to 0.40 mm)
            Top "S" service limit .... 0.0275 in (0.7 mm)
            Middle ring (if equipped) .... 0.0079 to 0.0137 in (0.2 to 0.35 mm)
        Oil ring .... 0.0079 to 0.0275 in (0.020 to 0.070 mm)
    Metro
        Compression rings
            Top – standard .... 0.0079 to 0.0129 in (0.20 to 0.30 mm)
            Top – service limit .... 0.0275 in (0.7 mm)
            Middle ring – standard .... 0.0079 to 0.0137 in (0.2 to 0.30 mm)
            Middle ring – service limit .... 0.0275 in (0.7 mm)
        Oil ring .... 0.0079 to 0.0275 in (0.020 to 0.060 mm)
Piston ring side clearance
    No. 1 (top) compression ring .... 0.0012 to 0.0027 in (0.03 to 0.07 mm)
    No. 2 compression ring .... 0.0008 to 0.0023 in (0.02 to 0.06 mm)

Torque specifications*

Ft-lbs (unless otherwise indicated)

Main bearing cap bolts .... 36 to 41
Connecting rod cap nuts .... 24 to 26
Rear oil seal housing screws .... 84 to 108 in-lbs

* Note: *Refer to Part A for additional torque specifications.*

---

1   General information

Included in this portion of Chapter 2 are the general overhaul procedures for the cylinder head and internal engine components.

The information ranges from advice concerning preparation for an overhaul and the purchase of replacement parts to detailed, step-by-step procedures covering removal and installation of internal engine components and the inspection of parts.

The following Sections have been written based on the assumption the engine has been removed from the vehicle. For information concerning in-vehicle engine repairs, as well as removal and installation of the external components necessary for the overhaul, see Part A of this Chapter and Section 7 of this Part.

The Specifications included in this Part are only those necessary for the inspection and overhaul procedures which follow. Refer to Part A for additional Specifications.

2   Engine overhaul – general information

Refer to illustrations 2.4a and 2.4b

It's not always easy to determine when, or if, an engine should be completely overhauled, as a number of factors must be considered.

High mileage is not necessarily an indication an overhaul is needed, while low mileage doesn't preclude the need for an overhaul. Frequency of servicing is probably the most important consideration. An engine that's had regular and frequent oil and filter changes, as well as other required maintenance, will most likely give many thousands of miles of reliable service. Conversely, a neglected engine may require an overhaul very early in its life.

Excessive oil consumption is an indication that piston rings, valve seals and/or valve guides are in need of attention. Make sure oil leaks aren't responsible before deciding the rings and/or guides are bad. Perform a compression check to determine the extent of the work required (see Section 3).

2B

2.4a   Remove the oil pressure sending unit (arrow) located above the oil filter (the filter has been removed for this photo) . . .

2.4b   . . . and install an oil pressure gauge

Check the oil pressure with a gauge installed in place of the oil pressure sending unit **(see illustrations)** and compare it to this Chapter's Specifications. If it's extremely low, the bearings and/or oil pump are probably worn out.

Loss of power, rough running, knocking or metallic engine noises, excessive valve train noise and high fuel consumption rates may also point to the need for an overhaul, especially if they're all present at the same time. If a complete tune-up doesn't remedy the situation, major mechanical work is the only solution.

An engine overhaul involves restoring the internal parts to the specifications of a new engine. During an overhaul, the piston rings are replaced and the cylinder walls are reconditioned (rebored and/or honed). If a rebore is done by an automotive machine shop, new oversize pistons will also be installed. The main bearings and connecting rod bearings are generally replaced with new ones and, if necessary, the crankshaft may be reground to restore the journals. Generally, the valves are serviced as well, since they're usually in less-than-perfect condition at this point.

While the engine is being overhauled, other components, such as the distributor, starter and alternator, can be rebuilt as well. The end result should be a like-new engine that will give many trouble-free miles. **Note:** *Critical cooling system components such as the hoses, drivebelts, thermostat and water pump MUST be replaced with new parts when an engine is overhauled. The radiator should be checked carefully to ensure it isn't clogged or leaking (see Chapter 3).*

Before beginning the engine overhaul, read through the entire procedure to familiarize yourself with the scope and requirements of the job. Overhauling an engine isn't difficult if you follow all of the instructions carefully, have the necessary tools and equipment and pay close attention to all specifications; however, it can be time consuming. Plan on the vehicle being tied up for a minimum of two weeks, especially if parts must be taken to an automotive machine shop for repair or reconditioning. Check on availability of parts and make sure any necessary special tools and equipment are obtained in advance. Most work can be done with typical hand tools, although a number of precision measuring tools are required for inspecting parts to determine if they must be replaced. Often an automotive machine shop will handle the inspection of parts and offer advice concerning reconditioning and replacement. **Note:** *Always wait until the engine has been completely disassembled and all components, especially the engine block, have been inspected before deciding what service and repair operations must be performed by an automotive machine shop. Since the block's condition will be the major factor to consider when determining whether to overhaul the original engine or buy a rebuilt one, never purchase parts or have machine work done on other components until the block has been thoroughly inspected. As a general rule, time is the primary cost of an overhaul, so it doesn't pay to install worn or substandard parts.*

As a final note, to ensure maximum life and minimum trouble from a rebuilt engine, everything must be assembled with care in a spotlessly clean environment.

3.6   A compression gauge with a threaded fitting for the spark plug hole is preferred over the type that requires hand pressure to maintain the seal – be sure to open the throttle and choke valves as far as possible during the compression check!

3   Cylinder compression check

Refer to illustration 3.6

1   A compression check will tell you what mechanical condition the upper end (pistons, rings, valves, head gasket) of the engine is in. Specifically, it can tell you if the compression is down due to leakage caused by worn piston rings, defective valves and seats or a blown head gasket. **Note:** *The engine must be at normal operating temperature and the battery must be fully charged for this check. Also, if the engine is equipped with a carburetor, the choke valve must be all the way open to get an accurate compression reading (if the engine's warm, the choke should be open).*

2   Begin by cleaning the area around the spark plugs before you remove them (compressed air should be used, if available, otherwise a small brush or even a bicycle tire pump will work). The idea is to prevent dirt from getting into the cylinders as the compression check is being done.

3   Remove all of the spark plugs from the engine (see Chapter 1).

4   Block the throttle wide open.

5   Detach the coil wire from the center of the distributor cap and ground it on the engine block. Use a jumper wire with alligator clips on each end to ensure a good ground. On EFI equipped vehicles, the fuel pump circuit should also be disabled (see Chapter 4).

6   Install the compression gauge in the number one spark plug hole **(see illustration)**.

7   Crank the engine over at least seven compression strokes and watch the gauge. The compression should build up quickly in a healthy engine. Low compression on the first stroke, followed by gradually increasing pressure on successive strokes, indicates worn piston rings. A low compression reading on the first stroke, which doesn't build up during successive strokes, indicates leaking valves or a blown head gasket (a cracked head could also be the cause). Deposits on the valve seats can also cause low compression. Record the highest gauge reading obtained.

8   Repeat the procedure for the remaining cylinders and compare the results to this Chapter's Specifications.

9   If any of the readings are low, add some engine oil (about three squirts from a plunger-type oil can) to each cylinder, through the spark plug hole, and repeat the test.

10   If the compression increases after the oil is added, the piston rings are definitely worn. If the compression doesn't increase significantly, the leakage is occurring at the valves or head gasket. Leakage past the valves may be caused by burned valve seats and/or faces or warped, cracked or bent valves.

11   If two adjacent cylinders have equally low compression, there's a strong possibility the head gasket between them is blown. The appearance of coolant in the combustion chambers or the crankcase would verify this condition.

12   If one cylinder is slightly lower than the others, and the engine has a slightly rough idle, a worn lobe on the camshaft could be the cause.

13   If the compression is unusually high, the combustion chambers are probably coated with carbon deposits. If that's the case, the cylinder head should be removed and decarbonized.

14   If compression is way down or varies greatly between cylinders, it would be a good idea to have a leak-down test performed by an automotive repair shop. This test will pinpoint exactly where the leakage is occurring and how severe it is.

4   Engine removal – methods and precautions

If you've decided that an engine must be removed for overhaul or major repair work, several preliminary steps should be taken.

Locating a suitable place to work is extremely important. Adequate work space, along with storage space for the vehicle, will be needed. If a shop or garage isn't available, at the very least a flat, level, clean work surface made of concrete or asphalt is required.

Cleaning the engine compartment and engine before beginning the removal procedure will help keep tools clean and organized.

An engine hoist or A-frame will also be necessary. Make sure the equipment is rated in excess of the combined weight of the engine and accessories. Safety is of primary importance, considering the potential hazards involved in lifting the engine out of the vehicle.

If the engine is being removed by a novice, a helper should be available. Advice and aid from someone more experienced would also be helpful. There are many instances when one person cannot simultaneously perform all of the operations required when lifting the engine out of the vehicle.

Plan the operation ahead of time. Arrange for or obtain all of the tools and equipment you'll need prior to beginning the job. Some of the equipment necessary to perform engine removal and installation safely and with relative ease are (in addition to an engine hoist) a heavy duty floor jack, complete sets of wrenches and sockets as described in the front of this manual, wooden blocks and plenty of rags and cleaning solvent for mopping up spilled oil, coolant and gasoline. If the hoist must be rented, be sure to arrange for it in advance and perform all of the operations possible without it beforehand. This will save you money and time.

Plan for the vehicle to be out of use for quite a while. A machine shop will be required to perform some of the work which the do-it-yourselfer can't accomplish without special equipment. These shops often have a busy schedule, so it would be a good idea to consult them before removing the engine in order to accurately estimate the amount of time required to rebuild or repair components that may need work.

Always be extremely careful when removing and installing the engine.

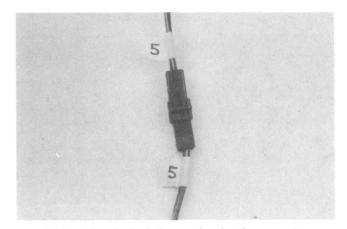

5.5   Label each wire before unplugging the connector

Serious injury can result from careless actions. Plan ahead, take your time and a job of this nature, although major, can be accomplished successfully.

5   Engine – removal and installation

2B

Refer to illustrations 5.5, 5.23a and 5.23b

Warning: *The air conditioning system is under high pressure! If you have to disconnect air conditioning hoses for engine removal, first have a dealer service department or service station discharge the system. Carefully note the routing of air conditioning system refrigerant lines before beginning engine removal to see if line disconnection, and therefore professional discharging, is necessary.*

Removal

1   Refer to Chapter 4 and relieve the fuel system pressure (EFI equipped vehicles only), then disconnect the negative cable from the battery.

2   Cover the fenders and cowl and remove the hood (see Chapter 11). Special pads are available to protect the fenders, but an old bedspread or blanket will also work.

3   Remove the air cleaner assembly.

4   Drain the cooling system (see Chapter 1).

5   Label the vacuum lines, emissions system hoses, wiring connectors, ground straps and fuel lines, to ensure correct reinstallation, then detach them. Pieces of masking tape with numbers or letters written on them work well **(see illustration)**. If there's any possibility of confusion, make a sketch of the engine compartment and clearly label the lines, hoses and wires.

6   Label and detach all coolant hoses from the engine.

7   Remove the cooling fan, shroud and radiator (see Chapter 3).

8   Remove the drivebelts (see Chapter 1).

9   Disconnect the fuel lines running from the engine to the chassis (see Chapter 4). Plug or cap all open fittings/lines. **Warning:** *Gasoline is extremely flammable, so extra precautions must be taken when working on any part of the fuel system. DO NOT smoke or allow open flames or bare light bulbs near the vehicle. Also, don't work in a garage if a natural gas appliance with a pilot light is present.*

10   Disconnect the throttle linkage (and TV linkage cable, if equipped) from the engine (see Chapter 4).

11   On air conditioned models, unbolt the compressor (see Chapter 3) and set it aside. Do not disconnect the hoses unless absolutely necessary.

12   Drain the engine oil (see Chapter 1) and remove the filter.

13   Remove the starter motor (see Chapter 5).

14   Remove the alternator (see Chapter 5).

15   Unbolt the exhaust system from the engine (see Chapter 4).

16   If you're working on a vehicle with an automatic transaxle, refer to Chapter 7 and remove the torque converter-to-driveplate fasteners.

5.23a   Pull the engine sideways to separate it from the transaxle, . . .

5.23b   . . . then slowly raise the engine until it clears the body

17   Support the transaxle with a jack. Position a block of wood between them to prevent damage to the transaxle. Special transaxle jacks with safety chains are available – use one if possible.
18   Attach an engine sling or a length of chain to the lifting brackets on the engine.
19   Roll the hoist into position and connect the sling to it. Take up the slack in the sling or chain, but don't lift the engine. **Warning:** *DO NOT place any part of your body under the engine when it's supported only by a hoist or other lifting device.*
20   Remove the transaxle-to-engine block bolts.
21   Remove the engine mount-to-frame bolts.
22   Recheck to be sure nothing is still connecting the engine to the transaxle or vehicle. Disconnect anything still remaining.
23   Raise the engine slightly. Carefully work it sideways to separate it from the transaxle **(see illustration)**. If you're working on a vehicle with an automatic transaxle, be sure the torque converter stays in the transaxle (clamp a pair of vise-grips to the housing to keep the converter from sliding out). If you're working on a vehicle with a manual transaxle, the input shaft must be completely disengaged from the clutch. Slowly raise the engine out of the engine compartment **(see illustration)**. Check carefully to make sure nothing is hanging up.
24   Remove the flywheel/driveplate and mount the engine on an engine stand.

Installation

25   Check the engine and transaxle mounts. If they're worn or damaged, replace them.
26   If you're working on a manual transaxle equipped vehicle, install the clutch and pressure plate (see Chapter 8). Now is a good time to install a new clutch.
27   Carefully lower the engine into the engine compartment – make sure the engine mounts line up.
28   If you're working on an automatic transaxle equipped vehicle, guide the torque converter into the crankshaft following the procedure outlined in Chapter 7.
29   If you're working on a manual transaxle equipped vehicle, apply a dab of high-temperature grease to the input shaft and guide it into the crankshaft pilot bearing until the bellhousing is flush with the engine block. **Caution:** *DO NOT use the bolts to force the transaxle and engine together!*
31   Reinstall the remaining components in the reverse order of removal.
32   Add coolant, oil and transaxle fluid as needed.
33   Run the engine and check for leaks and proper operation of all accessories, then install the hood and test drive the vehicle.
34   Have the air conditioning system recharged and leak tested, if it was discharged.

6   Engine rebuilding alternatives

The do-it-yourselfer is faced with a number of options when performing an engine overhaul. The decision to replace the engine block, piston/connecting rod assemblies and crankshaft depends on a number of factors, with the number one consideration being the condition of the block. Other considerations are cost, access to machine shop facilities, parts availability, time required to complete the project and the extent of prior mechanical experience on the part of the do-it-yourselfer.
Some of the rebuilding alternatives include:
Individual parts – If the inspection procedures reveal the engine block and most engine components are in reusable condition, purchasing individual parts may be the most economical alternative. The block, crankshaft and piston/connecting rod assemblies should all be inspected carefully. Even if the block shows little wear, the cylinder bores should be surface honed.
Short block – A short block consists of an engine block with a crankshaft and piston/connecting rod assemblies already installed. All new bearings are incorporated and all clearances will be correct. The existing cylinder head and external parts can be bolted to the short block with little or no machine shop work necessary.
Long block – A long block consists of a short block plus an oil pump, oil pan, cylinder head, valve cover, camshaft and valve train components, timing sprockets, belt and timing cover. All components are installed with new bearings, seals and gaskets incorporated throughout. The installation of manifolds and external parts is all that's necessary.

Give careful thought to which alternative is best for you and discuss the situation with local automotive machine shops, auto parts dealers and experienced rebuilders before ordering or purchasing replacement parts.

7   Engine overhaul – disassembly sequence

Refer to illustration 7.5

1   It's much easier to disassemble and work on the engine if it's mounted on a portable engine stand. A stand can often be rented quite cheaply from an equipment rental yard. Before the engine is mounted on a stand, the flywheel/driveplate and rear oil seal housing should be removed from the engine.
2   If a stand isn't available, it's possible to disassemble the engine with it blocked up on the floor. Be extra careful not to tip or drop the engine when working without a stand.
3   If you're going to obtain a rebuilt engine, all external components must come off first, to be transferred to the replacement engine, just as

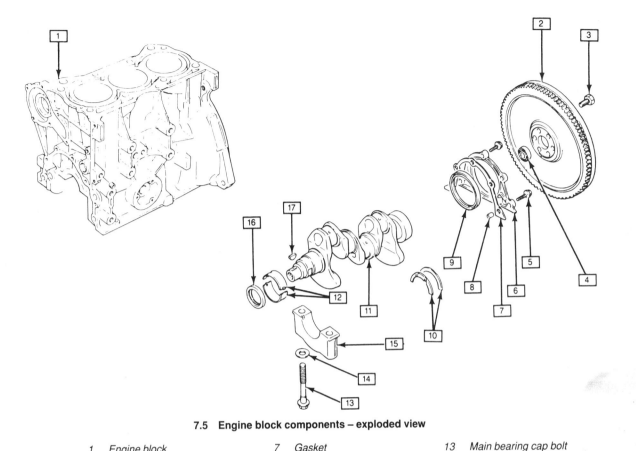

7.5 Engine block components – exploded view

1	Engine block	7	Gasket	13	Main bearing cap bolt
2	Flywheel	8	Dowel pin	14	Washer
3	Flywheel bolt	9	Rear main oil seal	15	Main bearing cap
4	Pilot bearing	10	Crankshaft thrust bearings	16	Front oil seal
5	Bolt/screw	11	Crankshaft	17	Crankshaft pulley key
6	Rear main oil seal housing	12	Main bearing		

2B

they will if you're doing a complete engine overhaul yourself. These include:

Alternator and brackets
Emissions control components
Distributor, spark plug wires and spark plugs
Thermostat and housing cover
Water pump
EFI components or carburetor
Intake/exhaust manifolds
Oil filter
Engine mounts
Clutch and flywheel/driveplate

Note: *When removing the external components from the engine, pay close attention to details that may be helpful or important during installation. Note the installed position of gaskets, seals, spacers, pins, brackets, washers, bolts and other small items.*

4   If you're obtaining a short block, which consists of the engine block, crankshaft, pistons and connecting rods all assembled, then the cylinder head, oil pan and oil pump will have to be removed as well. See Engine rebuilding alternatives for additional information regarding the different possibilities to be considered.

5   If you're planning a complete overhaul, the engine must be disassembled and the internal components **(see illustration)** removed in the following order:

Valve cover
Intake and exhaust manifolds

Timing belt and sprockets
Rocker arms and shafts or lifters
Cylinder head
Oil pan
Oil pump
Piston/connecting rod assemblies
Crankshaft and main bearings

6   Before beginning the disassembly and overhaul procedures, make sure the following items are available. Also, refer to Engine overhaul – reassembly sequence for a list of tools and materials needed for engine reassembly.

Common hand tools
Small cardboard boxes or plastic bags for storing parts
Gasket scraper
Ridge reamer
Micrometers
Telescoping gauges
Dial indicator set
Valve spring compressor
Cylinder surfacing hone
Piston ring groove cleaning tool
Electric drill
Tap and die set
Wire brushes
Oil gallery brushes
Cleaning solvent

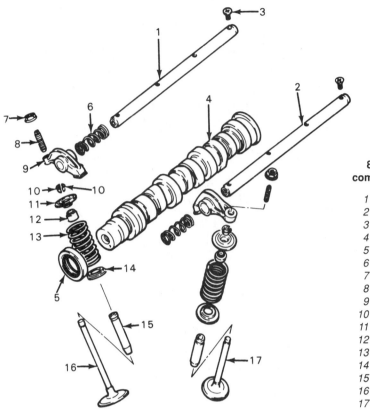

8.1a   Sprint valvetrain components – exploded view

1 Intake rocker arm shaft
2 Exhaust rocker arm shaft
3 Screw
4 Camshaft
5 Camshaft oil seal
6 Rocker arm spring
7 Locknut
8 Valve adjusting screw
9 Rocker arm
10 Keeper
11 Valve spring retainer
12 Valve stem seal
13 Valve spring
14 Valve spring seat
15 Valve guide
16 Intake valve
17 Exhaust valve

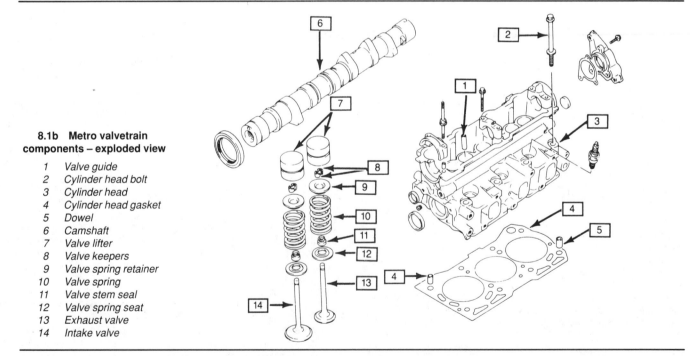

8.1b   Metro valvetrain components – exploded view

1 Valve guide
2 Cylinder head bolt
3 Cylinder head
4 Cylinder head gasket
5 Dowel
6 Camshaft
7 Valve lifter
8 Valve keepers
9 Valve spring retainer
10 Valve spring
11 Valve stem seal
12 Valve spring seat
13 Exhaust valve
14 Intake valve

8   Cylinder head – disassembly

Refer to illustrations 8.1a, 8.1b, 8.4, 8.5, 8.6a and 8.6b

Note: *New and rebuilt cylinder heads are commonly available for most engines at dealerships and auto parts stores. Due to the fact that some specialized tools are necessary for the disassembly and inspection procedures, and replacement parts may not be readily available, it may be more practical and economical for the home mechanic to purchase a re-*

placement head rather than taking the time to disassemble, inspect and recondition the original.

1   Cylinder head disassembly involves removal of the camshaft, intake and exhaust valves and related components **(see illustrations)**. Label the parts or store them separately so they can be reinstalled in their original locations.

2   Remove the timing belt sprocket as described in Chapter 2, Part A, Section 7.

8.4 A small plastic bag, with an appropriate label, can be used to store the valve train components so they can be kept together and reinstalled in the original location

8.5 Use a valve spring compressor to compress the spring, then remove the keepers from the valve stem (Sprint show, Metro similar)

8.6a The valve seals can be pulled off with pliers

8.6b If the valve won't pull through the guide, deburr the edge of the stem end and the area around the top of the keeper groove with a file

3   On Sprint models, if they're still in place, remove the camshaft, rocker arms and shafts from the cylinder head (see Chapter 2, Part A, Section 10). On Metro models, remove the camshaft and lifters (see Chapter 2, Part A, Section 11).

4   Before the valves are removed, arrange to label and store them, along with their related components, so they can be kept separate and reinstalled in the same valve guides they are removed from **(see illustration)**.

5   Compress the springs on the first valve with a spring compressor and remove the keepers **(see illustration)**. Carefully release the valve spring compressor and remove the retainer, the spring and the spring seat (if used).

6   Pull the valve out of the head, then remove the oil seal from the guide **(see illustration)**. If the valve binds in the guide (won't pull through), push it back into the head and deburr the area around the keeper groove with a fine file or whetstone **(see illustration)**.

7   Repeat the procedure for the remaining valves. Remember to keep all the parts for each valve together so they can be reinstalled in the same locations.

8   Once the valves and related components have been removed and stored in an organized manner, the head should be thoroughly cleaned and inspected. If a complete engine overhaul is being done, finish the engine disassembly procedure before beginning the cylinder head cleaning and inspection process.

9   Cylinder head – cleaning and inspection

Refer to illustrations 9.12, 9.14, 9.15, 9.16, 9.17 and 9.18

1   Thorough cleaning of the cylinder head and related valve train components, followed by a detailed inspection, will enable you to decide how much valve service work must be done during the engine overhaul. **Note:** *If the engine was severely overheated, the cylinder head is probably warped (see Step 12).*

Cleaning

2   Scrape all traces of old gasket material and sealing compound off the head gasket, intake manifold and exhaust manifold sealing surfaces. Be very careful not to gouge the cylinder head. Special gasket removal solvents that soften gaskets and make removal much easier are available at auto parts stores.

3   Remove all built up scale from the coolant passages.

4   Run a stiff wire brush through the various holes to remove deposits that may have formed in them.

5   Run an appropriate size tap into each of the threaded holes to remove corrosion and thread sealant that may be present. If compressed air is available, use it to clear the holes of debris produced by this operation. **Warning:** *Wear eye protection when using compressed air!*

6   On Sprint models, clean the rocker arm shaft oil holes with a wire and compressed air (if available). **Warning:** *Wear eye protection!*

7   Clean the cylinder head with solvent and dry it thoroughly. Compressed air will speed the drying process and ensure that all holes and recessed areas are clean. **Note:** *Decarbonizing chemicals are available and may prove very useful when cleaning cylinder heads and valve train components. They are very caustic and should be used with caution. Be sure to follow the instructions on the container.*

8   Clean the camshaft, rocker arms and rocker shafts (if equipped) with solvent and dry them thoroughly (don't mix them up during the cleaning process). Compressed air will speed the drying process and can be used to clean out the oil passages.

9   Clean all the valve springs, spring seats, keepers and retainers with solvent and dry them thoroughly. Do the components from one valve at a time to avoid mixing up the parts.

10   Scrape off any heavy deposits that may have formed on the valves, then use a motorized wire brush to remove deposits from the valve heads and stems. Again, make sure the valves don't get mixed up.

Inspection

Note: *Be sure to perform all of the following inspection procedures before concluding that machine shop work is required. Make a list of the items that need attention.*

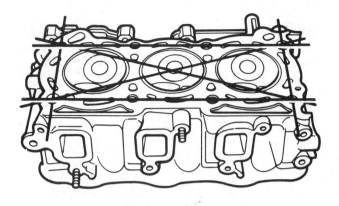

9.12   Check the cylinder head gasket surface for warpage by trying to slip a feeler gauge under the straightedge (see this Chapter's Specifications for the maximum warpage allowed and use a feeler gauge of that thickness)

9.14   A dial indicator can be used to determine the valve stem-to-guide clearance (move the valve stem as indicated by the arrows)

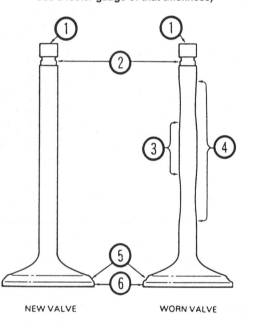

9.15   Check for valve wear at the points shown here

1	Valve tip	4	Stem (most worn area)
2	Keeper groove	5	Valve face
3	Stem (least worn area)	6	Margin

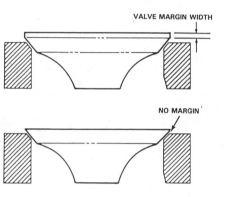

9.16   The margin width on each valve must be as specified (if no margin exists, the valve cannot be reused)

Cylinder head

11   Inspect the head very carefully for cracks, evidence of coolant leakage and other damage. If cracks are found, check with an automotive machine shop concerning repair. If repair isn't possible, a new cylinder head should be obtained.

12   Using a straightedge and feeler gauge, check the head gasket mating surface, the intake manifold mating surface and the exhaust manifold mating surface of the cylinder head for warpage (see illustration). If the warpage exceeds the limit listed in this Chapter's Specifications, it can be resurfaced at an automotive machine shop.

13   Examine the valve seats in each of the combustion chambers. If they're pitted, cracked or burned, the head will require valve service that's beyond the scope of the home mechanic.

14   Check the valve stem-to-guide clearance by measuring the lateral movement of the valve stem with a dial indicator attached securely to the head (see illustration). The valve must be in the guide and approximately 1/16-inch off the seat. The total valve stem movement indicated by the gauge needle must be divided by two to obtain the actual clearance. After this is done, if there's still some doubt regarding the condition of the valve guides they should be checked by an automotive machine shop (the cost should be minimal).

Valves

15   Carefully inspect each valve face for uneven wear, deformation, cracks, pits and burned areas (see illustration). Check the valve stem for scuffing and galling and the neck for cracks. Rotate the valve and check for any obvious indication that it's bent. Look for pits and excessive wear on the end of the stem. The presence of any of these conditions indicates the need for valve service by an automotive machine shop.

16   Measure the margin width on each valve (see illustration). Any valve with a margin narrower than specified will have to be replaced with a new one.

Valve components

17   Check each valve spring for wear (on the ends) and pits. Measure the free length and compare it to the Specifications in this Chapter (see illustration). Any springs that are shorter than specified have sagged and should not be reused. The tension of all springs should be checked with a special fixture before deciding they're suitable for use in a rebuilt engine (take the springs to an automotive machine shop for this check).

18   Stand each spring on a flat surface and check it for squareness (see illustration). If any of the springs are distorted or sagged, replace all of them with new parts.

19   Check the spring retainers and keepers for obvious wear and cracks. Any questionable parts should be replaced with new ones, as extensive damage will occur if they fail during engine operation.

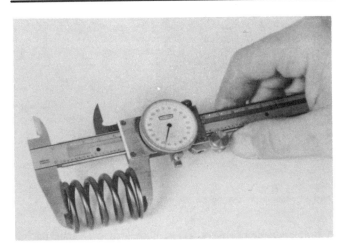

9.17   Measure the free length of each valve spring with a dial or vernier caliper

9.18   Check each valve spring for squareness

2B

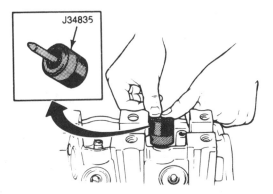

11.3a   Special tool J34835 is recommended for valve seal installation on Sprints, . . .

11.3b   . . . but a deep socket and a hammer can be used if the tool isn't available – don't hammer on the seals once they're seated

Rocker arms and camshaft
20   Refer to Chapter 2, Part A, Section 10 when inspecting these components.

10   Valves – servicing

1   Because of the complex nature of the job and the special tools and equipment needed, servicing of the valves, the valve seats and the valve guides, commonly known as a valve job, should be done by a professional.
2   The home mechanic can remove and disassemble the head, do the initial cleaning and inspection, then reassemble and deliver it to a dealer service department or an automotive machine shop for the actual service work. Doing the inspection will enable you to see what condition the head and valvetrain components are in and will ensure that you know what work and new parts are required when dealing with an automotive machine shop.
3   The dealer service department, or automotive machine shop, will remove the valves and springs, recondition or replace the valves and valve seats, recondition the valve guides, check and replace the valve springs, spring retainers and keepers (as necessary), replace the valve seals with new ones, reassemble the valve components and make sure the installed

spring height is correct. The cylinder head gasket surface will also be resurfaced if it's warped.
4   After the valve job has been performed by a professional, the head will be in like-new condition. When it's returned, be sure to clean it again before installation on the engine to remove any metal particles and abrasive grit that may still be present from the valve service or head resurfacing operations. Use compressed air, if available, to blow out all the oil holes and passages.

11   Cylinder head – reassembly

Refer to illustrations 11.3a, 11.3b, 11.5, 11.6 and 11.8

1   Regardless of whether or not the head was sent to an automotive repair shop for valve servicing, make sure it's clean before beginning reassembly.
2   If the head was sent out for valve servicing, the valves and related components will already be in place. Begin the reassembly procedure with Step 8.
3   Install new seals on each of the valve guides. Using a hammer and a deep socket or seal installation tool, gently tap each seal into place until it's completely seated on the guide (**see illustrations**). Don't twist or cock the seals during installation or they won't seal properly on the valve stems.
4   Beginning at one end of the head, lubricate and install the first valve. Apply moly-base grease or clean engine oil to the valve stem.

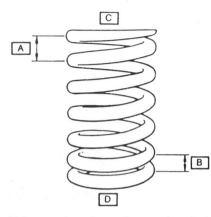

11.5   Make sure the valve springs are installed with the small-pitch coils next to the cylinder head

A   *Large-pitch coils*   C   *Valve spring retainer side*
B   *Small-pitch coils*   D   *Cylinder head side*

11.6   Keepers don't always stay in place, so apply a small dab of grease to each one as shown here before installation – it'll hold them in place on the valve stem as the spring is released

11.8   Be sure to check the valve spring installed height (the distance from the top of the seat/shims to the top of the spring)

5   Drop the spring seat or shim(s) (if used) over the valve guide and set the valve spring and retainer in place **(see illustration)**.
6   Compress the springs with a valve spring compressor and carefully install the keepers in the groove, then slowly release the compressor and make sure the keepers seat properly. Apply a small dab of grease to each keeper to hold it in place if necessary **(see illustration)**.
7   Repeat the procedure for the remaining valves. Be sure to return the components to their original locations – don't mix them up!
8   Check the installed valve spring height with a ruler graduated in 1/32-inch increments or a dial caliper. If the head was sent out for service work, the installed height should be correct (but don't automatically assume it is). The measurement is taken from the top of each spring seat or shim(s) to the bottom of the retainer **(see illustration)**. If the height is greater than specified, shims can be added under the springs to correct it. **Caution:** *Don't, under any circumstances, shim the springs to the point where the installed height is less than specified.*
9   Refer to Chapter 2, Part A, to install the camshaft, rocker arms, springs and shafts on Sprint models or the lifters and camshaft on Metro models.
10   Reinstall the distributor case with a new O-ring.

---

12   Pistons/connecting rods – removal

Refer to illustrations 12.1, 12.3 and 12.6
Note: *Prior to removing the piston/connecting rod assemblies, remove the cylinder head, the oil pan and the oil pickup by referring to the appropriate Sections in Chapter 2, Part A.*

12.1   A ridge reamer is required to remove the ridge from the top of each cylinder – do this before removing the pistons!

1   Use your fingernail to feel if a ridge has formed at the upper limit of ring travel (about 1/4-inch down from the top of each cylinder). If carbon deposits or cylinder wear have produced ridges, they must be completely removed with a special tool **(see illustration)**. Follow the manufacturer's instructions provided with the tool. Failure to remove the ridges before attempting to remove the piston/connecting rod assemblies may result in piston breakage.
2   After the cylinder ridges have been removed, turn the engine upside-down so the crankshaft is facing up.
3   Before the connecting rods are removed, check the endplay with feeler gauges. Slide them between the first connecting rod and the crankshaft throw until the play is removed **(see illustration)**. The endplay is equal to the thickness of the feeler gauge(s). If the endplay exceeds the service limit, new connecting rods will be required. If new rods (or a new crankshaft) are installed, the endplay may fall under the specified minimum (if it does, the rods will have to be machined to restore it – consult an automotive machine shop for advice if necessary). Repeat the procedure for the remaining connecting rods.
4   Check the connecting rods and caps for identification marks. If they aren't plainly marked, use a small center punch to make the appropriate number of indentations on each rod and cap (1, 2 or 3, depending on the cylinder they're associated with).
5   Loosen each of the connecting rod cap nuts 1/4-turn at a time until they can be removed by hand. Remove the number one connecting rod cap and bearing insert. Don't drop the bearing insert out of the cap.
6   Slip a short length of plastic or rubber hose over each connecting rod cap bolt to protect the crankshaft journal and cylinder wall as the piston is removed **(see illustration)**.
7   Remove the bearing insert and push the connecting rod/piston assembly out through the top of the engine. Use a wooden hammer handle to

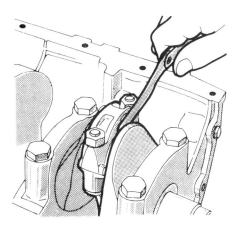

12.3   Check the connecting rod endplay with a feeler gauge as shown here

12.6   To prevent damage to the crankshaft journals and cylinder walls, slip a section of hose over the rod bolts before removing the pistons

13.1   Checking crankshaft endplay with a dial indicator

2B

push on the upper bearing surface in the connecting rod. If resistance is felt, double-check to make sure all of the ridge was removed from the cylinder.

8   Repeat the procedure for the remaining cylinders.

9   After removal, reassemble the connecting rod caps and bearing inserts in their respective connecting rods and install the cap nuts finger-tight. Leaving the old bearing inserts in place until reassembly will help prevent the connecting rod bearing surfaces from being accidentally nicked or gouged.

10   Don't separate the pistons from the connecting rods (see Section 17 for additional information).

13   Crankshaft – removal

Refer to illustrations 13.1 and 13.4

Note: *The crankshaft can be removed only after the engine has been removed from the vehicle. It's assumed the flywheel or driveplate, crankshaft pulley, timing belt, oil pan, oil pump and piston/connecting rod assemblies have already been removed. The rear oil seal housing must be unbolted and separated from the block before proceeding with crankshaft removal.*

1   Before the crankshaft is removed, check the endplay. Mount a dial indicator with the stem in line with the crankshaft and just touching one of the crank throws **(see illustration)**.

2   Push the crankshaft all the way to the rear and zero the dial indicator. Next, pry the crankshaft to the front as far as possible and check the reading on the dial indicator. The distance that it moves is the endplay. If it's greater than specified, check the crankshaft thrust surfaces for wear. If no wear is evident, new thrust bearings should correct the endplay.

3   If a dial indicator isn't available, feeler gauges can be used. Gently pry or push the crankshaft all the way to the front of the engine. Slip feeler gauges between the crankshaft and the front face of the thrust bearing to determine the clearance. The thrust bearings are located on both sides of the third main bearing saddle in the block (not in the bearing cap).

4   Check the main bearing caps to see if they're marked to indicate their locations. They should be numbered consecutively from the front of the engine to the rear. If they aren't, mark them with number stamping dies or a center punch. Main bearing caps generally have a cast-in arrow, which points to the front of the engine **(see illustration)**. Loosen the main bearing cap bolts 1/4-turn at a time each, until they can be removed by hand. Note if any stud bolts are used and make sure they're returned to their original locations when the crankshaft is reinstalled.

5   Gently tap the caps with a soft-face hammer, then separate them from the engine block. If necessary, use the bolts as levers to remove the caps. Try not to drop the bearing inserts if they come out with the caps.

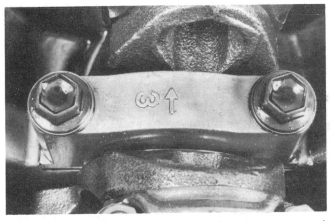

13.4   The main bearing caps are numbered from front-to-rear and the arrows indicate the front of the engine

6   Carefully lift the crankshaft out of the engine. With the bearing inserts in place in the engine block and main bearing caps, return the caps to their respective locations on the engine block and tighten the bolts finger-tight.

14   Engine block – cleaning

Refer to illustration 14.8

Caution: *The core plugs (also known as freeze or soft plugs) may be difficult or impossible to retrieve if they're driven into the block coolant passages.*

1   Remove the engine mount brackets and any components still attached to the engine block.

2   Using a gasket scraper, remove all traces of gasket material from the engine block. Be very careful not to nick or gouge the gasket sealing surfaces.

3   Remove the main bearing caps and separate the bearing inserts from the caps and the engine block. Tag the bearings, indicating which cylinder they were removed from and whether they were in the cap or the block, then set them aside.

4   Remove all of the threaded oil gallery plugs from the block. The plugs are usually very tight – they may have to be drilled out and the holes re-tapped. Use new plugs when the engine is reassembled.

5   If the engine is extremely dirty it should be taken to an automotive machine shop to be cleaned.

6   After the block is returned, clean all oil holes and oil galleries one more time. Brushes specifically designed for this purpose are available at most auto parts stores. Flush the passages with warm water until the water runs clear, dry the block thoroughly and wipe all machined surfaces with a light,

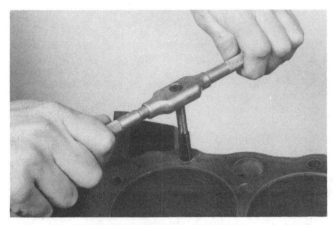

14.8   All bolt holes in the block – particularly the main bearing cap and head bolt holes – should be cleaned and restored with a tap (be sure to remove debris from the holes after this is done)

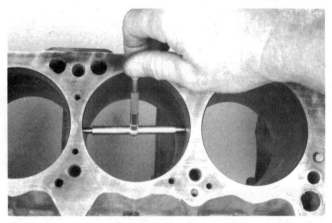

15.4b   The ability to "feel" when the telescoping gauge is at the correct point will be developed over time, so work slowly and repeat the check until you're satisfied the bore measurement is accurate

rust preventive oil. If you have access to compressed air, use it to speed the drying process and to blow out all the oil holes and galleries. **Warning:** *Wear eye protection when using compressed air!*

7   If the block isn't extremely dirty or sludged up, you can do an adequate cleaning job with solvent, followed with hot soapy water, and a stiff brush. Take plenty of time and do a thorough job. Regardless of the cleaning method used, be sure to clean all oil holes and galleries very thoroughly, dry the block completely and coat all machined surfaces with light oil.

8   The threaded holes in the block must be clean to ensure accurate torque readings during reassembly. Run the proper size tap into each of the holes to remove rust, corrosion, thread sealant or sludge and restore damaged threads **(see illustration)**. If possible, use compressed air to clear the holes of debris produced by this operation. Now is a good time to clean the threads on the head bolts and the main bearing cap bolts as well.

9   Reinstall the main bearing caps and tighten the bolts finger-tight.

10   Apply non-hardening sealant (such as Permatex no. 2 or Teflon pipe sealant) to the new oil gallery plugs and thread them into the holes in the block. Make sure they're tightened securely.

11   If the engine isn't going to be reassembled right away, cover it with a large plastic trash bag to keep it clean.

---

15   Engine block – inspection

Refer to illustrations 15.4a, 15.4b, 15.4c and 15.13

1   Before the block is inspected, it should be cleaned as described in Section 14.

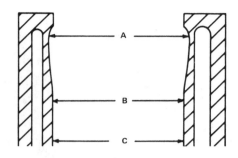

15.4a   Measure the diameter of each cylinder just under the wear ridge (A), at the center (B) and at the bottom (C)

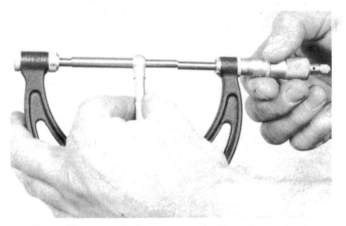

15.4c   The gauge is then measured with a micrometer to determine the bore size

2   Visually check the block for cracks, rust and corrosion. Look for stripped threads in the threaded holes. It's also a good idea to have the block checked for hidden cracks by an automotive machine shop that has the special equipment to do this type of work. If defects are found, have the block repaired, if possible, or replaced.

3   Check the cylinder bores for scuffing and scoring.

4   Measure the diameter of each cylinder at the top (just under the ridge area), center and bottom of the cylinder bore, parallel to the crankshaft axis **(see illustrations)**.

5   Next, measure each cylinder's diameter at the same three locations across the crankshaft axis. Compare the results to the Specifications.

6   If the required precision measuring tools aren't available, the piston-to-cylinder clearances can be obtained, though not quite as accurately, using feeler gauge stock. Feeler gauge stock comes in 12-inch lengths and various thicknesses and is generally available at auto parts stores.

7   To check the clearance, select a feeler gauge with a thickness equal to the recommended piston-to-bore clearance and slip it into the cylinder along with the matching piston. The piston must be positioned exactly as it normally would be. The feeler gauge must be between the piston and cylinder on one of the thrust faces (90-degrees to the piston pin bore).

8   The piston should slip through the cylinder (with the feeler gauge in place) with moderate pressure.

9   If it falls through or slides through easily, the clearance is excessive and a new piston will be required. If the piston binds at the lower end of the cylinder and is loose toward the top, the cylinder is tapered. If tight spots are encountered as the piston/feeler gauge is rotated in the cylinder, the cylinder is out-of-round.

10   Repeat the procedure for the remaining pistons and cylinders.

11   If the cylinder walls are badly scuffed or scored, or if they're out-of-round or tapered beyond the limits given in the Specifications, have the engine block rebored and honed at an automotive machine shop. If a re-bore is done, oversize pistons and rings will be required.

12   If the cylinders are in reasonably good condition and not worn to the outside of the limits, and if the piston-to-cylinder clearances can be main-

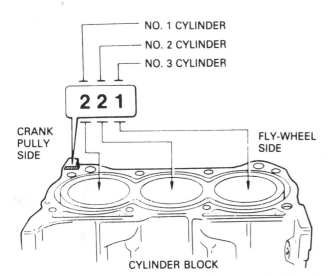

15.13   Code numbers are stamped on the engine block head gasket surface near the timing belt end – the numbers indicate the piston size installed in the respective cylinders

16.3a   A "bottle brush" hone will produce better results if you've never honed cylinders before

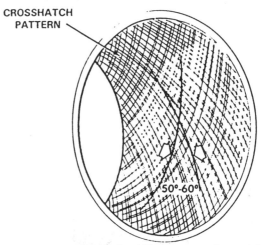

16.3b   The cylinder hone should leave a smooth, crosshatch pattern with the lines intersecting at approximately a 60-degree angle

2B

tained properly, then they don't have to be rebored. Honing is all that's necessary (see Section 16).

13   Engines are originally equipped with either one of two sizes of standard pistons. The engine blocks are stamped with number codes to indicate the piston size installed at the factory (**see illustration**). Consult the Specifications for dimensions.

16   Cylinder honing

Refer to illustrations 16.3a and 16.3b

1   Prior to engine reassembly, the cylinder bores must be honed so the new piston rings will seat correctly and provide the best possible combustion chamber seal. **Note:** *If you don't have the tools or don't want to tackle the honing operation, most automotive machine shops will do it for a reasonable fee.*

2   Before honing the cylinders, install the main bearing caps and tighten the bolts to the specified torque.

3   Two types of cylinder hones are commonly available – the flex hone or "bottle brush" type and the more traditional surfacing hone with spring-loaded stones. Both will do the job, but for the less experienced mechanic the "bottle brush" hone will probably be easier to use. You'll also need some kerosene or honing oil, rags and an electric drill. Proceed as follows:

a) Mount the hone in the drill, compress the stones and slip it into the first cylinder (**see illustration**). Be sure to wear safety goggles or a face shield!

b) Lubricate the cylinder with plenty of honing oil, turn on the drill and move the hone up-and-down in the cylinder at a pace that will produce a fine crosshatch pattern on the cylinder walls. Ideally, the crosshatch lines should intersect at approximately a 60-degree angle (**see illustration**). Be sure to use plenty of lubricant and don't take off any more material than absolutely necessary to produce the desired finish. **Note:** *Piston ring manufacturers may specify a smaller crosshatch angle than the traditional 60-degrees – read and follow any instructions included with the new rings.*

c) Don't withdraw the hone from the cylinder while it's running. Instead, shut off the drill and continue moving the hone up-and-down in the cylinder until it comes to a complete stop, then compress the stones and withdraw the hone. If you're using a "bottle brush" type hone, stop the drill motor, then turn the chuck in the normal direction of rotation while withdrawing the hone from the cylinder.

d) Wipe the oil out of the cylinder and repeat the procedure for the remaining cylinders.

4   After the honing job is complete, chamfer the top edges of the cylinder bores with a small file so the rings won't catch when the pistons are installed. Be very careful not to nick the cylinder walls with the end of the file.

5   The entire engine block must be washed again very thoroughly with warm, soapy water to remove all traces of the abrasive grit produced during the honing operation. **Note:** *The bores can be considered clean when a lint-free white cloth – dampened with clean engine oil – used to wipe them out doesn't pick up any more honing residue, which will show up as gray areas on the cloth.* Be sure to run a brush through all oil holes and galleries and flush them with running water.

6   After rinsing, dry the block and apply a coat of light rust preventive oil to all machined surfaces. Wrap the block in a plastic trash bag to keep it clean and set it aside until reassembly.

17   Pistons/connecting rods – inspection

Refer to illustrations 17.4a, 17.4b, 17.10, 17.11a and 17.11b

1   Before the inspection process can be carried out, the piston/connecting rod assemblies must be cleaned and the original piston rings removed from the pistons. **Note:** *Always use new piston rings when the engine is reassembled.*

2   Using a piston ring installation tool, carefully remove the rings from the pistons. Be careful not to nick or gouge the pistons in the process.

17.4a   The piston ring grooves can be cleaned with a special tool, as shown here, . . .

17.4b   . . . or a section of a broken ring

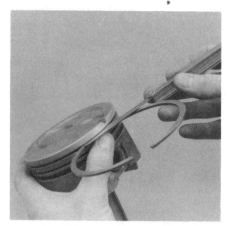

17.10   Check the ring side clearance with a feeler gauge at several points around the groove

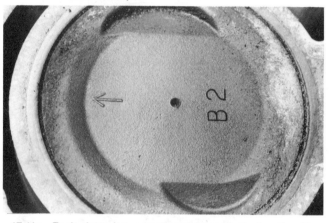

17.11a   Each piston has a number stamped in the top (1 or 2) – the arrow points to the front of the engine and the letter (B) is a production code

17.11b   Measure the piston diameter at a 90-degree angle to the piston pin and in line with it

3   Scrape all traces of carbon from the top of the piston. A hand-held wire brush or a piece of fine emery cloth can be used once the majority of deposits have been scraped away. Do not, under any circumstances, use a wire brush mounted in an electric drill to remove deposits from the pistons. The piston material is soft and may be eroded away by the wire brush.

4   Use a piston ring groove cleaning tool to remove carbon deposits from the ring grooves. If a tool isn't available, a piece broken off the old ring will do the job. Be very careful to remove only the carbon deposits – don't remove any metal and do not nick or scratch the sides of the ring grooves **(see illustrations)**.

5   Once the deposits have been removed, clean the piston/rod assemblies with solvent and dry them with compressed air (if available). Make sure the oil return holes in the back sides of the ring grooves are clear.

6   If the pistons and cylinder walls aren't damaged or worn excessively, and if the engine block is not rebored, new pistons won't be necessary. Normal piston wear appears as even vertical wear on the piston thrust surfaces and slight looseness of the top ring in its groove. New piston rings, however, should always be used when an engine is rebuilt.

7   Carefully inspect each piston for cracks around the skirt, at the pin bosses and at the ring lands.

8   Look for scoring and scuffing on the thrust faces of the skirt, holes in the piston crown and burned areas at the edge of the crown. If the skirt is scored or scuffed, the engine may have been suffering from overheating and/or abnormal combustion, which caused excessively high operating temperatures. The cooling and lubrication systems should be checked thoroughly. A hole in the piston crown is an indication that abnormal combustion (preignition) was occurring. Burned areas at the edge of the piston crown are usually evidence of spark knock (detonation). If any of the above problems exist, the causes must be corrected or the damage will

occur again. The causes may include intake air leaks, incorrect fuel/air mixture, incorrect ignition timing and EGR system malfunctions.

9   Corrosion of the piston, in the form of small pits, indicates coolant is leaking into the combustion chamber and/or the crankcase. Again, the cause must be corrected or the problem may persist in the rebuilt engine.

10   Measure the piston ring side clearance by laying a new piston ring in each ring groove and slipping a feeler gauge in beside it **(see illustration)**. Check the clearance at three or four locations around each groove. Be sure to use the correct ring for each groove – they are different. If the side clearance is greater than specified, new pistons will have to be used.

11   Check the piston-to-bore clearance by measuring the bore (see Section 15) and the piston diameter. Either of two standard size pistons may be installed at the factory. Each piston has a number stamped on top **(see illustration)**. There are also numbers stamped into the block **(see illustration 15.13)**. The numbers (either 1 or 2) on the pistons and block designate the bore size. Make sure the pistons and bores are correctly matched. Measure the piston across the skirt, at a 90-degree angle to the piston pin **(see illustration)**. Take the measurement 0.450-inch (11.5 mm) up from the bottom of the skirt on Metro LSI models, 0.600-inch (15 mm) up on all other models. Subtract the piston diameter from the bore diameter to obtain the clearance. If it's greater than specified, the block will have to be rebored and new pistons and rings installed.

12   Check the piston-to-rod clearance by twisting the piston and rod in opposite directions. Any noticeable play indicates excessive wear, which must be corrected. The piston/connecting rod assemblies should be taken to an automotive machine shop to have the pistons and rods resized and new pins installed.

13   If the pistons must be removed from the connecting rods for any reason, they should be taken to an automotive machine shop. While they are

18.1   The oil holes should be chamfered so sharp edges don't gouge or scratch the new bearings

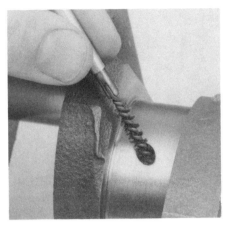

18.2   Use a wire or stiff plastic bristle brush to clean the oil passages in the crankshaft

18.4   Rubbing a penny lengthwise on each journal will reveal its condition – if copper rubs off and is embedded in the crankshaft, the journals should be reground

18.6   Measure the diameter of each crankshaft journal at several points to detect taper and out-of-round conditions

18.8   If the seals have worn grooves in the crankshaft journals, or if the seal contact surfaces are nicked or scratched, the new seals will leak

there have the connecting rods checked for bend and twist, since automotive machine shops have special equipment for this purpose. **Note:** *Unless new pistons and/or connecting rods must be installed, do not disassemble the pistons and connecting rods.*

14   Check the connecting rods for cracks and other damage. Temporarily remove the rod caps, lift out the old bearing inserts, wipe the rod and cap bearing surfaces clean and inspect them for nicks, gouges and scratches. After checking the rods, replace the old bearings, slip the caps into place and tighten the nuts finger-tight. **Note:** *If the engine is being rebuilt because of a connecting rod knock, be sure to install new rods.*

18   Crankshaft – inspection

Refer to illustrations 18.1, 18.2, 18.4, 18.6 and 18.8

1   Remove all burrs from the crankshaft oil holes with a stone, file or scraper **(see illustration)**.

2   Clean the crankshaft with solvent and dry it with compressed air (if available). Be sure to clean the oil holes with a stiff brush **(see illustration)** and flush them with solvent.

3   Check the main and connecting rod bearing journals for uneven wear, scoring, pits and cracks.

4   Rub a penny across each journal several times **(see illustration)**. If a journal picks up copper from the penny, it's too rough and must be reground.

5   Check the rest of the crankshaft for cracks and other damage. It

should be magnafluxed to reveal hidden cracks – an automotive machine shop will handle the procedure.

6   Using a micrometer, measure the diameter of the main and connecting rod journals and compare the results to the Specifications **(see illustration)**. By measuring the diameter at a number of points around each journal's circumference, you'll be able to determine whether or not the journal is out-of-round. Take the measurement at each end of the journal, near the crank throws, to determine if the journal is tapered.

7   If the crankshaft journals are damaged, tapered, out-of-round or worn beyond the limits given in the Specifications, have the crankshaft reground by an automotive machine shop. Be sure to use the correct size bearing inserts if the crankshaft is reconditioned.

8   Check the oil seal journals at each end of the crankshaft for wear and damage. If the seal has worn a groove in the journal, or if it's nicked or scratched **(see illustration)**, the new seal may leak when the engine is reassembled. In some cases, an automotive machine shop may be able to repair the journal by pressing on a thin sleeve. If repair isn't feasible, a new or different crankshaft should be installed.

9   Refer to Section 19 and examine the main and rod bearing inserts.

19   Main and connecting rod bearings – inspection and selection

Inspection

Refer to illustration 19.1

1   Even though the main and connecting rod bearings should be replaced with new ones during the engine overhaul, the old bearings should

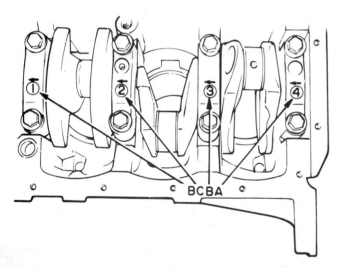

19.1   Typical bearing failures

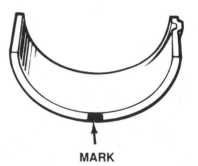

19.9   Standard size main bearings have one paint mark
undersize bearings have two paint marks – the colors indicate
the bearing thickness at the center

		NUMERAL STAMPED ON CRANK WEB (JOURNAL DIAMETER)		
		1	2	3
Letter stamped on mating surface	A	Green	Black	Colorless
	B	Black	Colorless	Yellow
	C	Colorless	Yellow	Blue
	New standard bearing to be installed.			

19.12   Use this table to find the correct bearing color code

19.10   The letters (A, B or C) stamped into the oil pan mating
surface indicate the sizes of the main bearing bores in the
block – again, the arrows show which bearing each letter is
associated with

be retained for close examination, as they may reveal valuable information about the condition of the engine (**see illustration**).

2   Bearing failure occurs because of lack of lubrication, the presence of dirt or other foreign particles, overloading the engine and corrosion. Regardless of the cause of bearing failure, it must be corrected before the engine is reassembled to prevent it from happening again.

3   When examining the bearings, remove them from the engine block, the main bearing caps, the connecting rods and the rod caps and lay them out on a clean surface in the same general position as their location in the engine. This will enable you to match any bearing problems with the corresponding crankshaft journal.

4   Dirt and other foreign particles get into the engine in a variety of ways. It may be left in the engine during assembly, or it may pass through filters or the PCV system. It may get into the oil, and from there into the bearings. Metal chips from machining operations and normal engine wear are often present. Abrasives are sometimes left in engine components after reconditioning, especially when parts are not thoroughly cleaned using the proper cleaning methods. Whatever the source, these foreign objects often end up embedded in the soft bearing material and are easily recognized. Large particles will not embed in the bearing and will score or gouge the bearing and journal. The best prevention for this cause of bearing failure is to clean all parts thoroughly and keep everything spotlessly clean during engine assembly. Frequent and regular engine oil and filter changes are also recommended.

5   Lack of lubrication (or lubrication breakdown) has a number of interrelated causes. Excessive heat (which thins the oil), overloading (which squeezes the oil from the bearing face) and oil leakage or throw off (from excessive bearing clearances, worn oil pump or high engine speeds) all contribute to lubrication breakdown. Blocked oil passages, which usually are the result of misaligned oil holes in a bearing shell, will also oil starve a bearing and destroy it. When lack of lubrication is the cause of bearing failure, the bearing material is wiped or extruded from the steel backing of the bearing. Temperatures may increase to the point where the steel backing turns blue from overheating.

6   Driving habits can have a definite effect on bearing life. Full throttle, low speed operation (lugging the engine) puts very high loads on bearings, which tends to squeeze out the oil film. These loads cause the bearings to flex, which produces fine cracks in the bearing face (fatigue failure). Eventually the bearing material will loosen in pieces and tear away from the steel backing. Short trip driving leads to corrosion of bearings because insufficient engine heat is produced to drive off the condensed water and corrosive gases. These products collect in the engine oil, forming acid and sludge. As the oil is carried to the engine bearings, the acid attacks and corrodes the bearing material.

20.2a Carbureted engine – radiator side

20.2b Carbureted engine – timing belt end

7   Incorrect bearing installation during engine assembly will lead to bearing failure as well. Tight fitting bearings leave insufficient bearing oil clearance and will result in oil starvation. Dirt or foreign particles trapped behind a bearing insert result in high spots on the bearing which lead to failure.

Selection

Refer to illustrations 19.9, 19.10 and 19.12

8   If the original bearings are worn or damaged, or if the oil clearances are incorrect (Section 22 or 24), the following procedures should be used to select the correct new bearings for engine reassembly. However, if the crankshaft has been reground, new undersize bearings must be installed – the following procedure should not be used if undersize bearings are required! The automotive machine shop that reconditions the crankshaft will provide or help you select the correct size bearings. Regardless of how the bearing sizes are determined, use the oil clearance, measured with Plasti-gage, as a guide to ensure the bearings are the right size.

Main bearings

9   If you need to use a STANDARD size main bearing, install one that has the same color code as the original bearing **(see illustration)**.
10   If the color code on the original main bearing has been obscured, first locate the number on the crankshaft web that designates the crankshaft journal diameter **(see illustration)**.
11   Next, locate the main bearing bore grade letters stamped into the oil pan mating surface on the engine block **(see illustration 19.10)**.
12   Use the accompanying chart to determine the correct color code **(see illustration)**. **Note:** *The actual main bearing bore sizes, bearing thicknesses and journal diameters designated by the number, letter and color codes are listed in this Chapter's Specifications.*

Connecting rod bearings

13   Two kinds of rod bearings are available from dealers; standard size and a 0.25 mm (0.0098-inch) undersize bearing. The undersize bearing has "US025" stamped on the back. Standard size bearings have no marks.

All bearings

14   Remember, the oil clearance is the final judge when selecting new bearings. If you have any questions or are unsure which bearings to use, get help from a dealer parts or service department.

20.2c Carbureted engine – firewall side

1   Before beginning engine reassembly, make sure you have all the necessary new parts, gaskets and seals as well as the following items on hand:
Common hand tools
A 1/2-inch drive torque wrench
Piston ring installation tool
Piston ring compressor
Short lengths of rubber or plastic hose to fit over connecting rod bolts
Plastigage
Feeler gauges
A fine-tooth file
New engine oil
Engine assembly lube or moly-base grease
Gasket sealant
Thread locking compound
2   To save time and avoid problems, engine reassembly must be done in the following general order **(see illustrations)**:
Piston rings
Crankshaft and main bearings
Piston/connecting rod assemblies
Oil pump
Oil pan
Cylinder head
Camshaft

20   Engine overhaul – reassembly sequence

Refer to illustrations 20.2a, 20.2b and 20.2c

2B

21.3   When checking piston ring end gap, the ring must be square in the cylinder bore (this is done by pushing the ring down with the top of a piston as shown)

21.4   With the ring square in the cylinder, measure the end gap with a feeler gauge

21.5   If the end gap is too small, clamp a file in a vise and file the ring ends (from the outside in only) to enlarge the gap slightly

21.9a   Installing the spacer/expander in the oil control ring groove

21.9b   DO NOT use a piston ring installation tool when installing the oil ring side rails

Rocker arms and shafts (Sprint only)
Timing belt and sprockets
Timing belt cover
Intake and exhaust manifolds
Valve cover
Engine rear plate
Flywheel/driveplate

21   Piston rings – installation

Refer to illustrations 21.3, 21.4, 21.5, 21.9a, 21.9b, 21.11 and 21.12

1   Before installing the new piston rings, the ring end gaps must be checked. It's assumed the piston ring side clearance has been checked and verified correct (see Section 17).

2   Lay out the piston/connecting rod assemblies and the new ring sets so the ring sets will be matched with the same piston and cylinder during the end gap measurement and engine assembly.

3   Insert the top (number one) ring into the first cylinder and square it up with the cylinder walls by pushing it in with the top of the piston **(see illustration)**. The ring should be near the bottom of the cylinder, at the lower limit of ring travel.

4   To measure the end gap, slip feeler gauges between the ends of the ring until a gauge equal to the gap width is found **(see illustration)**. The feeler gauge should slide between the ring ends with a slight amount of drag. Compare the measurement to the Specifications. If the gap is larger or smaller than specified, double-check to make sure you have the correct rings before proceeding.

5   If the gap is too small, it must be enlarged or the ring ends may come in contact with each other during engine operation, which can cause serious damage to the engine. The end gap can be increased by filing the ring ends very carefully with a fine file. Mount the file in a vise equipped with soft jaws, slip the ring over the file with the ends contacting the file face and slowly move the ring to remove material from the ends. When performing this operation, file only from the outside in **(see illustration)**.

6   Excess end gap isn't critical unless it's greater than 0.040-inch. Again, double-check to make sure you have the correct rings for the engine.

7   Repeat the procedure for each ring that will be installed in the first cylinder and for each ring in the remaining cylinders. Remember to keep rings, pistons and cylinders matched up.

8   Once the ring end gaps have been checked/corrected, the rings can be installed on the pistons.

9   The oil control ring (lowest one on the piston) is installed first. It's usually composed of three separate components. Slip the spacer/expander into the groove **(see illustration)**. If an anti-rotation tang is used, make sure it's inserted into the drilled hole in the ring groove. Next, install the lower side rail. Don't use a piston ring installation tool on the oil ring side rails, as they may be damaged. Instead, place one end of the side rail into the groove between the spacer/expander and the ring land, hold it firmly in place and slide a finger around the piston while pushing the rail into the groove **(see illustration)**. Next, install the upper side rail in the same manner.

10   After the three oil ring components have been installed, check to make sure both the upper and lower side rails can be turned smoothly in the ring groove.

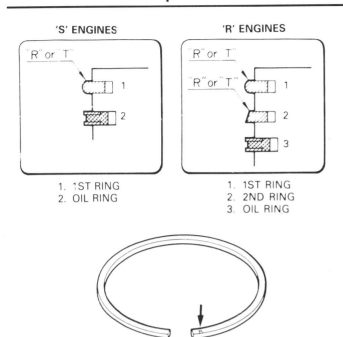

1. 'S' ENGINES
   1. 1ST RING
   2. OIL RING

'R' ENGINES
   1. 1ST RING
   2. 2ND RING
   3. OIL RING

21.11 Most compression rings are marked with an R or T on top (some models only have one per piston)

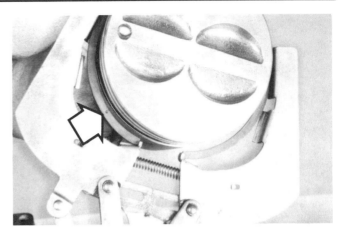

21.12 Installing the compression rings with a ring expander – the mark (arrow) must face up

11 The number two (middle) ring (if equipped) is installed next. It's usually stamped with a mark (such as a "T" or "R") which must face up, toward the top of the piston (see illustration). **Note:** *Some pistons are only equipped with two rings. Always follow the instructions printed on the ring package or box – different manufacturers may require different approaches. Do not mix up the top and middle rings, as they have different cross-sections.*

12 Use a piston ring installation tool and make sure the identification mark is facing the top of the piston, then slip the ring into the middle groove on the piston (see illustration). Don't expand the ring any more than necessary to slide it over the piston.

13 Install the number one (top) ring in the same manner. Make sure the mark is facing up. Be careful not to confuse the number one and number two rings.

14 Repeat the procedure for the remaining pistons and rings.

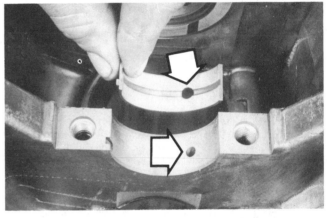

22.5 Make sure the oil holes (arrows) align

22 Crankshaft – installation and main bearing oil clearance check

Refer to illustrations 22.5, 22.6, 22.11 and 22.15

1 Crankshaft installation is the first step in engine reassembly. It's assumed at this point that the engine block and crankshaft have been cleaned, inspected and repaired or reconditioned.

2 Position the engine with the bottom facing up.

3 Remove the main bearing cap bolts and lift out the caps. Lay them out in the proper order to ensure correct installation.

4 If they're still in place, remove the original bearing inserts from the block and the main bearing caps. Wipe the bearing surfaces of the block and caps with a clean, lint-free cloth. They must be kept spotlessly clean.

Main bearing oil clearance check

5 Clean the back sides of the new main bearing inserts and lay one in each main bearing saddle in the block. If one of the bearing inserts from each set has a large groove in it, make sure the grooved insert is installed in the block. Lay the other bearing from each set in the corresponding main bearing cap. Make sure the tab on the bearing insert fits into the recess in the block or cap. **Caution:** *The oil holes in the block must line up with the oil holes in the bearing insert* **(see illustration)**. *Do not hammer the bearing*

22.6 Install the thrust bearings on both sides of the bearing saddle in the block; be sure the oil grooves face out

into place and don't nick or gouge the bearing faces. No lubrication should be used at this time.

6 The thrust bearings must be installed in the number three saddle in the block (see illustration).

7 Clean the faces of the bearings in the block and the crankshaft main bearing journals with a clean, lint-free cloth.

8 Check or clean the oil holes in the crankshaft, as any dirt here can go only one way – straight through the new bearings.

9 Once you're certain the crankshaft is clean, carefully lay it in position in the main bearings.

10 Before the crankshaft can be permanently installed, the main bearing oil clearance must be checked.

2B

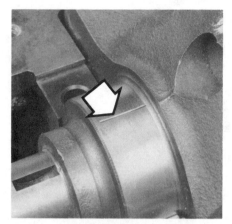

22.11   Lay the Plastigage strips (arrow) on the main bearing journals, parallel to the crankshaft centerline

22.15   Compare the width of the crushed Plastigage to the scale on the envelope to determine the main bearing oil clearance (always take the measurement at the widest point of the Plastigage); be sure to use the correct scale – standard and metric ones are included

23.3   After removing the housing from the block, support it on a couple of wood blocks and drive out the old seal with a hammer and punch

11   Cut several pieces of the appropriate size Plastigage (they must be slightly shorter than the width of the main bearings) and place one piece on each crankshaft main bearing journal, parallel to the journal axis (see illustration).

12   Clean the faces of the bearings in the caps and install the caps in their respective positions (don't mix them up) with the arrows pointing toward the front of the engine. Don't disturb the Plastigage.

13   Starting with the inner mains and working out toward the ends, tighten the main bearing cap bolts, in three steps, to the torque listed in this Chapter's Specifications. Don't rotate the crankshaft at any time during this operation.

14   Remove the bolts and carefully lift off the main bearing caps. Keep them in order. Don't disturb the Plastigage or rotate the crankshaft. If any of the main bearing caps are difficult to remove, tap them gently from side-to-side with a soft-face hammer to loosen them.

15   Compare the width of the crushed Plastigage on each journal to the scale printed on the Plastigage envelope to obtain the main bearing oil clearance (see illustration). Check the Specifications to make sure it's correct.

16   If the clearance is not as specified, the bearing inserts may be the wrong size (which means different ones will be required). Before deciding different inserts are needed, make sure no dirt or oil was between the bearing inserts and the caps or block when the clearance was measured. If the Plastigage was wider at one end than the other, the journal may be tapered (refer to Section 18).

17   Carefully scrape all traces of the Plastigage material off the main bearing journals and/or the bearing faces. Use your fingernail or the edge of a credit card – don't nick or scratch the bearing faces.

Final crankshaft installation

18   Carefully lift the crankshaft out of the engine.

19   Clean the bearing faces in the block, then apply a thin, uniform layer of moly-base grease or engine assembly lube to each of the bearing surfaces and the thrust bearings.

20   Make sure the crankshaft journals are clean, then lay the crankshaft back in place in the block.

21   Clean the faces of the bearings in the caps, then apply lubricant to them.

22   Install the caps in their respective positions with the arrows pointing toward the front of the engine.

23   Install the bolts.

24   Tighten all except the thrust bearing cap bolts to the torque listed in this Chapter's Specifications (work from the center out and approach the final torque in three steps).

25   Tighten the thrust bearing cap bolts to 10-to-12 ft-lbs.

23.4   Drive the new seal into the housing with a block of wood or a section of pipe, if you have one large enough – make sure you don't cock the seal in the bore.

26   Tap the ends of the crankshaft forward and backward with a lead or brass hammer to line up the main bearing and crankshaft thrust surfaces.

27   Retighten all main bearing cap bolts to the specified torque, starting at the third main and working out toward the ends.

28   On manual transaxle equipped models, install a new pilot bearing in the end of the crankshaft (see Chapter 8).

29   Rotate the crankshaft a number of times by hand to check for any obvious binding.

30   The final step is to check the crankshaft endplay with a feeler gauge or a dial indicator as described in Section 13. The endplay should be correct if the crankshaft thrust faces aren't worn or damaged and new bearings have been installed.

---

23   Rear main oil seal installation

Refer to illustrations 23.3 and 23.4

1   All models are equipped with a one-piece seal that fits into a housing attached to the block. The crankshaft must be installed first and the main bearing caps bolted in place, then the new seal should be installed in the housing and the housing bolted to the block.

2   Before installing the seal and housing, check the seal contact surface very carefully for scratches and nicks that could damage the new seal lip and cause oil leaks. If the crankshaft is damaged, the only alternative is a new or different crankshaft.

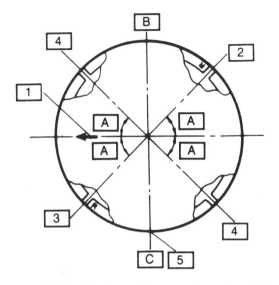

24.5 Position the ring end gaps as shown here before installing the piston/connecting rod assemblies in the engine

A	45-degrees	2	First ring end gap
B	Intake side	3	Second ring end gap
C	Exhaust side	4	Oil ring rail gaps
1	Arrow mark	5	Oil ring spacer gap

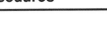
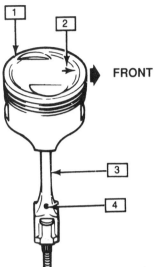

24.9 The arrow on the piston must point to the front (crankshaft pulley) end of the engine and the oil hole in the connecting rod must be on the intake manifold side

1	Piston	3	Connecting rod
2	Arrow mark	4	Oil hole

2B

3   The old seal can be removed from the housing with a hammer and punch by driving it out from the back side **(see illustration)**. Be sure to note how far it's recessed into the housing bore before removing it; the new seal will have to be recessed an equal amount. Be very careful not to scratch or otherwise damage the bore in the housing or oil leaks could develop.

4   Make sure the housing is clean, then apply a thin coat of engine oil to the outer edge of the new seal. The seal must be pressed squarely into the housing bore, so hammering directly on it isn't recommended. If you don't have access to a press, tap the seal into place with a hammer and a block of wood **(see illustration)**. The block of wood must be thick enough to distribute the force evenly around the entire circumference of the seal. Work slowly and make sure the seal enters the bore squarely.

5   The seal lips must be lubricated with multi-purpose grease or engine assembly lube before the seal/housing is slipped over the crankshaft and bolted to the block. Use a new gasket – no sealant is required – and make sure the dowel pins are in place before installing the housing.

6   Tighten the screws a little at a time to the torque listed in this Chapter's Specifications.

24 Pistons/connecting rods – installation and rod bearing oil clearance check

Refer to illustrations 24.5, 24.9, 24.11, 24.13 and 24.17

1   Before installing the piston/connecting rod assemblies, the cylinder walls must be perfectly clean, the top edge of each cylinder must be chamfered, and the crankshaft must be in place.

2   Remove the cap from the end of the number one connecting rod (refer to the marks made during removal). Remove the original bearing inserts and wipe the bearing surfaces of the connecting rod and cap with a clean, lint-free cloth. They must be kept spotlessly clean.

Connecting rod bearing oil clearance check

3   Clean the back side of the new upper bearing insert, then lay it in place in the connecting rod. Make sure the tab on the bearing fits into the recess in the rod. Don't hammer the bearing insert into place and be very careful

not to nick or gouge the bearing face. Don't lubricate the bearing at this time.

4   Clean the back side of the other bearing insert and install it in the rod cap. Again, make sure the tab on the bearing fits into the recess in the cap, and don't apply any lubricant. It's critically important that the mating surfaces of the bearing and connecting rod are perfectly clean and oil free when they're assembled.

5   Position the piston ring gaps around the piston as shown **(see illustration)**.

6   Slip a section of plastic or rubber hose over each connecting rod cap bolt.

7   Lubricate the piston and rings with clean engine oil and attach a piston ring compressor to the piston. Leave the skirt protruding about 1/4-inch to guide the piston into the cylinder. The rings must be compressed until they're flush with the piston.

8   Rotate the crankshaft until the number one connecting rod journal is at BDC (bottom dead center) and apply a coat of engine oil to the cylinder walls.

9   With the arrow on top of the piston facing the front of the engine **(see illustration)**, gently insert the piston/connecting rod assembly into the number one cylinder bore and rest the bottom edge of the ring compressor on the engine block.

10   Tap the top edge of the ring compressor to make sure it's contacting the block around its entire circumference.

11   Gently tap on the top of the piston with the end of a wooden or plastic hammer handle **(see illustration)** while guiding the end of the connecting rod into place on the crankshaft journal. The piston rings may try to pop out of the ring compressor just before entering the cylinder bore, so keep some downward pressure on the ring compressor. Work slowly, and if any resistance is felt as the piston enters the cylinder, stop immediately. Find out what's hanging up and fix it before proceeding. Do not, for any reason, force the piston into the cylinder – you might break a ring and/or the piston.

12   Once the piston/connecting rod assembly is installed, the connecting rod bearing oil clearance must be checked before the rod cap is permanently bolted in place.

13   Cut a piece of the appropriate size Plastigage slightly shorter than the width of the connecting rod bearing and lay it in place on the number one connecting rod journal, parallel to the journal axis **(see illustration)**.

14 Clean the connecting rod cap bearing face, remove the protective hoses from the connecting rod bolts and install the rod cap. Make sure the mating mark on the cap is on the same side as the mark on the connecting rod.

15 Install the nuts and tighten them to the specified torque, working up to it in three steps. **Note:** *Use a thin-wall socket to avoid erroneous torque readings that can result if the socket is wedged between the rod cap and nut. If the socket tends to wedge itself between the nut and the cap, lift up on it slightly until it no longer contacts the cap. Do not rotate the crankshaft at any time during this operation.*

16 Remove the nuts and detach the rod cap, being very careful not to disturb the Plastigage.

17 Compare the width of the crushed Plastigage to the scale printed on the Plastigage envelope to obtain the oil clearance **(see illustration)**. Compare it to this Chapter's Specifications to make sure the clearance is correct.

18 If the clearance is not as specified, the bearing inserts may be the wrong size (which means different ones will be required). Before deciding different inserts are needed, make sure no dirt or oil was between the bearing inserts and the connecting rod or cap when the clearance was measured. Also, recheck the journal diameter. If the Plastigage was wider at one end than the other, the journal may be tapered (refer to Section 18).

Final connecting rod installation

19 Carefully scrape all traces of the Plastigage material off the rod journal and/or bearing face. Be very careful not to scratch the bearing – use your fingernail or the edge of a credit card.

20 Make sure the bearing faces are perfectly clean, then apply a uniform layer of clean moly-base grease or engine assembly lube to both of them. You'll have to push the piston into the cylinder to expose the face of the bearing insert in the connecting rod – be sure to slip the protective hoses over the rod bolts first.

21 Slide the connecting rod back into place on the journal, remove the protective hoses from the rod cap bolts, install the rod cap and tighten the nuts to the specified torque. Again, work up to the torque in three steps.

22 Repeat the entire procedure for the remaining pistons/connecting rods.

23 The important points to remember are:
  a) Keep the back sides of the bearing inserts and the insides of the connecting rods and caps perfectly clean when assembling them.
  b) Make sure you have the correct piston/rod assembly for each cylinder.
  c) The arrow on the piston must face the front of the engine.
  d) Lubricate the cylinder walls with clean oil.
  e) Lubricate the bearing faces when installing the rod caps after the oil clearance has been checked.

24 After all the piston/connecting rod assemblies have been properly installed, rotate the crankshaft a number of times by hand to check for any obvious binding.

25 As a final step, the connecting rod endplay must be checked. Refer to Section 12 for this procedure.

26 Compare the measured endplay to the Specifications to make sure it's correct. If it was correct before disassembly and the original crankshaft and rods were reinstalled, it should still be right. If new rods or a new crankshaft were installed, the endplay may be inadequate. If so, the rods will have to be removed and taken to an automotive machine shop for resizing.

27 Install the remaining components in the reverse order of removal. Refer to Section 20 and Part A of this Chapter for additional information.

---

25   Initial start-up and break-in after overhaul

Warning: *Have a fire extinguisher handy when starting the engine for the first time.*

1 Once the engine has been installed in the vehicle, double-check the engine oil and coolant levels.

2 With the spark plugs out of the engine and the ignition system disabled (see Section 3), crank the engine until the oil pressure warning light goes out.

3 Install the spark plugs, hook up the plug wires and restore the ignition system functions (see Section 3).

4 Start the engine. It may take a few moments for the fuel system to build up pressure, but the engine should start without a great deal of effort. **Note:** *If backfiring occurs through the carburetor or throttle body, recheck the valve timing and ignition timing.*

5 After the engine starts, it should be allowed to warm up to normal operating temperature. While the engine is warming up, use the time to check carefully for fuel, oil and coolant leaks.

6 Shut the engine off and recheck the engine oil and coolant levels.

7 Drive the vehicle to an area with minimum traffic, accelerate at full throttle from 30 to 50 mph, then allow the vehicle to slow to 30 mph with the throttle closed. Repeat the procedure 10 or 12 times. This will load the piston rings and cause them to seat properly against the cylinder walls. Check again for oil and coolant leaks.

8 Drive the vehicle gently for the first 500 miles (no sustained high speeds) and keep a constant check on the oil level. It's not unusual for an engine to use oil during the break-in period.

9 At approximately 500 to 600 miles, change the oil and filter.

10 For the next few hundred miles, drive the vehicle normally. Don't pamper it or abuse it.

11 After 2000 miles, change the oil and filter again and consider the engine broken in.

24.11   The piston can be driven (gently) into the cylinder bore with the end of a wooden or plastic hammer handle

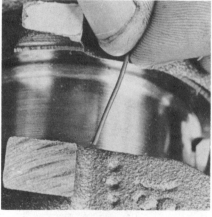

24.13   Lay the Plastigage strips on each rod bearing journal, parallel to the crankshaft centerline

24.17   Measuring the width of the crushed Plastigage to determine the rod bearing oil clearance (be sure to use the correct scale – standard and metric ones are included)

Chapter 3   Cooling, heating and air conditioning systems

Contents

Specifications

General

Radiator cap pressure rating .... 13 psi
Thermostat rating (opening temperature) .... 180-degrees F (82-degrees C)
Cooling system capacity .... See Chapter 1
Refrigerant capacity .... 1.3 to 1.7 lbs

Torque specifications

	Ft-lbs
Water pump-to-engine block bolts	11
Water pump pulley bolts	17
Thermostat housing bolts	20
Coolant inlet pipe nuts	14

---

1   General information

Engine cooling system

All vehicles covered by this manual employ a pressurized engine cooling system with thermostatically-controlled coolant circulation. An impeller-type water pump mounted on the drivebelt end of the block pumps coolant through the engine. The coolant flows around each cylinder and toward the transaxle end of the engine. Cast-in coolant passages direct coolant around the intake and exhaust ports, near the spark plug areas and in close proximity to the exhaust valve guides.

A wax pellet-type thermostat is located in a housing near the transaxle end of the engine. During warm up, the closed thermostat prevents coolant from circulating through the radiator. As the engine nears normal operating temperature, the thermostat opens and allows hot coolant to travel through the radiator, where it's cooled before returning to the engine.

The cooling system is sealed by a pressure type radiator cap, which raises the boiling point of the coolant and increases the cooling efficiency of the radiator. If the system pressure exceeds the cap pressure relief value, the excess pressure in the system forces the spring-loaded valve inside the cap off its seat and allows the coolant to escape through the overflow tube into a coolant reservoir. When the system cools, the excess coolant is automatically drawn from the reservoir back into the radiator.

The coolant reservoir does double duty as both the point at which fresh coolant is added to the cooling system to maintain the proper fluid level and as a holding tank for overheated coolant.

This type of cooling system is known as a closed design because coolant that escapes past the pressure cap is saved and reused.

Heater

The heater consists of a blower fan and heater core located in the heater box, the hoses connecting the heater core to the engine cooling system and the heater/air conditioning control head on the dashboard. Hot engine coolant is circulated through the heater core. When the heater is activated, a flap door opens to expose the heater box to the passenger compartment. A fan switch on the control head activates the blower motor, which forces air through the core, heating the air.

Air conditioning system

The air conditioning system consists of a condenser mounted in front of the radiator, an evaporator mounted adjacent to the heater core, a compressor mounted on the engine, a receiver-drier which contains a high pressure relief valve and the plumbing connecting all of the above components.

A blower fan forces the warmer air of the passenger compartment through the evaporator core (sort of a radiator-in-reverse), transferring the heat from the air to the refrigerant. The liquid refrigerant boils off into low pressure vapor, taking the heat with it when it leaves the evaporator.

2   Antifreeze – general information

Warning: *Do not allow antifreeze to come in contact with your skin or painted surfaces of the vehicle. Rinse off spills immediately with plenty of water. Never leave antifreeze lying around in an open container or in a puddle in the driveway or on the garage floor. Children and pets are attracted by it's sweet smell. Antifreeze is fatal if ingested in sufficient quantity. Check with local authorities before disposing of used antifreeze. Many communities have collection centers which will see that antifreeze is disposed of safely. Antifreeze is also combustible, so don't store or use it near open flames.*

The cooling system should be filled with a water/ethylene glycol based antifreeze solution, which will prevent freezing down to at least -20-degrees F, or lower if local climate requires it. It also provides protection against corrosion and increases the coolant boiling point.

The cooling system should be drained, flushed and refilled at the specified intervals (see Chapter 1). Old or contaminated antifreeze solutions are likely to cause damage and encourage the formation of corrosion and scale in the system. Use distilled water with the antifreeze.

Before adding antifreeze, check all hose connections, because antifreeze tends to search out and leak through very minute openings. Engines don't normally consume coolant, so if the level goes down, find the cause and correct it.

The exact mixture of antifreeze-to-water which you should use depends on the relative weather conditions. The mixture should contain at least 50-percent antifreeze, but should never contain more than 70-percent antifreeze. Consult the mixture ratio chart on the antifreeze container before adding coolant. Hydrometers are available at most auto parts stores to test the coolant. Use antifreeze which meets the vehicle manufacturer's specifications.

3   Thermostat – check and replacement

Warning: *Do not remove the radiator cap, drain the coolant or replace the thermostat until the engine has cooled completely.*

Check

1   Before assuming the thermostat is to blame for a cooling system problem, check the coolant level, drivebelt tension (see Chapter 1) and temperature gauge operation.
2   If the engine seems to be taking a long time to warm up (based on heater output or temperature gauge operation), the thermostat is probably

stuck open – replace it with a new one.
3   If the engine runs hot, use your hand to check the temperature of the upper radiator hose. If the hose isn't hot, but the engine is, the thermostat is probably stuck closed, preventing the coolant inside the engine from escaping to the radiator. Replace the thermostat. **Caution:** *Don't drive the vehicle without a thermostat. The lack of a thermostat may cause the computer to stay in open loop, causing emissions and fuel economy to suffer.*
4   If the upper radiator hose is hot, it means the coolant is flowing and the thermostat is open. Consult the *Troubleshooting* section at the front of this manual for cooling system diagnosis.

Replacement

Refer to illustrations 3.10, 3.11a, 3.11b and 3.13
5   Disconnect the negative battery cable from the battery.
6   Drain the cooling system (see Chapter 1). If the coolant is relatively new or in good condition, save it and reuse it.
7   Remove the air cleaner.
8   Follow the upper radiator hose to the engine to locate the thermostat housing. Loosen the hose clamp, then detach the hose from the fitting. If it's stuck, grasp it near the end with a pair of adjustable pliers and twist it to break the seal, then pull it off. If the hose is old or deteriorated, cut it off and install a new one.
9   If the outer surface of the large fitting that mates with the hose is deteriorated (corroded, pitted, etc.) it may be damaged further by hose removal. If it is, the thermostat housing cover will have to be replaced.
10   On Sprint models, unplug the electrical connector for the engine cooling fan switch **(see illustration)**.
11   Remove the bolts and detach the housing cover and bracket, if equipped **(see illustrations)**. If the cover is stuck, tap it with a soft-face hammer to jar it loose. Be prepared for some coolant to spill as the gasket seal is broken.
12   Note how it's installed (which end is facing the engine), then remove the thermostat. Thoroughly clean the sealing surfaces.
13   Install the new thermostat in the housing. Make sure the air bleed is positioned correctly and the spring end is directed into the engine **(see illustration)**.
14   Install a new gasket over the thermostat.
15   Install the cover and bolts. Tighten the bolts to the torque listed in this Chapter's Specifications.
16   Reattach the hose to the fitting and tighten the hose clamp securely.
17   Refill the cooling system (see Chapter 1).
18   Start the engine and allow it to reach normal operating temperature, then check for leaks and proper thermostat operation (as described in Steps 2 through 4).

4   Engine cooling fan – check and replacement

Refer to illustrations 4.5a, 4.5b, 4.8a, 4.8b, 4.9 and 4.10
Check

1   The engine cooling fan is controlled by a temperature switch mounted in the thermostat housing cover. When the coolant reaches a predetermined temperature, the switch opens the ground return for the fan motor relay, completing the circuit.
2   First, check the fuses (see Chapter 12).
3   To test the fan motor, unplug the motor connector and use fused jumper wires to connect the fan directly to the battery. If the fan still doesn't work, replace the motor.
4   If the motor tested okay, the fault lies in the coolant temperature switch, the fan relay or the wiring harness (see Chapter 12).
5   Test the temperature switch by unplugging the connector and bridging the terminals in the wire harness **(see illustrations)** with the ignition switch On.
6   If the fan does not operate, check the wiring and the relay (see Chapter 12).

Replacement

7   Disconnect the negative cable from the battery, then remove the air cleaner intake duct.

3.10   If you're working on a Sprint, unplug the electrical connector and remove the bolts (arrows) to get at the thermostat

3.11a   On Metros, the thermostat and housing are located under the distributor

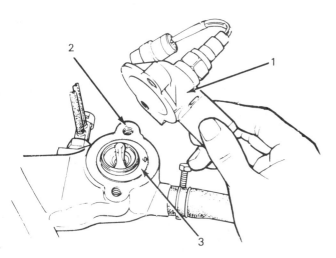

3.11b   Detach the thermostat cover (1) to get at the gasket (2) and thermostat (3) (Sprint shown, Metro similar)

3.13   Thermostat installation details

1   *Thermostat*
2   *Air bleed valve*
3   *Heater inlet hose*

4.5a   To check the engine cooling fan temperature switch, unplug the connector . . .

4.5b   . . . and bridge the terminals with a jumper wire

3

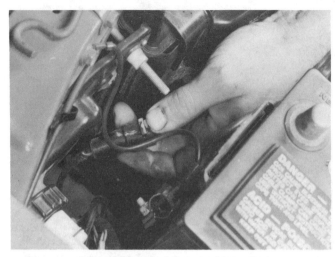

4.8a   Unplug the fan motor connector

4.8b   Remove the fan shroud mounting bolts (arrows)

4.9   Remove the nut and detach the fan blade assembly from the motor shaft

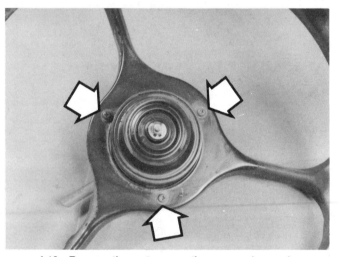

4.10   Remove the motor mounting screws (arrows)

8   Unplug the wires and detach the hoses, then unbolt the fan shroud at the top and bottom **(see illustrations)**. **Note:** *Refer to Chapter 1 and drain the coolant before removing the radiator hoses.*

9   Lift the fan assembly out of the engine compartment. Remove the nut and detach the fan blade assembly from the motor shaft **(see illustration)**.

10   Take out the screws holding the fan motor to the bracket and detach the motor **(see illustration)**.

11   Installation is the reverse of removal.

---

5   Radiator – removal and installation

Refer to illustrations 5.7 and 5.11
Warning: *Wait until the engine is completely cool before beginning this procedure.*

Removal

1   Disconnect the negative battery cable from the battery.

2   Raise the front of the vehicle and support it securely on jackstands.

3   Drain the cooling system (see Chapter 1). If the coolant is relatively new or in good condition, save it and reuse it.

4   Loosen the hose clamps, then detach the radiator hoses from the fittings. If they're stuck, grasp each hose near the end with a pair of adjust-

able pliers and twist it to break the seal, then pull it off – be careful not to damage the radiator fittings! If the hoses are old or deteriorated, cut them off and install new ones.

5   Disconnect the coolant reservoir hose from the radiator filler neck.

6   Remove the cooling fan as described in Section 4.

7   If the vehicle is equipped with an automatic transaxle, disconnect the cooler lines **(see illustration)** and plug the lines and fittings.

8   Carefully lift out the radiator. Don't spill coolant on the vehicle or scratch the paint.

9   With the radiator removed, it can be inspected for leaks and damage. If it needs repair, have a radiator shop or dealer service department perform the work as special techniques are required.

10   Bugs and dirt can be removed from the radiator with a garden hose or a soft brush. Don't bend the cooling fins as this is done.

Installation

11   Installation is the reverse of the removal procedure. Be sure the rubber cushions are seated properly **(see illustration)**.

12   After installation, fill the cooling system with the recommended mixture of antifreeze and water. Refer to Chapter 1 if necessary.

13   Start the engine and check for leaks. Allow the engine to reach normal operating temperature, indicated by the upper radiator hose becoming hot. Recheck the coolant level and add more if required.

14   If you're working on an automatic transaxle equipped vehicle, check and add fluid as needed.

5.7   On automatic transaxle models, disconnect the cooling lines from the bottom of the radiator (one on each side)

5.11   Be sure the rubber cushions are seated properly before reinstalling the radiator

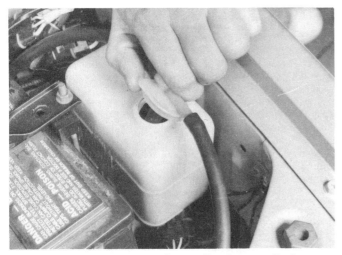

6.1   Lift the coolant reservoir cap off and remove the hose

6.2   The coolant reservoir slips out of/into the bracket

3

6   Coolant reservoir – removal and installation

Refer to illustrations 6.1 and 6.2

1   Lift the cap off the coolant reservoir and withdraw the overflow hose **(see illustration)**.
2   Lift the coolant reservoir straight up to remove it **(see illustration)**.
3   Installation is the reverse of removal.

7   Water pump – check

Refer to illustrations 7.4 and 7.5

1   A failure in the water pump can cause serious engine damage due to overheating.
2   There are three ways to check the operation of the water pump while it's installed on the engine. If the pump is defective, it should be replaced with a new or rebuilt unit.
3   With the engine running at normal operating temperature, squeeze the upper radiator hose. If the water pump is working properly, a pressure surge should be felt as the hose is released.
4   Water pumps are equipped with weep or vent holes. If a failure occurs in the pump seal, coolant will leak from the hole. In most cases you'll need a flashlight to find the hole on the water pump to check for leaks **(see illustration)**.

7.4   The water pump weep hole (arrow) will drip coolant when the seal on the pump shaft fails (pulley removed for clarity)

7.5   Rock the shaft up-and-down to check for play

8.6   Water pump mounting bolts (arrows) – when installing the pump, install new rubber seals in the ridge gaps at the top and bottom of the pump

8   Compare the new pump to the old one to make sure they're identical.
9   Remove all traces of old gasket material from the sealing surfaces **(see illustration)**.
10   Use a bead of RTV sealant to hold the pump gasket in place. Carefully mate the pump to the engine. Slip a couple of bolts through the pump mounting holes to hold the pump in place.
11   Install the remaining bolts. Tighten them to the torque listed in this Chapter's Specifications in 1/4-turn increments. Don't overtighten them or the pump may be damaged.
12   Place new rubber seals between the water pump and oil pump and between the water pump and cylinder head. Reinstall all parts removed for access to the pump.
13   Refill the cooling system and check the drivebelt tension (see Chapter 1). Run the engine and check for leaks.

8.9   Remove all traces of old gasket material from the engine block before installing the new pump

5   If the water pump shaft bearings fail there may be a howling sound at the drivebelt end of the engine while it's running. Shaft wear can be felt if the water pump pulley is rocked up-and-down **(see illustration)**. Don't mistake drivebelt slippage, which causes a squealing sound, for water pump bearing failure.

---

8   Water pump – replacement

Refer to illustrations 8.6 and 8.9
Warning: *Wait until the engine is completely cool before beginning this procedure.*
1   Disconnect the negative battery cable from the battery.
2   Drain the cooling system (see Chapter 1). If the coolant is relatively new or in good condition, save it and reuse it.
3   Loosen the water pump pulley bolts.
4   Refer to Chapter 1 and remove the drivebelt(s). Remove the pulley from the end of the water pump shaft.
5   Remove the timing belt (see Chapter 2, Part A).
6   Remove the bolts **(see illustration)** and detach the water pump from the engine. Note the locations of the various brackets and the different lengths/diameters of the bolts as they're removed to ensure correct installation.
7   Clean the bolt threads and the threaded holes in the engine to remove corrosion and sealant.

---

9   Coolant temperature sending unit – check and replacement

Refer to illustrations 9.3a and 9.3b
Warning: *The engine must be completely cool before removing the sending unit.*

Check

1   If the coolant temperature gauge is inoperative, check the fuses first (see Chapter 12).
2   If the temperature indicator shows excessive temperature after running a while, see the *Troubleshooting* section in the front of the manual.
3   If the temperature gauge indicates Hot shortly after the engine is started cold, disconnect the wire at the coolant temperature sending unit **(see illustrations)**. If the gauge reading drops, replace the sending unit. If the reading remains high, the wire to the gauge may be shorted to ground or the gauge is faulty.
4   If the coolant temperature gauge fails to indicate after the engine has been warmed up (approximately 10 minutes) and the fuses checked out okay, shut off the engine. Disconnect the wire at the sending unit and, using a jumper wire, connect it to a clean ground on the engine. Turn on the ignition without starting the engine. If the gauge now indicates Hot, replace the sending unit.
5   If the gauge still doesn't work, the circuit may be open or the gauge may be faulty. See Chapter 12 for additional information.

Replacement

6   With the engine completely cool, remove the cap from the radiator to release any pressure, then reinstall the cap. This reduces coolant loss during sending unit replacement.
7   Disconnect the wire from the sending unit.

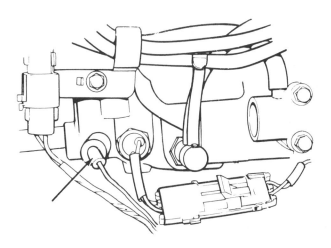

9.3a If you're working on a Sprint, the coolant temperature sending unit is located on the firewall side of the intake manifold below the thermostat

9.3b If you're working on a Metro, the coolant temperature sending unit is located in the intake manifold near the base of the throttle body (arrow)

3

10.2 Unplug the hose and electrical connector from the motor, remove the three screws, then maneuver the blower unit out from under the dash

10.5 The blower fan is attached to the motor shaft with a nut (arrow)

8   Prepare the new sending unit for installation by applying a Teflon tape or light coat of sealant to the threads.
9   Unscrew the sending unit from the engine and quickly install the new one to prevent coolant loss.
10   Tighten the sending unit securely and connect the wire.
11   Refill the cooling system and run the engine. Check for leaks and proper gauge operation.

---

10 Blower unit – removal and installation

Sprint

Refer to illustrations 10.2 and 10.5
1   Disconnect the negative cable from the battery.
2   The blower unit is located above and to the right of the accelerator pedal. Disconnect the wiring from the blower and remove the rubber air duct running between the motor and the blower housing (**see illustration**).
3   Remove the screws holding the blower unit to the vehicle and lower the unit from the dash.
4   Remove the three mounting screws and lift the motor out of the hous-

ing.
5   If you're replacing the motor, detach the fan (**see illustration**) and transfer it to the new motor.
6   Installation is the reverse of removal. Run the blower and check for proper operation.

Metro

Refer to illustrations 10.10, 10.12 and 10.13
7   Disconnect the negative cable from the battery.
8   The blower unit is located on the passenger's side of the dash, behind the glove box. Remove the two screws from the glove box striker and detach the striker.
9   Detach the rear upper glove box panel.
10   Disconnect the wire from the blower and remove the rubber air hose running between the motor and the blower housing (**see illustration**).
11   Disconnect the fresh/recirculated control cable from the blower case assembly.
12   Remove the three blower case mounting screws (**see illustration**) and lower the case from the vehicle.
13   Remove the three mounting screws (**see illustration**) and lift the motor out of the housing.
14   Follow Steps 5 and 6 above.

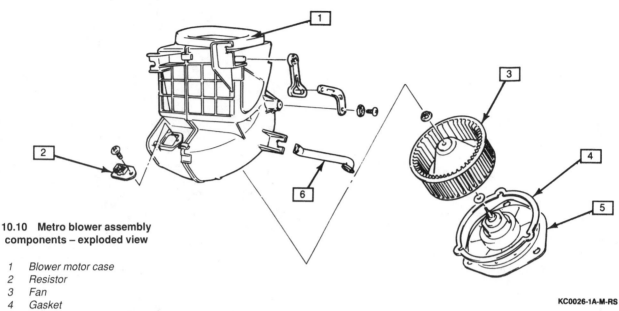

**10.10   Metro blower assembly
components – exploded view**

1   Blower motor case
2   Resistor
3   Fan
4   Gasket
5   Motor assembly
6   Air hose

KC0026-1A-M-RS

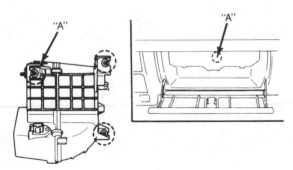

KC0027-1A-M-RS

10.12   Blower case mounting screw locations

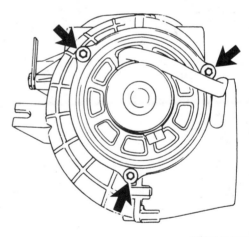

KC0028-1A-M-RS

10.13   Blower motor mounting screw locations (arrows)

---

11   Heater core – removal and installation

*Refer to illustrations 11.3, 11.6a, 11.6b, 11.7a, 11.7b, 11.8, 11.9a, 11.9b
and 11.10*

1   Disconnect the negative cable from the battery.
2   Drain the cooling system (see Chapter 1).
3   Working in the engine compartment, disconnect the heater hoses
where they enter the firewall **(see illustration)**.
4   Remove the instrument cluster (see Chapter 11).
5   Remove the heater controls (see Section 12). Be sure to mark the locations of the cable clamps on the cables to ensure correct adjustment
upon reinstallation.
6   Remove the instrument panel assembly **(see illustrations)**.
7   Label and detach the air ducts, wiring and controls still attached to the
heater housing **(see illustrations)**.

11.3   Disconnect the heater hoses at the firewall

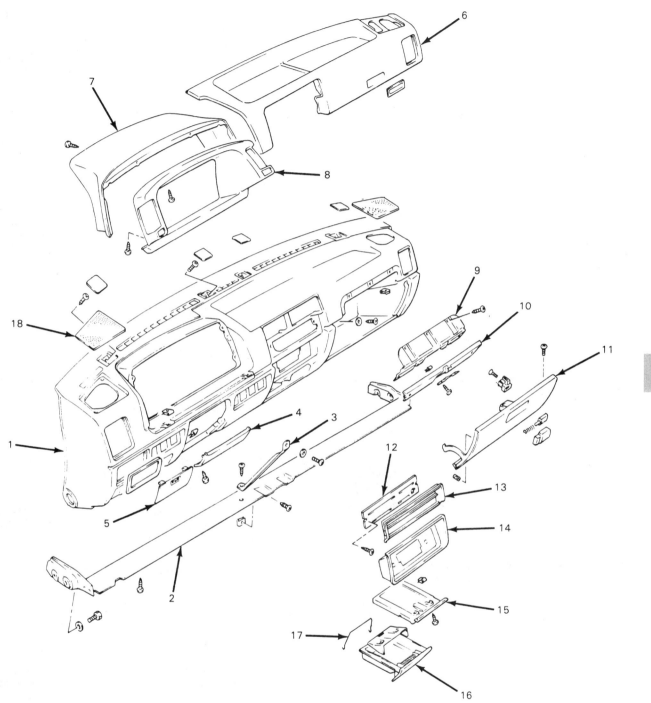

11.6a   Instrument panel components – exploded view (Sprint)

1	Main panel	10	Pad support
2	Instrument panel member	11	Glove box lid
3	Main brace	12	Heater control lever panel
4	Steering column hole cover	13	Panel garnish
5	Fuse case cover	14	Radio hole garnish
6	Instrument panel pad	15	Front ashtray
7	Cluster bezel	16	Ashtray case
8	Switch panel	17	Protector spring
9	Extension	18	Speaker garnish

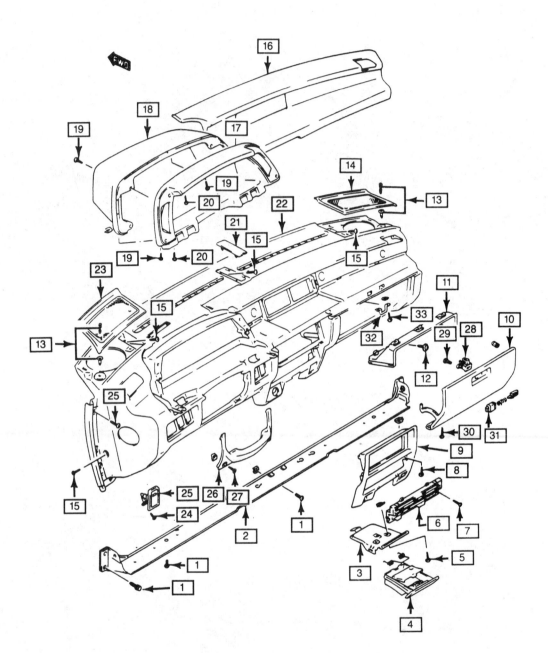

11.6b   Instrument panel components – exploded view (Metro)

1	Support member mounting screw	12	Screw	23	(LH) front speaker garnish panel
2	Support member	13	Garnish cover push pins	24	Hood latch release lever mounting screw
3	Ashtray upper plate	14	(RH) front speaker garnish cover	25	Hood latch release lever assembly
4	Ashtray assembly	15	Main panel attaching screws	26	Lower steering column panel
5	Screw	16	Instrument panel pad	27	Screw
6	Heater control panel	17	Cluster switch panel	28	Glovebox latch assembly
7	Mounting screw	18	Cluster bezel	29	Latch assembly screw
8	Bezel attaching screw	19	Screws	30	Glovebox door screw
9	Bezel	20	Screws	31	Glovebox latch button
10	Glove box door	21	Instrument main panel access panel	32	Glovebox striker
11	Glove box upper panel	22	Instrument main panel	33	Glovebox striker mounting screw

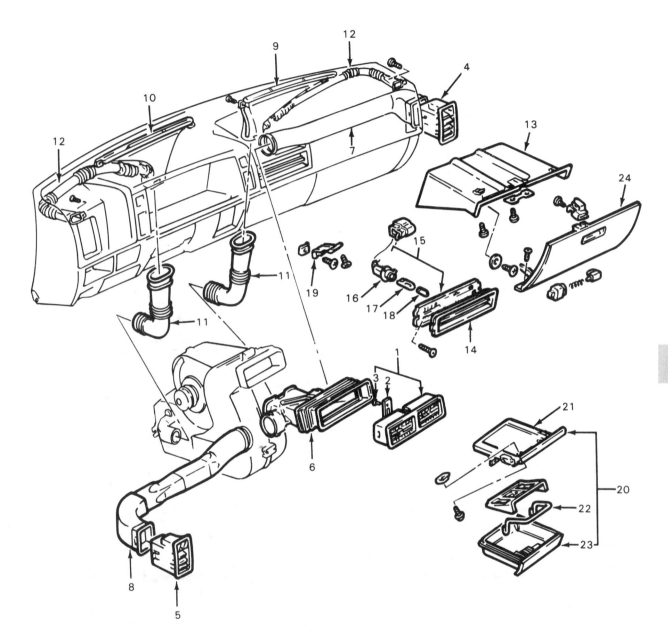

11.7a   Heater system components – exploded view (Sprint)

1	Center vent louver	10	Defroster nozzle (L)	18	Heater control bulb cap
2	Center vent holder	11	Defroster hose	19	Instrument panel
3	Screw	12	Side demister hose		member stay
4	Right side vent louver	13	Instrument panel	20	Front ashtray
5	Left side vent louver		upper compartment	21	Ashtray upper plate
6	Center vent duct	14	Heater control panel plate	22	Protector spring
7	Right side vent duct	15	Heater control lever panel	23	Ashtray case
8	Left side vent duct	16	Control lever lead wire	24	Glove box lid
9	Defroster nozzle (R)	17	Heater control bulb		

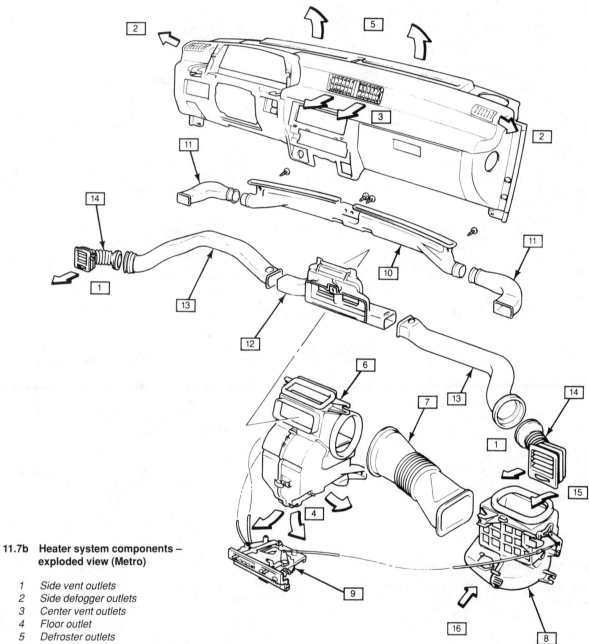

**11.7b Heater system components –
exploded view (Metro)**

1   Side vent outlets
2   Side defogger outlets
3   Center vent outlets
4   Floor outlet
5   Defroster outlets
6   Heater case
7   Air duct
8   Blower motor case
9   Heater control assembly
10 Defroster nozzle
11 Side demister ducts
12 Center vent duct
13 Side vent ducts
14 Side vent joints
15 Outside air
16 Inside air

8 Unbolt the heater assembly from the firewall **(see illustration)**.
9 Remove the screws and clips and separate the two halves of the heater assembly **(see illustrations)**.
10 Take out the the old heater core **(see illustration)** and install the new one.
11 Reassemble the heater unit and check the operation of the control flaps. If any parts bind, correct the problem before installation.
12 Reinstall the remaining parts in the reverse order of removal.
13 Refill the cooling system, reconnect the battery and run the engine. Check for leaks and proper system operation.

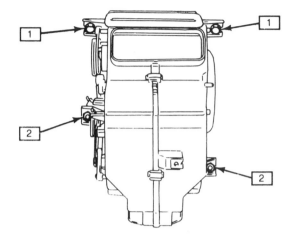

11.8 Metro heater case mounting details

1 Mounting bolts   2 Mounting nuts

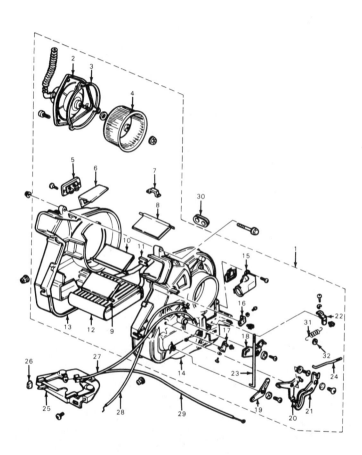

11.9a Heater case components – exploded view (Sprint)

1	Heater assembly	18	Temperature lever
2	Blower motor	19	Link lever
3	Seal	20	Mode lever
4	Blower fan	21	Link no. 2 lever
5	Resistor	22	Defroster link plate
6	Resistor plate	23	Vent link shaft
7	Case clamp	24	Defroster link shaft
8	Defroster damper	25	Heater control lever assembly
9	Temperature damper		
10	Vent damper	26	Control level knob
11	Heater pipe cover	27	Air control cable
12	Heater core	28	Heat control cable
13	Heater left case	29	Fresh air control cable
14	Heater right case	30	Heater grommet
15	Duct	31	Defroster link spring
16	Vent link plate	32	Defroster link spring washer
17	Temperature lever		

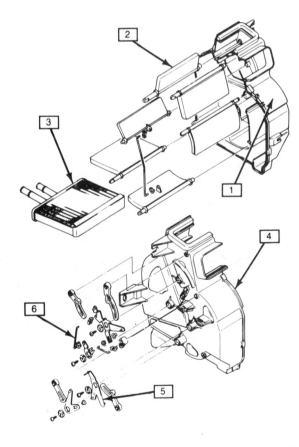

11.9b Heater case components – exploded view (Metro)

1 Heater case
2 Control door (damper)
3 Heater core
4 Heater case
5 Control lever linkage
6 Control shaft

3

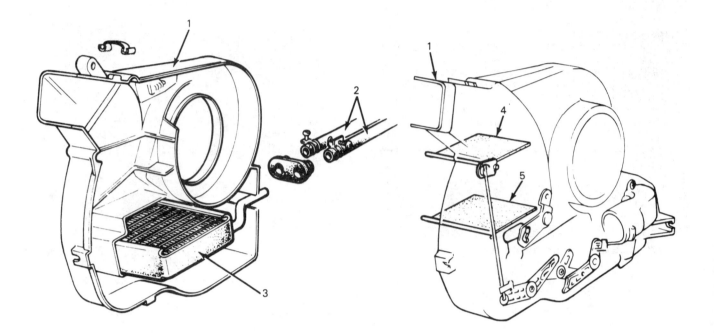

11.10 Once the cases are separated, the heater core can be slipped out

1	Heater cases	3 Heater core	5 Temperature damper
2	Water hoses	4 Vent damper	

12.3a Remove the trim panels . . .

12.3b . . . and pull off the knobs

12 Air conditioner and heater control assembly – removal, installation and cable adjustment

Refer to illustrations 12.3a, 12.3b, 12.6, 12.7 and 12.8

1 Disconnect the negative cable from the battery.
2 Remove the ashtray assembly (if necessary) by removing the two upper mounting screws.
3 Pull off the control knobs and detach the trim panels which surround the radio and heater control assembly, as necessary **(see illustrations)**.
4 Remove the radio (see Chapter 12).
5 Remove the glove compartment.
6 Remove the control mounting screws **(see illustration)**.

7 Carefully pull and tilt the unit out of the dash as far as the cables allow **(see illustration)**.
8 Check the cable housings for indentations where the clamps grip them. Mark the cable housing with paint if no indentation is visible. Remove the clamps and detach the control cables. If necessary, disconnect the control cables at the ends opposite from the control by detaching the cable clamps and separating the cables from the operating levers **(see illustration)**.
9 Unplug the wiring connectors and lift the control from the vehicle.
10 Installation is the reverse of removal.
11 Normally, if a control cable is reattached where the clamp mark is, the lever will be adjusted properly. If the lever requires adjustment, remove the clamp and move the cable until the control lever moves freely through its normal range of motion.

12.6   Remove the control panel mounting screws (arrows)

12.7   Carefully pull the control unit out for access to the cables

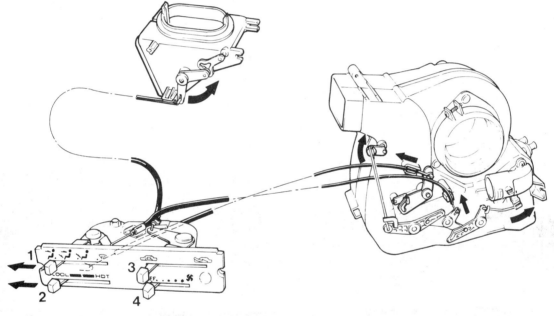

12.8   Sprint heater control cable details – position the levers as shown during installation and adjustment

1 *Mode control lever*	3 *Cir-Fresh control lever*
2 *Cool-Hot control lever*	4 *Blower speed control lever*

13   Air conditioning system – check and maintenance

Refer to illustrations 13.7, 13.8, 13.9 and 13.11

Warning: *The air conditioning system is under high pressure. Do not loosen any hose fittings or remove any components until after the system has been discharged by a dealer service department or service station. Always wear eye protection when disconnecting air conditioning system fittings.*

Check

1   The following maintenance checks should be performed on a regular basis to ensure the air conditioner continues to operate at peak efficiency.

   a) Check the compressor drivebelt. If it's worn or deteriorated, replace it (see Chapter 1).

   b) Check the drivebelt tension and, if necessary, adjust it (see Chapter 1).

   c) Check the system hoses. Look for cracks, bubbles, hard spots and deterioration. Inspect the hoses and all fittings for oil bubbles and seepage. If there's any evidence of wear, damage or leaks, replace the hose(s).

   d) Inspect the condenser fins for leaves, bugs and other debris. Use a "fin comb" or compressed air to clean the condenser.

   e) Make sure the system has the correct refrigerant charge.

   f) Check the evaporator housing drain tube for blockage.

2   It's a good idea to operate the system for about 10 minutes at least once a month, particularly during the winter. Long term non-use can cause hardening, and subsequent failure, of the seals.

3   Because of the complexity of the air conditioning system and the special equipment necessary to service it, in-depth troubleshooting and repairs are not included in this manual. However, simple checks and component replacement procedures are provided in this Chapter.

4   The most common cause of poor cooling is simply a low system refrigerant charge. If a noticeable drop in cool air output occurs, one of the following quick checks will help determine if the refrigerant level is low.

13.7   Check the sight glass (arrow) in the top of the receiver-drier

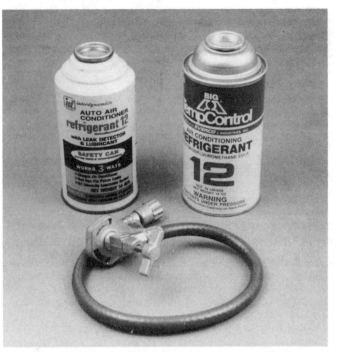

13.8   A typical charging kit consists of a 14-oz can of refrigerant, a can tap valve and a short section of service hose which can be attached to the system low side service valve – make sure at least one can of refrigerant you buy contains dye, like the one on the left

5   Warm the engine up to normal operating temperature.

6   Place the air conditioning temperature selector at the coldest setting and put the blower at the highest setting. Open the doors (to make sure the air conditioning system doesn't cycle off as soon as it cools the passenger compartment).

7   When the compressor engages, the clutch will make an audible click and the center of the clutch will rotate – inspect the sight glass (**see illustration**). If the refrigerant looks foamy, it's low. Charge the system as described later in this Section.

Adding refrigerant

8   Buy an automotive charging kit at an auto parts store. A charging kit includes a 14-ounce can of refrigerant, a tap valve and a short section of hose that can be attached between the tap valve and the system low side service valve (**see illustration**). Because one can of refrigerant may not be sufficient to bring the system charge up to the proper level, it's a good idea to buy a few additional cans. Make sure the first can contains red refrigerant dye. If the system is leaking, the red dye will leak out with the refrigerant and help pinpoint the location of the leak. **Warning:** *Never add more than three cans of refrigerant to the system.*

9   Connect the charging kit by following the manufacturer's instructions (**see illustration**). **Warning:** *DO NOT connect the charging kit hose to the system high side! Wear eye protection.*

10   Warm up the engine and turn on the air conditioner. Keep the charging kit hose away from the fan and other moving parts.

11   Place a thermometer in the dashboard vent nearest the evaporator (**see illustration**) and add refrigerant until the indicated temperature is around 40 to 45-degrees F or the system is full.

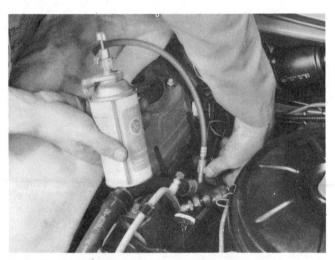

13.9   Connect the charging kit to the low pressure side – it's the one with the larger diameter tubing

---

14   Air conditioning receiver/drier – removal and installation

Refer to illustrations 14.3, 14.5a and 14.5b
Warning: *The air conditioning system is under high pressure. Do not loosen any fittings or remove any components until after the system has been discharged by a dealer service department or service station. Always wear eye protection when disconnecting air conditioning system fittings.*

13.11   Measure the output air temperature with a thermometer placed in the vent

14.3   Disconnect the refrigerant lines (arrows) – Sprint shown, Metro similar

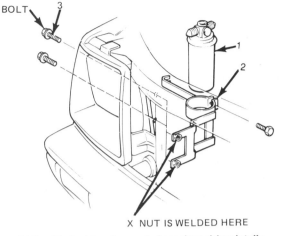

14.5a   Typical front-mounted receiver-drier details

1   Receiver-drier   3   Bolts
2   Bracket

1   The receiver/drier, which acts as a reservoir and filter for the refrigerant, is located either between the grille and radiator on the driver's side or adjacent to the timing belt end of the engine.
2   Remove the grille for access, if necessary (see Chapter 11).
3   Detach the two refrigerant lines from the receiver/drier (see illustration).
4   Immediately cap the open fittings to prevent the entry of dirt and moisture.
5   Unbolt the receiver/drier (see illustrations) and lift it out of the vehicle.
6   Install new O-rings (if equipped) on the lines and lubricate them with clean refrigerant oil.
7   Installation is the reverse of removal. Note: Do not remove the sealing caps until you're ready to reconnect the lines. Do not mistake the inlet (marked IN) and the outlet (marked OUT) connections.
8   If a new receiver/drier is installed, add 0.4 US fluid ounces (10 cc's) of refrigerant oil to the system.
9   Have the system evacuated, charged and leak tested by the shop that discharged it.

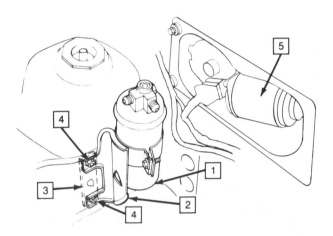

14.5b   Typical rear-mounted receiver-drier details

1   Receiver-drier   4   Nut
2   Bracket   5   Wiper motor
3   Brace

15   Air conditioning compressor – removal and installation

Refer to illustrations 15.6 and 15.7

Warning: The air conditioning system is under high pressure. Do not loosen any fittings or remove any components until after the system has been discharged by a dealer service department or service station. Always wear eye protection when disconnecting air conditioning system fittings.

1   Disconnect the negative cable from the battery.
2   Set the parking brake and block the rear tires.
3   Raise the front of the vehicle and support it securely on jackstands.
4   Unbolt the lower splash shield and remove the compressor drivebelt (see Chapter 1).
5   Disconnect the wiring from the compressor.
6   Detach the refrigerant lines from the compressor (see illustration) and immediately cap the open fittings to prevent the entry of dirt and moisture.
7   Remove the mounting bolts (see illustration) and lower the compressor from the engine compartment. Note: Keep the compressor level during handling and storage. If the compressor seized or you find metal particles in the refrigerant lines, the system must be flushed out by an air conditioning technician and the receiver/drier must be replaced.

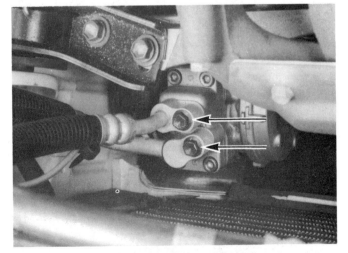

15.6   Unbolt the refrigerant lines (arrows) from the compressor – Metro shown, Sprint similar

8   Prior to installation, turn the center of the clutch six times to disperse any oil that has collected in the head.

9   Install the compressor in the reverse order of removal. Use Loctite (or equivalent) on the bolt threads.

10   If you're installing a new compressor, refer to the manufacturer's instructions for adding refrigerant oil to the system.

11   Have the system evacuated, charged and leak tested by the shop that discharged it.

16   Air conditioning condenser – removal and installation

Refer to illustrations 16.2, 16.3 and 16.6

Warning: *The air conditioning system is under high pressure. Do not loosen any fittings or remove any components until after the system has been discharged by a dealer service department or service station. Always wear eye protection when disconnecting air conditioning system fittings.*

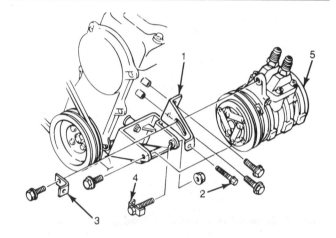

15.7   Compressor and related components – exploded view

1	*Compressor adjuster*	*4*	*Compressor bolt*
2	*Adjusting bolt*	*5*	*Compressor*
3	*Adjusting bolt lever*		

16.3   Auxiliary electric fan mounting details – the fan can be removed along with the condenser or by itself

1   Remove the grille (see Chapter 11).

2   Remove the vertical brace **(see illustration)**.

3   Remove the auxiliary electric fan **(see illustration)**.

4   Disconnect the refrigerant lines from the condenser assembly. Be sure to use a back-up wrench to avoid twisting the lines.

5   Immediately cap the open fittings to prevent the entry of dirt and moisture.

6   Unbolt the condenser **(see illustration)** and lift it out of the vehicle. Store it upright to prevent oil loss.

7   Installation is the reverse of removal.

8   If a new condenser was installed, add 0.7 to 1.0 ounces (20 to 30 cc's) of refrigerant oil to the system.

9   Have the system evacuated, charged and leak tested by the shop that discharged it.

16.2   Detach the vertical brace

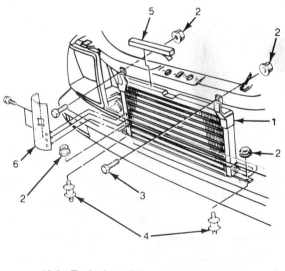

16.6   Typical condenser mounting details

1	*Condenser*	*4*	*Studs*
2	*Nuts*	*5*	*Condenser packing*
3	*Bolt*	*6*	*Condenser cover*

Chapter 4   Fuel and exhaust systems

Contents

Specifications

Choke valve-to-carburetor bore clearance (Sprint models only)
  At 77-degrees F (25-degrees C) .... 0.004 to 0.019 in (0.1 to 0.5 mm)
  At 95-degrees F (35-degrees C) .... 0.030 to 0.060 in (0.7 to 1.7 mm)
Fuel pressure (Metro models only)
  Idling .... 13 to 20 psi
  Engine OFF and ignition ON .... 23 to 30.5 psi

Torque specifications   Ft-lbs
Throttle body mounting bolts/nuts .... 14 to 16
Carburetor mounting bolts 18

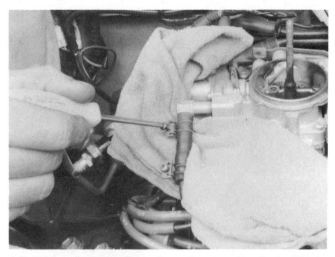

2.4   Place a rag directly under and surrounding the fuel line connection that will be removed

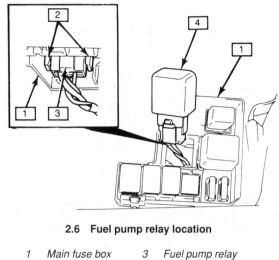

2.6   Fuel pump relay location

1	*Main fuse box*	3	*Fuel pump relay*
2	*Lock tabs*		*electrical connector*
		4	*Fuel pump relay*

1   General information

The fuel system consists of a rear mounted tank, combination metal and rubber fuel hoses, an engine mounted mechanical fuel pump or an electric fuel pump, and either a two stage, two venturi carburetor or an electronic fuel injection system.

The exhaust system is composed of an exhaust manifold, the catalytic converter and a combination muffler and tailpipe assembly.

The emission control systems modify the functions of both the exhaust and fuel systems. There may be some cross-references throughout this Chapter to sections in Chapter 6 because the emissions control systems are integral with the induction and exhaust systems.

Extreme caution should be exercised when dealing with either the fuel or exhaust system. Fuel is a primary element for combustion. Be very careful! The exhaust system is also an area for exercising caution as it operates at very high temperatures. Serious burns can result from even momentary contact with any part of the exhaust system and the fire potential is ever present.

2   Fuel pressure relief procedure

Warning: *Gasoline is extremely flammable, so take extra precautions when you work on any part of the fuel system. Don't smoke or allow open flames or bare light bulbs near the work area, and don't work in a garage where a natural gas-type appliance (such as a water heater or clothes dryer) with a pilot light is present. If you spill any fuel on your skin, rinse it off immediately with soap and water. When you perform any kind of work on the fuel system, wear safety glasses and have a Class B type fire extinguisher on hand.*

All models

1   Always relieve the fuel pressure before disconnecting any fuel system component to minimize the risk of fire and personal injury.
2   Unscrew the fuel filler cap to release the pressure caused by fuel vapor.

Carbureted models

Refer to illustration 2.4
3   Place rags under the connector or clamp that unites the fuel filter and the fuel line.
4   Loosen the clamp and remove the fuel line. Gently twist the fuel line and allow the fuel to drip into the rags **(see illustration)**. Cover the lines completely with the rags while simultaneously twisting the fuel line.

Fuel-injected models

Refer to illustration 2.6
5   Position the shifter in Park (automatic transaxle) or Neutral (manual transaxle) and block the rear wheels.
6   Remove the fuel pump relay **(see illustration)** from the main fuse panel (see Chapter 12).
7   Start the engine, allowing it to run until it stalls. Crank it over five or six times. Reinstall the relay, but don't turn the ignition key on until after all work to the fuel system has been performed, otherwise the fuel system will pressure-up again.
8   Even though fuel pressure should now be safely relieved, it's always a good idea to place a rag over any fuel fitting before loosening it.

3   Fuel lines and fittings – inspection and replacement

Warning: *Gasoline is extremely flammable, so take extra precautions when you work on any part of the fuel system. Don't smoke or allow open flames or bare light bulbs near the work area, and don't work in a garage where a natural gas-type appliance (such as a water heater or clothes dryer) with a pilot light is present. If you spill any fuel on your skin, rinse it off immediately with soap and water. When you perform any kind of work on the fuel system, wear safety glasses and have a Class B type fire extinguisher on hand.*

Inspection

1   Once in a while, you will have to raise the vehicle to service or replace some component. Whenever you work under the vehicle, always inspect fuel lines and all fittings and connections for damage or deterioration.
2   Check all hoses and pipes for cracks, kinks, deformation or obstructions.
3   Make sure all hoses and pipe clips attach their associated hoses or pipes securely to the underside of the vehicle.
4   Verify all hose clamps attaching rubber hoses to metal fuel lines or pipes are snug enough to assure a tight fit between the hoses and pipes.

Replacement

Refer to illustration 3.6
5   If you must replace any damaged sections, use original equipment replacement hoses or pipes constructed from exactly the same material as the section you are replacing. Do not install substitutes constructed from inferior or inappropriate material or you could cause a fuel leak or a fire.

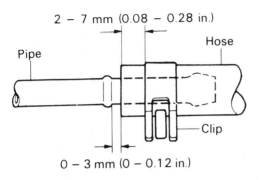

2 – 7 mm (0.08 – 0.28 in.)
Pipe
Hose
Clip
0 – 3 mm (0 – 0.12 in.)

3.6 When attaching a section of rubber hose to a metal fuel line, be sure to overlap the hose as shown and secure it to the line with a new hose clamp of the proper type

4.15 Connect a fuel pressure gauge onto the inlet side of the TBI fuel line and the TBI unit.

6   Always, before detaching or disassembling any part of the fuel line system, note the routing of all hoses and pipes and the orientation of all clamps and clips to assure that replacement sections are installed in exactly the same manner. When attaching hoses to metal lines, overlap them as shown (see illustration).

7   Before detaching any part of the fuel system, be sure to relieve the fuel line and tank pressure (see Section 2).

8   While you're under the vehicle, it's a good idea to check the condition of the fuel filter – make sure that it's not clogged or damaged (see Chapter 1).

4   Fuel pump/fuel system pressure – check

Warning: *Gasoline is extremely flammable, so take extra precautions when you work on any part of the fuel system. Don't smoke or allow open flames or bare light bulbs near the work area, and don't work in a garage where a natural gas-type appliance (such as a water heater or clothes dryer) with a pilot light is present. If you spill any fuel on your skin, rinse it off immediately with soap and water. When you perform any kind of work on the fuel system, wear safety glasses and have a Class B type fire extinguisher on hand.*

Note: *The following checks assume the fuel filter is in good condition. If you doubt it's condition, install a new one (see Chapter 1).*

1   Check that there is adequate fuel in the fuel tank. If you doubt the reading on the gauge, insert a long wooden dowel at the filler opening; it will serve as a dipstick.

Carbureted models
Preliminary check

2   If you suspect insufficient fuel delivery, first inspect all fuel lines to ensure that the problem is not simply a leak in a line.

3   If there are no leaks evident in the fuel lines, inspect the fuel pump itself. The following checks will tell you if the fuel pump is leaking and whether it is pumping fuel.

4   Remove the air cleaner housing.

Fuel pump output check

5   Hook up a remote starter switch in accordance with the manufacturer's instructions. If you don't have a remote starter switch, you will need an assistant to help you with this and the following procedure.

6   Trace the fuel outlet hose from the pump to the carburetor and detach it at the carburetor.

7   Attach the cable to the negative terminal of the battery.

8   Detach the wires from the primary terminals of the ignition coil (see Chapter 5).

9   Place a metal container under the open end of the fuel pump outlet hose.

10   Direct the fuel pump outlet hose into the container while cranking the engine for a few seconds with the remote starter (or while an assistant cranks the engine with the ignition key).

11   If fuel is emitted in well defined spurts, the pump is operating satisfactorily. If fuel dribbles or trickles out the hose, the pump is defective. Replace it (see Section 5).

Fuel-injected models
Fuel pump operational check

Note: *On 1989 and later models, the fuel pump is located inside the fuel tank.*

12   Set the parking brake and have an assistant turn the ignition switch to the On position while you listen at the fuel pump. You should hear a whirring sound, lasting for a couple of seconds. Start the engine. The whirring sound should now be continuous (although harder to hear with the engine running). If there is no whirring sound, either the fuel pump or the fuel main relay circuit is defective.

Pressure check

Refer to illustrations 4.15

13   Relieve the fuel pressure (see Section 2).

14   Remove the air cleaner assembly.

15   Remove the fuel line from the TBI unit and attach a fuel pressure gauge **(see illustration)** between the fuel feed line and the throttle body. Clamp the lines securely to make sure there will not be any leaks.

16   Start the engine. With the engine idling, measure the fuel pressure. It should be as listed in this Chapter's Specifications.

17   Shut the engine Off and turn the key to the On position and measure the fuel pressure. It should be as listed in this Chapter's Specifications. If the fuel pressure is not within specification, check for a pinched or clogged fuel return hose or pipe.

18   If the pressure is lower than specified, inspect the fuel filter – make sure it's not clogged. Look for a pinched or clogged fuel hose between the fuel tank and the fuel pump.

19   If there are no problems with any of the above-listed components, check the fuel pump (see below).

Fuel pump check

Refer to illustration 4.23

20   If you suspect a problem with the fuel pump, verify the pump actually runs. Have an assistant turn the ignition switch to ON – you should hear a brief whirring noise as the pump comes on and pressurizes the system. Have the assistant start the engine. This time you should hear a constant whirring sound from the pump (but it's more difficult to hear with the engine running).

21   If the pump does not come on (makes no sound), proceed to the next step.

22   Remove the rear seat (see Chapter 11).

4

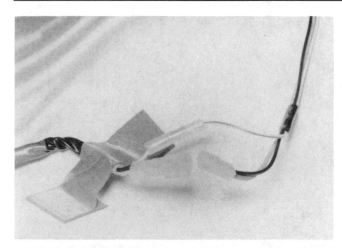

4.23   Do not mistake the fuel sender connector (yellow/black wire) with the fuel pump connector (red and black wires)

23   Detach the black and red wire connector **(see illustration)**. Make sure the ignition switch is turned Off before disconnecting the wires.
24   Touch the positive probe of a voltmeter to the red wire and the negative probe to the black wire, then turn on the ignition switch and verify there is voltage available.
25   If voltage is available, replace the fuel pump (see Section 5).
26   If no voltage is available, check the main relay (see Chapter 12).

5   Fuel pump – removal and installation

Warning: *Gasoline is extremely flammable, so take extra precautions when you work on any part of the fuel system. Don't smoke or allow open flames or bare light bulbs near the work area, and don't work in a garage where a natural gas-type appliance (such as a water heater or clothes dryer) with a pilot light is present. If you spill any fuel on your skin, rinse it off immediately with soap and water. When you perform any kind of work on the fuel system, wear safety glasses and have a Class B type fire extinguisher on hand.*

1   Disconnect the cable from the negative terminal of the battery.
2   Relieve the fuel system pressure (see Section 2).

Mechanical pump (carbureted models)

Refer to illustration 5.6

3   Relieve the fuel tank pressure by removing the fuel filler cap.
4   Locate the fuel pump mounted on the left rear corner of the cylinder head. Place rags underneath the pump to catch any spilled fuel.
5   Loosen hose clamps and slide them down the hoses, past the fittings. Disconnect the hoses from the pump, using a twisting motion as you pull them from the fittings. Immediately plug the hoses to prevent leakage of fuel and the entry of dirt.
6   Unscrew the fasteners that retain the pump to the cylinder head **(see illustration)**, then detach the pump from the head. Inspect the fuel pump arm for wear. Coat it with clean engine oil before installing it.
7   Using a gasket scraper or putty knife, remove all traces of old gasket material from the mating surfaces on the cylinder head (and the fuel pump, if the same one will be reinstalled). While scraping, be careful not to gouge the soft aluminum surfaces.
8   Installation is the reverse of the removal procedure, but be sure to use a new gasket and tighten the mounting fasteners securely.

Electric pump (fuel-injected models)

Refer to illustration 5.11

9   Remove the fuel tank following the procedure described in Section 6.
10   Remove the fuel feed lines and the clamps and hoses from the fuel return lines.
11   Remove the retaining screws, then lift the assembly out of the fuel tank **(see illustration)**.

5.6   Remove the fuel pump nuts (arrows) from the base of the pump (the other nut is not visible)

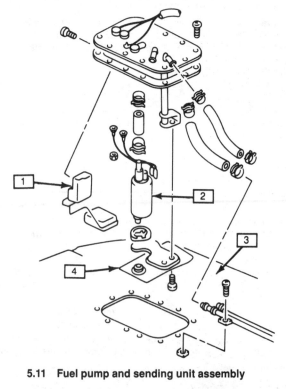

5.11   Fuel pump and sending unit assembly

1	Sending unit	3	Fuel tank
2	Fuel pump	4	Fuel filter

12   Remove the one bolt that secures the fuel pump motor assembly **(see illustration 5.11)**.
13   Remove the two fuel pump electrical connectors and remove the fuel pump.
14   Installation is the reverse of the removal procedure. Be sure to replace the sending unit gasket if it shows any signs of deterioration.

6   Fuel tank – removal and installation

Refer to illustrations 6.7, 6.8a and 6.8b

Warning: *Gasoline is extremely flammable, so take extra precautions when you work on any part of the fuel system. Don't smoke or allow open flames or bare light bulbs near the work area, and don't work in a garage* where a natural gas-type appliance (such as a water heater or clothes dryer) with a pilot light is present. If you spill any fuel on your skin, rinse it off immediately with soap and water. When you perform any kind of work on the fuel system, wear safety glasses and have a Class B type fire extinguisher on hand.

Note: The following procedure is much easier to perform if the fuel tank is empty. Some tanks have a drain plug for this purpose. If the tank does not have a drain plug, drive the vehicle until the tank is nearly empty (if possible) or siphon the fuel from the tank using a siphoning kit (available at most auto parts stores).

1   Remove the fuel filler cap to relieve fuel tank pressure.
2   Relieve the fuel pressure (see Section 2).
3   Detach the cable from the negative terminal of the battery.
4   If the tank has a drain plug, remove it and allow the fuel to drain into an approved gasoline container.
5   Raise the vehicle and place it securely on jackstands.
6   On 1989 and later Metro models, remove the rear seat cushions from the vehicle (if equipped). Disconnect the fuel pump wire harness and remove the grommet and harness through the floor pan.
7   On 1985 through 1988 Sprint models, remove the three fuel hoses from the pipes **(see illustration)**.
8   Disconnect the fuel lines, the vapor return lines and the fuel filler neck **(see illustrations)**. **Note:** The fuel lines are usually different diameters, so reattachment is simplified. If you have any doubts, however, clearly label the lines and the fittings. Be sure to plug the hoses to prevent leakage and contamination of the fuel system.
9   Support the fuel tank with a floor jack. Position a piece of wood between the jack head and the fuel tank to protect the tank.
10   Disconnect the fuel tank brackets and bolts.
11   Lower the tank enough to disconnect the electrical wires and ground strap from the fuel pump/fuel gauge sending unit, if you have not already done so.
12   Remove the tank from the vehicle.
13   Installation is the reverse of removal.

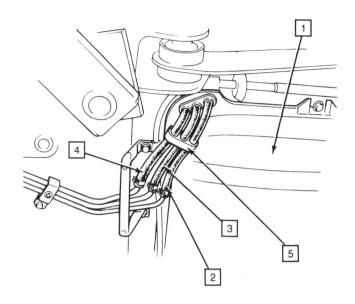

6.7   On Sprint models, remove the three fuel hoses from the lines

1   Fuel tank
2   Fuel return hose (to carburetor)
3   Vapor vent hose (to canister)
4   Fuel hose (to fuel filter)
5   Clamp

4

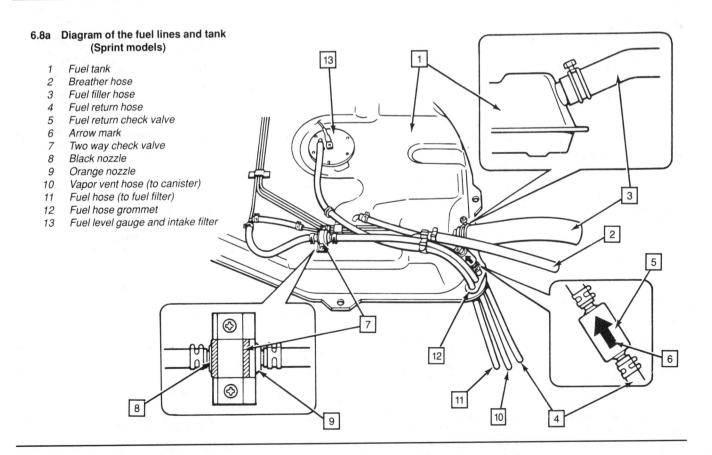

6.8a   Diagram of the fuel lines and tank (Sprint models)

1   Fuel tank
2   Breather hose
3   Fuel filler hose
4   Fuel return hose
5   Fuel return check valve
6   Arrow mark
7   Two way check valve
8   Black nozzle
9   Orange nozzle
10   Vapor vent hose (to canister)
11   Fuel hose (to fuel filter)
12   Fuel hose grommet
13   Fuel level gauge and intake filter

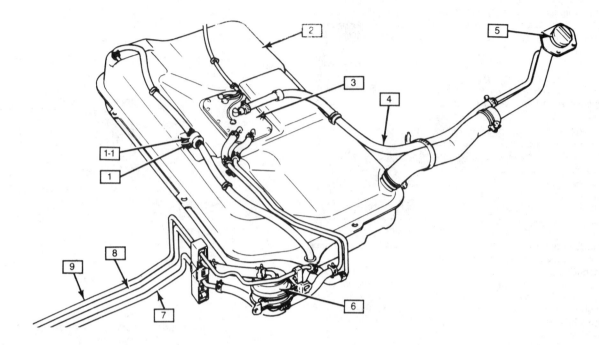

6.8b   Diagram of the fuel lines and tank (Metro models)

1	2-way check valve	3	Fuel pump and sending unit
1-1	Black side	4	Breather hose
2	Fuel tank	5	Fuel filler cap

6	Fuel filter
7	Fuel vapor line
8	Fuel feed line
9	Fuel return line

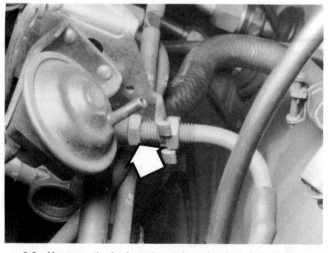

8.2   Unscrew the locknut (arrow) on the threaded portion of the cable

8.3   Grasp the throttle lever arm with a pair of needle nose pliers and rotate it to put some slack in the cable, then slip the cable end out of the slot in the arm

7   Fuel tank cleaning and repair – general information

1   Any repairs to the fuel tank or filler neck should be carried out by a professional who has experience in this critical and potentially dangerous work. Even after cleaning and flushing of the fuel system, explosive fumes can remain and ignite during repair of the tank.

2   If the fuel tank is removed from the vehicle, it should not be placed in an area where sparks or open flames could ignite the fumes coming out of the tank. Be especially careful inside garages where a natural gas-type appliance is located, because the pilot light could cause an explosion.

8   Throttle cable – removal, installation and adjustment

Refer to illustrations 8.2, 8.3 and 8.5

Removal

1   Detach the cable from the negative terminal of the battery.

2   Unscrew the locknut on the threaded portion of the throttle cable at the carburetor or throttle body **(see illustration)**.

3   Grasp the throttle lever arm and rotate it to put some slack in the throttle cable, then slip the cable end out of its slot in the arm **(see illustration)**.

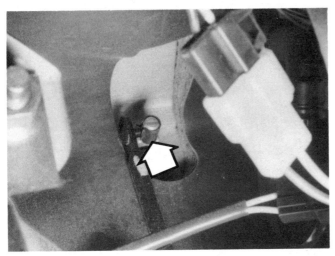

8.5 Remove the retaining clip (arrow) from end of the throttle cable by sliding it out

4 Trace the throttle cable to the firewall, detaching it from all brackets.
5 The cable is secured to the firewall with a retaining clip **(see illustration)** that must be removed from inside the vehicle, directly above the the throttle pedal.
6 Detach the throttle cable from the accelerator pedal.
7 From inside the vehicle, pull the cable through the firewall.

Installation and adjustment

8 Installation is the reverse of removal.
9 To adjust the cable, fully depress the accelerator pedal and check that the throttle is fully opened.
10 If not fully opened, loosen the locknuts, depress the accelerator pedal and adjust the cable so full throttle can be attained.
11 Tighten the locknuts and recheck the adjustment. Make sure the throttle closes fully when the pedal isn't depressed.

---

9 Carburetor – diagnosis and overhaul (Sprint models only)

Warning: *Gasoline is extremely flammable, so take extra precautions when you work on any part of the fuel system. Don't smoke or allow open flames or bare light bulbs near the work area, and don't work in a garage where a natural gas-type appliance (such as a water heater or clothes dryer) with a pilot light is present. If you spill any fuel on your skin, rinse it off immediately with soap and water. When you perform any kind of work on the fuel system, wear safety glasses and have a Class B type fire extinguisher on hand.*

General diagnosis

1 A thorough road test and check of carburetor adjustments should be done before any major carburetor service work. Specifications for some adjustments are listed on the Vehicle Emissions Control Information (VECI) label found in the engine compartment.
2 Carburetor problems usually show up as flooding, hard starting, stalling, severe backfiring and poor acceleration. A carburetor that's leaking fuel and/or covered with wet looking deposits definitely needs attention.
3 Some performance complaints directed at the carburetor are actually a result of loose, out-of-adjustment or malfunctioning engine or electrical components. Others develop when vacuum hoses leak, are disconnected or are incorrectly routed. The proper approach to analyzing carburetor problems should include the following items:
  a) Inspect all vacuum hoses and actuators for leaks and correct installation (see Chapters 1 and 6).
  b) Tighten the intake manifold and carburetor mounting nuts/bolts evenly and securely.

  c) Perform a cylinder compression test (see Chapter 2).
  d) Clean or replace the spark plugs as necessary (see Chapter 1).
  e) Check the spark plug wires (see Chapter 1).
  f) Inspect the ignition primary wires.
  g) Check the ignition timing (follow the instructions printed on the Emissions Control Information label).
  h) Check the fuel pump (see Section 4).
  i) Check the heat control valve in the air cleaner for proper operation (see Chapter 1).
  j) Check/replace the air filter element (see Chapter 1).
  k) Check the PCV system (see Chapters 1 and 6).
  l) Check/replace the fuel filter (see Chapter 1). Also, the strainer in the tank could be restricted.
  m) Check for a plugged exhaust system.
  n) Check EGR valve operation (see Chapter 6).
  o) Check the choke – it should be completely open at normal engine operating temperature (see Chapter 1).
  p) Check for fuel leaks and kinked or dented fuel lines (see Chapters 1 and 4)
  q) Check accelerator pump operation with the engine off (remove the air cleaner cover and operate the throttle as you look into the carburetor throat – you should see a stream of gasoline enter the carburetor).
  r) Check for incorrect fuel or bad gasoline.
  s) Check the valve clearances (if applicable) and camshaft lobe lift (see Chapters 1 and 2)
  t) Have a dealer service department or repair shop check the electronic engine and carburetor controls.
4 Diagnosing carburetor problems may require that the engine be started and run with the air cleaner off. While running the engine without the air cleaner, backfires are possible. This situation is likely to occur if the carburetor is malfunctioning, but just the removal of the air cleaner can lean the fuel/air mixture enough to produce an engine backfire. **Warning:** *Don't position any part of your body, especially your face, directly over the carburetor during inspection and servicing procedures. Wear eye protection!*

Overhaul

Refer to illustration 9.5

5 Once it's determined that the carburetor needs an overhaul **(see illustration)**, several options are available. If you're going to attempt to overhaul the carburetor yourself, first obtain a good quality carburetor rebuild kit (which will include all necessary gaskets, internal parts, instructions and a parts list). You'll also need some special solvent and a means of blowing out the internal passages of the carburetor with air.
6 An alternative is to obtain a new or rebuilt carburetor. They're readily available from dealers and auto parts stores. Make absolutely sure the exchange carburetor is identical to the original. A tag is usually attached to the top of the carburetor or a number is stamped on the float bowl. It will help determine the exact type of carburetor you have. When obtaining a rebuilt carburetor or a rebuild kit, make sure the kit or carburetor matches your application exactly. Seemingly insignificant differences can make a large difference in engine performance.
7 If you choose to overhaul your own carburetor, allow enough time to disassemble it carefully, soak the necessary parts in the cleaning solvent (usually for at least one-half day or according to the instructions listed on the carburetor cleaner) and reassemble it, which will usually take much longer than disassembly. When disassembling the carburetor, match each part with the illustration in the carburetor kit and lay the parts out in order on a clean work surface. Overhauls by inexperienced mechanics can result in an engine which runs poorly or not at all. To avoid this, use care and patience when disassembling the carburetor so you can reassemble it correctly.
8 Because carburetor designs are constantly modified by the manufacturer in order to meet increasingly more stringent emissions regulations, the overhaul procedures in this Chapter may not apply exactly to your vehicle. You'll receive a detailed, well illustrated set of instructions with any carburetor overhaul kit; they'll apply in a more specific manner to the carburetor on your vehicle.

4

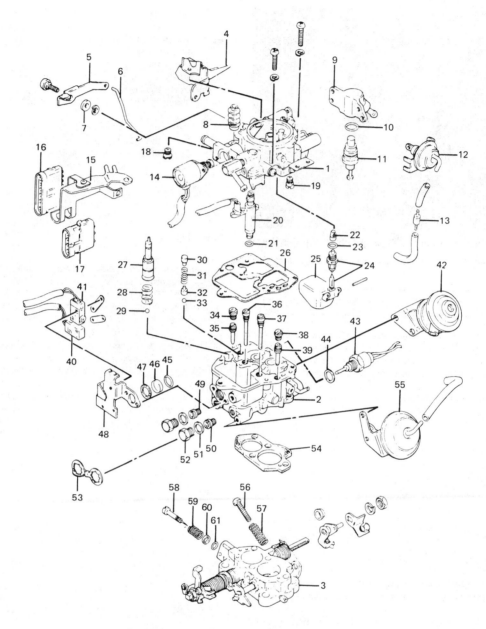

9.5   Exploded view of the MR08 carburetor

1	Air horn	17	Connector (4 terminals)	30	Injector weight	45	Level gauge seal
2	Float chamber	18	Primary slow air	31	Injector spring	46	Level gauge
3	Throttle chamber		No. 1 bleeder	32	Injector weight	47	Level gauge gasket
4	Cable bracket	19	Secondary slow	33	Ball	48	Micro switch bracket
5	Pump lever		air bleeder	34	Primary slow air	49	Primary main jet
6	Pump rod	20	Mixture control		No. 2 bleeder	50	Secondary main jet
7	Washer		solenoid valve	35	Primary slow jet	51	Drain plug gasket
8	Choke lever guide	21	Solenoid valve seal	36	Primary main air bleeder	52	Drain plug
9	Thermo element holder	22	Needle valve filter	37	Secondary main	53	Lock plate
10	Seal	23	Needle valve gasket		air bleeder	54	Insulator
11	Thermo element	24	Needle valve	38	Plug	55	Secondary diaphragm
12	Choke piston	25	Float	39	Secondary slow jet	56	Throttle adjust screw
13	Delay valve	26	Air horn gasket	40	Idle micro switch	57	Spring
14	Switch vent solenoid	27	Pump piston	41	Wide open micro switch	58	Mixture adjust screw
15	Connector holder	28	Air horn gasket	42	Idle up actuator	59	Spring
16	Connector (6 terminals)	29	Ball	43	Solenoid valve (fuel cut)	60	Washer
				44	Washer	61	Seal

10.5   Clearly label all vacuum hoses before disconnecting them

10.8   Because of the difficult angles and the lack of room at the base of the carburetor, a curved, open end wrench is the best tool for reaching the carburetor nuts.

---

10   Carburetor – removal and installation (Sprint models only)

Warning: *Gasoline is extremely flammable, so take extra precautions when you work on any part of the fuel system. Don't smoke or allow open flames or bare light bulbs near the work area, and don't work in a garage where a natural gas-type appliance (such as a water heater or clothes dryer) with a pilot light is present. If you spill any fuel on your skin, rinse it off immediately with soap and water. When you perform any kind of work on the fuel system, wear safety glasses and have a Class B type fire extinguisher on hand.*

Removal

Refer to illustrations 10.5 and 10.8

1   Remove the fuel tank cap to relieve the tank pressure.
2   Remove the air cleaner from the carburetor. Be sure to label all vacuum hoses attached to the air cleaner housing.
3   Disconnect the throttle cable from the throttle lever (see Section 8).
4   If the vehicle is equipped with an automatic transaxle, disconnect the TV cable from the throttle lever.
5   Clearly label all vacuum hoses and fittings, then disconnect the hoses **(see illustration).**
6   Disconnect the fuel line from the carburetor.
7   Label the wires and terminals, then unplug all wire harness connectors.
8   Remove the mounting fasteners **(see illustration)**, remove the EGR modulator bracket (see Chapter 6) and lift the carburetor from the intake manifold. Remove the carburetor mounting gasket. Stuff a shop rag into the intake manifold openings.

Installation

9   Use a gasket scraper to remove all traces of gasket material and sealant from the intake manifold, being careful not to damage the surface (and the carburetor, if it's being reinstalled). Clean the mating surfaces with lacquer thinner or acetone.
10   Place a new gasket on the intake manifold and the carburetor baseplate.
11   Position the carburetor on the gasket and install the mounting fasteners.
12   To prevent carburetor distortion or damage, tighten the fasteners, in a criss-cross pattern, 1/4 turn at a time, until the torque listed in this Chapter's Specifications is reached.
13   The remaining installation steps are the reverse of removal.
14   Check and, if necessary, adjust the idle speed (see Chapter 1).
15   If the vehicle is equipped with an automatic transaxle, refer to Chapter 7, Part B for the TV cable adjustment procedure.
16   Start the engine and check carefully for fuel leaks.

11.2   Using a feeler gauge (arrow), check the clearance of the choke plate to the carburetor bore

---

11   Carburetor – adjustments (Sprint models only)

Warning: *Gasoline is extremely flammable, so take extra precautions when you work on any part of the fuel system. Don't smoke or allow open flames or bare light bulbs near the work area, and don't work in a garage where a natural gas-type appliance (such as a water heater or clothes dryer) with a pilot light is present. If you spill any fuel on your skin, rinse it off immediately with soap and water. When you perform any kind of work on the fuel system, wear safety glasses and have a Class B type fire extinguisher on hand.*

Note: *If your vehicle's engine is hard to start or does not start at all, has an unstable idle or poor driveability and you suspect the carburetor is malfunctioning, it's best to first take the vehicle to a dealer service department that has the equipment necessary to diagnose this highly complicated system. The following procedures are intended to help the home mechanic verify proper operation of components, make minor adjustments, and replace some components. They are not intended as troubleshooting procedures.*

Choke check and adjustment

Refer to illustrations 11.2 and 11.5

1   Remove the air cleaner assembly. With the engine stopped and cold, hold the throttle open and depress the choke plate with your finger – it should move smoothly. The choke should be almost fully closed if the ambient air temperature is below 77-degrees F (25-degrees C) and the engine is cold.
2   Check the clearance of the choke plate to the carburetor bore **(see illustration)** and compare your reading with those listed in this Chapter's

4

11.5   With the idle-up actuator removed, rotate the fast idle cam to align the hole in the cam with the hole in the bracket – insert a punch through the two holes to hold the cam in this position – the choke lever can now be adjusted with a pair of pliers

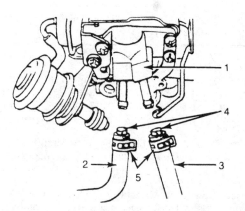

11.10   Plug the hoses on the thermo element holder

1	Carburetor thermo element holder	3	Choke number 2 hose
2	Choke number 1 hose	4	Plug
		5	Clamp

Specifications section. If the clearances are too small or too large, lubricate the choke linkage and take another measurement. **Note:** *If the air temperature is very warm, use the alternate specification to check the carburetor bore clearance. If the air temperature is at around 85 degrees F, calculate a midpoint value using the two other specifications.*

3   Start the engine and allow it to warm to normal operating temperature. Depress and release the accelerator once. The choke should now be fully open. If it's not, and the plate-to-bore clearance is correct, there's a problem with the choke linkage or operating mechanism.

4   If the plate-to-bore clearance is not as specified, remove the carburetor (see Section 10) and adjust the choke lever as follows.

5   Remove the idle-up actuator from the carburetor, turn the fast idle cam counter-clockwise and insert a pin into the cam and bracket to lock them into place **(see illustration)**.

6   Using a pair of pliers, bend the choke lever up or down until the choke-to-bore clearance is set to the specified amount. Bending the tab up causes the choke valve to close, while bending it down allows it to open a little more **(see illustration 11.5)**.

7   Reinstall the carburetor and check the choke again.

Accelerator pump

8   Remove the air intake case. With the engine Off, operate the throttle linkage through its full range of travel while looking down the throat of the carburetor (you may have to hold the choke plate open). A healthy stream of fuel should squirt out of the pump discharge nozzle. If fuel just dribbles out or there is no squirt at all, the accelerator pump is defective or the discharge passage is clogged. In either case, an overhaul of the carburetor is required.

Fast idle adjustment

Refer to illustrations 11.10 and 11.11

9   Allow the engine to cool for at least four hours. The ambient temperature should be below 77-degrees F. Drain the coolant (see Chapter 3).

10   Disconnect the hoses from the choke thermo-element holder and plug them **(see illustration)**. Be sure to use clamps to prevent leakage at the seal ends.

11   After the carburetor has cooled, check to see that the mark on the fast idle cam and the center of the cam follower are in alignment **(see illustration)**.

12   Install the radiator drain plug and refill the cooling system (see Chapter 3). Check the hoses for any leaks.

13   With the engine running at idle speed, force the fast idle cam to pivot around until the mark on the cam centers with the cam follower (refer to Step 11) and check the idle speed. It should be 2100 to 2700 rpm. **Note:** *If necessary, pivot the fast idle cam using a pair of pliers.*

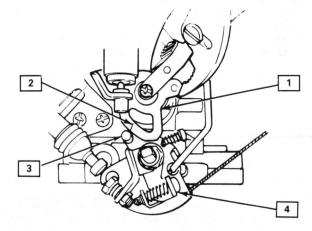

11.11   With the carburetor cool, make sure the mark on the fast idle cam is aligned with the center of the cam follower

1	Fast idle cam	3	Cam follower
2	Mark on cam	4	Fast idle adjusting screw

14   Adjust the fast idle by turning the fast idle screw **(see illustration 11.11)**.

15   Allow the engine to cool and install the cooling lines back onto the choke thermo-element holder. Installation is the reverse of removal.

Idle-up adjustment

Refer to illustration 11.17

Note: *The idle-up adjustment must be performed when the cooling fan is not running.*

16   Run the engine until it reaches normal operating temperature. Connect a tachometer and verify that the idle speed is as specified (see Chapter 1).

17   Turn the parking lamps On and check to see that the idle-up actuator rod moves down. Now turn the headlights On and check the engine rpm (the heater fan, rear defogger and air conditioner must be turned Off). It should increase to 750 – 850 rpm. If it doesn't increase, turn the adjusting screw **(see illustration)**. **Note:** *On vehicles equipped with an automatic transaxle, the idle-up actuator also should function with the brake pedal depressed and the shift selector in Drive.*

12 Electronic Fuel Injection (EFI) system – general information (Metro models only)

Refer to illustration 12.2

Electronic fuel injection provides optimum mixture ratios at all stages of combustion and offers immediate throttle response characteristics. It also enables the engine to run at the leanest possible air/fuel mixture ratio, reducing exhaust gas emissions.

A Throttle Body Injection (TBI) unit replaces a conventional carburetor atop the intake manifold **(see illustration)**. It is controlled by the Electronic Control Module (ECM), which monitors engine performance and adjusts the air/fuel mixture accordingly (see Chapter 6 for a complete description of the fuel control system).

An electric fuel pump – located in the fuel tank with the fuel gauge sending unit – pumps fuel to the fuel injection system through the fuel feed line and an in-line fuel filter. A pressure regulator keeps fuel available at a constant pressure. Fuel in excess of injector needs is returned to the fuel tank by a separate line.

The basic TBI unit is made up of the throttle body housing, a fuel injector, a fuel pressure regulator, the throttle opener (which controls the throttle valve opening so that it's a little bit wider when the engine is starting than when it's at an idle), the throttle position sensor, an air valve (which lets an additional amount of air past the throttle plate during cold engine operation) and the idle speed control solenoid valve (which controls the idle speed according to the ECM).

The fuel injector is a solenoid operated device controlled by the ECM. The ECM turns on the solenoid, which lifts a normally closed needle valve

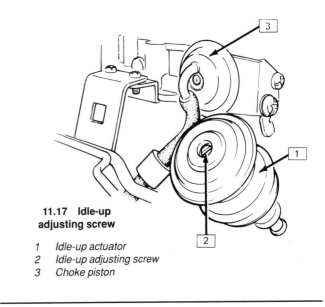

11.17 Idle-up adjusting screw

1 *Idle-up actuator*
2 *Idle-up adjusting screw*
3 *Choke piston*

off its seat. The fuel, which is under pressure, is injected in a conical spray pattern at the walls of the throttle body bore above the throttle valve. The fuel which is not used by the injector passes through the pressure regulator before being returned to the fuel tank.

4

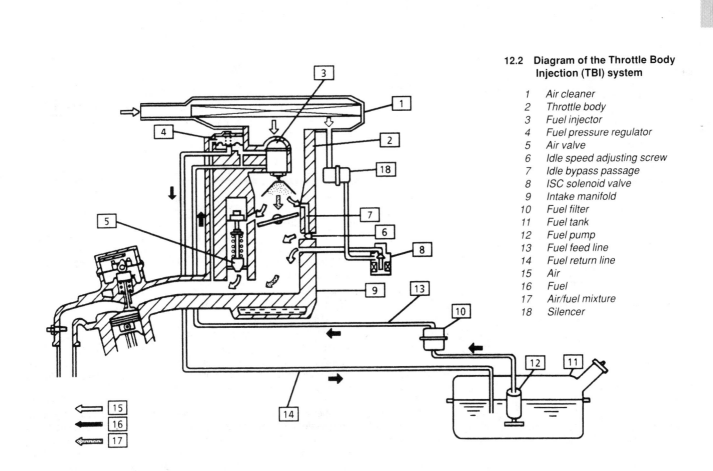

12.2 Diagram of the Throttle Body Injection (TBI) system

1 *Air cleaner*
2 *Throttle body*
3 *Fuel injector*
4 *Fuel pressure regulator*
5 *Air valve*
6 *Idle speed adjusting screw*
7 *Idle bypass passage*
8 *ISC solenoid valve*
9 *Intake manifold*
10 *Fuel filter*
11 *Fuel tank*
12 *Fuel pump*
13 *Fuel feed line*
14 *Fuel return line*
15 *Air*
16 *Fuel*
17 *Air/fuel mixture*
18 *Silencer*

14.6a   Remove the two long TBI unit attaching bolts (arrows)

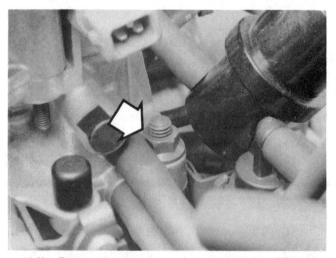

14.6b   Remove the two nuts on the backside of the TBI unit (arrow) – the other mounting nut is not visible in this photo

13   Electronic Fuel Injection (EFI) system – check

Warning: *Gasoline is extremely flammable, so take extra precautions when you work on any part of the fuel system. Don't smoke or allow open flames or bare light bulbs near the work area, and don't work in a garage where a natural gas-type appliance (such as a water heater or clothes dryer) with a pilot light is present. If you spill any fuel on your skin, rinse it off immediately with soap and water. When you perform any kind of work on the fuel tank, wear safety glasses and have a Class B type fire extinguisher on hand.*

Preliminary checks

1   Check the ground wire connections on the intake manifold for tightness. Check all electrical connectors that are related to the system. Loose connectors and poor grounds can cause many problems that resemble more serious malfunctions.
2   Check to see that the battery is fully charged, as the control unit and sensors depend on an accurate supply voltage in order to properly meter the fuel.
3   Check the air filter element – a dirty or partially blocked filter will severly impede performance and economy (see Chapter 1).

4   If a blown fuse is found, replace it and see if it blows again. If it does, search for a grounded wire in the harness to the fuel pump.
5   Check the condition of the vacuum hoses attached to the throttle body and intake manifold. Vacuum leaks can result in an excessively lean mixture.
6   Check the fuel system pressure (see Section 4).
7   Set the parking brake, remove the air cleaner top plate and with the engine idling in Park, observe the operating fuel injector. The spray pattern should be even and conical in shape. The spray should touch the throttle body bore.
  a) If the spray is weak or uneven, the injector is clogged or faulty. Gasoline additives designed to clean fuel injectors can sometimes clear a clogged injector. If not, a dealer service department has more effective cleaning equipment.
  b) If an injector is not operating at all, check its electrical connector. If the connection is good and the injector is receiving voltage, but the injector still doesn't work, the injector is faulty.
8   The remainder of the system checks should be left to a dealer service department or other qualified repair shop, as there is a chance that the control unit may be damaged if they are not performed properly.

14   Throttle Body Injection (TBI) unit – removal and installation

Warning: *Gasoline is extremely flammable, so take extra precautions when you work on any part of the fuel system. Don't smoke or allow open flames or bare light bulbs near the work area, and don't work in a garage where a natural gas-type appliance (such as a water heater or clothes dryer) with a pilot light is present. If you spill any fuel on your skin, rinse it off immediately with soap and water. When you perform any kind of work on the fuel tank, wear safety glasses and have a Class B type fire extinguisher on hand.*

Removal

Refer to illustration 14.6a and 14.6b

1   Disconnect the cable from the negative terminal of the battery.
2   Relieve the fuel system pressure (see Section 2).
3   Following the procedure described in Section 8, disconnect the throttle cable from the throttle lever at the TBI unit.
4   Disconnect the fuel feed and return lines from the TBI unit.
5   Label and disconnect any electrical connectors and vacuum hoses.
6   Remove the attaching bolts and lift the TBI unit from the intake manifold **(see illustrations)**.

Installation

7   Using a gasket scraper or a putty knife, remove all traces of old gasket material and sealant from the intake manifold (and throttle body, if the same one will be installed). While scraping, be careful not to gouge the soft aluminum surfaces.
8   Installation is the reverse of the removal procedure, but be sure to use a new base gasket, and tighten the bolts to the torque listed in this Chapter's Specifications.

15   Throttle Body Injection (TBI) unit – component check and replacement

Warning: *Gasoline is extremely flammable, so take extra precautions when you work on any part of the fuel system. Don't smoke or allow open flames or bare light bulbs near the work area, and don't work in a garage where a natural gas-type appliance (such as a water heater or clothes dryer) with a pilot light is present. If you spill any fuel on your skin, rinse it off immediately with soap and water. When you perform any kind of work on the fuel tank, wear safety glasses and have a Class B type fire extinguisher on hand.*

Note: *All TBI components and parts (except IAC valve, pressure regulator diaphragm and any rubber pieces) should be cleaned in a cold immersion cleaner such as Carbon X or equivalent.*

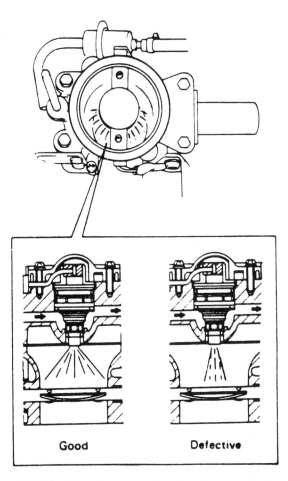

15.2 The fuel injector should emit a strong, conical spray of fuel against the walls of the TBI unit bore

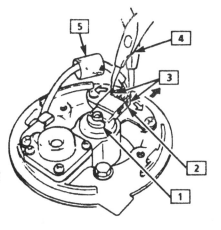

15.4 Disconnecting electrical connector

1	Injector	4	Snap-ring pliers
2	Coupler	5	Coupler cover
3	Claw		

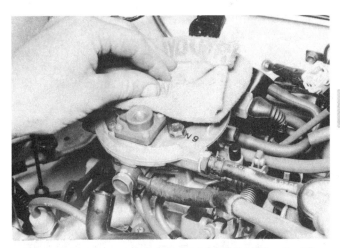

15.9a Apply compressed air to the inlet of the TBI unit while simultaneously holding a rag over the injector to catch any fuel that might blow up past the seals at the moment the injector releases from the bore

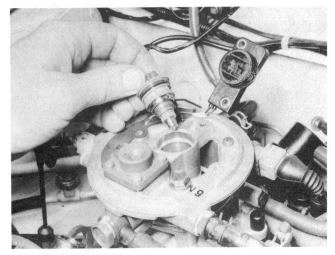

15.9b Carefully lift the injector from the TBI unit

Fuel injector

Refer to illustrations 15.2, 15.4, 15.9a, 15.9b and 15.11

1   Unbolt the air cleaner assembly from the top of the throttle body and move it aside.

2   Start the engine and carefully peer down into the throttle body (wear safety goggles), checking the injector spray pattern. It should be an even, conical pattern **(see illustration)** – if it isn't, the injector must be replaced with a new one.

3   Shut off the engine and make sure the injection of fuel stops as well. The injector should not leak more than one drop per minute – if it does, replace it.

4   Disconnect the electrical connector from the injector **(see illustration)**.

5   To replace the fuel injector, begin by relieving the fuel system pressure (see Section 2).

6   Disconnect the cable from the negative terminal of the battery.

7   Disconnect the fuel feed line from the throttle body. Remove the two injector cover screws and lift the cover from the injector.

8   Disconnect the injector electrical connector, release the harness clamp and dislodge the grommet from the throttle body housing.

9   To remove the injector from the throttle body, carefully direct compressed air into the fuel inlet port while pulling up on the injector **(see illustrations)**. **Caution:** *Apply the compressed air gradually, using only enough to ease the injector out of the throttle body. Do not exceed 85 psi, or damage to the injector and other components may occur. Also, once the injector has been removed, handle it carefully and don't immerse it in solvent to clean it.*

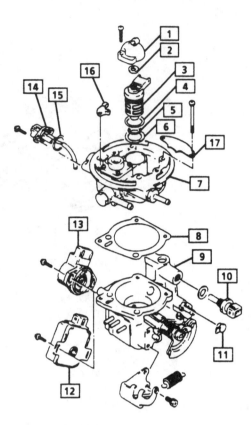

15.11 Throttle body injector assembly

1   *Injector cover*
2   *Upper insulator*
3   *Fuel injector*
4   *Upper O-ring*
5   *Lower O-ring*
6   *Lower insulator*
7   *Throttle upper body*
8   *Gasket*
9   *Throttle lower body*
10 *WTS*
11 *Idle speed adjusting screw cap*
12 *TS (M/T model only)*
13 *TPS (A/T model only)*
14 *Injector sub wire coupler*
15 *O-ring*
16 *Clamp*
17 *Plate*

15.17 Use a Torx driver to remove the bolts that secure the fuel pressure regulator to the body of the TBI unit

15.18 Carefully inspect the rubber diaphragm for rips or defects

10 Check the fuel filters on the injector for dirt particles. If there is any residue, clean the filters and check the fuel tank and lines for contamination.

11 Before installing the injector, lubricate the O-rings with light oil (if you are reinstalling the same injector, use new O-rings). Push the injector firmly into its bore, making sure the wiring harness is pointing toward its slot in the throttle body housing **(see illustration)**. Push the grommet on the wiring harness into the slot.

12 Install the injector cover and tighten the screws securely.

13 Hook up the cable to the negative battery terminal. Connect the injector electrical connector and pressurize the fuel system by turning the ignition key to the On position. Check the fuel feed line and the injector for leakage.

14 Install the air cleaner assembly.

Fuel pressure regulator

Refer to illustration 15.17 and 5.18

Note: *Checking the fuel pressure requires the use of some special adapters not normally available to the home mechanic. If the necessary tools are not available (see Section 4), the fuel pressure should be checked by a dealer service department or other service facility with the necessary hardware. If the regulator has been determined to be faulty, replace it using the following procedure.*

15 Disconnect the cable from the negative terminal of the battery.

16 Relieve the fuel system pressure (see Section 2).

17 Remove the screws that secure the regulator to the throttle body using a Torx drive (T-20) **(see illustration)**, then pull the regulator straight up.

18 Check the diaphragm **(see illustration)** for cuts or defects and also make sure the spring is intact and not twisted or damaged.

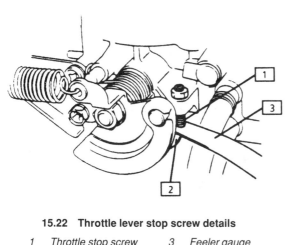

15.22   Throttle lever stop screw details

1   Throttle stop screw   3   Feeler gauge
2   Throttle lever

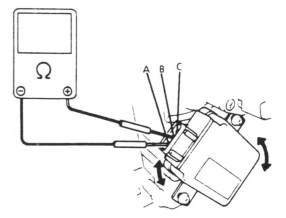

15.25   Adjusting the throttle switch

19   Install the new fuel pressure regulator straight into the throttle body. Tighten the screws securely.
20   Install the fuel return line, tightening the hose clamp securely.
21   Connect the cable to the negative battery terminal, pressurize the fuel system by turning the ignition switch to the On position and check around the regulator for fuel leaks.

Throttle switch (TS) (manual transaxle models only)
Refer to illustration 15.22

22   To check the throttle switch, disconnect the TS electrical connector and insert a 0.012 inch (0.3 mm) feeler gauge between the throttle lever stop screw and throttle lever **(see illustration)**.
23   There should be continuity **(see illustration 15.25)**. If there is no continuity, adjust the switch.

Adjustment
Refer to illustration 15.25

24   To adjust the throttle switch (TS), insert a 0.024 inch (0.6 mm) feeler gauge between the throttle lever stop screw and the throttle lever.
25   Connect an ohmmeter between terminal A and terminal B **(see illustration)**.
26   Loosen the throttle switch (TS) bolts and move the switch clockwise until the ohmmeter reads open (no continuity). Tighten the screws to 18 in-lbs.
27   Check that there is no continuity with a 0.35 inch (0.9 mm) feeler gauge between the throttle lever stop screw and throttle lever.
28   Check that there is continuity with a 0.12 inch (0.3 mm) feeler gauge between the throttle lever stop screw and throttle lever.
29   If the readings are correct, reinstall the electrical connector and the air cleaner assembly.

Throttle position sensor (TPS)
(automatic transaxle-equipped models)
Refer to illustrations 15.31

30   Disconnect the cable from the negative terminal of the battery.
31   Unplug the TPS electrical connector and check the resistance between the terminals when the throttle is fully open and fully closed **(see illustration)**. If the readings aren't as specified, adjust the throttle position sensor. If the correct readings cannot be obtained even after adjustment, then replace the sensor.
32   To adjust the sensor, insert a 0.012 inch (0.3 mm) feeler gauge between the throttle lever stop screw and the throttle lever **(see illustration 15.22)**.

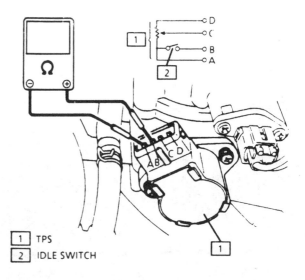
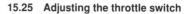

1   TPS
2   IDLE SWITCH

TERMINALS	CONDITION	RESISTANCE
Between A and B terminals (Idle Switch)	When throttle lever-to-stop screw clearance is 0.3 mm (0.012 in.)	0
	When throttle lever-to-stop screw clearance is 0.9 mm (0.035 in.)	Continuity
Between A and D terminals	Throttle valve is at idle position	4.37 - 8.13 kΩ
Between A and C terminals	Throttle valve is at idle position	240 - 1140 Ω
	Throttle valve is fully opened	3.17 - 6.6 kΩ

15.31   TPS output check (models with automatic transaxles only)

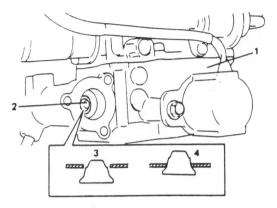

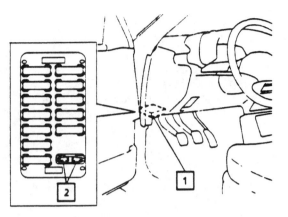

15.38   With the cap removed you can check the position of the air valve – it should be open when the engine is cool and closed when it is hot

1 Throttle body	*3 Air valve open position*
2 Air valve	*4 Air valve closed position*

15.42   Diagnosis switch terminal

1   Junction fuse block
2   Diagnosis terminal

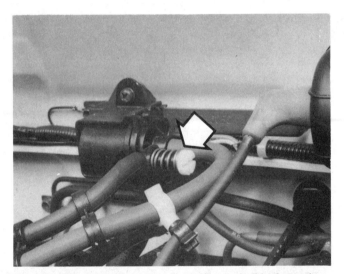

15.43   The VSV (arrow) is located on the firewall in the engine compartment (1990 Metro shown)

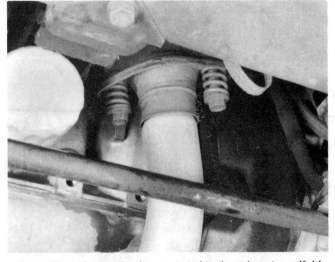

16.1a   The exhaust pipe is connected to the exhaust manifold with two nuts – there is a gasket under the flange which should be replaced whenever the pipe is unbolted from the manifold

33   Connect an ohmmeter between terminal A and terminal B **(see illustration 15.31)**.

34   Loosen the throttle position sensor (TPS) bolts and move the switch counter-clockwise until the ohmmeter reads 0 ohms (continuity). Tighten the screws to 18 in-lbs.

35   Check that there is no continuity with a 0.35 inch (0.9 mm) feeler gauge between the throttle lever stop screw and throttle lever.

36   If the readings are correct, replace the electrical connector and the air cleaner assembly.

Air valve

Refer to illustration 15.38

37   The air valve permits an additional amount of air to bypass the throttle plate when the engine is cold (when the coolant is less than 140-degrees F). This raises the engine rpm to a fast idle. If the engine doesn't run at a fast idle when it is cold, or if it doesn't idle down when warm, check the operation of the air valve as follows.

38   With the engine cold, remove the air valve cap from the TBI unit. Look inside and confirm that the air valve is open **(see illustration)**.

39   Install the air valve cap and run the engine until it reaches normal operating temperature. Remove the cap once again – the valve should be closed.

40   If the air valve doesn't operate as described, it should be replaced with a new one. When installing the air valve cap, use a new gasket.

Idle speed/air conditioning VSV adjustment

Refer to illustration 15.42 and 15.43

41   With the engine operating at normal temperature, connect a tachometer and switch the air conditioner On.

42   Install the spare fuse into the diagnosis switch terminal **(see illustration)**.

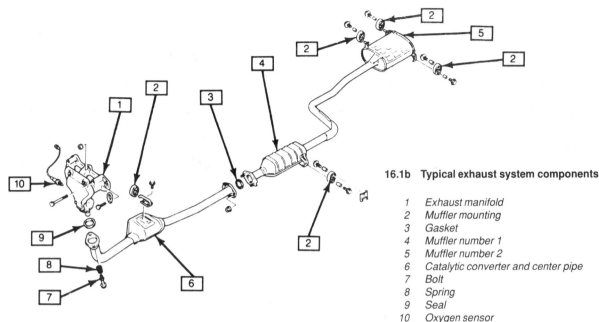

16.1b   Typical exhaust system components

1   Exhaust manifold
2   Muffler mounting
3   Gasket
4   Muffler number 1
5   Muffler number 2
6   Catalytic converter and center pipe
7   Bolt
8   Spring
9   Seal
10 Oxygen sensor

4

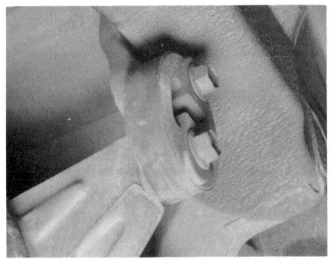

16.1c   Here's a typical exhaust system hanger – they should be inspected for cracks and replaced if deteriorated

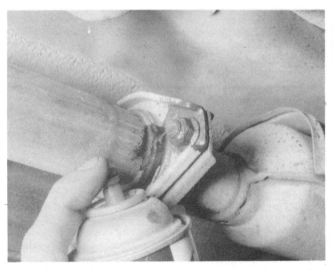

16.1d   Exhaust system bolts and nuts, particularly those on the exhaust manifold and catalytic converters, can be very difficult to loosen – spraying them with a penetrant will free up the threads

43   Check and adjust the idle speed by adjusting the A/C vacuum switch valve (VSV) idle screw to the proper specification **(see illustration)**.
   Automatic transaxle . . . 850 ± 50 rpm
   Manual transaxle . . . 900 ± 50 rpm
44   Remove the spare fuse from the diagnosis switch terminal.
45   Adjust the idle speed to the rpm listed in the Chapter 1 Specifications (refer to idle speed adjustment in Chapter 1).

16   Exhaust system servicing – general information

Refer to illustrations 16.1a, 16.1b, 16.1c and 16.1d
Warning: *Inspection and repair of exhaust system components should be*

done only after enough time has elapsed after driving the vehicle to allow the system components to cool completely. Also, when working under the vehicle, make sure it is securely supported on jackstands.

1   The exhaust system consists of the exhaust manifold, catalytic converter, the muffler, the tailpipe and all connecting pipes, brackets, hangers and clamps **(see illustrations)**. The exhaust system is attached to the body with mounting brackets and rubber hangers. If any of these parts are damaged or deteriorated, excessive noise and vibration will be transmitted to the body.
2   Conduct regular inspections of the exhaust system will keep it safe and quiet. Look for any damaged or bent parts, open seams, holes, loose connections, excessive corrosion or other defects which could allow exhaust fumes to enter the vehicle. Deteriorated exhaust system components should not be repaired – they should be replaced with new parts.

3   If the exhaust system components are extremely corroded or rusted together, they will probably have to be cut from the exhaust system. The convenient way to accomplish this is to have a muffler repair shop remove the corroded sections with a cutting torch. If, however, you want to save money by doing it yourself (and you don't have an oxy/acetylene welding outfit with a cutting torch), simply cut off the old components with a hacksaw. If you have compressed air, special pneumatic cutting chisels can also be used. If you do decide to tackle the job at home, be sure to wear eye protection to protect your eyes from metal chips and work gloves to protect your hands.

4   Here are some simple guidelines to apply when repairing the exhaust system:

a) Work from the back to the front when removing exhaust system components.

b) Apply penetrating oil to the exhaust system component fasteners to make them easier to remove.

c) Use new gaskets, hangers and clamps when installing exhaust system components.

d) Apply anti-seize compound to the threads of all exhaust system fasteners during reassembly.

e) Be sure to allow sufficient clearance between newly installed parts and all points on the underbody to avoid overheating the floor pan and possibly damaging the interior carpet and insulation. Pay particularly close attention to the catalytic converter and its heat shield. **Warning:** *The catalytic converter operates at very high temperatures! Wait until it cools before attempting to remove the converter. Failure to do so could result in serious burns.*

1   General information

The engine electrical systems include all ignition, charging and starting components. Because of their engine-related functions, these components are discussed separately from chassis electrical devices such as the lights, the instruments, etc. (which are included in Chapter 12).

Always observe the following precautions when working on the electrical systems:

a) Be extremely careful when servicing engine electrical components. They are easily damaged if checked, connected or handled improperly.

b) Never leave the ignition switch on for long periods of time with the engine off.

c) Don't disconnect the battery cables while the engine is running.

d) Maintain correct polarity when connecting a battery cable from another vehicle during jump starting.

e) Always disconnect the negative cable first and hook it up last or the battery may be shorted by the tool being used to loosen the cable clamps.

It's also a good idea to review the safety-related information regarding the engine electrical systems located in the Safety first section near the front of this manual before beginning any operation included in this Chapter.

2   Battery – removal and installation

Refer to illustration 2.1

1   **Caution:** *Always disconnect the negative cable first and hook it up last or the battery may be shorted by the tool being used to loosen the cable clamps. Disconnect both cables from the battery terminals* **(see illustration).**

2   Remove the battery hold-down clamp or strap.

3   Lift out the battery. Be careful – it's heavy.

4   While the battery is out, inspect the carrier (tray) for corrosion (see Chapter 1).

5   If you are replacing the battery, make sure that you get one that's identical, with the same dimensions, amperage rating, cold cranking rating, etc.

6   Installation is the reverse of removal.

2.1   To remove the battery, disconnect both cables from the battery terminals (arrows) – negative cable first, then the positive cable – then remove the nuts from the battery hold-down plate and remove the plate

3   Battery – emergency jump starting

Refer to the *Booster battery (jump) starting* procedure at the front of this manual.

4   Battery cables – check and replacement

1   Periodically inspect the entire length of each battery cable for damage, cracked or burned insulation and corrosion. Poor battery cable connections can cause starting problems and decreased engine performance.

2   Check the cable-to-terminal connections at the ends of the cables for cracks, loose wire strands and corrosion. The presence of white, fluffy deposits under the insulation at the cable terminal connection is a sign that the cable is corroded and should be replaced. Check the terminals for distortion, missing mounting bolts and corrosion.

3   When removing the cables, always disconnect the negative cable first and hook it up last or the battery may be shorted by the tool used to loosen the cable clamps. Even if only the positive cable is being replaced, be sure to disconnect the negative cable from the battery first (see Chapter 1 for further information regarding battery cable removal).

4   Disconnect the old cables from the battery, then trace each of them to their opposite ends and detach them from the starter solenoid and ground terminals. Note the routing of each cable to ensure correct installation.

5   If you are replacing either or both of the old cables, take them with you when buying new cables. It is vitally important that you replace the cables with identical parts. Cables have characteristics that make them easy to identify: positive cables are usually red, larger in cross-section and have a larger diameter battery post clamp; ground cables are usually black, smaller in cross-section and have a slightly smaller diameter clamp for the negative post.

6   Clean the threads of the solenoid or ground connection with a wire brush to remove rust and corrosion. Apply a light coat of battery terminal corrosion inhibitor, or petroleum jelly, to the threads to prevent future corrosion.

7   Attach the cable to the solenoid or ground connection and tighten the mounting nut/bolt securely.

8   Before connecting a new cable to the battery, make sure that it reaches the battery post without having to be stretched.

9   Connect the positive cable first, followed by the negative cable.

5   Ignition system – general information and precautions

The ignition system includes the ignition switch, the battery, the module (Chevrolet Sprint) or the igniter (Geo Metro), the coil, the primary (low voltage) and secondary (high voltage) wiring circuits, the distributor and the spark plugs. On all Chevy Sprints and Geo Metro LSi models, the spark advance is controlled by vacuum and centrifugal advance units. On Geo Metro Base and XFi models, the ignition system is controlled by the Electronic Control Module (ECM). Using data provided by information sensors which monitor various engine functions (such as rpm, intake air volume, engine temperature, etc.) the ECM ensures a perfectly timed spark under all conditions.

When working on the ignition system, take the following precautions:

a) Don't keep the ignition switch on for more than 10 seconds if the engine won't start;

b) Always connect a tachometer in accordance with the manufacturer's instructions. Some tachometers may be incompatible with this ignition system. Consult a dealer service department before buying a tachometer for use with this vehicle.

c) Never allow the ignition coil terminals to touch ground. Grounding the coil could result in damage to the module/igniter and/or the ignition coil.

d) Don't disconnect the battery when the engine is running.

e) Make sure that the module/igniter is properly grounded.

Chapter 5   Engine electrical systems

Contents

5

Specifications

Coil

Chevy Sprint
  Primary resistance .... 1.06 to 1.43 ohms
  Secondary resistance .... 10.8 to 16.2 k-ohms
Geo Metro
  Primary resistance .... 1.33 to 1.55 ohms
  Secondary resistance .... 10.7 to 14.5 k-ohms

Distributor

Pole piece/signal rotor air gap .... 0.008 to 0.015 in (0.2 to 0.4 mm)
Pick-up coil/generator assembly resistance
  Vacuum/centrifugal advance distributor .... 130 to 190 ohms
  Electronic spark control distributor .... 140 to 180 ohms

Ignition timing

Chevy Sprint
  Manual transaxle .... 10-degrees BTDC at 700 to 800 rpm
  Automatic transaxle .... 6-degrees BTDC at 800 to 900 rpm
Geo Metro .... Refer to VECI label under hood

6.2   An inexpensive spark tester like this unit is the safest and most convenient way to find out if you've got spark – simply unplug each wire (one at a time to prevent mixing up the leads), plug in the tester, clip it to a good ground, like a valve cover bolt, crank the engine and see if a spark jumps across the gap

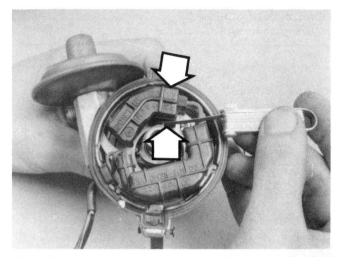

7.2a   To measure the air gap on a vacuum/centrifugal advance distributor, insert a feeler gauge between a tooth of the pole piece (lower arrow) and the pick-up coil (upper arrow)

3   Crank the engine and watch the end of the tester or spark plug wire to see if bright blue, well-defined sparks occur. If you're not using a calibrated tester, have an assistant crank the engine for you. **Warning:** *Keep clear of drivebelts and other moving engine components that could injure you.*
4   If sparks occur, sufficient voltage is reaching the plug to fire it (repeat the check at the remaining plug wires to verify the wires, distributor cap and rotor are OK). However, the plugs themselves may be fouled, so remove them and check them as described in Chapter 1.
5   If no sparks or intermittent sparks occur, remove the distributor cap and check the cap and rotor as described in Chapter 1. If moisture is present, dry out the cap and rotor, then reinstall the cap.
6   If there's still no spark, detach the coil secondary wire from the distributor cap and hook it up to the tester (reattach the plug wire to the spark plug), then repeat the spark check. Again, if you don't have a tester, hold the end of the wire about 1/4-inch from a good ground. If sparks occur now, the distributor cap, rotor or plug wire(s) may be defective.
7   On all models, if no sparks occur, check the wire connections at the coil to make sure they're clean and tight. Check for voltage to the coil. Make any necessary repairs, then repeat the check again.
8   If there's still no spark, the coil-to-cap wire may be bad (check the resistance with an ohmmeter – it should be 7000 ohms per foot or less). If a known good wire doesn't make any difference in the test results, the ignition module may be defective.

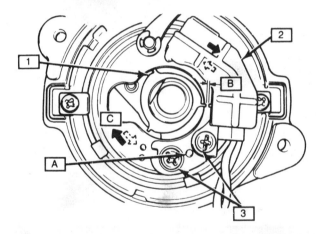

7.2b   To measure the air gap on an electronic spark control distributor, insert a feeler gauge between a ridge of the signal rotor and the pick-up coil

A	Locater pivot	1	Signal rotor
B	Signal rotor air gap	2	Pick-up coil
C	Turn pick-up coil with base plate to adjust air gap	3	Screw with lockwasher and washer

6   Ignition system – check

Refer to illustration 6.2

Warning: *Because of the very high voltage generated by the ignition system, extreme care should be taken when this check is performed.*

1   If the engine turns over but won't start, disconnect the spark plug wire from any spark plug and attach it to a calibrated ignition tester (available at most auto parts stores).
2   Connect the clip of a spark tester to a bolt or metal bracket on the engine **(see illustration)**. If you're unable to obtain a calibrated ignition tester, remove the wire from one of the spark plugs and, using an insulated tool, hold the end of the wire about 1/4-inch from a good ground.

7   Distributor air gap – check and adjustment

Refer to illustrations 7.2a, 7.2b and 7.3

1   Remove the distributor cap and rotor (see Chapter 1).
2   Using a feeler gauge, measure the air gap between a tooth of the pole piece and the pick-up coil on a vacuum/centrifugal advance distributor **(see illustration)**. On an electronic spark control distributor, measure the gap between a ridge of the signal rotor and the generator assembly **(see illustration)**. Compare your measurement to the air gap listed in this Chapter's Specifications. If the air gap is incorrect, adjust it.
3   To adjust the air gap on a vacuum/centrifugal advance distributor, first remove the module/igniter (see Section 11) and loosen the two screws which attach the pick-up coil **(see illustration)**. There is no module or igniter inside the electronic spark control distributor – simply loosen the generator assembly retaining screws **(see illustration 7.2b)** to adjust the gap.
4   Using a screwdriver, move the pick-up coil/generator assembly until the gap is within specification, then retighten the pick-up coil/generator assembly screws and recheck the gap. Install the module/igniter (if equipped), the rotor and the distributor cap.

5

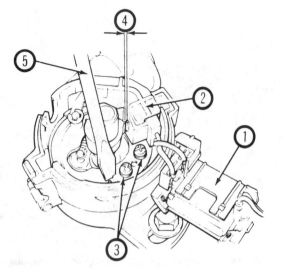

7.3   To adjust the air gap on a vacuum/centrifugal advance distributor, remove the module, loosen the pick-up coil retaining screws, move the pick-up coil assembly until the gap is correct, then retighten the screws

1 Module	*4 Pole piece air gap*
2 Pick-up coil	*5 Screwdriver*
3 Pick-up coil retaining screws	

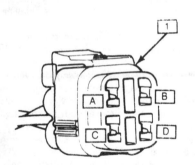

8.10   Diagnostic connector (models with electronic spark control distributor)

A A/F duty check terminal	*D Test switch terminal*
B Diagnosis switch terminal	*1 Diagnostic connector*
C Ground	

8   Ignition timing – check and adjustment

Vacuum/centrifugal advance distributor

Refer to illustration 8.6

1   Make sure the headlights, heater fan, engine cooling fan, rear defogger (if equipped) and air conditioner (if equipped) are off. If one of them is on, the idle up system operates and the engine idle speed will be higher than specified.
2   Start the engine and warm it up to normal operating temperature.
3   Check and, if necessary, adjust the idle speed (see Chapter 1).
4   If the vehicle is a Geo Metro LSi model, detach the vacuum hose at the intake manifold gas filter (it's screwed into the manifold near the timing belt cover). Plug the filter.
5   Hook up a timing light to the number one spark plug wire in accordance with the manufacturer's instructions.
6   With the engine running at the specified idle speed (see Chapter 1),

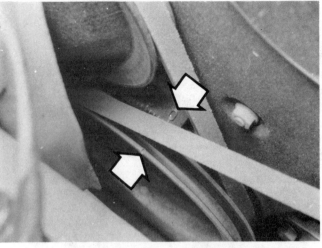

8.6   Typical stationary timing mark (upper arrow) and notch (lower arrow) in pulley

point the timing light at the stationary timing mark. The notch in the pulley should line up with the stationary mark **(see illustration)**. (The number of degrees of timing advance is listed in this Chapter's Specifications for Chevy Sprint models; refer to the VECI label in the engine compartment on Geo models.)
7   If the mark isn't aligned with the notch in the pulley, loosen the distributor hold-down bolts and turn the distributor housing to advance or retard the timing. Turning the distributor clockwise advances the timing; turning it counterclockwise retards the timing. When the timing is set, tighten the hold-down bolts. Recheck your work and repeat the procedure if necessary. Remove the timing light.
8   If the timing can't be adjusted properly, look for a vacuum leak, then check the vacuum advance unit (see Section 13) and the centrifugal advance unit (see Section 14).
9   If the vehicle is a Geo Metro LSi model, reattach the vacuum hose to the fuel filter at the intake manifold.

Electronic spark control distributor

Refer to illustration 8.10

10   Remove the protective cap from the diagnostic connector **(see illustration)**, which is located next to the ignition coil.
11   Insert a jumper wire between terminals C and D of the diagnostic connector.
12   Hook up a timing light to the number one spark plug wire in accordance with the manufacturer's instructions.
13   Start the engine and aim the timing light at the stationary timing mark. The line on the pulley should line up with the timing mark. If it doesn't, loosen the distributor hold-down bolts and rotate the distributor – clockwise to retard, counterclockwise to advance – until the notch in the pulley is aligned with the timing mark. Tighten the hold-down bolts and recheck your work. (The specifications for ignition timing are on the VECI label in the engine compartment.)
14   Turn off the ignition switch, remove the jumper wire from the diagnostic connector and reinstall the protective cap.

9   Ignition coil – check and replacement

Refer to illustrations 9.4, 9.5, 9.6a and 9.6b

1   Locate the ignition coil on the engine compartment firewall.
2   On Geo Metros, remove the ignition coil cap and, using a voltmeter, check for voltage at the coil positive terminal. If there's no battery voltage, check the engine wire harness, the connector for the ignition coil and the underhood fuse/relay center for a blown fuse (see Chapter 12 for information about the fuses in your vehicle).
3   Detach the cable from the negative terminal of the battery.

9.4   Remove the protective cap from the coil

9.5   Disconnect the high tension cable (1), the leads for the positive (2) and negative (3) primary terminals, remove the bolts (4 and 5) from the coil mounting bracket and remove the coil

9.6a   Measure the resistance between the primary terminals and compare your measurement with the resistance listed in this Chapter's Specifications – replace the coil if the indicated resistance is outside specification

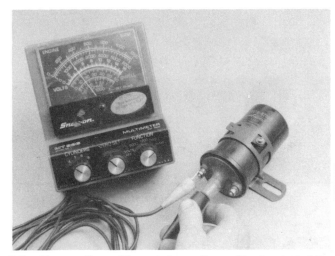

9.6b   Measure the resistance between the positive terminal of the primary side of the coil and the high tension lead, then compare your measurement with the resistance listed in this Chapter's Specifications – replace the coil if the indicated resistance is outside specification

4   Disconnect the coil high tension cable by gripping the boot firmly and turning it turn while pulling on the wire. Remove the protective cap from the coil **(see illustration)**. Disconnect the electrical connectors from the primary terminals of the coil.

5   Remove the coil from the firewall **(see illustration)**.

6   Using an ohmmeter, check the coil:
   a) Measure the resistance between the primary terminals **(see illustration)**. Compare your reading with the coil primary resistance listed in this Chapter's Specifications.
   b) Measure the resistance between the positive terminal and high tension terminal **(see illustration)**. Compare your reading with the coil secondary resistance listed in this Chapter's Specifications.

7   If either of the above tests yield resistance values outside the specified resistance, replace the coil. If the new coil doesn't come with a mounting bracket, loosen the clamp screw and slide the mounting bracket off the old coil and install it on the new one.

10   Distributor – removal and installation

Refer to illustration 10.2, 10.5a and 10.5b

Removal

1   Unplug the primary lead from the coil.
2   Unplug the electrical connector for the module/igniter **(see illustration)**. Follow the wires as they exit the distributor to find the connector.

10.2   Disconnect the electrical connector (arrow) for the module/igniter

10.5a   Put an alignment mark (arrow) directly below the rotor on the distributor base

10.5b   Put another alignment mark (left arrow) on the distributor base and the cylinder head, then remove the hold-down bolt(s) (right arrow) (Chevy Sprint distributor shown, Geo Metro distributor similar, but has two hold-down bolts)

Installation

Refer to illustration 10.8

Note: *If you turned the crankshaft while the distributor was out, position the engine at Top Dead Center (TDC) compression for cylinder number one by following the procedure in Chapter 2 Part A.*

7   Insert the distributor into the cylinder head in exactly the same relationship to the head that it was in when removed.

8   The dogs on the end of the distributor coupling **(see illustration)** are offset. If they won't drop into the slot in the camshaft, you may have to turn the rotor slightly. If that doesn't work, recheck the alignment marks between the distributor base and the head to verify that the distributor is in the same position it was in before removal. Also check the rotor to see if it's aligned with the mark you made on the edge of the distributor base.

9   Loosely install the hold-down bolts.

10   Install the distributor cap.

11   Plug in the module/igniter electrical connector.

12   Reattach the spark plug wires to the plugs (if removed).

13   Connect the cable to the negative terminal of the battery.

14   Check the ignition timing (see Section 8) and tighten the distributor hold-down bolts securely.

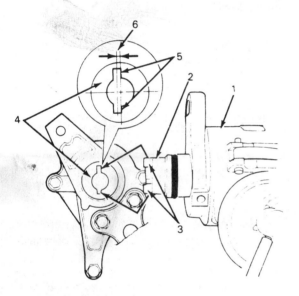

10.8   Installation details of a typical distributor (Chevy Sprint shown, Geo Metro similar)

1	Distributor	4	Camshaft
2	Coupling	5	Slot
3	Dog	6	Offset

3   Look for a raised "1" on the distributor cap. This marks the location for the number one cylinder spark plug wire terminal. If the cap does not have a mark for the number one terminal, locate the number one spark plug and trace the wire back to the terminal on the cap.

4   Remove the distributor cap (see Chapter 1) and turn the engine over until the rotor is pointing toward the number one spark plug terminal (see locating TDC procedure in Chapter 2).

5   Make a mark on the edge of the distributor base directly below the rotor tip and in line with it **(see illustration)**. Also, mark the distributor base and the cylinder head to ensure that the distributor is installed correctly **(see illustration)**.

6   Remove the distributor hold-down bolt(s) (Chevy Sprints have a single hold-down bolt; Geo Metros have two), then pull the distributor straight out to remove it. **Caution:** *DO NOT turn the crankshaft while the distributor is out of the engine, or the alignment marks will be useless.*

11   Module/igniter – check and replacement (vacuum/centrifugal advance distributor)

Refer to illustrations 11.3, 11.4, 11.5a, 11.5b, 11.6, 11.7, 11.9a and 11.9b

Note: *This component is referred to as a "module" on Chevy Sprints and an "igniter" on Geo Metros, but the procedures for checking and replacing it are the same.*

1   Remove the distributor cap and rotor (see Chapter 1).

2   Remove the distributor (see Section 10).

3   Remove the seal **(see illustration)**. If the seal is cracked or torn, discard it and get a new one.

4   Remove the module cover **(see illustration)**.

5   Remove the module screws **(see illustration)** and remove the module **(see illustration)**.

6   The module and the pick-up coil are connected by a pair of wires. One's red and the other's white. Disconnect both of them from the distributor base **(see illustration)** and unplug them from the module. Label each spade terminal on the module so you'll remember which one is for the red wire and which one is for the white wire.

7   Connect an ohmmeter, a test light and a 12-volt battery source to the module as shown **(see illustration)**. Set the ohmmeter to the R x 1 range. Touch the negative probe to the module terminal for the red wire and the positive probe to the terminal for the white wire. **Caution:** *Don't reverse the leads of the ohmmeter or you will damage the module circuitry.*

11.3   Remove the seal from the distributor base – if it's cracked or torn, replace it

11.4   Remove the cover from the module

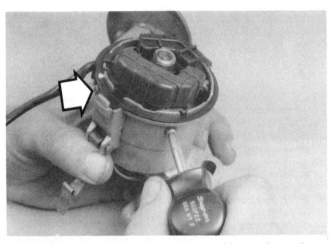

11.5a   Remove the module screws (screwdriver and arrow) . . .

11.5b   . . . and remove the module from the distributor

5

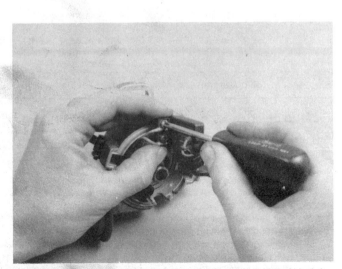

11.6   Detach the wires between the pickup coil and the module (one's red, the other is white) from the distributor base, then disconnect them from the module – be sure to label the terminals on the module so you don't reverse the wires during reassembly

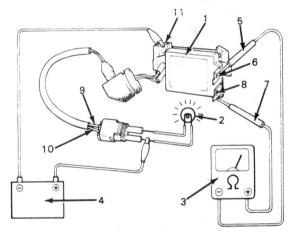

11.7   To check the module, hook it up as shown to the battery and an ohmmeter

1	Module	6	Terminal for red wire
2	Test light or bulb	7	Positive probe
3	Ohmmeter		of ohmmeter
4	Battery (must be 12 volts)	8	Terminal for white wire
5	Negative probe of	9	Brown wire
	ohmmeter	10	Black/white wire
		11	Ground

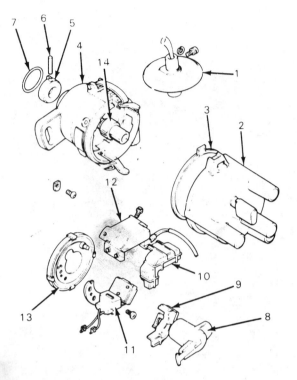

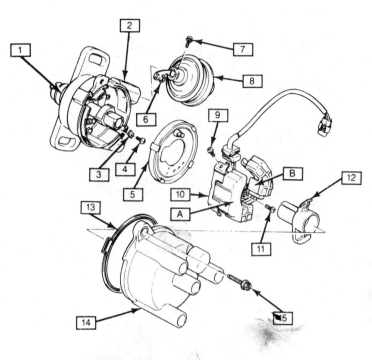

**11.9b Exploded view of a conventional
vacuum/centrifugal advance distributor (Geo Metro)**

A	Igniter	7	Vacuum controller
B	Pick-up coil		mounting screw
1	O-ring	8	Vacuum controller
2	Distributor housing	9	Igniter retaining screw
	and centrifugal advancer	10	Igniter with pick-up coil
3	Base plate washer	11	Pick-up coil screw
4	Screw	12	Rotor
5	Base plate	13	Cap seal
6	C-clip	14	Cap
		15	Cap screw

**11.9a Exploded view of a vacuum/centrifugal advance
distributor (Chevy Sprint)**

1	Vacuum advance unit	8	Rotor
2	Distributor cap	9	Pick-up coil dust cover
3	O-ring	10	Module dust cover
4	Distributor housing	11	Pick-up coil
5	Distributor coupling	12	Module
6	Pin	13	Pick-up coil base plate
7	Seal	14	Pole piece

8   If the bulb in the test light comes on, the module is working properly; if it doesn't come on, the module is faulty. Replace it.
9   Installation is the reverse of removal **(see illustrations)**. Make sure you don't reverse the red and white leads from the pick-up coil.

12   Pick-up coil/generator assembly – check and replacement

Pick-up coil (vacuum/centrifugal advance distributor)

Refer to illustrations 12.4 and 12.5
1   Remove the distributor cap and rotor (see Chapter 1).
2   Remove the distributor (see Section 10).
3   Remove the module, detach the dust cover from the module and disconnect the red and white wires from the module (see Section 11).
4   Remove the pick-up coil mounting screws **(see illustration)** and remove the pick-up coil **(see illustration)**.
5   Hook up an ohmmeter to the red and white wires as shown **(see illustration)** and measure the resistance of the pick-up coil. It should be within the range listed in this Chapter's Specifications. If it isn't, replace the pick-up coil.
6   Installation is the reverse of removal **(see illustration 11.9a or 11.9b)**. Make sure you don't reverse the red and white leads or you may damage the module or pick-up coil.

12.4 Remove the pick-up coil mounting screws (arrows) and detach the pick-up coil (vacuum/centrifugal advance distributor)

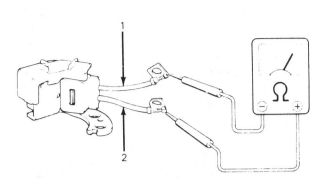

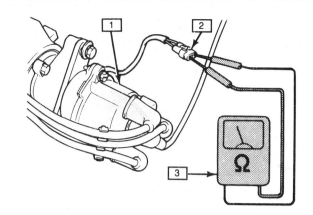

12.5   To check the pick-up coil on a vacuum/centrifugal advance distributor, touch the negative probe of an ohmmeter to the red wire and the positive probe to the white wire

12.7   To check the pick-up coil on an electronic spark control distributor (1), simply unplug the connector (2) for the pick-up coil lead, hook up an ohmmeter (3) as shown and measure the resistance

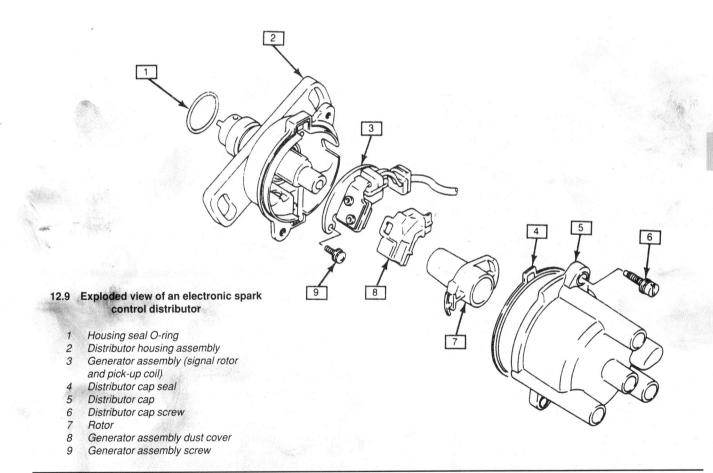

12.9   Exploded view of an electronic spark control distributor

1   Housing seal O-ring
2   Distributor housing assembly
3   Generator assembly (signal rotor and pick-up coil)
4   Distributor cap seal
5   Distributor cap
6   Distributor cap screw
7   Rotor
8   Generator assembly dust cover
9   Generator assembly screw

Generator assembly (electronic spark control distributor)

Refer to illustrations 12.7 and 12.9

7   Unplug the lead to the generator assembly, hook up an ohmmeter as shown **(see illustration)** and measure the resistance. It should be within the range listed in this Chapter's Specifications. If it isn't, replace the generator assembly.

8   To replace the generator assembly, remove the distributor cap, the distributor cap seal and the rotor (see Chapter 1).

9   Remove the dust cover from the generator assembly **(see illustration)**.

10   Remove the retaining screws from the generator assembly and remove the generator assembly.

11   Installation is the reverse of removal. Be sure to check and, if necessary, adjust the air gap (see Section 7) when you're done.

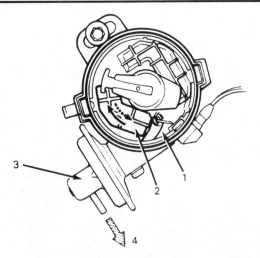

13.2   To test the vacuum advance unit, detach the vacuum
hose, attach a hand-held vacuum tester in its place, apply
about 15 inches (400 mm) Hg of vacuum and release it – the
pick-up coil base plate should return smoothly to its normal
(unadvanced) position – if it doesn't, either the base plate
needs lubrication or the vacuum unit is faulty

1   *Pick-up coil base plate*
2   *Pick-up coil*
3   *Vacuum advance unit*
4   *Vacuum source (hand-operated vacuum pump)*

13.6   Remove the vacuum advance unit retaining screw from the
distributor base

---

13   Vacuum advance unit – check and replacement

Refer to illustrations 13.2, 13.5, 13.6 and 13.7

1   Remove the distributor cap (see Chapter 1).
2   Detach the vacuum hose from the vacuum advance unit and attach a
vacuum tester in its place **(see illustration)**.
3   Apply about 15 inches (400 mm) Hg of vacuum, then release it. The
pick-up coil base plate should move smoothly. If it doesn't, try lubricating it
(see Section 14). If that doesn't work, replace the vacuum advance unit.
4   To replace the vacuum advance unit, remove the distributor (see Section 10), the rotor (see Chapter 1), the module/igniter (see Section 11) and
the pick-up coil (see Section 12).
5   Remove the C-clip that attaches the vacuum advance unit to the base
plate **(see illustration)**.

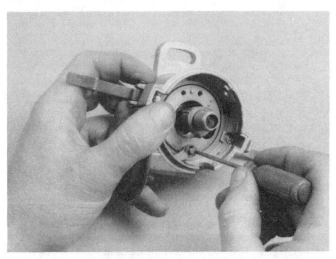

13.5   Pry off this C-clip from the post on the base plate

13.7   Rotate the base plate clockwise to disengage the advance
arm from the post, then remove the advance unit

6   Remove the vacuum advance unit retaining screw **(see illustration)**.
7   Rotate the base plate clockwise to disengage the advance arm from
the post **(see illustration)** and remove the advance unit.
8   Installation is the reverse of removal **(see illustration 11.9a or
11.9b)**. Be sure to check and, if necessary, adjust the air gap (see Section 7) and the ignition timing (see Section 8) when you're done.

---

14   Centrifugal advance – check and replacement

Refer to illustrations 14.4, 14.5 and 14.7

1   Remove the distributor cap (see Chapter 1).
2   Turn the rotor counterclockwise with your fingers, then release it. The
rotor should return (rotate clockwise) smoothly by spring force. If it
doesn't, remove and inspect the base plate.
3   To remove the base plate, remove the distributor (see Section 10),
pull off the rotor, the module/igniter (see Section 11), the pick-up coil (see
Section 12) and the vacuum advance unit (see Section 13).
4   Remove the two base plate screws **(see illustration)** and remove the
base plate. Do NOT attempt to disassemble the base plate.
5   Hold the outer ring of the base plate as shown, grasp the post for the
centrifugal advance arm with your thumb and index finger and turn the inner plate back and forth **(see illustration)**. It should rotate smoothly. If it
doesn't, replace it.

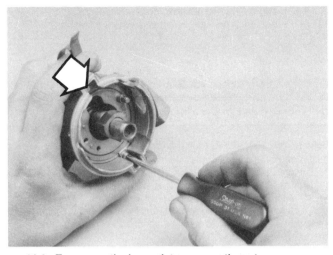

14.4 To remove the base plate, remove these two screws

14.5 To check the base plate, hold it in one hand and slowly turn the inner plate with the other – if the inner plate doesn't rotate smoothly, the bearings or the races are worn – replace the plate (it can't be rebuilt)

6   Inspect the centrifugal advance springs and weights. If they're dirty or corroded, spray them with contact cleaner and lubricate them with light oil.
7   Install the base plate in the distributor housing. Fit the four clips on the base plate into the four grooves in the distributor housing as shown (see illustration).
8   Installation is otherwise the reverse of removal. Be sure to check and, if necessary, adjust the air gap (see Section 7) and the ignition timing (see Section 8) when you're done.
9   If the distributor still fails to advance properly, the centrifugal advance assembly is sticking. This assembly isn't available individually; you'll have to replace the distributor base.

15   Charging system – general information and precautions

The charging system includes the alternator, an internal voltage regulator, a charge indicator, the battery, the fusible link and the wiring between all the components. The charging system supplies electrical power for the ignition system, the lights, the radio, etc. The alternator is driven by a drivebelt at the front of the engine.

The purpose of the voltage regulator is to limit the alternator's voltage to a preset value. This prevents power surges, circuit overloads, etc., during peak voltage output.

The fusible links are fuse-like units mounted on the relay panel in the engine compartment. See Chapter 12 for additional information regarding fusible links.

The charging system doesn't ordinarily require periodic maintenance. However, the drivebelt, battery and wires and connections should be inspected at the intervals outlined in Chapter 1.

The dashboard warning light should come on when the ignition key is turned to Start, then go off immediately. If it remains on, there is a malfunction in the charging system (see Section 16). Some vehicles are also equipped with a voltmeter. If the voltmeter indicates abnormally high or low voltage, check the charging system (see Section 16).

Be very careful when making electrical circuit connections to a vehicle equipped with an alternator and note the following:
a) When reconnecting wires to the alternator from the battery, be sure to note the polarity.
b) Before using arc welding equipment to repair any part of the vehicle, disconnect the wires from the alternator and the battery terminals.
c) Never start the engine with a battery charger connected.
d) Always disconnect both battery leads before using a battery charger.

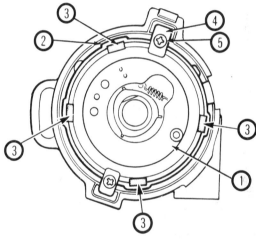

14.7 When you install the base plate, make sure the four clips are seated properly into their respective grooves in the distributor housing

1	Pick-up coil base plate	3	Clips
2	Groove	4	Base plate washer
		5	Base plate screw

e) The alternator is turned by an engine drivebelt which could cause serious injury if your hands, hair or clothes become entangled in it with the engine running.
f) Because the alternator is connected directly to the battery, it could arc or cause a fire if overloaded or shorted out.
g) Wrap a plastic bag over the alternator and secure it with rubberbands before steam cleaning the engine.

16   Charging system – check

1   If a malfunction occurs in the charging circuit, don't automatically assume the alternator is causing the problem.

First check the following items:

a) Check the drivebelt tension and condition (see Chapter 1). Replace it if it's worn or deteriorated.
b) Make sure the alternator mounting and adjustment bolts are tight.
c) Inspect the alternator wiring harness and the electrical connectors at the alternator and voltage regulator. They must be in good condition and tight.
d) Check the fusible link (if equipped) (see Chapter 12).
e) Start the engine and check the alternator for abnormal noises (a shrieking or squealing sound indicates a bad bearing).
f) Check the specific gravity of the battery electrolyte. If it's low, charge the battery (doesn't apply to maintenance free batteries).
g) Make sure the battery is fully charged (one bad cell in a battery can cause overcharging by the alternator).
h) Disconnect the battery cables (negative first, then positive). Inspect the battery posts and the cable clamps for corrosion. Clean them thoroughly if necessary (see Chapter 1). Reconnect the cable to the negative terminal.
i) With the key off, connect a test light between the negative battery post and the disconnected negative cable clamp.
   1) If the test light does not come on, reattach the clamp and proceed to the next Step.
   2) If the test light comes on, there is a short (drain) in the electrical system of the vehicle. The short must be repaired before the charging system can be checked.
   3) Disconnect the alternator wiring harness.
      (a) If the light goes out, the alternator is bad.
      (b) If the light stays on, pull each fuse until the light goes out (this will tell you which component is shorted).

2   Using a voltmeter, check the battery voltage with the engine off. It should be approximately 12-volts.
3   Start the engine and check the battery voltage again. It should now be approximately 14 to 15-volts.
4   Turn on the headlights. The voltage should drop, and then come back up, if the charging system is working properly.
5   If the voltage reading is more than the specified charging voltage, replace the voltage regulator (see Section 18). If the voltage is less, the alternator diode(s), stator or rectifier may be bad or the voltage regulator may be malfunctioning.

17   Alternator – removal and installation

Refer to illustrations 17.2, 17.4 and 17.5

1   Detach the cable from the negative terminal of the battery.
2   Detach the electrical connectors from the alternator **(see illustration)**.
3   Many new and rebuilt alternators DO NOT have a pulley installed, so you may have to switch the pulley from the old unit to the new/rebuilt one if you plan to buy an alternator. Find out the shop's policy regarding pulleys – some shops will perform this service free of charge, some won't. If you're going to have to do it yourself, loosen the pulley bolts now, before you remove the drivebelt.
4   Loosen the alternator adjustment bolt **(see illustration)**.
5   Raise the vehicle and loosen the pivot bolt **(see illustration)**.
6   Detach the drivebelt.
7   Remove the adjustment and pivot bolts and separate the alternator from the engine.
8   Remove the pulley, if necessary.
9   If you're replacing the alternator, take the old one with you when purchasing a replacement unit. Make sure the new/rebuilt unit looks identical to the old alternator. Look at the terminals – they should be the same in number, size and location as the terminals on the old alternator. Finally, look at the identification numbers – they will be stamped into the housing or printed on a tag attached to the housing. Make sure the numbers are the same on both alternators.
10   Install the pulley on the new/rebuilt alternator, if necessary.

11   Installation is otherwise the reverse of removal.
12   After the alternator is installed, adjust the drivebelt tension (see Chapter 1).
13   Check the charging voltage to verify proper operation of the alternator (see Section 16).

18   Voltage regulator and alternator brushes – replacement

Refer to illustrations 18.2, 18.4 and 18.5

1   Remove the alternator (see Section 17).
2   Remove the B terminal insulator nut and bushing **(see illustration)**.
3   Remove the three rear end cover nuts and remove the rear end cover.
4   If you're replacing the voltage regulator, remove the two 4 mm regulator mounting screws **(see illustration)** and the screw between the regulator and the brush holder (this screw attaches the regulator lead to the brush holder). Remove the regulator.
5   If you're replacing the brush holder, remove the three brush holder screws **(see illustration 18.4)** and remove and brush holder **(see illustration)**.
6   Installation is the reverse of removal. Don't forget to reattach the regulator lead to the brush holder.

19   Starting system – general information and precautions

Refer to illustration 19.2

The sole function of the starting system is to turn over the engine quickly enough to allow it to start.

The starting system consists of the battery, the ignition switch, the clutch start switch (manual transaxle) or the neutral start switch (automatic transaxle), the starter solenoid, the starter motor and the wires connecting them. The solenoid is mounted directly on the starter motor.

The solenoid/starter motor assembly is installed on the lower part of the engine, next to the transaxle bellhousing.

When the ignition key is turned to the Start position, the starter solenoid is actuated through the starter control circuit. The starter solenoid then connects the battery to the starter. The battery supplies the electrical energy to the starter motor, which does the actual work of cranking the engine.

The starter motor on a vehicle equipped with a manual transaxle can only be operated when the clutch pedal is depressed; the starter on a vehicle equipped with an automatic transaxle can only be operated when the transaxle selector lever is in Park or Neutral.

Always observe the following precautions when working on the starting system:

a) Excessive cranking of the starter motor can overheat it and cause serious damage. Never operate the starter motor for more than 15 seconds at a time without pausing to allow it to cool for at least two minutes.
b) The starter is connected directly to the battery and could arc or cause a fire if mishandled, overloaded or shorted out.
c) Always detach the cable from the negative terminal of the battery before working on the starting system.

20   Starter motor – testing in vehicle

Note: *Before diagnosing starter problems, make sure the battery is fully charged.*

1   If the starter motor does not turn at all when the switch is operated, make sure that the shift lever is in Neutral or Park (automatic transaxle) or that the clutch pedal is depressed (manual transaxle).
2   Make sure that the battery is charged and that all cables, both at the battery and starter solenoid terminals, are clean and secure.

17.2   Disconnect the wires (arrows) from the alternator

17.4   Remove the adjustment bolt (arrow) from the alternator

17.5   Support the alternator and remove the pivot bolt (arrow)

18.2   To get the back cover off the alternator, loosen the insulator nut   (upper right arrow), back it off far enough to slide the bushing clear of the cover, remove the three cover screws (other three arrows) and remove the cover

5

18.4   To replace the voltage regulator, remove the two mounting screws (two right arrows) and the screw between the brush holder and the regulator (secures the regulator lead to the brush holder) – to replace the brush holder, remove the three mounting screws (upper arrow and two lower arrows) . . .

18.5   . . . and remove the brush holder – when you install the new holder, don't forget to attach the lead for the voltage regulator with the screw between the holder and the regulator

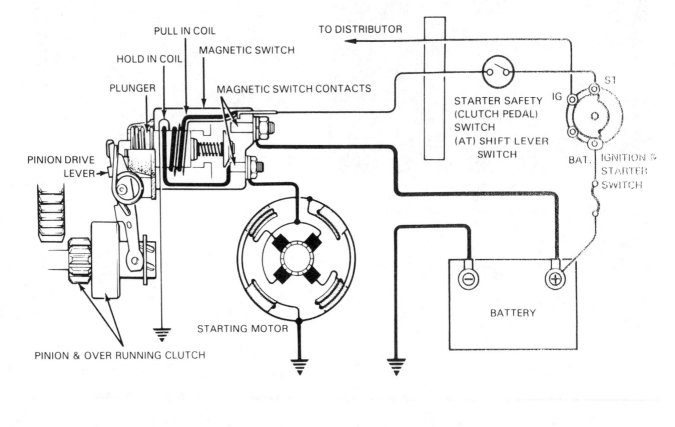

19.2   Typical starter circuit

3   If the starter motor spins but the engine is not cranking, the overrunning clutch in the starter motor is slipping and the starter motor must be replaced.

4   If, when the switch is actuated, the starter motor does not operate at all but the solenoid clicks, then the problem lies with either the battery, the main solenoid contacts or the starter motor itself (or the engine is seized).

5   If the solenoid plunger cannot be heard when the switch is actuated, the battery is bad, the fusible link is burned (the circuit is open) or the solenoid itself is defective.

6   To check the solenoid, connect a jumper lead between the battery (+) and the ignition switch wire terminal (the small terminal) on the solenoid. If the starter motor now operates, the solenoid is OK and the problem is in the ignition switch, neutral start switch or the wiring.

7   If the starter motor still does not operate, remove the starter/solenoid assembly for disassembly, testing and repair.

8   If the starter motor cranks the engine at an abnormally slow speed, first make sure the battery is fully charged and that all terminal connections are tight. If the engine is partially seized or has the wrong viscosity oil in it (in cold weather), it will crank slowly. Also, verify the battery's Cold Cranking Amp (CCA) rating is sufficient for the engine (an auto parts store can usually tell you what the minimum should be).

9   Run the engine until normal operating temperature is reached, then disconnect the coil wire from the distributor cap and ground it on the engine.

10   Connect a voltmeter positive lead to the positive battery post and connect the negative lead to the negative post. A fully charged battery should read about 12.6 volts. If the reading is lower, charge the battery before proceeding.

11   Crank the engine and take the voltmeter readings as soon as a steady figure is indicated. Do not allow the starter motor to turn for more than 15 seconds at a time. A reading of 9 volts or more, with the starter motor turning at normal cranking speed, is normal. If the reading is 9 volts or more but the cranking speed is slow, the solenoid contacts are burned, there is a bad connection or the starter motor is faulty. If the reading is less than 9 volts and the cranking speed is slow, the starter motor is bad or the battery is discharged.

21   Starter motor – removal and installation

Refer to illustrations 21.2, 21.3a and 21.3b

Note: *It's not necessary to raise the vehicle to get at the starter motor, which is located immediately behind the block and under the intake manifold.*

1   Detach the cable from the negative terminal of the battery.

2   Clearly label, then disconnect the wires from the terminals on the starter motor solenoid **(see illustration)**.

3   If you're also planning to replace the solenoid, you'll have to remove the entire starter assembly: Locate the starter drive housing bolts from the transaxle bellhousing (they face toward the driver's side of the vehicle) and remove them **(see illustrations)**.

21.2 Disconnect the wires (arrows) from the starter motor terminals – if you just want to replace the starter, remove the two long bolts (lower left arrows) that attach the starter motor to the drive housing

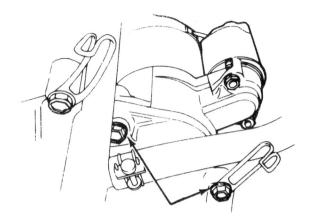

21.3a Starter drive housing mounting bolts (Chevy Sprint)

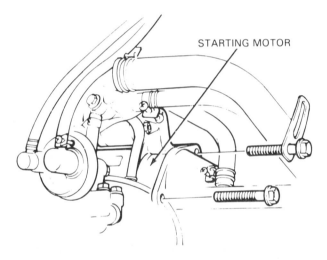

STARTING MOTOR

21.3b Starter drive housing mounting bolts (Geo Metro)

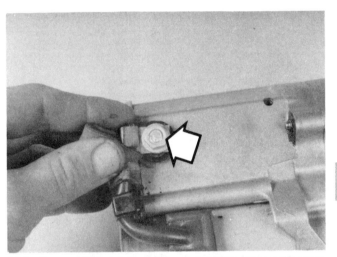

22.3 Remove the retaining nut (arrow) and disconnect the strap between the solenoid and the starter motor (starter assembly for automatic model shown – strap and terminals are located on the ends of the starter and solenoid on models with manual transaxles)

4 If you just want to replace the starter, it's not necessary to remove the entire starter assembly – simply remove the two long bolts that attach the starter motor to the drive housing (**see illustration 21.2**).
5 Installation is the reverse of removal.

22 Starter solenoid – removal and installation

Refer to illustrations 22.3, 22.4 and 22.5

1 Disconnect the cable from the negative terminal of the battery.
2 Remove the starter motor (see Section 21).
3 Remove the retaining nut and disconnect the strap from the solenoid to the starter motor terminal (**see illustration**). **Note:** *On vehicles with an automatic transaxle, the strap is attached between terminals on the sides of the starter motor and solenoid (as shown); on vehicles with a manual transaxle, you'll find the strap between terminals on the ends of the starter and solenoid (not shown).*
4 Remove the through-bolts which secure the solenoid to the starter drive housing (**see illustration**).

22.4 Remove the bolts which secure the solenoid to the starter motor

5   Pull up and out to disengage the plunger hook from the shift lever **(see illustration)** and remove the solenoid.
6   Installation is the reverse of removal. Be sure to grease the plunger hook and install the solenoid with the plunger hook facing up.

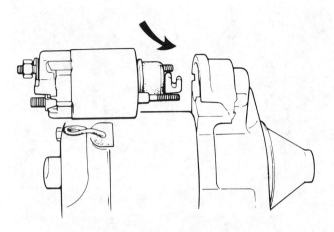

22.5   Pull up and out to disengage the plunger hook from the shift lever and remove the solenoid

Chapter 6   Emissions control systems

Contents

6

---

1   General information

Refer to illustrations 1.1a, 1.1b, 1.1c and 1.6

To minimize pollution of the atmosphere from incompletely burned and evaporating gases and to maintain good driveability and fuel economy, a number of emission control systems are used on these vehicles **(see illustrations)**. They include the:

Positive Crankcase Ventilation (PCV) system, which reduces hydrocarbons from crankcase blowby

Evaporative Emission Control (EVAP) system, which reduces evaporative hydrocarbons

Feedback system (some models), which reduces hydrocarbons and carbon monoxide by regulating the operating conditions of the engine

Exhaust Gas Recirculation (EGR) system, which reduces oxides of nitrogen emissions

Catalytic converter, which reduces hydrocarbons, carbon monoxide and oxides of nitrogen

Electronic Fuel Injection (EFI) system (some models), which reduces all exhaust emissions by regulating the operating conditions of the engine

The sections in this chapter include general descriptions, checking procedures within the scope of the home mechanic and component replacement procedures (when possible) for each of the systems listed above.

Before assuming an emissions control system is malfunctioning, check the fuel and ignition systems carefully (see Chapters 4 and 5). The diagnosis of some emission control devices requires specialized tools, equipment and training. If checking and servicing become too difficult or if a procedure is beyond the scope of your skills, consult your dealer service department.

This doesn't mean, however, that emission control systems are particularly difficult to maintain and repair. You can quickly and easily perform many checks and do most of the regular maintenance at home with common tune-up and hand tools. **Note:** *Because of a federally mandated extended warranty which covers the emission control system components, check with a dealer service department about warranty coverage before working on any emission related systems. Note: The most frequent cause of emissions problems is simply a loose or broken electrical connector or vacuum hose, so always check the electrical connectors and vacuum hoses first.*

Pay close attention to any special precautions outlined in this chapter. It should be noted that the illustrations of the various systems may not exactly match the system installed on your vehicle because of changes made by the manufacturer during production or from year to year.

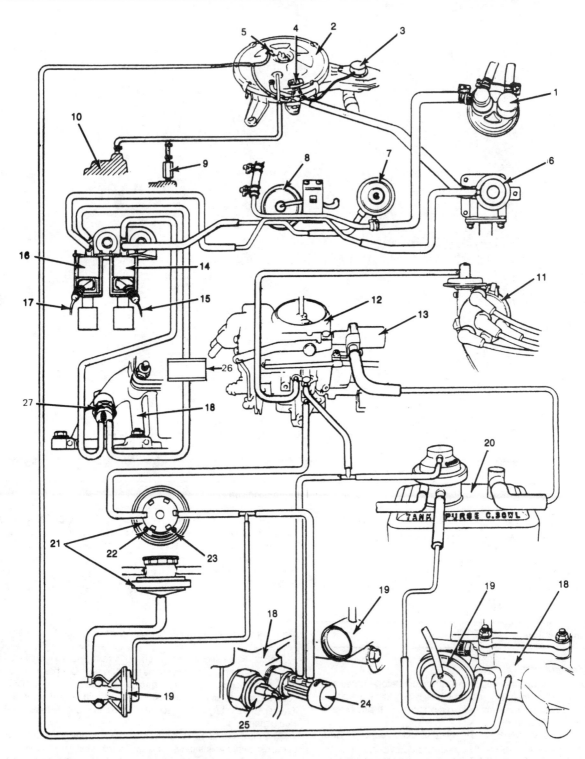

1.1a   Engine emission control systems schematic (1985 and 1986 Sprint models)

1	Fuel pump	10	Cylinder head cover	17	Blue wire	24	Bi-metal vacuum
2	Air cleaner	11	Distributor	18	Intake manifold		switching valve
3	Air control actuator	12	Carburetor	19	EGR valve	25	Thermal switch
4	Thermo sensor	13	Switch vent solenoid	20	Canister	26	VTV (Vacuum Transmitting
5	Hot idle compensator	14	Three way solenoid	21	EGR modulator		Valve) A/T only
6	Second air valve		valve (black)	22	P	27	Fuel filter
7	Idle-up actuator	15	Black wire	23	Q		
8	Secondary diaphragm	16	Three way solenoid				
9	PCV valve		valve (blue)				

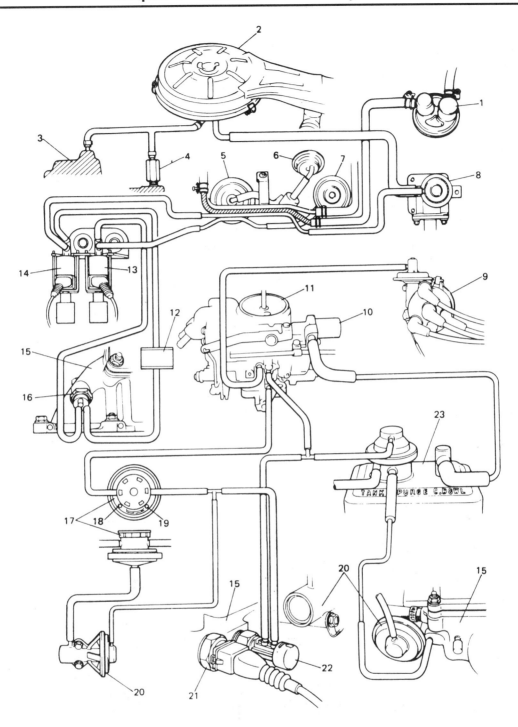

1.1b   Engine emission control system hose routing (1987 and 1988 Sprint models)

1 Fuel pump	10 Bowl vent solenoid	16 Filter
2 Air cleaner	11 Carburetor	17 EGR modulator
3 Cylinder head cover	12 Vacuum transmitting valve	18 "P" mark
4 PCV valve	(A/T only)	19 "Q" mark
5 Secondary diaphragm	13 Three way solenoid valve	20 EGR valve
(carburetor)	(black) for idle-up actuator	21 Coolant temperature sensor
6 Choke opener (carburetor)	14 Three way solenoid valve	22 Bi-metal vacuum switching
7 Idle-up actuator (carburetor)	(blue) for second air valve	valve (BVSV)
8 Second air valve	15 Intake manifold	23 Canister
9 Distributor		

6

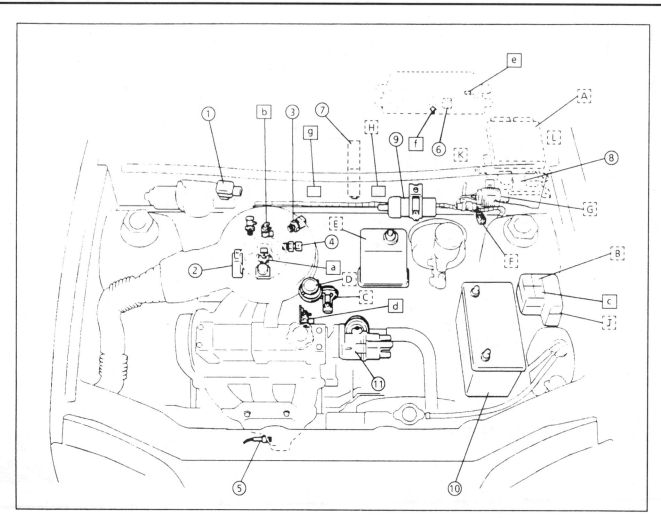

  INFORMATION SENSORS	CONTROLLED DEVICES	NOT ECM CONNECTED
1. MAP	a: Fuel injector	A: ECM
2. TS or TPS	b: ISC solenoid valve	B: Main relay
3. MAT	c: Fuel pump relay	C: EGR modulator*
4. CTS	d: EGR VSV*	D: EGR valve*
5. Oxygen sensor	e: "CHECK ENGINE" light	E: Canister
6. Speed sensor	f: Shift Light (For M/T model)	F: Monitor coupler
7. A/T control module (For A/T model)	g: A/C VSV (If equipped)	G: Injector resistor
8. Passenger compartment fuse block (Diagnosis switch terminal)		H: A/C Amplifier
9. Ignition coil		J: Engine compartment relay/fuse block
10. Battery		K: Electric load diode module (A/T) (91 only)
11. Distributor		L: Electric load diode module (M/T) (91) only

* CALIFORNIA AND XFI ONLY

1.1c   Component locations on a fuel-injected engine (1989 through 1991).

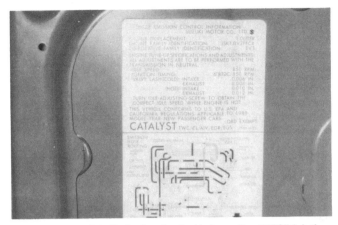

1.6   The Vehicle Emission Control Information (VECI) label contains tune-up specifications and vital information regarding the location of the emission control devices and vacuum hose routing

The Vehicle Emissions Control Information (VECI) label is located in the engine compartment **(see illustration)**. This label contains important emissions specifications and setting procedures, and a vacuum hose schematic with emissions components identified. When servicing the engine or emissions systems, the VECI label in your particular vehicle should always be checked for up-to-date information.

2   Electronic control system – description and precautions

Description

The computerized emission control system (the EFI system on fuel-injected engines and the Feedback system on carbureted engines) controls the fuel injection system or feedback carburetor system by means of a microcomputer known as the Electronic Control Module (ECM).

The ECM receives signals from various sensors which monitor changing engine operating conditions such as intake air volume, intake air temperature, coolant temperature, engine rpm, acceleration/deceleration, exhaust oxygen content, etc. These signals are utilized by the ECM to determine the correct injection duration or the air/fuel mixture in the carburetor or TBI unit.

The system is analogous to the central nervous system in the human body: The sensors (nerve endings) constantly relay signals to the ECM (brain), which processes the data and, if necessary, sends out a command to change the operating parameters of the engine (body).

Here's a specific example of how one portion of this system operates: An oxygen sensor, located in the exhaust manifold, constantly monitors the oxygen content of the exhaust gas. If the percentage of oxygen in the exhaust gas is incorrect, an electrical signal is sent to the ECM. The ECM takes this information, processes it and then sends a command to the fuel injection system or carburetor telling it to change the air/fuel mixture. This happens in a fraction of a second and it goes on continuously when the engine is running. The end result is an air/fuel mixture ratio which is constantly maintained at a predetermined ratio, regardless of driving conditions.

In the event of a sensor malfunction, a backup circuit will take over to provide driveability until the problem is identified and fixed.

Precautions

a) Always disconnect the power by either turning off the ignition switch or disconnecting the battery terminals before removing any wiring connectors related to the computerized engine control system.

b) When installing a battery, be particularly careful to avoid reversing the positive and negative battery cables.

c) Do not subject EFI, emissions related components, carburetor

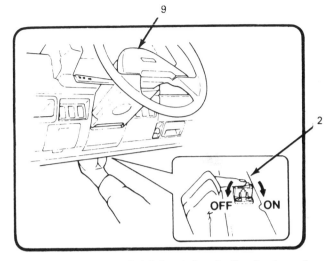

3.3a   The diagnostic switch is located under the steering column on 1987 and 1988 models

components or the ECM to severe impact during removal or installation.

d) Do not be careless during troubleshooting. Even slight terminal contact can invalidate a testing procedure and damage one of the numerous transistor circuits.

e) Never attempt to work on the ECM or open the ECM cover. The ECM is protected by a government mandated extended warranty that will be nullified if you tamper with or damage the ECM.

f) If you are inspecting electronic control system components during rainy weather, make sure that water does not enter any part. When washing the engine compartment, do not spray these parts or their connectors with water.

3   Diagnosis system – general information and obtaining code output

6

Note: *This procedure applies to 1987 and later models only.*

General information

The ECM contains a built-in self-diagnosis system which detects and identifies malfunctions occurring in the network. When the ECM detects a problem, three things happen: the Check Engine light comes on, the trouble is identified and a diagnostic code is recorded and stored. The ECM stores the failure code assigned to the specific problem area until the diagnosis system is cancelled by turning the diagnostic switch Off (1987 and 1988 models) or by removing the tail lamp fuse from the fuse block (1989 and later models).

The Check Engine warning light, which is located on the instrument panel, comes on when the ignition switch is turned to On and the engine is not running. When the engine is started, the warning light should go out. If the light remains on, the diagnosis system has detected a malfunction in the system.

Obtaining diagnosis code output

Refer to illustrations 3.3a and 3.3b

1   To obtain an output of diagnostic codes, verify first that the battery voltage is above 11 volts, the throttle is fully closed, the transaxle is in Neutral, the accessory switches are off and the engine is at normal operating temperature.

2   Turn the ignition switch to OFF. Do not start the engine. **Caution:** *The ignition key must be in the OFF position when disconnecting or reconnecting power to the ECM.*

3   On 1987 and 1988 models, turn the diagnosis switch located under the steering column area **(see illustration)**. On 1989 and later models,

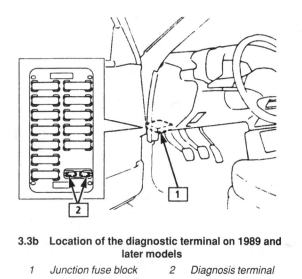

3.3b   Location of the diagnostic terminal on 1989 and later models

1   Junction fuse block   2   Diagnosis terminal

insert the spare fuse into the diagnostic terminal of the fuse block (**see illustration**).

4   Turn the ignition key ON. Read the diagnosis code as indicated by the number of flashes of the "Check Engine" light on the dash (see the accompanying chart). Normal system operation is indicated by Code 12 (no malfunctions) for all models. The "Check Engine" light displays a Code 12 by blinking the corresponding pattern one time only.

5   If there are any malfunctions in the system, their corresponding trouble codes are stored in computer memory and the light will blink the requisite number of times for the indicated trouble codes. If there's more than one trouble code in the memory, they'll be displayed in numerical order (from lowest to highest) with a pause interval between each one. After the code with the largest number flashes has been displayed, there will be another pause and then the sequence will begin all over again.

6   To ensure correct interpretation of the blinking "Check Engine" light, watch carefully for the interval between the end of one code and the beginning of the next (otherwise, you will become confused by the apparent number of blinks and misinterpret the display). The length of this interval varies with the model year.

Cancelling a diagnostic code

7   After the malfunctioning component has been repaired/replaced, the trouble code(s) stored in computer memory must be cancelled. To accomplish this, simply turn the diagnostic switch to OFF (1987 and 1988 models) or remove the tail lamp fuse (1988 and later models) from the fuse block with the ignition switch off. **Note:** *On 1988 and later models, the 30A main fuse will cancel the memory in the radio and the clock when removed. Use only the tail lamp fuse to cancel the codes in the ECM.*

8   Cancellation can also be affected by removing the cable from the battery negative terminal, but other memory systems (such as the clock) will also be cancelled.

9   If the diagnosis code is not cancelled it will be stored by the ECM and appear with any new codes in the event of future trouble.

10   Should it become necessary to work on engine components requiring removal of the battery terminal, first check to see if a diagnostic code has been recorded.

1987 and 1988 Chevrolet Sprint trouble codes		
Trouble codes	**Circuit or system**	**Probable cause**
Code 12 (1 flash, pause, 2 flashes)	Normal	This code will flash whenever the ECM is activated by turning the diagnostic switch ON, turning the ignition key ON and there are no codes stored in the ECM.
Code 13 (1 flash, pause, 3 flashes)	Oxygen sensor circuit (open circuit)	Check the wiring and connectors from the oxygen sensor Replace the oxygen sensor.*
Code 14 (1 flash, pause, 4 flashes)	Coolant temperature sensor (high temperature)	If the engine is experiencing overheating problems the problem must be rectified before continuing. Check all wiring and connectors associated with the coolant temperature sensor. Replace the coolant temperature sensor.*
Code 21 (2 flashes, pause, 1 flash)	Throttle position switches	Check for a faulty WOT or Idle switch. Check all wiring and connections between the switches and the ECM.
Code 23 (2 flashes, pause, 3 flashes)	Intake air temperature sensor	Check the Intake air temperature sensor and the circuit.
Code 32 (3 flashes, pause, 2 flashes)	Ambient pressure sensor	Ambient pressure sensor (located inside the ECM) is faulty
Code 51 (5 flashes, pause, 1 flash)	ECM	ECM faulty
Code 52 (5 flashes, pause, 2 flashes)	Fuel cut solenoid	Fuel cut solenoid or its circuit faulty. Also check ECM
Code 53 (5 flashes, pause, 3 flashes)	Second air solenoid	Second air three–way–solenoid or its circuit is faulty Also check ECM
Code 54 (5 flashes, pause, 4 flashes)	Mixture control solenoid	Mixture control solenoid or its circuit faulty. Also check ECM
Code 55 (5 flashes, pause, 5 flashes)	Bowl vent solenoid	Bowl vent solenoid or its circuit is faulty Also check ECM

1989 and later Geo Metro trouble codes		
Trouble codes	**Circuit or system**	**Probable cause**
Code 12 (1 flash, pause, 2 flashes)	Normal	This code will flash whenever the diagnostic terminal in the fuse block is activated, the ignition switched to ON and there are no other codes stored in the ECM .
Code 13 (1 flash, pause, 3 flashes)	Oxygen sensor circuit (open circuit)	Check the wiring and connectors from the oxygen sensor. Replace the oxygen sensor.*
Code 14 (1 flash, pause, 4 flashes)	Coolant sensor circuit (low temperature)	Check all wiring and connectors associated with the coolant temperature sensor. Replace the coolant temperature sensor.*
Code 15 (1 flash, pause, 5 flashes)	Coolant sensor circuit (high temperature)	If the engine is experiencing overheating problems the problem must be rectified before continuing. Then check the wiring connections at the ECM.
Code 21 (2 flashes, pause, 1 flash)	Throttle switch (Manual transmission only)	Check for a defective idle switch or WOT switch. Check all wiring and connections between the TS and the ECM. Adjust or replace the TS (see Chapter 4).*
Code 21 (2 flashes, pause, 1 flashes)	Throttle position sensor (Automatic transmission only)	Check the TPS adjustment (Chapter 4). Check the ECM connector. Replace the TPS (Chapter 4).*
Code 22 (2 flashes, pause, 2 flashes)	Throttle position sensor (Automatic transmission only)	Check the TPS adjustment (Chapter 4). Check the ECM connector. Replace the TPS (Chapter 4).*
Code 23 (2 flashes, pause, 3 flashes)	Manifold air temperature sensor	Check the MAT sensor, wiring and connectors for an open sensor circuit. Replace the MAT sensor.*
Code 25 (2 flashes, pause, 5 flashes)	Manifold air temperature sensor	Check the MAT sensor, wiring and connectors for an open sensor circuit. Replace the MAT sensor.*
Code 24 (2 flashes, pause, 4 flashes)	Vehicle speed sensor	A fault in this circuit should be indicated only when the vehicle is in motion. Check and repair the speedometer if it is not functioning.
Code 31 (3 flashes, pause, 1 flash)	MAP sensor	Check the circuit for bare wire (stripped insulator) or damaged electrical connectors. Replace the MAP sensor if necessary.
Code 32 (3 flashes, pause, 2 flashes)	MAP sensor	Check the GRN/BLK wire from the MAP sensor connector for an open circuit. Inspect the MAP sensor and the electrical connections
Code 41 (4 flashes, pause, 1 flash)	Ignition signal	Inspect and repair any damaged electrical connectors and wire in the harness. Note: The "Check Engine" light will not come on for this code.
Code 42 (4 flashes, pause, 2 flashes)	Crank angle sensor (Metro w/ ESA ignition only)	Check for a faulty connector or circuit. Also an improper air gap in the distributor (see Chapter 5)
Code 51 (4 flashes, pause, 2 flashes)	EGR system – CA only (Metro w/ ESA ignition only)	Check for a faulty connector or circuit. Also a high resistance in the solenoid coil

6

* Component replacement may not cure the problem in all cases. For this reason, you may want to seek professional advice before purchasing replacement parts.

4   Information sensors

Note: *Most of the components described in this section are protected by a Federally-mandated extended warranty. See your dealer for the details regarding your vehicle. It therefore makes little sense to either check or replace any of these parts yourself as long as they are still under warranty. However, once the warranty has expired, you may wish to perform some of the component checks and/or replacement procedures in this Chapter to save money.*

Carburetor-equipped models

1   See Chapter 4 for information on the carburetor system.

Oxygen sensor (all models)

2   The oxygen sensor is located in the exhaust manifold. It's purpose is to detect the concentration of oxygen in the exhaust gases. On some models, a second oxygen sensor is located in the catalytic converter. This sensor rechecks the emission level after the exhaust gases pass through the converter and feeds the results back to the main oxygen sensor so the air/fuel ratio is maintained as precisely as possible.

3   An open or shorted oxygen circuit will set a code 13.

4   See Chapter 1 for the oxygen sensor replacement procedure.

Coolant temperature sensor (all models)

Refer to illustrations 4.6a and 4.6b

5   The coolant temperature sensor is a thermistor (a resistor which varies the value of its voltage output in accordance with temperature changes). A failure in the coolant sensor or circuit will set a code 14 or 15 (1989 through 1991 Metro only). The coolant temperature sensor is located in the intake manifold near the EGR valve (1987 and 1988 models) or on the side of the TBI unit (1989 and later models).

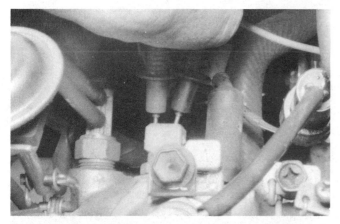

4.6a   Use an ohmmeter to observe the change in resistance of the coolant temperature sensor as the engine is warmed-up

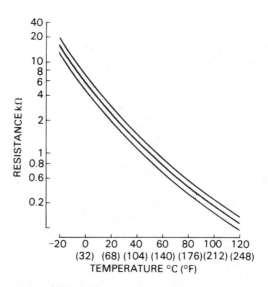

4.6b   Compare the indicated resistance to the resistance values specified on this graph – note as the temperature increases (as the engine warms up), resistance decreases

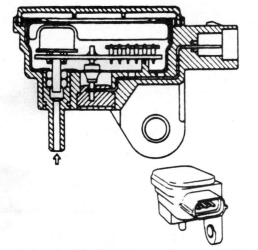

4.9   A typical Manifold Absolute Pressure (MAP) sensor

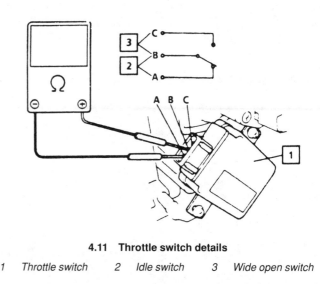

4.11   Throttle switch details

| 1 | Throttle switch | 2 | Idle switch | 3 | Wide open switch |

6   To check the coolant temperature sensor, unplug the electrical connector and use an ohmmeter to measure the resistance between the two terminals **(see illustrations)**.

7   If the indicated resistance is not as specified, replace the sensor. Be sure to use Teflon tape or thread sealant on the threads of the new sensor to prevent leaks.

Fuel-injected models

Manifold Air Temperature (MAT) sensor

8   The manifold air temperature (MAT) sensor, located in the side of the air cleaner housing, is a thermistor which constantly measures the temperature of the air entering the intake manifold. As air temperature varies, the ECM, by monitoring the MAT sensor, adjusts the amount of fuel according to the air temperature. A failure in the MAT sensor or circuit will set a code 24. The diagnosis of the MAT sensor should be left to a dealer service department.

Manifold Absolute Pressure (MAP) sensor

Refer to illustration 4.9

9   The Manifold Absolute Pressure (MAP) sensor **(see illustration)** monitors the intake manifold pressure changes resulting from changes in engine load and speed, then converts the information into a voltage reading. The ECM uses the MAP sensor to control fuel delivery, ISC solenoid valve, shift-up indicator light and the EGR VSV (if equipped).

10   Check for proper vacuum, tight hose connections or damaged electrical connectors. The only service possible is unit replacement if the diagnosis shows that the MAP sensor faulty.

Throttle Switch (TS) (manual transaxle models)

Refer to illustration 4.11

11   The Throttle Switch (TS) is located on the throttle body **(see illustration)**. By monitoring the output voltage from the TS, the ECM can determine fuel delivery based on throttle valve angle (driver demand). The Throttle Switch consists of two contact points; one detects the idle condition while the other detects the wide open throttle condition. A failure in the TS or circuit will set a code 21. If the TS requires diagnosis or replacement, it should be done by a dealer service department (because of the need for special tools and test equipment).

Throttle Position Sensor (TPS) (automatic transaxle models)

Refer to illustration 4.12

12   The Throttle Position sensor (TPS) is located on the throttle body **(see illustration)**. By monitoring the output voltage from the TPS, the ECM can determine fuel delivery based on throttle valve angle (driver demand). A failure in the TPS or circuit will set a code 21 or 22. If the TPS requires diag-

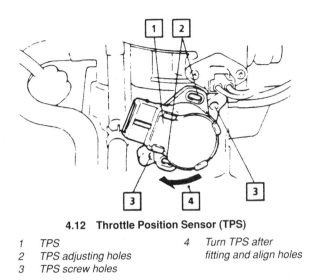

4.12 Throttle Position Sensor (TPS)

1 TPS
2 TPS adjusting holes
3 TPS screw holes
4 Turn TPS after fitting and align holes

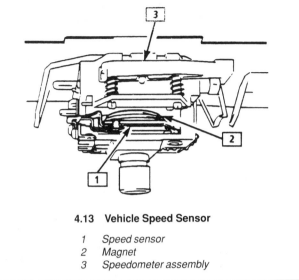

4.13 Vehicle Speed Sensor

1 Speed sensor
2 Magnet
3 Speedometer assembly

nosis or replacement, it should be done by a dealer service department (because of the need for special tools and test equipment).

Vehicle Speed Sensor (VSS)

Refer to illustration 4.13

13 The Vehicle Speed Sensor (VSS) consists of the lead switch and magnet that's built into the speedometer (**see illustration**). As the magnet turns with the speedometer cable, its magnetic force causes the lead switch to turn on and off. This pulsing voltage signal is sent to the ECM which is converted into miles per hour. If a failure occurs, a code 24 will be set. Diagnosis and repair should be left to a dealer service department.

Crank angle sensor

14 The Crank Angle Sensor is located in the distributor and consists of a signal generator and signal rotor. As the signal rotor turns, pulsing AC voltage is generated in the pick-up coil. This pulse signal is sent to the ECM

where it is used to calculate the engine speed and also as one of the signals to control various devices.

---

5 Evaporative Emission Control (EVAP) system

General description

Refer to illustrations 5.2a and 5.2b

1 This system is designed to trap and store fuel that evaporates from the fuel tank, carburetor and intake manifold that would normally enter the atmosphere in the form of hydrocarbon (HC) emissions.

2 The Evaporative Emission Control (EVAP) system consists of a char-coal-filled canister, the lines connecting the canister to the fuel tank and a thermo switch (**see illustrations**).

6

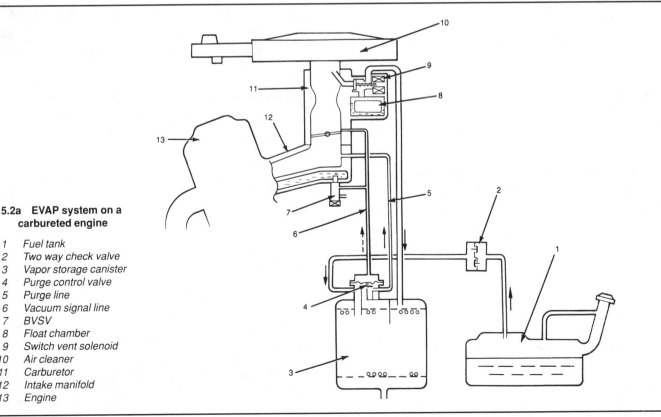

5.2a EVAP system on a carbureted engine

1 Fuel tank
2 Two way check valve
3 Vapor storage canister
4 Purge control valve
5 Purge line
6 Vacuum signal line
7 BVSV
8 Float chamber
9 Switch vent solenoid
10 Air cleaner
11 Carburetor
12 Intake manifold
13 Engine

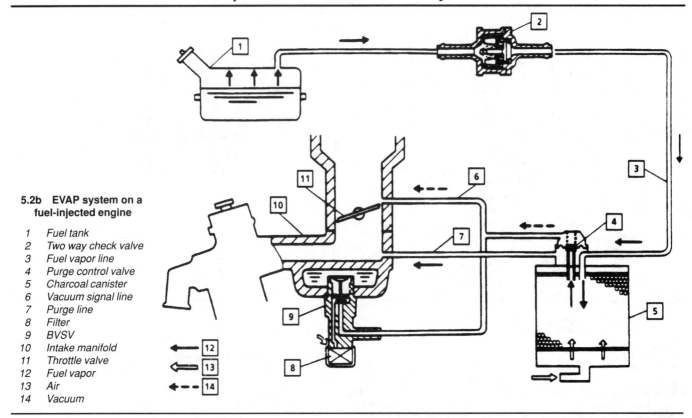

5.2b   EVAP system on a fuel-injected engine

1   Fuel tank
2   Two way check valve
3   Fuel vapor line
4   Purge control valve
5   Charcoal canister
6   Vacuum signal line
7   Purge line
8   Filter
9   BVSV
10   Intake manifold
11   Throttle valve
12   Fuel vapor
13   Air
14   Vacuum

3   Fuel vapors are transferred from the fuel tank and carburetor to a canister where they're stored when the engine isn't running. When the engine is running, the fuel vapors are purged from the canister by intake air flow and consumed in the normal combustion process.

4   A bi-metal thermo switch (BVSV) controls the canister purge. When the coolant temperature is low, the BVSV closes and does not allow ported vacuum to the canister purge control valve. When the coolant has reached operating temperature, the BVSV allows vacuum to the canister purge control valve which in turn allows the vapor from the canister to be sucked through the purge control valve and valve line into the intake manifold to be burned by the engine.

Checking

5   Poor idle, stalling and poor driveability can be caused by an inoperative purge valve, a damaged canister, split or cracked hoses or hoses connected to the wrong fittings. Check the fuel filler cap for a damaged or deformed gasket (see Chapter 1).

6   Evidence of fuel loss or fuel odor can be caused by liquid fuel leaking from fuel lines, a cracked or damaged canister, an inoperative purge valve, disconnected, misrouted, kinked, deteriorated or damaged vapor or control hoses.

7   Inspect each hose attached to the canister for kinks, leaks and cracks along its entire length. Repair or replace as necessary.

8   Inspect the canister. If it's cracked or damaged, replace it.

9   Look for fuel leaking from the bottom of the canister. If fuel is leaking, replace the canister and check the hoses and hose routing.

10   Further testing should be left to a dealer service department.

Charcoal canister replacement

Refer to illustration 5.12

11   Detach the negative cable from the battery.

12   Clearly label, then detach the vacuum hoses from the canister **(see illustration)**.

13   Remove the canister mounting bolts and lift it out of the vehicle.

14   Installation is the reverse of removal.

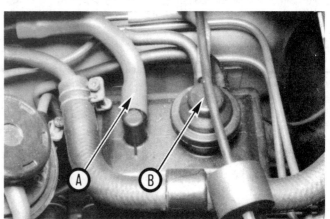

5.12   Charcoal canister mounting details

A   Carburetor vent line   *B   Purge control valve*

---

6   Exhaust Gas Recirculation (EGR) system

General description

Refer to illustrations 6.2 and 6.3

1   To reduce oxides of nitrogen emissions, some of the exhaust gases are recirculated through the EGR valve to the intake manifold to lower combustion temperatures.

2   On carburetor-equipped models, the EGR system **(see illustration)** consists of the EGR valve, EGR vacuum modulator and a bi-metal vacuum switching valve (BVSV). The EGR valve, which is operated by ported vacuum recirculates gases in accordance with engine load (intake air volume). To eliminate recirculation at idle, the vacuum signal is ported above the idle throttle position. During cold engine operation, the thermovalve opens, bleeding off ported vacuum and keeping the EGR valve closed.

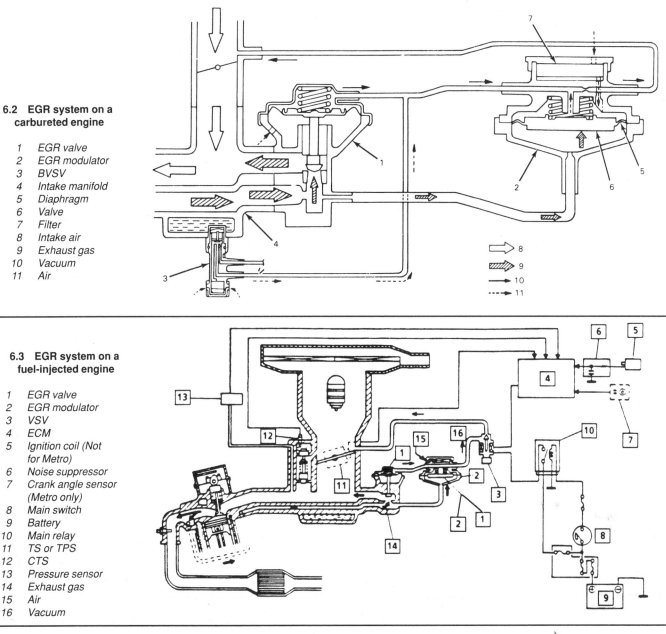

6.2 EGR system on a carbureted engine

1   EGR valve
2   EGR modulator
3   BVSV
4   Intake manifold
5   Diaphragm
6   Valve
7   Filter
8   Intake air
9   Exhaust gas
10 Vacuum
11 Air

6.3 EGR system on a fuel-injected engine

1   EGR valve
2   EGR modulator
3   VSV
4   ECM
5   Ignition coil (Not for Metro)
6   Noise suppressor
7   Crank angle sensor (Metro only)
8   Main switch
9   Battery
10 Main relay
11 TS or TPS
12 CTS
13 Pressure sensor
14 Exhaust gas
15 Air
16 Vacuum

6

When the engine coolant temperature exceeds the set temperature of the BVSV, it closes and ported vacuum is applied to the EGR valve. The EGR vacuum modulator controls the EGR valve by controlling the vacuum signal to the EGR valve with an atmospheric bleed. This bleed is controlled by the amount of exhaust pressure which acts on the bottom of the EGR vacuum modulator.

3   On fuel-injected models, the EGR system **(see illustration)** consists of the EGR valve, the EGR modulator, vacuum switching valve (VSV), the Electronic Control Module (ECM) and various sensors. The ECM memory is programmed to produce the ideal EGR valve lift for each operating condition.

Check

EGR valve
Refer to illustration 6.4

Warning: *The EGR valve becomes very hot during engine operation – wear gloves when checking the valves to avoid burning your fingers.*

4   Check the EGR valve diaphragm by pushing on it slightly with your finger **(see illustration)**. The diaphragm should move and not be frozen in one spot.

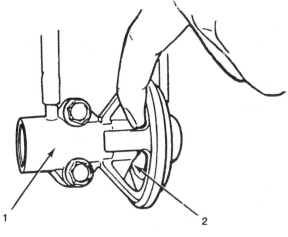

6.4 Gently push the EGR diaphragm with your finger

1   EGR valve   2   Diaphragm

6.7a To remove the EGR vacuum modulator filter for cleaning, remove this cap . . .

6.7b . . . then pull out the filter and blow it out with compressed air

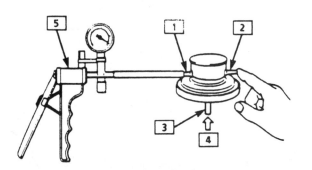

6.9 The EGR modulator should hold vacuum when it is applied to port P, port Q is plugged and the air is blown into port A

1	Port P	3	Port A	5	Vacuum pump
2	Port Q	4	Air		gauge

6.13 Label each vacuum hose before removing them from the EGR modulator

5   Start the engine and allow it to idle. Detach the vacuum hose from the EGR valve and attach a hand vacuum pump in its place.

6   Apply vacuum to the EGR valve. Vacuum should remain steady and the engine should run poorly.

    a) If the vacuum doesn't remain steady and the engine doesn't run poorly, replace the EGR valve and recheck it.

    b) If the vacuum remains steady but the engine doesn't run poorly, re-move the EGR valve and check the valve and the intake manifold for blockage. Clean or replace parts as necessary and recheck.

6.11 The EGR valve is located at the base of the intake manifold (carburetor removed for clarity)

EGR vacuum modulator valve

Refer to illustrations 6.7a, 6.7b and 6.9

7   Remove the valve (see Step 13 below). Pull the cover off and check the filters **(see illustrations)**. Clean them with compressed air, reinstall the cover and the modulator.

8   Plug one of the vacuum ports on the side of the valve and blow into the other port. Air should pass through the valve and come out the filter at the top of the valve.

9   Connect a vacuum pump to the modulator **(see illustration)**, plug the other vacuum port with your finger then blow into the port on the bottom. Operate the pump – the modulator should hold vacuum as long as air is being blown into the bottom port.

10   Any further checking of the EGR systems requires special tools and test equipment. Take the vehicle to a dealer service department for check-ing.

Component replacement

EGR valve

Refer to illustration 6.11

11   Disconnect the threaded fitting that attaches the EGR pipe to the EGR valve, remove the two EGR valve mounting bolts **(see illustration)**, remove the EGR valve from the intake manifold and check it for sticking and heavy carbon deposits. If the valve is sticking or clogged with depos-its, clean or replace it.

12   Installation is the reverse of removal.

EGR vacuum modulator valve

Refer to illustration 6.13

13   Label and disconnect the vacuum hoses **(see illustration)** and re-move the EGR vacuum modulator from its bracket.

14   Installation is the reverse of removal.

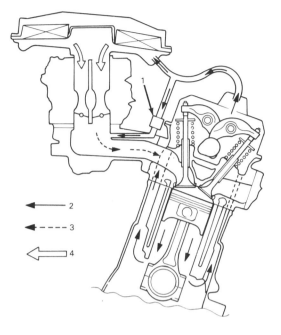

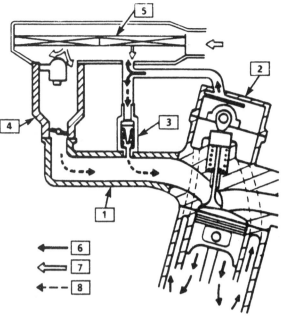

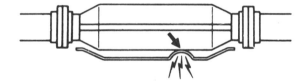

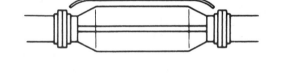

7.1a   PCV system on a carbureted engine

1	PCV valve	3	Mixture
2	Blow-by gas	4	Fresh air

7.1b   PCV system on a fuel-injected engine

1	Intake manifold	4	Throttle body	7	Fresh air
2	Cylinder head cover	5	Air cleaner	8	Blow-by gas and
3	PCV valve	6	Blow-by gas		fresh air mixture

8.3   If the catalytic converter is mounted under the vehicle, periodically inspect the shield for dents and other damage – if a dent is deep enough to touch the surface of the converter, replace the shield

8.4   If the catalytic converter is mounted under the vehicle, periodically inspect the heat insulator to make sure there is adequate clearance between it and the converter

7   Positive Crankcase Ventilation (PCV) system

Refer to illustrations 7.1a and 7.1b

1   To reduce hydrocarbon (HC) emissions, crankcase blow-by gas is routed to the intake manifold for combustion in the cylinders **(see illustrations)**.

2   The main components of the PCV system are the PCV valve, a fresh air filtered inlet and the vacuum hoses connecting these components with the engine.

3   To maintain idle quality, the PCV valve restricts the flow when the intake manifold vacuum is high. If abnormal operating conditions arise, the system is designed to allow excessive amounts of blow-by gases to flow back through the crankcase vent tube into the air cleaner to be consumed by normal combustion.

4   Checking and replacement of the PCV valve is covered in Chapter 1.

8   Catalytic converter

Note: *Because of a federally mandated extended warranty which covers emissions-related components such as the catalytic converter, check with*

a dealer service department before replacing the converter at your own expense.

General description

1   To reduce hydrocarbon, carbon monoxide and oxides of nitrogen emissions, all vehicles are equipped with a three-way catalyst system which oxidizes and reduces these chemicals, converting them into harmless nitrogen, carbon dioxide and water.

Checking

Refer to illustrations 8.3 and 8.4

2   Periodically inspect the catalytic converter-to-exhaust pipe mating flanges and bolts. Make sure that there are no loose bolts and no leaks between the flanges.

3   Look for dents in or damage to the catalytic converter protector **(see illustration)**. If any part of the protector is damaged or dented enough to touch the converter, repair or replace it.

4   Inspect the heat insulator for damage. Make sure that there is adequate clearance between the heat insulator and the catalytic converter **(see illustration)**.

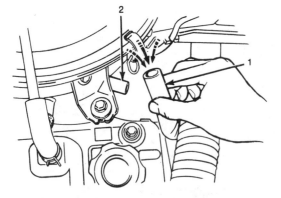

9.2   Remove the second air hose from the air cleaner

1   *Second air hose*
2   *Air cleaner*

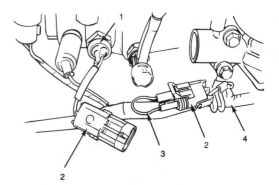

9.6   Use a jumper wire to connect the terminals on the coupler

1   *Thermal switch*   3   *Lead wire*
2   *Coupler disconnected*   4   *Wire harness*

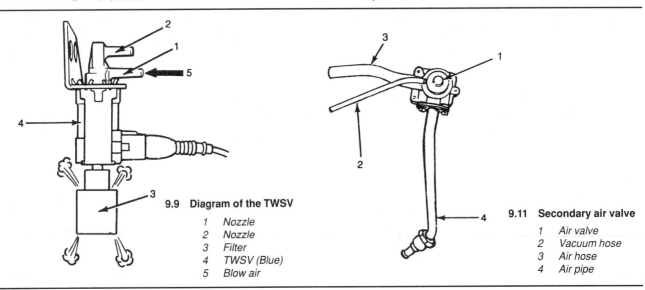

9.9   Diagram of the TWSV

1   *Nozzle*
2   *Nozzle*
3   *Filter*
4   *TWSV (Blue)*
5   *Blow air*

9.11   Secondary air valve

1   *Air valve*
2   *Vacuum hose*
3   *Air hose*
4   *Air pipe*

Replacement

5   To replace the catalytic converter, refer to Chapter 4.

9   Pulse Air Control system

General information

1   Additional oxygen is needed to aid the oxidation of HC and CO in the catalytic converter. The Pulse Air Control system supplies secondary air into the exhaust manifold when the engine coolant temperature is low or during deceleration. The air control valve is a simple reed-type valve that opens when exhaust gas pressure is low. When open, oxygen-rich air is drawn into the exhaust from the air cleaner to aid the converter with the oxidation process. When the exhaust gas pressure is high, the reed valve is closed (because of the high exhaust pressure) and prevents backflow of the exhaust gases. The alternating conditions cause the system to "pulse".

Checking

Non-ECM controlled (1985 and 1986 models only)

Refer to illustrations 9.2, 9.6, 9.9 and 9.11

2   Disconnect the second air hose from the air cleaner when the engine is cold **(see illustration)**.
3   Start the engine and allow it to idle. Air should be drawn into the hose and a bubbling sound should be heard from the inside of the hose.
4   Allow the engine to warm up to operating temperature. There should

be no air drawn into the hose (no bubbling sound heard).
5   Accelerate the engine to 3,000 rpms and release the pedal quickly. Air should be drawn into the hose (bubbling sound is heard).
6   Check the operation of the thermal switch. Disconnect the coupler of the thermal switch and jump the terminals with a wire lead **(see illustration)**. Air should be drawn into the hose during idle (bubbling sound should be heard).
7   If the thermal switch is defective, replace it with a new unit. Reconnect the air hose and the thermal switch connector.
8   Check the operation of the Three Way Solenoid Valve. Disconnect the two vacuum hoses from the TWSV (Blue).
9   Blow air into nozzle no. 1. Air should come out of no. 3 but not out of no. 2 **(see illustration)**.
10   Use an external source of power or connect leads from the battery and apply 12 volts to the TWSV. Blow air into no. 1. Air should come out of no. 2. Replace the valve with a new unit if it is faulty.
11   Check the operation of the Secondary Air Valve (SAV). Remove the SAV with the air pipe **(see illustration)**.
12   While applying vacuum to the diaphragm of the SAV, blow into the air hose. Air should come out of the pipe. Blow air into the pipe. There should not be any air coming out of the hose.
13   If the SAV is faulty, replace it with a new unit.

ECM controlled (1987 and 1988 models only)

Refer to illustrations 9.14

14   Check for cracked hoses, pipes, damaged electrical connectors or any exposed wires in the electrical harness **(see illustration)**. Have the system checked by a dealer service department or other repair shop.

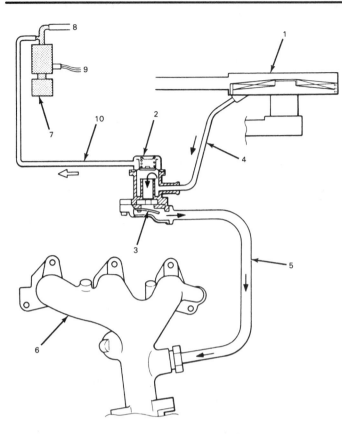

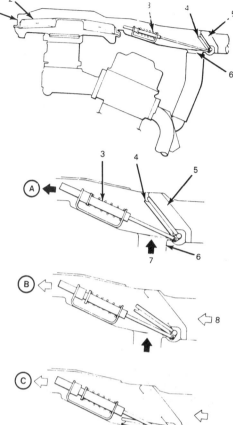

9.14   Diagram of the ECM controlled Pulse air control system

1	Air cleaner	7	Three way solenoid
2	Second air cleaner		valve (Blue)
3	Reed valve	8	To intake manifold
4	Air hose	9	To ECM
5	Air pipe	10	Vacuum hose
6	Exhaust manifold		

Component replacement

Non-ECM controlled (1985 and 1986 models only)

15   To replace the thermal switch, use an open end wrench or a box end wrench to remove the switch **(see illustration 9.6)**.

16   To replace the Three Way Solenoid Valve (TWSV), disconnect the vacuum lines and electrical connector from the valve **(see illustration 9.9)**.

17   Remove the bolts that hold the TWSV to the firewall. Replace it with a new unit.

18   To replace the Secondary Air Valve, use an open end wrench and separate the flanged nut from the exhaust manifold. Spray penetrating lubricant onto the pipe threads. Remove the bracket that holds the air valve to the engine and remove the SAV assembly.

ECM controlled (1987 and 1988 models only)

19   If the Three Way Solenoid Valve (TWSV) is diagnosed as faulty, remove the bolts that retain it to the firewall. Replace the valve with a new unit.

20   Replace any damaged hoses or electrical connectors.

---

10   Intake air temperature control system

Refer to illustrations 10.1a and 10.1b

General description

1   The Intake Air Temperature Control system consists of a thermo wax and damper mounted in the snorkel of the air cleaner **(see illustration)**.

10.1a   Intake air temperature control system

1	Air cleaner	7	Warm air
2	Air cleaner element	8	Cold air
3	Thermo-wax	A	Warm air delivery mode
4	Damper	B	Regulating mode
5	Cold air duct	C	Cold air delivery mode
6	Warm air duct		

6

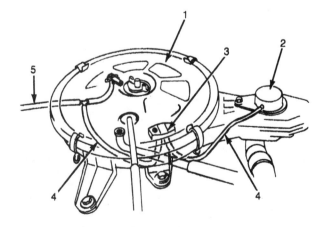

10.1b   Thermostatically Controlled Air Cleaner system

1	Air cleaner	4	Vacuum hose
2	Air control actuator	5	To intake manifold
3	Thermo sensor		

Note: *On early models (1985 and 1986), the system is slightly different and is referred to as the Thermostatically Controlled Air Cleaner (TCAC) system* **(see illustrations)**.

2   This system controls the intake air temperature by mixing the warm air (pre-heated air) and cold air (non-preheated air) to improve fuel vaporization and engine warm-up characteristics.

3   With the engine temperature cold, the thermo-wax contracts and closes the air duct that allows cold air into the air cleaner (cold air duct) and opens the duct that allows warm air from near the exhaust manifold into the air cleaner (warm air duct).

4   As the engine is warmed up, the temperature of the incoming air causes the thermo-wax to expand. Gradually, the cold air duct is opened to allow the cool air to mix with the warm air. The temperature of the intake air is controlled to maximize the efficiency of the air/fuel mixture. An improperly functioning IATC system can result in poor cold or hot driveability and excessive emissions.

Check

Air Control Actuator (ACA) and damper
(1985 and 1986 models only)

Refer to illustration 10.5

5   With the engine off, disconnect the warm air hose from the air intake housing and feel the damper **(see illustration)** – it should be shut (covering the warm air inlet duct).

6   Start the engine. If the air cleaner is cold, the damper should now open up. Allow the engine to warm up to normal operating temperature – the door should begin to close, allowing cool air to pass into the air intake housing.

7   If the damper doesn't move as described above, disconnect the vacuum hose to the ACA and connect a hand-held vacuum pump to it. Apply vacuum and feel for the damper to open – if it doesn't, replace the ACA.

Thermo sensor

8   If the damper valve does open, check the thermo sensor. Disconnect the two hoses from the sensor, which is located on the air cleaner lid **(see illustration 10.5)**.

9   Measure the air temperature around the sensor and write it down. Attach a length of hose to one side of the sensor, cover the other port with your finger and blow into the hose. If the recorded temperature is above 104-degrees F (45-degrees C), air should bleed out of the valve, indicating the valve is open.

10   If the temperature is below 77-degrees F (25-degrees C), no air should come out. If the thermo sensor doesn't work as described, replace it.

Component replacement
Air control actuator (ACA)

11   Pull the warm air duct out of the outlet on the air intake housing. Disconnect the vacuum hose from the ACA.

12   Remove the mounting bolt from the ACA, then pull the ACA out. Lift the ACA to disconnect the rod from the damper door.

13   When installing the ACA, position the rod with the bent end pointing down, push in on the damper door, then engage the rod with the hole in the damper door. A small mirror and flashlight will be helpful when doing this.

14   Install the ACA into the hole.

15   Reconnect the vacuum hose and the warm air duct.

Thermo sensor

16   Unplug the vacuum hoses from the sensor. Remove the top of the air cleaner, along with the air intake case, from the carburetor.

17   Pry the spring clip off the ports on the thermo sensor and remove the sensor from the under side of the air cleaner lid.

18   Installation is the reverse of the removal procedure.

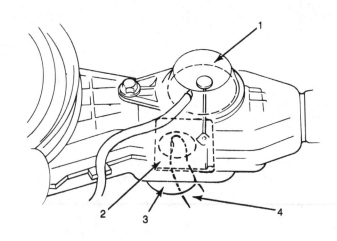

10.5   The damper should be closed with a warm engine condition

1	Air control actuator	3	Warm air duct
2	Damper	4	Finger

Chapter 7 Part A   Manual transaxle

Contents

Specifications

Lubricant type . . . .   See Chapter 1

Torque specifications   **Ft-lbs**
Transaxle-to-engine bolts   37
Shift housing nuts   23

---

1   General information

The vehicles covered by this manual are equipped with either a five-speed manual or a three-speed automatic transaxle. Information on the manual transaxle is in this Part of Chapter 7. Service procedures for the automatic transaxle are in Chapter 7, Part B.

The manual transaxle is a compact, two-piece, lightweight aluminum alloy housing containing both the transmission and differential assemblies. Because of the complexity, unavailability of replacement parts and special tools necessary, internal repair procedures for the manual transaxle are not recommended for the home mechanic. For readers who wish to tackle a transaxle rebuild, exploded views are provided. The bulk of information in this Chapter is devoted to removal and installation procedures.

---

2   Shift lever – adjustment

Refer to illustration 2.2

1   The shift lever is properly adjusted if, when in Neutral, it rests in the center of the shift pattern. If it doesn't, the shift lever position must be adjusted to center it.

2   Loosen the shift assembly housing nuts and guide plate bolts, then move the guide plate forward or back so the shift lever in the middle of the plate is at a right angle **(see illustration)**.

3   Once the shift lever is centered, tighten the guide plate bolts, followed by the housing nuts.

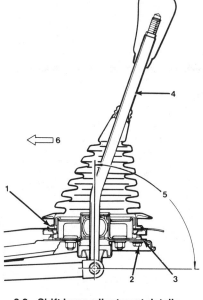

7A

2.2   Shift lever adjustment details

1	*Shift lever housing nut*	4	*Shift lever*
2	*Guide plate bolt*	5	*Right angle*
3	*Guide plate*	6	*Front*

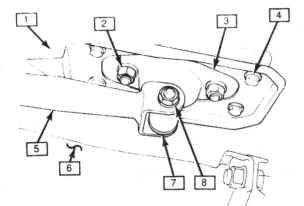

3.3   Shift lever to shift rod and chassis details

1	Shift assembly	5	Shift rod
	extension rod	6	Exhaust pipe
2	Housing nut	7	Shift control lever
3	Guide plate	8	Shift rod nut and bolt
4	Guide plate bolt		

3   Shift lever assembly – removal and installation

Refer to illustration 3.3

1   Remove the shifter boot and center console (Chapter 12).
2   Raise the vehicle and support it securely on jackstands.
3   From under the vehicle, remove the nut and bolt, detach the control rod from the shift lever, then remove the four guide plate bolts **(see illustration)**.
4   From inside the vehicle, remove the two lever cover screws (if equipped).
5   Scribe around the shift lever housing with a marking pen so it can be reinstalled to the same position, remove the four housing nuts, then push the control lever boots in the hole in the floor.
6   Move the control rod out of the way and remove the shift lever assembly by lowering it through the hole in the floor.
7   Installation is the reverse of removal.

4   Manual transaxle – removal and installation

Removal

1   Disconnect the negative cable from the battery.
2   Raise the vehicle and support it securely on jackstands.
3   Drain the transaxle fluid (see Chapter 1).
4   Disconnect the shift and clutch linkage from the transaxle.
5   Remove the starter motor and, on Geo models, the starter plate.
6   Detach the speedometer cable and electrical connectors from the transaxle.
7   Remove the exhaust system components as necessary for clearance.
8   Support the engine. This can be done from above with an engine hoist, or by placing a jack (with a block of wood as an insulator) under the engine oil pan. The engine must remain supported at all times while the transaxle is out of the vehicle!
9   Remove any chassis or suspension components that will interfere with transaxle removal (see Chapter 10).

10   Disconnect the driveaxles from the transaxle (see Chapter 8).
11   Support the transaxle with a jack, then remove the bolts securing the transaxle to the engine.
12   Remove the transaxle mount nuts and bolts.
13   Make a final check that all wires and hoses have been disconnected from the transaxle, then carefully pull the transaxle and jack away from the engine.
14   Once the input shaft is clear, lower the transaxle and remove it from under the vehicle. **Caution:** *Do not depress the clutch pedal while the transaxle is out of the vehicle.*
15   With the transaxle removed, the clutch components are now accessible and can be inspected. In most cases, new clutch components should be routinely installed when the transaxle is removed.

Installation

16   If removed, install the clutch components (see Chapter 8).
17   With the transaxle secured to the jack with a chain, raise it into position behind the engine, then carefully slide it forward, engaging the input shaft with the clutch plate hub splines. Do not use excessive force to install the transaxle – if the input shaft does not slide into place, readjust the angle of the transaxle so it is level and/or turn the input shaft so the splines engage properly with the clutch plate hub.
18   Install the transaxle-to-engine bolts. Tighten the bolts securely.
19   Install the transaxle mount nuts or bolts.
20   Install the chassis and suspension components which were removed. Tighten all nuts and bolts securely.
21   Remove the jacks supporting the transaxle and engine.
22   Install the various items removed previously, referring to Chapter 8 for installation of the driveaxles and Chapter 4 for information regarding the exhaust system components.
23   Make a final check that all wires, hoses, linkages and the speedometer cable have been connected and that the transaxle has been filled with lubricant to the proper level (see Chapter 1).
24   Connect the negative battery cable. Road test the vehicle for proper operation and check for leaks.

5   Manual transaxle overhaul – general information

Refer to illustrations 5.4a and 5.4b

Overhauling a manual transaxle is a difficult job for the do-it-yourselfer. It involves the disassembly and reassembly of many small parts. Numerous clearances must be precisely measured and, if necessary, changed with select fit spacers and snap-rings. As a result, if transaxle problems arise, it can be removed and installed by a competent do-it-yourselfer, but overhaul should be left to a transmission repair shop. Rebuilt transaxles may be available – check with a dealer parts department and auto parts stores. At any rate, the time and money involved in an overhaul is almost sure to exceed the cost of a rebuilt unit.

Nevertheless, it's not impossible for an inexperienced mechanic to rebuild a transaxle if the special tools are available and the job is done in a deliberate step-by-step manner so nothing is overlooked.

The tools necessary for an overhaul include internal and external snap-ring pliers, a bearing puller, a slide hammer, a set of pin punches, a dial indicator and possibly a hydraulic press. In addition, a large, sturdy workbench and a vise or transaxle stand will be required.

During disassembly of the transaxle, make careful notes of how each piece comes off, where it fits in relation to other pieces and what holds it in place. Exploded views are included **(see illustrations)** to show where the parts go – but actually noting how they're installed when you remove the parts will make it much easier to get the transaxle back together.

Before taking the transaxle apart for repair, it will help if you have some idea what area of the transaxle is malfunctioning. Certain problems can be closely tied to specific areas in the transaxle, which can make component examination and replacement easier. Refer to the *Troubleshooting* section at the front of this manual for information regarding possible sources of trouble.

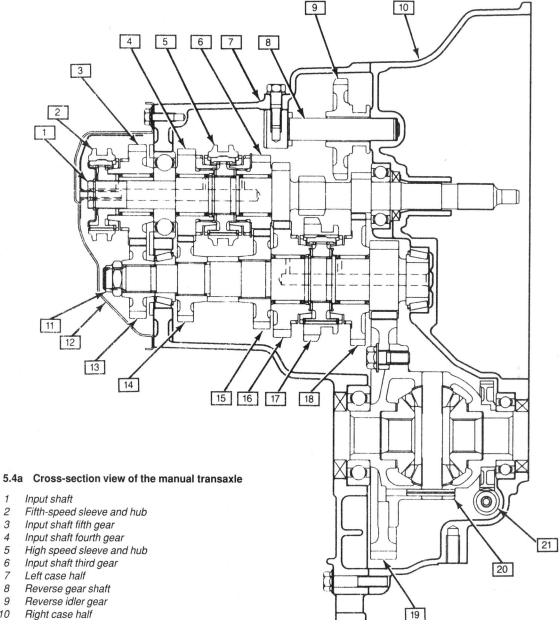

5.4a Cross-section view of the manual transaxle

1   Input shaft
2   Fifth-speed sleeve and hub
3   Input shaft fifth gear
4   Input shaft fourth gear
5   High speed sleeve and hub
6   Input shaft third gear
7   Left case half
8   Reverse gear shaft
9   Reverse idler gear
10   Right case half
11   Countershaft
12   Left cover
13   Countershaft fifth gear
14   Countershaft fourth gear
15   Countershaft third gear
16   Countershaft second gear
17   Low speed sleeve and hub
18   Countershaft first gear
19   Final gear
20   Differential case
21   Speedometer driven gear

7A

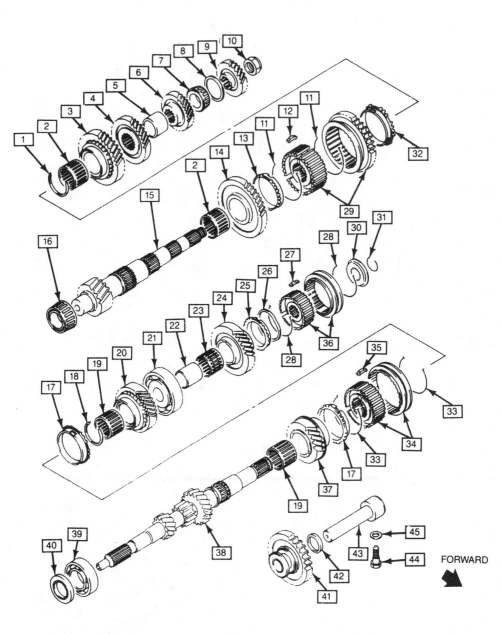

5.4b   Five-speed manual transaxle gearshafts – exploded view

1	Snap-ring	16	Countershaft right hand bearing	31	Snap-ring
2	First and second gear bearing	17	High speed synchronizer ring	32	Second gear synchronizer ring
3	Countershaft second gear	18	Snap-ring	33	High speed synchronizer spring
4	Countershaft third gear	19	Third and fourth gear bearing	34	High speed sleeve and hub
5	Third and fourth gear spacer	20	Input shaft fourth gear	35	High speed synchronizer key
6	Countershaft fourth gear	21	Input shaft left hand bearing	36	Fifth speed sleeve and hub
7	Countershaft left hand bearing	22	Fifth gear spacer	37	Input shaft third gear
8	Bearing set shim	23	Fifth gear bearing	38	Input shaft
9	Countershaft fifth gear	24	Input shaft fifth gear	39	Input shaft right hand bearing
10	Countershaft nut	25	Fifth speed synchronizer ring	40	Oil seal
11	Low speed synchronizer spring	26	Synchronizer ring spring	41	Reverse idler gear
12	Low speed synchronizer key	27	Fifth synchronizer key	42	Reverse shaft washer
13	First gear synchronizer ring	28	Fifth synchronizer spring	43	Reverse gear shaft
14	Countershaft first gear	29	Low speed sleeve and hub	44	Reverse shaft bolt
15	Countershaft	30	Fifth synchronizer hub plate	45	Washer

Chapter 7 Part B Automatic transaxle

Contents

Specifications

General
Fluid type . . . . See Chapter 1
Throttle valve (TV) cable boot-to-inner cable
  stopper clearance . . . . 0 to 0.002 in (0 to 0.05 mm)
Torque converter flange nut-to-transaxle
  face clearance . . . . 27/32 in (21.4 mm)

Torque specifications   **Ft-lbs**
Transaxle-to-engine bolts 40
Torque converter-to-driveplate bolts 14

1   General information

All vehicles covered in this manual come equipped with either a five-speed manual or a three-speed automatic transaxle. All information on the automatic transaxle is included in this Part of Chapter 7. Information for the manual transaxle can be found in Part A of this Chapter.

Due to the complexity of the automatic transaxles covered in this manual and the need for special equipment to perform most service operations, this Chapter contains only general diagnosis, routine maintenance, adjustment and removal and installation procedures.

If the transaxle requires major repair work, it should be left to a dealer service department or an automotive or transmission repair shop. You can, however, remove and install the transaxle yourself and save the expense, even if the repair work is done by a transmission shop.

2   Diagnosis – general

Note: *Automatic transaxle malfunctions may be caused by five general conditions: poor engine performance, improper adjustments, hydraulic malfunctions, mechanical malfunctions or malfunctions in the computer or its signal network. Diagnosis of these problems should always begin with a check of the easily repaired items: fluid level and condition (see Chapter 1), shift linkage adjustment and throttle linkage adjustment. Next, perform a road test to determine if the problem has been corrected or if more diagnosis is necessary. If the problem persists after the preliminary tests and corrections are completed, additional diagnosis should be done by a dealer service department or transmission repair shop. Refer to the Troubleshooting Section at the front of this manual for information on symptoms of transaxle problems.*

Preliminary checks

1   Drive the vehicle to warm the transaxle to normal operating temperature.

2   Check the fluid level as described in Chapter 1:
  a) If the fluid level is unusually low, add enough fluid to bring the level within the designated area of the dipstick, then check for external leaks (see below).
  b) If the fluid level is abnormally high, drain off the excess, then check the drained fluid for contamination by coolant. The presence of engine coolant in the automatic transmission fluid indicates that a failure has occurred in the internal radiator walls that separate the coolant from the transmission fluid (see Chapter 3).
  c) If the fluid is foaming, drain it and refill the transaxle, then check for coolant in the fluid, or a high fluid level.

3   Check the engine idle speed. **Note:** *If the engine is malfunctioning, do not proceed with the preliminary checks until it has been repaired and runs normally.*

4   Check the throttle valve cable for freedom of movement. Adjust it if necessary (see Section 5). **Note:** *The throttle cable may function properly when the engine is shut off and cold, but it may malfunction once the engine is hot. Check it cold and at normal engine operating temperature.*

5   Inspect the shift cable (see Section 3). Make sure that it's properly adjusted and that the linkage operates smoothly.

Fluid leak diagnosis

6   Most fluid leaks are easy to locate visually. Repair usually consists of replacing a seal or gasket. If a leak is difficult to find, the following procedure may help.

7   Identify the fluid. Make sure it's transmission fluid and not engine oil or brake fluid (automatic transmission fluid is a deep red color).

8   Try to pinpoint the source of the leak. Drive the vehicle several miles, then park it over a large sheet of cardboard. After a minute or two, you should be able to locate the leak by determining the source of the fluid dripping onto the cardboard.

9   Make a careful visual inspection of the suspected component and the area immediately around it. Pay particular attention to gasket mating surfaces. A mirror is often helpful for finding leaks in areas that are hard to see.

10   If the leak still cannot be found, clean the suspected area thoroughly with a degreaser or solvent, then dry it.

11   Drive the vehicle for several miles at normal operating temperature and varying speeds. After driving the vehicle, visually inspect the suspected component again.

12   Once the leak has been located, the cause must be determined before it can be properly repaired. If a gasket is replaced but the sealing flange is bent, the new gasket will not stop the leak. The bent flange must be straightened.

13   Before attempting to repair a leak, check to make sure that the following conditions are corrected or they may cause another leak. **Note:** *Some of the following conditions cannot be fixed without highly specialized tools and expertise. Such problems must be referred to a transmission shop or a dealer service department.*

Gasket leaks

14   Check the pan periodically. Make sure the bolts are tight, no bolts are missing, the gasket is in good condition and the pan is flat (dents in the pan may indicate damage to the valve body inside).

15   If the pan gasket is leaking, the fluid level or the fluid pressure may be too high, the vent may be plugged, the pan bolts may be too tight, the pan sealing flange may be warped, the sealing surface of the transaxle housing may be damaged, the gasket may be damaged or the transaxle casting may be cracked or porous. If sealant instead of gasket material has been used to form a seal between the pan and the transaxle housing, it may be the wrong sealant.

Seal leaks

16   If a transaxle seal is leaking, the fluid level or pressure may be too high, the vent may be plugged, the seal bore may be damaged, the seal itself may be damaged or improperly installed, the surface of the shaft protruding through the seal may be damaged or a loose bearing may be causing excessive shaft movement.

17   Make sure the dipstick tube seal is in good condition and the tube is properly seated. Periodically check the area around the speedometer gear or sensor for leakage. If transmission fluid is evident, check the O-ring for damage.

Case leaks

18   If the case itself appears to be leaking, the casting is porous and will have to be repaired or replaced.

19   Make sure the oil cooler hose fittings are tight and in good condition. Fluid comes out vent pipe or fill tube

20   If this condition occurs, the transaxle is overfilled, there is coolant in the fluid, the case is porous, the dipstick is incorrect, the vent is plugged or the drain back holes are plugged.

3   Shift cable – check and adjustment

Refer to illustration 3.3

Check

1   With the engine running and your foot firmly on the brake, place the shift lever in each detent and make sure the transaxle shifts into the corresponding gear as the indicator is moved.

Adjustment

2   Raise the vehicle and support it securely on jackstands.

3   Loosen the cable nut on the manual shift lever at the transaxle **(see illustration)**.

4   Move the transaxle shift lever to the Neutral position.

5   Move the shift lever inside the vehicle to the Neutral position.

6   Turn the adjusting nut until it contacts the shift cable joint, then tighten the cable nut securely.

7   Check the operation of the transaxle in each shift lever position (try to start the engine in each gear – the starter should operate in the Park and Neutral positions only).

the engine is started and won't allow the ignition key to be removed except in Park. The system is operated by the backdrive cable which connects the ignition switch and the shifter and a solenoid. Should it be necessary to shift from Park to another detent position with the key removed, such as when the battery is dead or the key is unavailable, a manual release knob is provided to release the backdrive mechanism.

Adjustment

2   Remove the console (see Chapter 11).
3   With the shift lever in Park, completely loosen nuts 3 and 4 on the backdrive cable **(see illustration)**.
4   Pull the cable casing forward until there is no deflection on the inner cable, hand tighten nut 3 first, then nut 4. Tighten the nuts securely.
5   After adjustment, make sure that when the shift lever is in Park the ignition key can be turned from the Accessory to the Lock position, then removed. When the shift lever is in any other position than Park, it should not be possible to turn the key from Accessory to Lock.

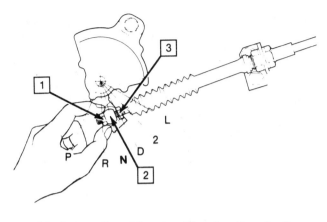

3.3   Loosen the cable nut and then turn the adjusting nut until it contacts the shift cable joint

1	Adjusting nut	3	Cable nut
2	Shift cable joint		

4   Backdrive system – description and adjustment

Refer to illustration 4.3

Description

1   The backdrive system ensures that the shift lever in Park whenever

5   Throttle valve (TV) cable – check and adjustment

Refer to illustration 5.3

1   Warm up the engine to normal operating temperature. Shut off the engine and remove the TV cable cover.
2   Have an assistant hold the accelerator pedal down while you watch the TV cable link in the engine compartment to make sure it opens fully.
3   If the link doesn't open all the way, use a feeler gauge to check the TV cable boot-to-inner cable clearance **(see illustration)**. Compare this clearance measurement to the Specifications at the beginning of this Chapter.

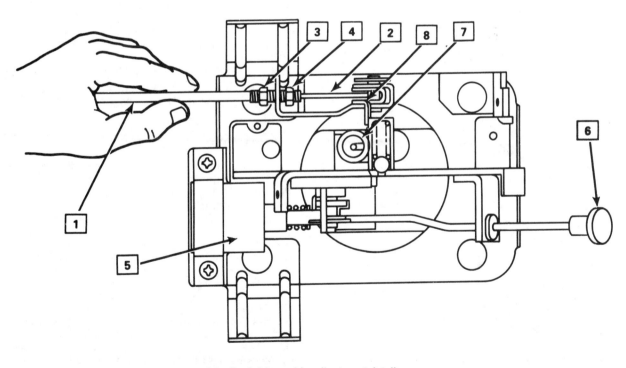

4.3   Backdrive cable adjustment details

1	Backdrive cable casing	4	Nut	7	Shift lever
2	Backdrive cable	5	Solenoid	8	Key release plate
3	Nut	6	Manual release knob		

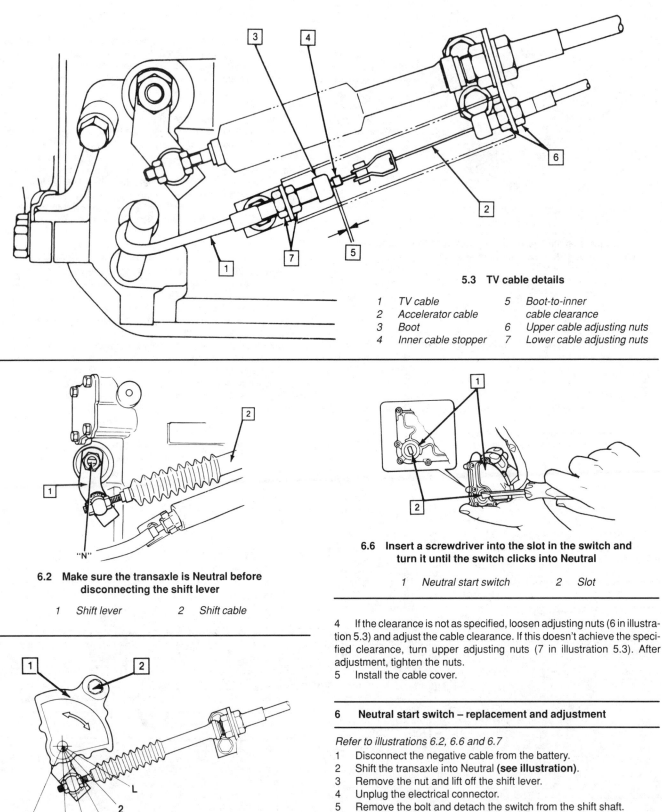

5.3   TV cable details

1	TV cable	5	Boot-to-inner
2	Accelerator cable		cable clearance
3	Boot	6	Upper cable adjusting nuts
4	Inner cable stopper	7	Lower cable adjusting nuts

6.2   Make sure the transaxle is Neutral before disconnecting the shift lever

1	Shift lever	2	Shift cable

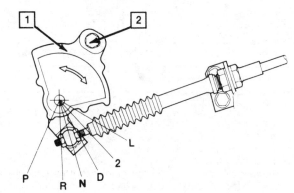

6.7   Rotate the switch until it clicks into Neutral before tightening the bolt

1	Neutral start switch	2	Bolt

6.6   Insert a screwdriver into the slot in the switch and turn it until the switch clicks into Neutral

1	Neutral start switch	2	Slot

4   If the clearance is not as specified, loosen adjusting nuts (6 in illustration 5.3) and adjust the cable clearance. If this doesn't achieve the specified clearance, turn upper adjusting nuts (7 in illustration 5.3). After adjustment, tighten the nuts.
5   Install the cable cover.

6   Neutral start switch – replacement and adjustment

Refer to illustrations 6.2, 6.6 and 6.7
1   Disconnect the negative cable from the battery.
2   Shift the transaxle into Neutral **(see illustration)**.
3   Remove the nut and lift off the shift lever.
4   Unplug the electrical connector.
5   Remove the bolt and detach the switch from the shift shaft.
6   Before installing the switch, insert a screwdriver into the switch slot and turn the screwdriver until you hear a click **(see illustration)**.
7   Push the switch onto the shaft and rotate it until the switch clicks, indicating that it is in Neutral, then install the bolt **(see illustration)**. Tighten the bolt securely.
8   Connect the negative battery cable and verify that the engine will start only in Neutral or Park.

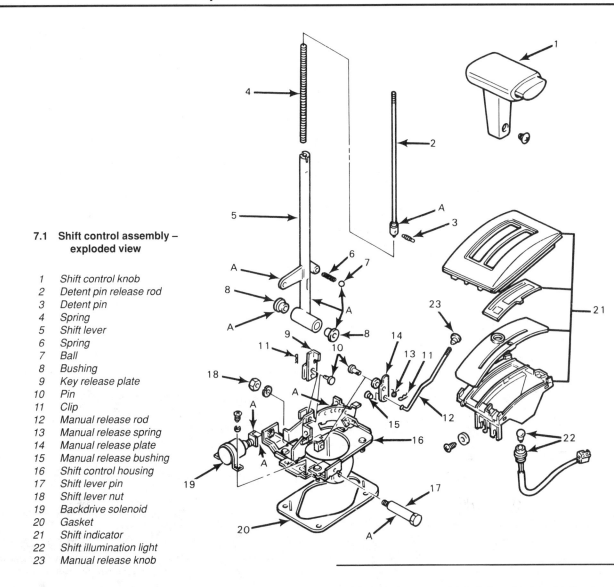

7.1 Shift control assembly – exploded view

1   Shift control knob
2   Detent pin release rod
3   Detent pin
4   Spring
5   Shift lever
6   Spring
7   Ball
8   Bushing
9   Key release plate
10   Pin
11   Clip
12   Manual release rod
13   Manual release spring
14   Manual release plate
15   Manual release bushing
16   Shift control housing
17   Shift lever pin
18   Shift lever nut
19   Backdrive solenoid
20   Gasket
21   Shift indicator
22   Shift illumination light
23   Manual release knob

7   Shift control assembly – removal and installation

Refer to illustration 7.1

1   Remove the shift control knob, the center console, the shift indicator and the housing **(see illustration)**.
2   Remove the cotter pin, pull out the pin and detach the cable from the shift control assembly.
3   Detach the backdrive cable.
4   Unplug the electrical connectors.
5   From under the vehicle, remove the four shift control assembly mounting nuts.
6   Remove the shift control assembly.
7   Installation is the reverse of removal.

8   Shift cable – replacement

Refer to illustrations 8.3 and 8.4

1   Detach the cable from the negative battery terminal.
2   Remove the center console (see Chapter 11).
3   Detach the shift cable from the shift control assembly **(see illustration)**.

4   Loosen the nuts and detach the cable from the floor bracket **(see illustration)**.
5   Raise the vehicle and place it securely on jackstands.
6   Remove the nut and detach the shift cable from the shift lever.
7   Detach the shift cable from the bracket on the transaxle.
8   Detach the shift cable from the cable clips on the crossmember.
9   Remove the cable from under the vehicle.
10   Installation is the reverse of removal. After installation, adjust the cable as described in Section 3.

9   Oil seals – replacement

Refer to illustrations 9.10a and 9.10b

1   Oil leaks frequently occur due to wear of the driveaxle oil seals, and/or the speedometer cable or drive gear O-ring. Replacement of these seals is relatively easy, since the repairs can usually be performed without removing the transaxle from the vehicle.
2   The driveaxle oil seals are located at the sides of the transaxle, where the driveaxles are attached. If leakage at the seal is suspected, raise the vehicle and support it securely on jackstands. If the seal is leaking, lubricant will be found on the sides of the transaxle.
3   Refer to Chapter 8 and remove the driveaxles.
4   Using a screwdriver or pry bar, carefully pry the oil seal out of the transaxle bore.

7B

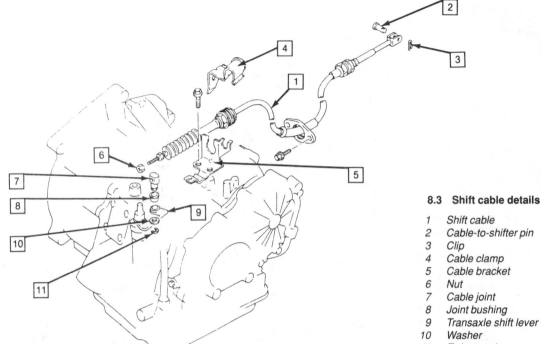

8.3   Shift cable details

1   *Shift cable*
2   *Cable-to-shifter pin*
3   *Clip*
4   *Cable clamp*
5   *Cable bracket*
6   *Nut*
7   *Cable joint*
8   *Joint bushing*
9   *Transaxle shift lever*
10 *Washer*
11 *E-ring retainer*

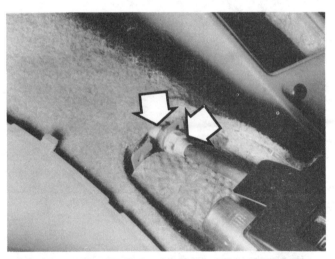

8.4   Loosen the nuts (arrows) and detach the cable from the floor bracket

9.10a   On Sprint models, use a small screwdriver to remove the O-ring from the end of the speedometer cable

5   If the oil seal cannot be removed with a screwdriver or pry bar, a special oil seal removal tool (available at auto parts stores) will be required.
6   Using a large section of pipe or a large deep socket as a drift, install the new oil seal. Drive it into the bore squarely and make sure it's completely seated.
7   Install the driveaxle(s). Be careful not to damage the lip of the new seal.
8   The speedometer cable and driven gear housing or speed sensor connection is located on the transaxle housing. Look for lubricant around the cable housing to determine if the grommet is leaking.
9   Disconnect the speedometer cable from the transaxle. On Sprint models, grasp the speedometer cable securely near the connection to the transaxle and pull out sharply to disconnect it. On Geo models, remove the bolt and separate the driven gear from the transaxle.
10   On Sprint models, remove the bolt in the transaxle, withdraw the cable end, and use a small screwdriver to replace the O-ring. On Geo models, use a hooked tool to remove the O-ring from the driven gear housing, press the new one in evenly and reinstall the speedometer cable assembly **(see illustrations)**.

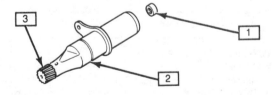

9.10b   Use a hooked piece of wire to remove the grommet from the speedometer gear housing (Metro)

1   *O-ring*   3   *Speedometer gear*
2   *Gear housing*

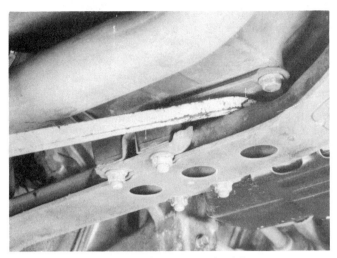

10.1   Pry on the transaxle mount to check for movement

10   Transaxle mounts – check and replacement

Refer to illustration 10.1

1   Insert a large screwdriver or pry bar between each mount and the transaxle and pry up while watching the mount **(see illustration)**.
2   If the rubber separates from the metal plate on the mount, or the case moves up, but not down (mount bottomed out), replace the mount.
3   To replace a mount, support the transaxle with a jack, remove the nuts and bolts and detach the mount. It may be necessary to raise the transaxle slightly to provide enough clearance to remove the mount.
4   Installation is the reverse of removal.

11   Automatic transaxle – removal and installation

Refer to illustrations 11.6 and 11.21

Removal

1   Disconnect the negative cable from the battery. Remove the battery and tray.
2   Raise the vehicle and support it securely on jackstands.
3   Drain the transaxle fluid (see Chapter 1).
4   Remove the torque converter cover.
5   Mark the relationship of the torque converter and driveplate with white paint so they can be installed in the same position.
6   Remove the torque converter-to-driveplate bolts **(see illustration)**. Turn the crankshaft pulley bolt for access to each bolt.
7   Remove the starter motor (see Chapter 5).
8   Disconnect the driveaxles from the transaxle (see Chapter 8).
9   Disconnect the speedometer cable.
10   Disconnect the wire harness from the transaxle.
11   Remove any exhaust components which will interfere with transaxle removal (see Chapter 4).
12   Disconnect the TV cable.
13   Disconnect the shift linkage.
14   Support the engine using a hoist from above or a jack and a block of wood under the oil pan to spread the load.
15   Support the transaxle with a jack – preferably a special jack made for this purpose. Safety chains will help steady the transaxle on the jack.
16   Remove any chassis or suspension components which will interfere with transaxle removal.
17   Remove the bolts securing the transaxle to the engine.
18   Remove the transaxle mount nuts and bolts.
19   Lower the transaxle slightly and disconnect and plug the transaxle cooler lines.

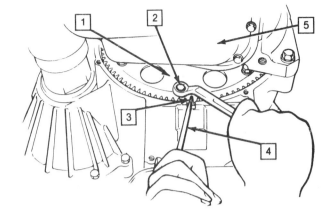

11.6   Lock the driveplate from turning by inserting a screwdriver through the notch in the transaxle case, then remove the torque converter bolts

1	*Driveplate*	*4*	*Screwdriver*
2	*Bolt*	*5*	*Engine oil pan*
3	*Notch*		

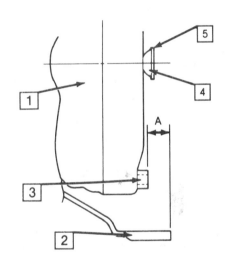

11.21   Torque converter installation details

1	*Torque converter*	*4*	*Cup*
2	*Transaxle case*	*5*	*Lubrication area*
3	*Flange nut*	*A*	*Specified distance*

20   Move the transaxle back to disengage it from the engine block dowel pins and make sure the torque converter is detached from the driveplate. Secure the torque converter to the transaxle so it will not fall out during removal. Lower the transaxle from the vehicle.

Installation

21   Prior to installation, make sure the torque converter hub is securely engaged in the pump. Measure the distance from the face of the torque converter flange nut to the face of the transaxle housing **(see illustration)**. If the measurement is not as specified at the beginning of this Chapter, it isn't seated properly. In necessary, remove the torque converter and reinstall it securely. After installation, lubricate the cup in the center of the torque cover with multi-purpose grease.
22   With the transaxle secured to the jack, raise it into position. Be sure to keep it level so the torque converter does not slide out. Connect the fluid cooler lines.

7B

23   Turn the torque converter to line up the drive studs with the holes in the driveplate. The white paint mark on the torque converter and the stud made in Step 5 must line up.

24   Move the transaxle forward carefully until the dowel pins and the torque converter are engaged.

25   Install the transaxle housing-to-engine bolts. Tighten them to the torque listed in this Chapter's Specifications.

26   Install the torque converter-to-driveplate bolts. Tighten the bolts to the specified torque.

27   Install any suspension and chassis components which were removed. Tighten the bolts and nuts to the torque listed in the Chapter 10 Specifications.

28   Remove the jacks supporting the transaxle and the engine.

29   Install the starter motor (see Chapter 5).

30   Connect the vacuum hose(s) (if equipped).

31   Connect the shift and TV linkage.

32   Plug in the transaxle electrical connectors.

33   Install the torque converter cover.

34   Connect the driveaxles (see Chapter 8).

35   Connect the speedometer cable.

36   Adjust the shift cable (see Section 3).

37   Install any exhaust system components that were removed or disconnected.

38   Lower the vehicle.

39   Fill the transaxle (see Chapter 1), run the vehicle and check for fluid leaks.

Chapter 8 Clutch and driveaxles

Contents

8

Specifications

Clutch release arm freeplay . . . . 5/64 to 11/64 in (2 to 4 mm)

Torque specifications

Ft-lbs

Driveaxle-to-hub nut . . . . 108.5 to 195.0
Pressure plate-to-flywheel bolts 17

1 General information

The information in this Chapter deals with the components from the rear of the engine to the front wheels, except for the transaxle, which is dealt with in the previous Chapter. For the purposes of this Chapter, these components are grouped into two categories – clutch and driveaxles. Separate Sections within this Chapter offer general descriptions and checking procedures for both groups.

Since nearly all the procedures covered in this Chapter involve working under the vehicle, make sure it's securely supported on sturdy jackstands or a hoist where the vehicle can be easily raised and lowered.

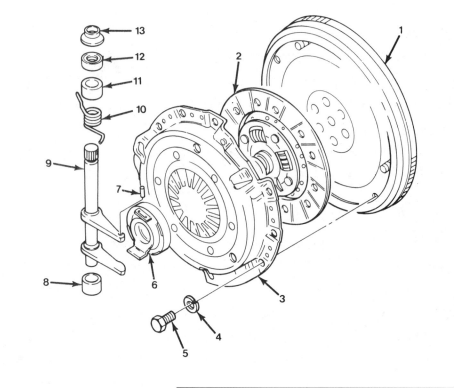

2.1   An exploded view of the clutch assembly

1   *Flywheel*
2   *Clutch disc*
3   *Clutch cover*
4   *Lockwasher*
5   *Bolt*
6   *Release bearing*
7   *Release fork pin*
8   *No. 2 bushing*
9   *Release shaft*
10   *Return spring*
11   *No. 1 bushing*
12   *Shaft seal*
13   *Shaft cover*

2   Clutch – description and check

Refer to illustration 2.1

1   All vehicles with a manual transaxle use a single dry plate, diaphragm spring type clutch **(see illustration)**. The clutch disc has a splined hub which allows it to slide along the splines of the transaxle input shaft. The clutch and pressure plate are held in contact by spring pressure exerted by the diaphragm in the pressure plate.

2   The clutch release system is cable-operated. It includes the clutch pedal with adjuster mechanism, a clutch cable which actuates the clutch release lever and the release bearing.

3   When pressure is applied to the clutch pedal to release the clutch, mechanical pressure is exerted against the outer end of the clutch release lever. As the lever pivots, the shaft fingers push against the release bearing. The bearing pushes against the fingers of the diaphragm spring of the pressure plate assembly, which in turn releases the clutch plate.

4   Terminology can be a problem when discussing the clutch components because common names are in some cases different from those used by the manufacturer. For example, the driven plate is also called the clutch plate or disc and the clutch release bearing is sometimes called a throwout bearing.

5   Other than replacement of components with obvious damage, some preliminary checks should be performed to diagnose clutch problems.

   a) To check "clutch spin down time," run the engine at normal idle speed with the transaxle in Neutral (clutch pedal up – engaged). Disengage the clutch (pedal down), wait several seconds and shift the transaxle into Reverse. No grinding noise should be heard. A grinding noise would most likely indicate a problem in the pressure plate or the clutch disc.

   b) To verify full clutch release, run the engine (with the parking brake applied to prevent movement) and hold the clutch pedal approximately 1/2-inch from the floor. Shift the transaxle between 1st gear and Reverse several times. If the shift is hard or the transaxle grinds, component failure is indicated.

   c) Visually inspect the pivot bushing at the top of the clutch pedal to make sure there is no binding or excessive play.

   d) A clutch pedal that's difficult to operate is most likely caused by a faulty clutch cable. Check the cable where it enters the housing for frayed wires, rust and other signs of corrosion. If it looks good, lubricate the cable with penetrating oil. If pedal operation improves, the cable is worn out. Replace it.

3   Clutch cable – removal, installation and adjustment

Removal and installation

Refer to illustration 3.2

1   Detach the cable from the negative battery terminal.

2   Remove the clutch cable retaining nut from the release arm **(see illustration)** and disconnect the cable from the release arm.

3   Remove the retaining bolts from the clutch cable bracket and detach the bracket from the cable.

4   Remove the retaining pin from the upper end of the clutch pedal and detach the cable clevis from the pedal.

5   Pull the cable through the firewall and remove it from the vehicle.

6   Inspect the cable for frayed areas, kinks, worn ends, excessive friction and broken boots. If there are any signs of damage or wear, replace the cable.

7   Grease the clevis and pin of the clutch cable and attach the cable to the clutch pedal. Installation is otherwise the reverse of removal. Adjust the cable when you're done.

Adjustment

Refer to illustrations 3.8 and 3.9

8   Loosen the locknut on the clutch pedal stop bolt **(see illustration)**. Turn the stop bolt until the clutch pedal is the same height as the brake pedal. Tighten the locknut.

9   Measure the freeplay at the clutch release arm **(see illustration)**. Compare your measurement to the freeplay listed in this Chapter's Specifications. If the freeplay at the release arm is out of specification, loosen or tighten the clutch cable joint nut **(see illustration 3.2)** to bring it within spec.

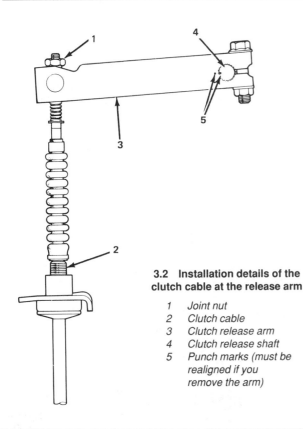

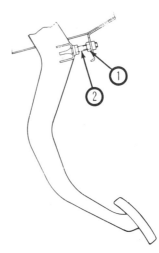

3.2   Installation details of the clutch cable at the release arm

1   Joint nut
2   Clutch cable
3   Clutch release arm
4   Clutch release shaft
5   Punch marks (must be realigned if you remove the arm)

3.8   To adjust the clutch pedal height, loosen the lock nut (1) and turn the stop bolt (2) until the pedal is parallel with the brake pedal, then tighten the locknut

---

4   Clutch components – removal, inspection and installation

Warning: *Dust produced by clutch wear and deposited on clutch components may contain asbestos, which is hazardous to your health. DO NOT blow it out with compressed air and DO NOT inhale it. DO NOT use gasoline or petroleum-based solvents to remove the dust. Brake system cleaner should be used to flush the dust into a drain pan. After the clutch components are wiped clean with a rag, dispose of the contaminated rags and cleaner in a covered, marked container.*

Removal

Refer to illustration 4.5

1   Access to the clutch components is normally accomplished by removing the transaxle, leaving the engine in the vehicle. If, of course, the engine is being removed for major overhaul, then check the clutch for wear and replace worn components as necessary. However, the relatively low cost of the clutch components compared to the time and trouble spent gaining access to them warrants their replacement anytime the engine or transaxle is removed, unless they are new or in near perfect condition. The following procedures are based on the assumption the engine will stay in place.

2   Referring to Chapter 7 Part A, remove the transaxle from the vehicle. Support the engine while the transaxle is out. Preferably, an engine hoist should be used to support it from above. However, if a jack is used underneath the engine, make sure a piece of wood is positioned between the jack and oil pan to spread the load. **Caution:** *The pickup for the oil pump is very close to the bottom of the oil pan. If the pan is bent or distorted in any way, engine oil starvation could occur.*

3   The release fork, shaft and bearing can remain attached to the transaxle housing for the time being.

4   To support the clutch disc during removal, install a clutch alignment tool through the clutch disc hub.

5   Carefully inspect the flywheel and pressure plate for indexing marks. The marks are usually an X, an O or a white letter. If you can't find a mark, scribe your own so the pressure plate and the flywheel will be in the same alignment during installation (**see illustration**).

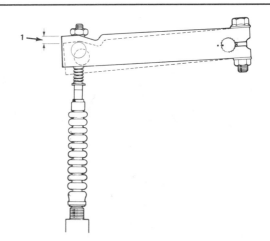

3.9   To measure the clutch release arm freeplay (1), place a six-inch steel ruler next to the end of the arm and move the arm up and down – measure the distance between the top and bottom of its travel and compare this measurement with the freeplay listed in this Chapter's Specifications

8

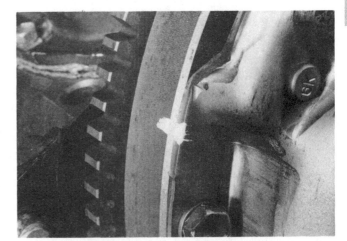

4.5   If you intend to reuse the same pressure plate, be sure to mark the pressure plate-to-flywheel relationship

4.10   Inspect the clutch disc for excessive wear and damage such as distorted lining material, chewed-up rivets, worn hub splines and distorted damper cushions or springs

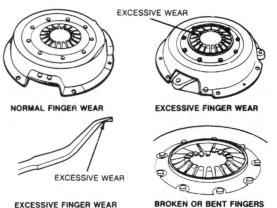

EXCESSIVE WEAR

NORMAL FINGER WEAR   EXCESSIVE FINGER WEAR

EXCESSIVE WEAR

EXCESSIVE FINGER WEAR   BROKEN OR BENT FINGERS

4.12a   Replace the pressure plate if any of these conditions are noted

4.12b   Inspect the pressure plate friction surface for score marks, cracks and evidence of overheating (blue spots)

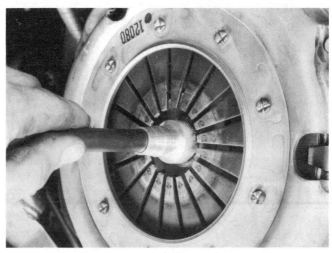

4.14   Center the clutch disc in the pressure plate with a clutch alignment tool

6   Turning each bolt 1/4-turn at a time, loosen the pressure plate-to-fly-wheel bolts. Work in a criss-cross pattern until all spring pressure is re-lieved. Then hold the pressure plate securely and completely remove the bolts, followed by the pressure plate and clutch disc.

Inspection

Refer to illustrations 4.10, 4.12a and 4.12b

7   Ordinarily, when a problem occurs in the clutch, it can be attributed to wear of the clutch driven plate assembly (clutch disc). However, all com-ponents should be inspected at this time.

8   Inspect the flywheel for cracks, heat checking, grooves and other ob-vious defects. If the imperfections are slight, a machine shop can machine the surface flat and smooth, which is highly recommended regardless of the surface appearance. Refer to Chapter 2 for the flywheel removal and installation procedure.

9   Inspect the pilot bearing (see Section 6).

10   Inspect the lining on the clutch disc. There should be at least 1/16-inch of lining above the rivet heads. Check for loose rivets, distortion, cracks, broken springs and other obvious damage **(see illustration)**. As men-tioned above, ordinarily the clutch disc is routinely replaced, so if in doubt about the condition, replace it with a new one.

11   The release bearing should also be replaced along with the clutch disc (see Section 5).

12   Check the machined surfaces and the diaphragm spring fingers of the pressure plate **(see illustrations)**. If the surface is grooved or otherwise damaged, replace the pressure plate. Also check for obvious damage, distortion, cracking, etc. Light glazing can be removed with medium grit emery cloth. If a new pressure plate is required, new and factory-rebuilt units are available.

Installation

Refer to illustration 4.14

13   Before installation, clean the flywheel and pressure plate machined surfaces with lacquer thinner or acetone. It's important that no oil or grease is on these surfaces or the lining of the clutch disc. Handle the parts only with clean hands.

14   Position the clutch disc and pressure plate against the flywheel with the clutch held in place with an alignment tool **(see illustration)**. Make sure it's installed properly (most replacement clutch plates will be marked "flywheel side" or something similar – if not marked, install the clutch disc with the damper springs toward the transaxle).

15   Tighten the pressure plate-to-flywheel bolts only finger tight, working around the pressure plate.

16   Center the clutch disc by ensuring the alignment tool extends through the splined hub and into the pilot bearing in the crankshaft. Wiggle the tool up, down or side-to-side as needed to bottom the tool in the pilot bearing. Tighten the pressure plate-to-flywheel bolts a little at a time, working in a criss-cross pattern to prevent distorting the cover. After all of the bolts are snug, tighten them to the torque listed in this Chapter's Specifications. Re-move the alignment tool.

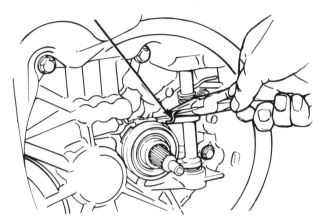

5.3   Using a pair of pliers, unhook the return spring (arrow) from the clutch release shaft fork

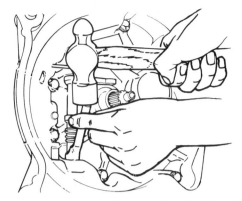

5.7   Tap out the release shaft seal and the No. 1 bushing with a bushing remover (arrow) or use a large socket with an outside diameter slightly smaller than the outside diameters of the seal and bushing

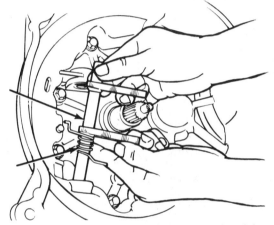

5.8   Remove the clutch release shaft (arrow) and the return spring (arrow) from the transaxle

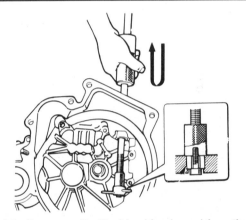

5.9   To remove the No. 2 bushing (arrow) from the transaxle, you'll need a special bushing remover (Tool J-34862, or equivalent) and a slide hammer

17   Using high-temperature grease, lubricate the inner groove of the release bearing (see Section 5). Also place grease on the release lever contact areas and the transaxle input shaft bearing retainer.

18   Install the clutch release bearing as described in Section 5.

19   Install the transaxle and all components removed previously. Tighten all fasteners to the proper torque specifications.

5   Clutch release bearing and fork – removal, inspection and installation

Warning: *Dust produced by clutch wear and deposited on clutch components may contain asbestos, which is hazardous to your health. DO NOT blow it out with compressed air and DO NOT inhale it. DO NOT use gasoline or petroleum-based solvents to remove the dust. Brake system cleaner should be used to flush the dust into a drain pan. After the clutch components are wiped clean with a rag, dispose of the contaminated rags and cleaner in a covered, marked container.*

Removal
Refer to illustrations 5.3, 5.7, 5.8 and 5.9

1   Disconnect the negative cable from the battery.

2   Remove the transaxle (see Chapter 7).

3   Note how the return spring is hooked onto the release shaft fork, then detach it from the shaft fork **(see illustration)**.

4   Slide the clutch release bearing off the transaxle input shaft.

5   Remove the nut and pinch bolt from the clutch release arm and remove the arm from the release shaft.

6   Remove the cover from the release shaft seal.

7   Remove the release shaft seal and No. 1 bushing **(see illustration)** with a bushing remover (Tool J-34861, or a similar tool).

8   Remove the release shaft and return spring from the transaxle **(see illustration)**.

9   Remove the No. 2 bushing from the transaxle with a bushing remover (Tool J-34862, or equivalent) and a slide hammer **(see illustration)**.

Inspection
Refer to illustration 5.10

10   Hold the center of the bearing and rotate the outer portion while applying pressure. If the bearing doesn't turn smoothly or if it's noisy, replace it. Wipe the bearing with a clean rag and inspect it for damage, wear and cracks. Don't immerse the bearing in solvent – it's sealed for life and to do so would ruin it. Also check the release lever and fork for cracks and other damage. Finally, inspect the bearing retainer **(see illustration)** for wear and damage. If it's damaged, replace the right transaxle case (see Chapter 7, Part A).

Installation
Refer to illustrations 5.11, 5.14 and 5.17

11   Tap the No. 2 bushing into the transaxle with a hammer and a large socket with an outside diameter slightly smaller than the outside diameter of the bushing **(see illustration)**. Grease the inside of the bushing.

12   Install the release shaft and spring.

8

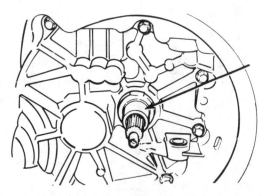

5.10   Inspect the bearing retainer (arrow) for wear and damage – if it's damaged or seriously worn, the right transaxle case must be replaced

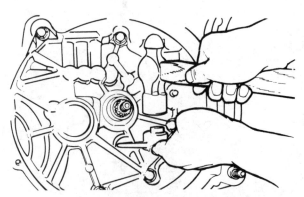

5.11   Tap the No. 2 bushing into place with a hammer and a large socket with an outside diameter slightly smaller than the outside diameter of the bushing

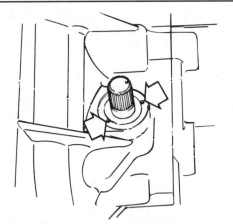

5.14   After the new seal is installed, stake the transaxle case against the sides of the seal at two points (arrows)

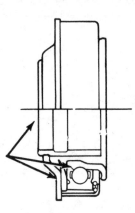

5.17   Lubricate the new release bearing at the indicated points (arrows)

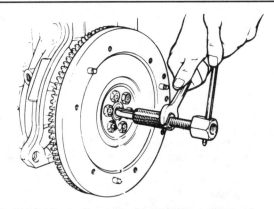

6.5   This is the factory puller (J-34839) for removing the pilot bearing

13   Grease the inside of the No. 1 bushing, slide it onto the end of the release shaft and, using a large socket with an outside diameter slightly smaller than the outside diameter of the bushing, tap the bushing into place.

14   Grease the lip of the new seal and drive the seal into place using a large socket with an outside diameter slightly smaller than the outside diameter of the seal. Stake the transaxle case against the seal at two points **(see illustration)**.

15   Slide the shaft seal cover onto the release shaft.

16   Install the clutch release arm. Be sure to align the punch mark on the release arm with the punch mark on the release shaft **(see illustration 3.2)**.

17   Grease the clutch release bearing **(see illustration)**, then slide it onto the input shaft.

18   Hook the return spring over the release shaft fork.

19   Install the transaxle (see Chapter 7, Part A).

20   Adjust the clutch cable (see Section 3).

---

6   Pilot bearing – inspection and replacement

Refer to illustrations 6.5, 6.8, 6.9 and 6.10

1   The clutch pilot bearing is a needle roller type bearing which is pressed into the rear of the crankshaft. It's greased at the factory and does not require additional lubrication. Its primary purpose is to support the front of the transaxle input shaft. Because of its inaccessibility, you should always inspect the pilot bearing any time the clutch components are removed. If you're in doubt about the condition of the pilot, replace it.

2   Remove the transaxle (see Chapter 7, Part A). **Note:** *If you have already removed the engine from the vehicle, disregard this Step.*

3   Remove the clutch components (see Section 4).

4   Inspect the pilot bearing for excessive wear, scoring, lack of grease, dryness or obvious damage. You'll need a flashlight to illuminate the recess. If the pilot bearing is damaged or worn, replace it.

5   The factory recommends removing the pilot bearing with a special puller **(see illustration)**, but an alternative method also works very well.

6   Find a solid steel bar which is slightly smaller in diameter than the bearing. Alternatives to a solid bar would be a wood dowel or a socket with a bolt fixed in place to make it solid.

6.8   Here's an alternative to the factory puller: Fill the cavity behind the pilot bushing with grease . . .

6.9   . . . then force the bushing out hydraulically with a steel rod slightly smaller than the bore in the bushing – when the hammer strikes the rod, the grease will transmit the force to the backside of the bushing and push it out

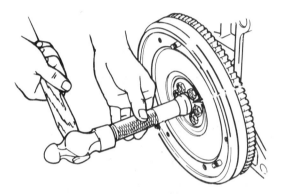

6.10   Install the new pilot bearing with a bushing driver (J-34848) or a socket with an outside diameter slightly smaller than the outside diameter of the pilot bearing

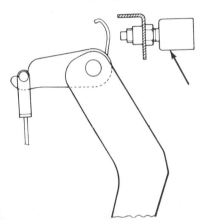

7.3   Once you find the clutch start switch (arrow) at the upper end of the clutch pedal, disconnect the electrical connector and loosen the locknut

7   Check the bar for fit – it should just slip into the bearing with very little clearance.

8   Pack the bearing and the area behind it (in the crankshaft recess) with heavy grease **(see illustration)**. Pack it tightly to eliminate as much air as possible.

9   Insert the bar into the bearing bore and strike the bar sharply with a hammer. This will force the grease to the back side of the bearing and push it out **(see illustration)**. Remove the bearing and clean all grease from the crankshaft recess.

10   To install the new bearing, lightly lubricate the outside surface with lithium-based grease, then drive it into the recess with a soft-face hammer **(see illustration)**. Make sure the seal faces out (the brand, size, etc. faces toward you).

11   Install the clutch components, transaxle and all other components removed previously, tightening all fasteners properly.

7   Clutch start switch – check and replacement

Refer to illustrations 7.3 and 7.4

1   Firmly apply the parking brake and put the gear shift lever in Neutral.

2   Reach under the dash and locate the clutch start switch at the upper end of the clutch pedal. Trace the switch leads back to their connector and unplug it.

3   Loosen the locknut and screw out the switch **(see illustration)**.

4   Push down the clutch pedal as far as it will go, then let it come up about 0.4 to 1.1 inches (10 to 30 mm) **(see illustration)**.

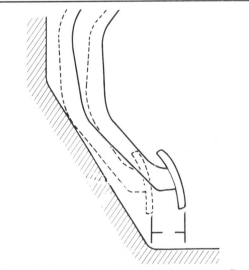

7.4   To check the clutch start switch, you must first position the clutch pedal at the proper height – push the pedal all the way to the floor, then let it back up about 0.4 to 1.1 inches (30 to 40 mm)

8

9.3   To prevent the hub from turning while you're breaking the hub nut loose, place a pry bar between two of the wheel studs

9.6a   Using a large prybar, carefully pry the inner CV joint from the differential side gear

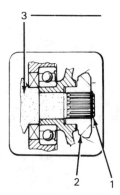

9.6b   In this cutaway view, you can see the snap-ring (1) that locks the inner CV joint stub axle into the differential side gear

5   Hook up an ohmmeter to the switch and slowly screw in the switch until the indicated resistance goes to zero – the switch is now on.
6   Hold the switch at this position and tighten the locknut securely. Recheck your resistance reading and make sure it occurs when the clutch pedal is 0.4 to 1.1 inches above the bottom of its travel.
7   Reconnect the lead wire.

---

8   Driveaxles – general information and inspection

Power is transmitted from the transaxle to the wheels through a pair of driveaxles. The inner end of each driveaxle is connected to its respective differential side gear in the transaxle by a splined stub axle which is an integral part of the inner CV joint. The splined stub axle at the outer end of each driveaxle is inserted through the steering knuckle and axle hub and secured by a large nut.

The inner CV joints are the sliding tripod type, which are capable of both angular and axial motion. Each inner joint assembly consists of a "spider" (tripod and bearings) and a CV joint housing. The tripod can slide freely in and out as the driveaxle moves up and down with the wheel. The inner CV joints are rebuildable (see Section 10).

The outer CV joints are the ball-and-cage type. Ball bearings run between an inner race and an outer race (the joint housing), and are held in proper relationship to each other by a cage. These CV joints are capable of angular – but not axial – movement. The outer joints are neither rebuildable nor removable. If one of them fails, a new driveaxle/outer joint assembly must be installed.

The boots should be inspected periodically for damage and leaking lubricant. Damaged CV joint boots must be replaced immediately or the joints can be damaged. Boot replacement involves the removal of the driveaxle (see Section 9). **Note:** *Some auto parts stores carry "split" type replacement boots, which can be installed without removing the driveaxle from the vehicle. This is a convenient alternative; however, the driveaxle should be removed and the CV joint disassembled and cleaned to ensure the joint is free from contaminants such as moisture and dirt, which will accelerated CV joint wear. The most common symptom of worn out or damaged CV joints, besides lubricant leaks, is a clicking noise in turns, a clunk when accelerating after coasting and vibration at highway speeds.*

To check for wear in the CV joints and driveaxle shafts, grasp each axle (one at a time) and rotate it in both directions while holding the CV joint housings and feeling for play (indicating worn splines or sloppy CV joints). Also check the driveaxle shafts for cracks, dents and distortion.

---

9   Driveaxles – removal and installation

Removal
Refer to illustrations 9.3, 9.6a and 9.6b
1   Remove the wheel cover and break loose the hub nut. Loosen the

wheel lug nuts, raise the front of the vehicle and support it securely on jackstands. Remove the front wheel.
2   Drain the oil from the transaxle (see Chapter 1).
3   Remove the cotter pin from the driveaxle hub nut and remove the nut. To prevent the hub from turning, place a pry bar between two of the wheel studs, then loosen the nut **(see illustration)**.
4   Remove both bolts from the stabilizer bar mounting bracket (see Chapter 10).
5   Remove the balljoint stud pinch bolt and detach the balljoint stud from the steering knuckle by pulling down on the stabilizer bar (see Chapter 10).
6   Using a large pry bar positioned between the transaxle housing and the CV joint housing, carefully pry the splined inner end of the driveaxle out of the differential side gear in the transaxle **(see illustration)**. A circlip in the end of the splined stub axle "locks" the driveaxle into the differential side gear **(see illustration)**. You'll feel this circlip pop loose when you pry on the CV joint. Once you've got the driveaxle disconnected from the transaxle, support the inner end with a piece of wire while you work on the outer end.
7   Push the outer end of the driveaxle out of the hub and steering knuckle. Use a puller if necessary.
8   Support the CV joints and carefully remove the driveaxle from the vehicle.

Installation
9   Pry the old circlip from the inner end of the driveaxle and install a new one. Lubricate the differential seal with multi-purpose grease, raise the driveaxle into position while supporting the CV joints and insert the splined end of the inner CV joint into the differential side gear. Make sure the stub axle is fully seated.
10   Apply a light coat of multi-purpose grease to the outer CV joint splines, pull out on the strut/steering knuckle assembly and install the stub axle into the hub.
11   Insert the balljoint stud into the steering knuckle and install the pinch bolt (see Chapter 10).
12   Install the hub nut. Lock the disc so it cannot turn, as described in Step 3, and tighten – but don't torque – the hub nut.
13   Grasp the inner CV joint housing (not the driveaxle) and try to pull it out to make sure the driveaxle is securely locked into place.
14   Install the wheel, install the wheel lug nuts, hand tighten them and lower the vehicle.
15   Tighten the wheel lug nuts to the torque listed in the Chapter 1 Specifications. Tighten the hub nut to the torque listed in this Chapter's Specifications. Install the wheel cover.

---

10   Driveaxle boot replacement and CV joint overhaul

Note: *If the CV joints are worn, indicating the need for an overhaul (usually due to torn boots), explore all options before beginning the job. Complete rebuilt driveaxles are available on an exchange basis, which eliminates*

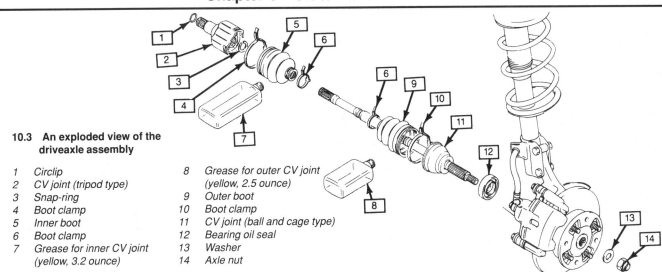

10.3   An exploded view of the driveaxle assembly

1	Circlip	8	Grease for outer CV joint
2	CV joint (tripod type)		(yellow, 2.5 ounce)
3	Snap-ring	9	Outer boot
4	Boot clamp	10	Boot clamp
5	Inner boot	11	CV joint (ball and cage type)
6	Boot clamp	12	Bearing oil seal
7	Grease for inner CV joint	13	Washer
	(yellow, 3.2 ounce)	14	Axle nut

much time and work. If you decide to rebuild a CV joint, check on the cost and availability of parts **before** disassembling the driveaxle.

1   Remove the driveaxle from the vehicle (see Section 9).

2   Mount the driveaxle in a vise. The jaws of the vise should be lined with wood or rags to prevent damage to the driveaxle.

Inner CV joint

Disassembly

Refer to illustrations 10.3, 10.4, 10.5 and 10.6

3   Cut off both boot clamps **(see illustration)** and slide the boot towards the center of the driveaxle.

4   Mark or paint alignment marks on the outer race and the tripod bearing assembly **(see illustration)** so they can be returned to their original position, then slide the outer race off the tripod bearing assembly.

5   Remove the snap-ring from the end of the axleshaft, then mark the relationship of the tripod bearing assembly to the axleshaft **(see illustration)**.

6   Secure the bearing rollers with tape, then remove the tripod bearing assembly from the axleshaft with a brass drift and a hammer **(see illustration)**. Remove the tape, but don't let the rollers fall off and get mixed up.

7   Remove the stop-ring, slide the old boot off the driveaxle and discard it.

Inspection

8   Clean the old grease from the outer race and the tripod bearing assembly. Paint or scribe marks on each bearing roller and its respective shaft to ensure proper reassembly, then carefully disassemble each sec-

tion of the tripod assembly, one at a time, and clean the needle bearings with solvent.

9   Inspect the rollers, tripod, bearings and outer race for scoring, pitting or other signs of abnormal wear, which will warrant the replacement of the inner CV joint.

Reassembly

Refer to illustrations 10.10, 10.16, 10.17a and 10.17b

10   Wrap the splines of the axleshaft with tape to avoid damaging the new boot, then slide the boot onto the axleshaft **(see illustration)**. Remove

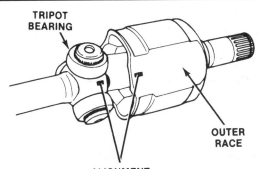

10.4   Scribe or paint alignment marks on the tripod assembly and the outer race, then slide the outer race off

8

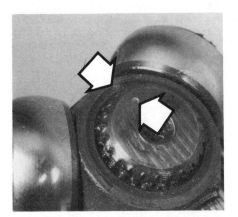

10.5   Remove the snap-ring from end of the axleshaft, then mark the relationship of the tripod to the axleshaft

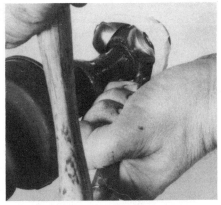

10.6   Secure the bearing rollers with tape and drive the tripod off the shaft with a hammer and a brass drift, then remove the stop-ring

10.10   Wrap the splined area of the axleshaft with tape to prevent damage to the boot when installing it

10.16   Equalize the pressure inside the boot by inserting a small, dull screwdriver between the boot and the outer race

10.17a   To install the new boot clamps, bend the tang down . . .

10.17b   . . . and flatten the tabs to hold it in place

the tape.

11   Align the match marks you made before disassembly and tap the tripod assembly onto the axleshaft with a hammer and brass drift.

12   Install the outer snap-ring.

13   Apply a coat of CV joint grease to the inner bearing surfaces to hold the needle bearings in place when reassembling the tripod assembly. Make sure each roller is installed on the same post as before.

14   Pack the outer race with half of the grease furnished with the new boot and place the remainder in the boot. Install the outer race. Make sure the marks you made on the tripod assembly and the outer race are aligned.

15   Seat the boot in the grooves in the outer race and the axleshaft.

16   With the driveaxle set to the proper length, equalize the pressure in the boot by inserting a blunt screwdriver between the boot and the outer race **(see illustration)**. Don't damage the boot with the tool.

17   Install and tighten the new boot clamps **(see illustrations)**.

18   Install the driveaxle assembly (see Section 9).

Outer CV joint and boot

Disassembly

19   Following Steps 3 through 7, remove the inner CV joint from the driveaxle and disassemble it.

20   Cut the boot clamps from the outer CV joint. Slide the boot off the shaft.

Inspection

Refer to illustration 10.22

21   Thoroughly wash the inner and outer CV joints in clean solvent and blow them dry with compressed air, if available. **Note:** *Because the outer joint can't be disassembled, it is difficult to wash away all the old grease and to rid the bearing of solvent once it's clean. But it is imperative that the job be done thoroughly, so take your time and do it right.*

22   Bend the outer CV joint housing at an angle to the axleshaft to expose the bearings, inner race and cage **(see illustration)**. Inspect the bearing surfaces for signs of wear. If the bearings are damaged or worn, replace the driveaxle.

Reassembly

23   Slide the new outer boot onto the axleshaft. It's a good idea to wrap tape around the splines of the shaft to prevent damage to the boot **(see illustration 9.10)**. When the boot is in position, add the specified amount of grease (included in the boot replacement kit) to the outer joint and the boot (pack the joint with as much grease as it will hold and put the rest into the boot). Slide the boot on the rest of the way and install the new clamps **(see illustrations 10.17a and 10.17b)**.

24   Clean and reassemble the inner CV joint by following Steps 8 through 17.

25   Install the driveaxle as outlined in Section 9.

10.22   After the old grease has been rinsed away and the solvent has been blown out with compressed air, rotate the outer joint assembly through its full range of motion and inspect the bearing surfaces for wear and damage – if any of the ball bearings, the race or the cage look damaged, replace the driveaxle and outer joint assembly

Chapter 9   Brakes

Contents

Specifications

General

Brake fluid type	See Chapter 1
Power brake booster pushrod-to-master cylinder	
piston clearance	0.004-0.020 in

Disc brakes

Minimum brake pad thickness	See Chapter 1
Brake disc	
Standard thickness	0.394 in (10.0 mm)
Minimum thickness*	0.315 in (8.0 mm)
Runout limit	
Metro	0.004 in (0.1 mm)
Sprint	0.003 in (0.07 mm)

Drum brakes

Drum inside diameter	
Standard	7.09 in (180 mm)
Maximum*	7.16 in (182 mm)

Refer to marks cast or stamped into the disc or drum (they supersede information printed here)

Torque specifications   Ft-lbs (unless otherwise indicated)

Caliper mounting bolts	
Metro	20.0
Sprint	17.5 to 26
Brake hose-to-caliper banjo fitting bolt	14.5 to 18
Brake disc-to-hub bolts	37
Front hub nut	See Chapter 8
Drum spindle nut	74
Master cylinder mounting nuts	120 in-lbs
Power booster mounting nuts	120 in-lbs
Wheel cylinder mounting bolts	90 to 108 in-lbs

9

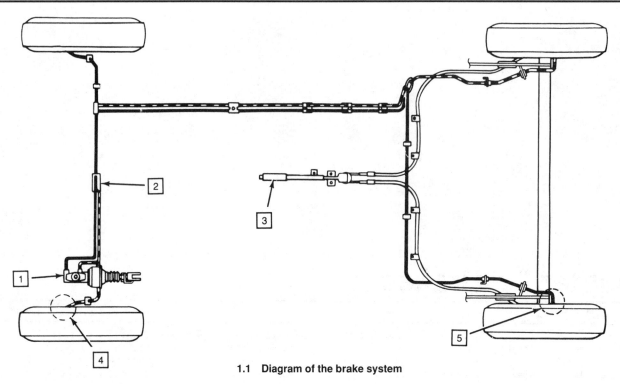

1.1   Diagram of the brake system

1	Master cylinder	5	Rear drum brake
2	Proportioning valve	6	Front
3	Parking brake lever	7	Rear
4	Front disc brake		

1   General information

Refer to illustration 1.1

The vehicles covered by this manual are equipped with hydraulically operated front and rear brake systems **(see illustration)**. The front brakes are disc type and the rear brakes are drum type. Both the front and rear brakes are self adjusting. The front disc brakes automatically compensate for pad wear, while the rear drum brakes incorporate an adjustment mechanism.

Hydraulic system

The hydraulic system consists of two separate circuits. The master cylinder has separate reservoirs for the two circuits and in the event of a leak or failure in one hydraulic circuit, the other circuit will remain operative. A visual warning of circuit failure or air in the system is given by a warning light on the dashboard.

Proportioning valve

A proportioning valve, located on the engine compartment on the firewall, consists of sections providing the following functions. The metering section limits pressure to the front brakes until a predetermined front input pressure is reached and until the rear brakes are activated. There is no restriction at inlet pressures below 3 psi, allowing pressure equalization during non-braking periods. The proportioning section proportions outlet pressure to the rear brakes after a predetermined rear input pressure has been reached, preventing early rear wheel lock-up under heavy brake loads. The valve is also designed to assure full pressure to one brake system should the other system fail.

Power brake booster

The power brake booster, utilizing engine manifold vacuum and atmospheric pressure to provide assistance to the hydraulically operated brakes, is mounted on the firewall in the engine compartment.

Parking brake

The parking brake operates the rear brakes only, through cable actuation. It's activated by a lever located in between the two front seats.

Service

After completing any operation involving disassembly of any part of the brake system, always test drive the vehicle to check for proper braking performance before resuming normal driving. When testing the brakes, perform the tests on a clean, dry flat surface. Conditions other than these can lead to inaccurate test results. Test the brakes at various speeds with both light and heavy pedal pressure. The vehicle should stop evenly without pulling to one side or the other. Avoid locking the brakes because this slides the tires and diminishes braking efficiency and control of the vehicle.

Tires, vehicle load and front-end alignment are factors which also affect braking performance.

2   Disc brake pads – replacement

Refer to illustrations 2.4, 2.5, 2.6a, 2.6b and 2.8

Warning: *Disc brake pads must be replaced on both front wheels at the same time – never replace the pads on only one wheel. Also, the dust created by the brake system may contain asbestos, which is harmful to your health. Never blow it out with compressed air and don't inhale any of it. An approved filtering mask should be worn when working on the brakes. Do not, under any circumstances, use petroleum based solvents to clean brake parts. Use brake cleaner or denatured alcohol only!*

Note: *When servicing the disc brakes, use only high quality, nationally recognized name brand pads.*

1   Remove the cover from the brake fluid reservoir.
2   Loosen the wheel lug nuts, raise the front of the vehicle and support it securely on jackstands.
3   Remove the front wheels. Work on one brake assembly at a time, using the assembled brake for reference if necessary.

2.4   Remove the caliper retaining bolts

2.5   Use rope or wire to support the caliper

2.6a   Remove the outer pad from the mounting bracket

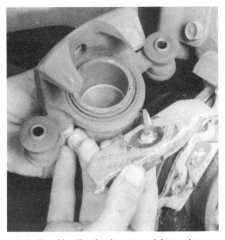

2.6b   Unclip the inner pad from the caliper piston

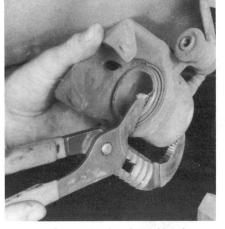

2.8   Compress the piston into the caliper to make room for the new pads

3.3   Unscrew the brake hose fitting bolt and detach the hose

4   Remove the caliper mounting bolts **(see illustration)**.
5   Remove the caliper from its mounting position and support it using wire or rope **(see illustration)**. Don't let it hang by the brake hose.
6   Remove the pads **(see illustrations)**.
7   Inspect the brake disc carefully as outlined in Section 4. If machining is necessary, follow the information in that Section to remove the disc.
8   Push the piston back into the bore to provide room for the new brake pads. A pair of slip joint pliers can be used to accomplish this **(see illustration)**. As the piston is depressed to the bottom of the caliper bore, the fluid in the master cylinder will rise. Make sure it doesn't overflow. If necessary, siphon off some of the fluid.
9   Position the pads in the caliper and install the assembly over the disc.
10   Install and tighten the caliper mounting bolts.
11   Install the wheels and lower the vehicle.
12   After the job has been completed, firmly depress the brake pedal a few times to bring the pads into contact with the disc. Check the brake fluid level and add some if necessary (see Chapter 1).
13   Check for fluid leakage and make sure the brakes operate normally before driving in traffic.

3   Disc brake caliper – removal, overhaul and installation

Refer to illustrations 3.3, 3.6, 3.8, 3.9 and 3.10
Warning: *Dust created by the brake system may contain asbestos, which is harmful to your health. Never blow it out with compressed air and don't*

inhale any of it. An approved filtering mask should be worn when working on the brakes. Do not, under any circumstances, use petroleum-based solvents to clean brake parts. Use brake cleaner or denatured alcohol only!

Note: *If an overhaul is indicated (usually because of fluid leakage) explore all options before beginning the job. New and factory rebuilt calipers are available on an exchange basis, which makes this job quite easy. If it's decided to rebuild the calipers, make sure a rebuild kit is available before proceeding. Always rebuild the calipers in pairs – never rebuild just one of them.*

Removal

1   Loosen the wheel lug nuts, raise the front of the vehicle and support it securely on jackstands.
2   Remove the front wheels.
3   Remove the brake hose inlet fitting bolt and detach the hose **(see illustration)**. Have a rag handy to catch spilled fluid and wrap a plastic bag tightly around the end of the hose to prevent fluid loss and contamination.
4   Remove the mounting bolts and detach the caliper from the vehicle. Separate the pads from the caliper (see Section 2).

Overhaul

5   Clean the exterior of the caliper with brake cleaner or denatured alcohol. Never use gasoline, kerosene or petroleum-based cleaning solvents. Place the caliper on a clean workbench.

9

3.6   Using a screwdriver, remove the dust boot retaining ring

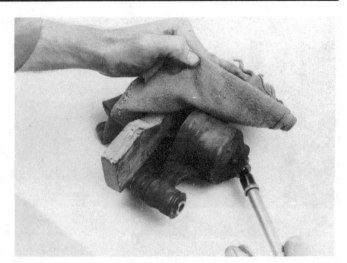

3.8   With the caliper padded to prevent damage, use compressed air to force the piston out of the bore – make sure your fingers aren't between the piston and the caliper

3.9   The piston seal should be removed with a plastic or wood tool to avoid damage to the bore and seal groove – a pencil will do the job

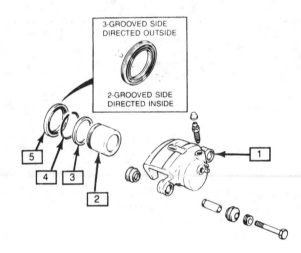

3.10   Exploded view of the caliper assembly

1	Caliper body	4	Boot retaining ring
2	Piston	5	Dust boot
3	Piston seal		

6   Carefully remove the ring retaining the dust boot to the caliper bore **(see illustration)**.
7   Carefully pry the dust boot out of the caliper bore.
8   Position a wood block or several shop rags in the caliper as a cushion, then use compressed air to remove the piston from the caliper **(see illustration)**. Use only enough air pressure to ease the piston out of the bore. If the piston is blown out, even with the cushion in place, it may be damaged. **Warning:** *Never place your fingers in front of the piston in an attempt to catch or protect it when applying compressed air, as serious injury could occur.*
9 Using a wood or plastic tool, remove the piston seal from the groove in the caliper bore **(see illustration)**. Metal tools may cause bore damage.
10   Remove the caliper bleeder screw, then remove the sleeves and bushings from the caliper ears. Discard all rubber parts **(see illustration)**.
11   Clean the remaining parts with brake system cleaner or denatured alcohol then blow them dry with compressed air.
12   Carefully examine the piston for nicks and burrs and loss of plating. If surface defects are present, the parts must be replaced.
13   Check the caliper bore in a similar way. Light polishing with crocus cloth is permissible to remove light corrosion and stains. Discard the mounting bolts if they're corroded or damaged.
14   When assembling, lubricate the piston bore and seal with clean brake fluid. Position the seal in the caliper bore groove.

15   Lubricate the piston with clean brake fluid, then install a new dust boot in the piston groove, with the fold toward the open end of the piston.
16   Insert the piston squarely into the caliper bore, then apply force to bottom it.
17   Position the dust boot in the cylinder groove and install the retaining ring.
18   Install the bleeder screw.
19   If the old bushings or pins will not clean up using crocus cloth, new ones should be installed. Old or new bushings or pins should be lubricated with silicone grease.
20   Install new rubber boots to the pins or bushings. Install the dust boot supports if equipped.

Installation

21   Inspect the mounting bolts for excessive corrosion.
22   Place the caliper in position over the disc and caliper mounting bracket, install the bolts and tighten them to the torque listed in this Chapter's Specifications.
23   Install the brake hose and inlet fitting bolt, using new copper washers, then tighten the bolt.

4.3   The brake pads on this vehicle were obviously neglected, as they wore down to the rivets and cut deep grooves in the disc – wear this severe will require replacement of the disc

4.4a   Use a dial indicator to check disc runout – if the reading exceeds the maximum allowable runout limit, the disc will have to be machined or replaced

4.4b   Remove the glaze from the disc surface with emery cloth – use a swirling motion

4.5a   The discard thickness is cast into the back of the disc (arrow)

4.5b   Use a micrometer to check the disc thickness

24   Be sure to bleed the brakes (see Section 10).
25   Install the wheels and lower the vehicle.
26   After the job has been completed, firmly depress the brake pedal a few times to bring the pads into contact with the disc.
27   Check brake operation before driving the vehicle in traffic.

---

4   Brake disc – inspection, removal and installation

Refer to illustrations 4.3, 4.4a, 4.4b, 4.5a, 4.5b, 4.6, 4.7, 4.9, 4.10, 4.12 and 4.13

Inspection

1   Loosen the wheel lug nuts, raise the vehicle and support it securely on jackstands. Remove the front wheels.
2   Remove the brake caliper as outlined in Section 3. It's not necessary to disconnect the brake hose. After removing the caliper bolts, suspend the caliper out of the way with a piece of wire or rope. Don't let the caliper hang by the hose and don't stretch or twist the hose.
3   Visually check the disc surface for score marks and other damage. Light scratches and shallow grooves are normal after use and may not al-

ways be detrimental to brake operation, but deep score marks – over 0.015-inch (0.38 mm) – require disc removal and refinishing by an automotive machine shop. Be sure to check both sides of the disc (**see illustration**). If pulsating has been noticed during application of the brakes, suspect disc runout. Be sure to check the wheel bearings to make sure they're in good shape and properly adjusted – a bad bearing can also cause runout.
4   To check disc runout, place a dial indicator at a point about 1/2-inch from the outer edge of the disc (**see illustration**). Set the indicator to zero and turn the disc. The indicator reading should not exceed the runout limit listed in this Chapter's Specifications. If it does, the disc should be refinished by an automotive machine shop. **Note:** *Professionals recommend resurfacing of brake discs regardless of the dial indicator reading (to produce a smooth, flat surface that will eliminate brake pedal pulsations and other undesirable symptoms related to questionable discs). At the very least, if you elect not to have the discs resurfaced, deglaze them with sandpaper or emery cloth (use a swirling motion to ensure a nondirectional finish)* (**see illustration**).
5   The disc must not be machined to a thickness less than the minimum refinish thickness listed in this Chapter's Specifications. The is cast into the inside of the disc (**see illustration**). The disc thickness can be checked with a micrometer (**see illustration**).

9

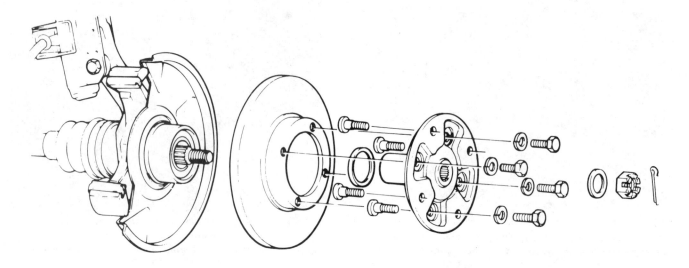

4.6   Exploded view of the disc and hub assembly

4.7   A pair of side cutters works well for removing the cotter pin

**4.9   Before removing the disc, reference mark its position to the
caliper mount (arrows)**

**4.10   Use a slide hammer with the proper adapter to remove
the disc**

Removal

6   While an assistant depresses the brake pedal, loosen the bolts retaining the disc **(see illustration)**.
7   Remove the cotter pin and hub nut **(see illustration)**.
8   Remove the caliper and pads (see Section 3).
9   Reference mark the position of the disc to the caliper mounting bracket **(see illustration)**.
10   Using a large slide hammer and proper adapter, pull off the disc and wheel hub **(see illustration)**.
11   Separate the disc from the hub.

Installation

12   Be sure the spacer on the hub is installed with the concave side to the disc **(see illustration)**.
13   Using the reference marks made during removal and the proper driver and hammer, install the disc and hub assembly to the position it was in before removal **(see illustration)**.
14   Install the castle nut and tighten it to the torque listed in this Chapter's Specifications. Install a new cotter pin. If necessary, turn the nut an additional amount to line up the slots in the nut with the hole in the driveaxle (don't loosen the nut to align the slots and hole).

4.12   Be sure the spacer on the rear of the hub is positioned with the concave side to the hub

4.13   Use the proper driver to install the disc and hub assembly

5.4   Nuts that don't have cotter pins have to be unstaked before they are loosened

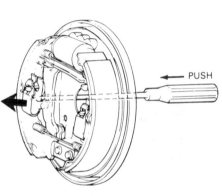

5.5   If the drum refuses to come off, try releasing the tension as shown – if the drum still won't come off . . .

5.6   . . . use a slide hammer to remove it

15   Install the caliper and brake pad assembly over the disc and position it on the steering knuckle (refer to Section 3 for the caliper installation procedure, if necessary). Tighten the caliper bolts to the torque listed in this Chapter's Specifications.

16   Install the wheel, then lower the vehicle to the ground. Tighten the lug nuts to the torque listed in the Chapter 1 Specifications.

17   Depress the brake pedal a few times to bring the brake pads into contact with the disc. Bleeding of the system will not be necessary unless the brake hose was disconnected from the caliper. Check the operation of the brakes carefully before placing the vehicle into normal service.

---

5   Drum brake shoes – replacement

Refer to illustrations 5.4, 5.5, 5.6, 5.7, 5.8, 5.12, 5.14 and 5.16

Warning: *Drum brake shoes must be replaced on both wheels at the same time – never replace the shoes on only one wheel. Also, the dust created by the brake system may contain asbestos, which is harmful to your health. Never blow it out with compressed air and don't inhale any of it. An approved filtering mask should be worn when working on the brakes. Do not, under any circumstances, use petroleum-based solvents to clean brake parts. Use brake cleaner or denatured alcohol only!*

Caution: *Whenever the brake shoes are replaced, the retractor and hold-down springs should also be replaced. Due to the continuous heating/cooling cycle that the springs are subjected to, they lose their tension over a period of time and may allow the shoes to drag on the drum and wear at a*

much faster rate than normal. When replacing the rear brake shoes, use only high quality nationally recognized brand-name parts.

1   Loosen the wheel lug nuts, raise the rear of the vehicle and support it securely on jackstands. Block the front wheels to keep the vehicle from rolling.

2   Release the parking brake.

3   Remove the wheel. **Note:** *All four rear brake shoes must be replaced at the same time, but to avoid mixing up parts, work on only one brake assembly at a time.*

4   Remove the cotter pin (if equipped) and the nut retaining the brake drum **(see illustration)**.

5   Remove the brake drums. **Note:** *If the drums cannot be pulled off with the parking brake completely released, the brake shoes will have to be retracted by removing the plug from the backing plate. Insert a screwdriver into the plug hole until its tip contacts the shoe hold-down spring* **(see illustration)**. *Push on the hold-down spring and release the parking brake lever from the hold-down spring.*

6   If the drum still will not come off, use a large slide hammer and the proper adapter to remove the drum **(see illustration)**.

7   Compress the hold-down spring while rotating the retaining pin. Remove the hold-down spring **(see illustration)**.

8   Remove the clip retaining the parking brake lever **(see illustration)**.

9   Remove the lower shoe return spring.

10   Remove the brake shoes from the backing plate and the parking brake lever.

11   Transfer the parts from the old brake shoes to the new shoes.

12   Clean the backing plate and apply high-temperature brake grease to the shoe contact areas of the backing plate **(see illustration)**.

9

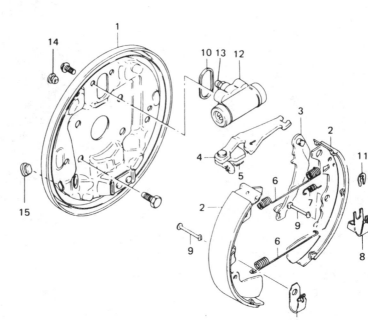

5.7   Exploded view of the rear brake assembly

1   Brake backing plate
2   Brake shoe
3   Parking brake shoe lever
4   Brake strut
5   Quadrant spring
6   Shoe return spring
7   Anti-rattle spring
8   Shoe hold-down spring
9   Shoe hold-down pin
10   Seal
11   Parking brake lever retaining clip
12   Wheel cylinder
13   Bleeder plug cap
14   Rubber plug
15   Rubber plug

5.8   Use a screwdriver to pry apart the ends of the clip retaining the parking brake lever to the shoe

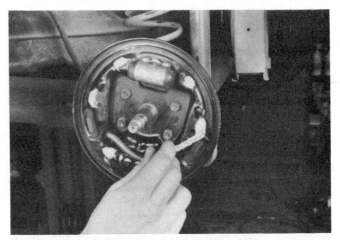

5.12   Use high-temperature brake grease to lubricate the shoe-to-backing plate contact surfaces

5.14   The drum discard dimension is cast into the inside of the drum

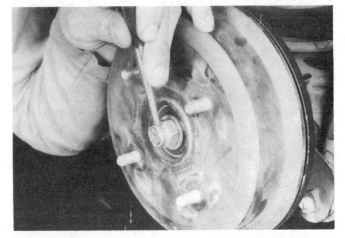

5.16   If your vehicle is not using a cotter pin on the drum retaining nut, be sure to stake the nut into the groove

6.1   Use a drift punch and hammer to remove the wheel bearings

13   Installation is the reverse of the removal procedure. Be sure to use a new clip to retain the parking brake lever.
14   Before reinstalling the drum it should be checked for cracks, score marks, deep scratches and hard spots, which will appear as small discolored areas. If the hard spots cannot be removed with fine emery cloth or if any of the other conditions listed above exist, the drum must be taken to an automotive machine shop to have it turned. **Note:** *Professionals recommend resurfacing the drums whenever a brake job is done. Resurfacing will eliminate the possibility of out-of-round drums. If the drums are worn so much that they can't be resurfaced without exceeding the maximum allowable diameter (cast into the drum)* **(see illustration)**, *then new ones will be required. At the very least, if you elect not to have the drums resurfaced, remove the glazing from the surface with emery cloth or sandpaper, using a swirling motion.*
15   Install the brake drum.
16   Install and tighten the drum retaining nuts. Nuts that don't use cotter pins have to be staked **(see illustration)**.
17   Mount the wheel, install the lug nuts, then lower the vehicle.
18   Make a number of forward and reverse stops to adjust the brakes until satisfactory pedal action is obtained.
19   Check brake operation before driving the vehicle in traffic.

6   Rear wheel bearings – replacement

Refer to illustrations 6.1, 6.2 and 6.3

1   With the rear drum removed (see Section 5), remove the bearings using a drift and a hammer **(see illustration)**.
2   If the spacer was removed, install it with the inner lip toward the studs. Fill the cavity between the bearings with wheel bearing grease **(see illustration)**. If the bearings didn't come packed with grease from the factory, push the same wheel bearing grease into the bearings until they are thoroughly packed.
3   Using the proper driver, install both the inner and outer bearings with the sealed sides facing out **(see illustration)**.

7   Wheel cylinder – removal, overhaul and installation

Refer to illustration 7.5
Note: *If an overhaul is indicated (usually because of fluid leakage or sticky operation) explore all options before beginning the job. New wheel cylinders are available, which makes this job quite easy. If it's decided to rebuild the wheel cylinder, make sure that a rebuild kit is available before proceeding. Never overhaul only one wheel cylinder – always rebuild both of them at the same time.*

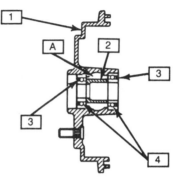

6.2   Wheel bearing installation details (cutaway view)

1   Brake drum   4   Wheel bearing
2   Spacer   A   Fill with wheel
3   Sealed side   bearing grease

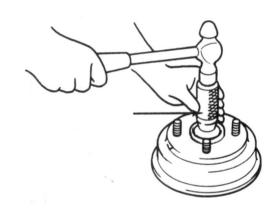

6.3   Use the proper driver to install the wheel bearings

Removal

1   Raise the rear of the vehicle and support it securely on jackstands. Block the front wheels to keep the vehicle from rolling.
2   Remove the brake shoe assembly (see Section 5).
3   Remove all dirt and foreign material from around the wheel cylinder.
4   Unscrew the brake line fitting, using a flare nut wrench, if available. Don't pull the brake line away from the wheel cylinder.
5   Remove the wheel cylinder mounting bolts **(see illustration)**.
6   Detach the wheel cylinder from the brake backing plate and place it on a clean workbench. Immediately plug the brake line to prevent fluid loss and contamination. **Note:** *If the brake shoe linings are contaminated with brake fluid, install new brake shoes.*

Overhaul

7   Remove the bleeder screw, cups, pistons, boots and spring assembly from the wheel cylinder body **(see illustration 7.5)**.
8   Clean the wheel cylinder with brake fluid, denatured alcohol or brake system cleaner. **Warning:** *Do not, under any circumstances, use petroleum-based solvents to clean brake parts!*
9   Use compressed air to remove excess fluid from the wheel cylinder and to blow out the passages.
10   Check the cylinder bore for corrosion and score marks. Crocus cloth can be used to remove light corrosion and stains, but the cylinder must be replaced with a new one if the defects cannot be removed easily, or if the bore is scored.

9

7.5 Details of the wheel cylinder

1   Backing plate
2   Seal
3   Bleeder screw cap
4   Wheel cylinder assembly

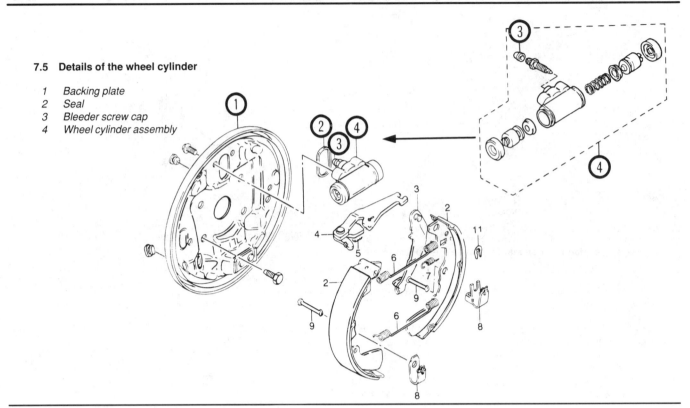

11   Lubricate the new cups with brake fluid.
12   Assemble the wheel cylinder components. Make sure the cup lips face in.

Installation

13   Place the wheel cylinder in position and install the bolts.
14   Connect the brake line and tighten the fitting. Install the brake shoe assembly.
15   Bleed the brakes (see Section 10).
16   Check brake operation before driving the vehicle in traffic.

8   Master cylinder – removal, overhaul and installation

Refer to illustrations 8.2, 8.6, 8.8, 8.9a and 8.9b

Removal

1   Clean around the reservoir cap and remove the brake fluid using a suction device such as a syringe.
2   Disconnect the brake lines from the master cylinder **(see illustration)**. **Note:** *Do not allow brake fluid to get on the painted surfaces.*
3   Remove the two nuts and washers mounting the master cylinder to the brake booster.
4   Remove the master cylinder.

Overhaul

5   Before attempting the overhaul of the master cylinder, obtain the proper rebuild kit, which will contain the necessary replacement parts and also any instructions which may be specific to your model.
6   Remove the fluid reservoir retaining screw **(see illustration)**.
7   Pull up on the reservoir and detach it from the master cylinder.
8   Remove the rubber grommets from the master cylinder **(see illustration)**.
9   Remove the snap-ring from the end of the master cylinder **(see illustrations)**.
10   Remove the primary piston by inverting the cylinder and tapping it against a wood block.
11   Remove the stopper bolt for the secondary piston **(see illustration 8.9b)**.

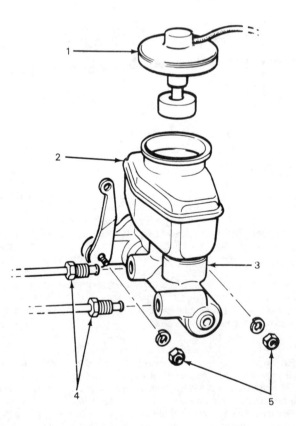

8.2   Master cylinder mounting details

1 Reservoir cap	4 Flare nuts
2 Reservoir	5 Attaching nuts
3 Master cylinder	

8.6   Remove the reservoir retaining screw (arrow)

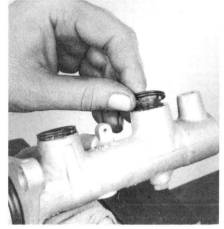

8.8   After the reservoir has been removed, pull the grommets off (if they're hardened, damaged or appear to have been leaking, replace them)

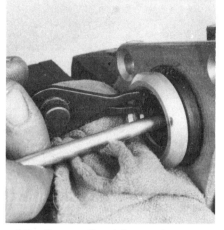

8.9a   Depress the pistons and remove the snap-ring with snap-ring pliers

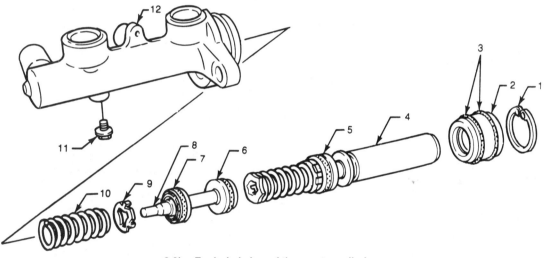

8.9b   Exploded view of the master cylinder

1	Snap-ring	5	Piston cup
2	Piston stopper	6	Secondary piston pressure cup
3	Piston stopper seals	7	Piston cup
4	Primary piston	8	Secondary piston

9	Secondary piston return spring seat
10	Secondary piston return spring
11	Secondary piston stopper bolt
12	Master cylinder body

12   Remove the secondary piston by inverting the cylinder and tapping it against a wood block.
13   Carefully inspect the bore of the master cylinder.
14   Any deep score marks or other damage will mean a new master cylinder is required. DO NOT attempt to hone the bore.
15   Replace all parts included in the rebuild kit, following any instructions in the kit.
16   Clean all reused parts with new brake fluid, brake system cleaner or denatured alcohol. Do not use any petroleum-based solvents during reassembly, lubricate all parts liberally with clean brake fluid.
17   Push the assembled components into the bore, bottoming them against the end of the master cylinder, then install the stopper bolt.
18   Install a new snap-ring, making sure it's seated properly in the groove.
19   Install the reservoir grommets and reservoir.
20   Before installing the master cylinder, it should be bench bled. Since you'll have to apply pressure to the master cylinder piston and, at the same time, control flow from the brake line outlets, the master cylinder should be

mounted in a vise, with the jaws of the vise clamping on the mounting flange.
21   Insert threaded plugs into the brake line outlet holes and snug them down so no air will leak past them, but not so tight that they can't be easily loosened.
22   Fill the reservoir with brake fluid of the recommended type (see Chapter 1).
23   Remove one plug and push the piston assembly into the bore to expel the air from the master cylinder. A large Phillips screwdriver can be used to push on the piston assembly.
24   To prevent air from being drawn back into the master cylinder, the plug must be replaced and snugged down before releasing the pressure on the piston.
25   Repeat the procedure until only brake fluid is expelled from the brake line outlet hole. When only brake fluid is expelled, repeat the procedure at the other outlet hole and plug. Be sure to keep the master cylinder reservoir filled with brake fluid to prevent the introduction of air into the system.

9

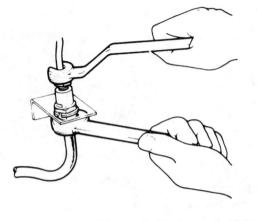

9.2   **Hold the hose with a wrench then loosen the fitting with a flare-nut wrench**

9.3   **Once the fitting has been completely loosened, remove the hose clip with a pair of pliers**

26   Since high pressure isn't involved in the bench bleeding procedure, an alternative to the removal and replacement of the plugs with each stroke of the piston assembly is available. Before pushing in on the piston assembly, remove the plug as described in Step 23. Before releasing the piston, however, instead of replacing the plug, simply put your finger tightly over the hole to keep air from being drawn back into the master cylinder. Wait several seconds for brake fluid to be drawn from the reservoir into the bore, then depress the piston again, removing your finger as brake fluid is expelled. Be sure to put your finger back over the hole each time before releasing the piston, and when the bleeding procedure is complete for that outlet, replace the plug and tighten it before going on to the other port.

Installation

27   Installation is the reverse of removal.
28   Fill the reservoir with brake fluid.
29   Bleed the brake system (see Section 10).

9   Brake hoses and lines – inspection and replacement

Inspection

1   About every six months, with the vehicle raised and supported securely on jackstands, the rubber hoses which connect the steel brake lines with the front and rear brake assemblies should be inspected for cracks, chafing of the outer cover, leaks, blisters and other damage. These are important and vulnerable parts of the brake system and inspection should be complete. A light and mirror will be helpful for a thorough check. If a hose exhibits any of the above conditions, replace it with a new one.

Replacement

Front brake hose

Refer to illustrations 9.2 and 9.3
2   Using a back-up wrench, disconnect the brake line from the hose fitting, being careful not to bend the frame bracket or brake line **(see illustration).**
3   Use a pair of pliers to remove the U-clip from the female fitting at the bracket, then detach the hose from the bracket **(see illustration).**
4   Unscrew the brake hose from the caliper.
5   To install the hose, first thread it into the caliper, tightening it securely.
6   Without twisting the hose, install the female fitting in the hose bracket. It will fit the bracket in only one position.
7   Install the U-clip retaining the female fitting to the frame bracket.
8   Using a back-up wrench, attach the brake line to the hose fitting.
9   When the brake hose installation is complete, there should be no kinks in the hose. Make sure the hose doesn't contact any part of the sus-

pension. Check this by turning the wheels to the extreme left and right positions. If the hose makes contact, remove it and correct the installation as necessary. Bleed the system (see Section 10).

Metal brake lines

10   When replacing brake lines be sure to use the correct parts. Don't use copper tubing for any brake system components. Purchase steel brake lines from a dealer or auto parts store.
11   Prefabricated brake line, with the tube ends already flared and fittings installed, is available at auto parts stores and dealers.
12   When installing the new line make sure it's securely supported in the brackets and has plenty of clearance between moving or hot components.
13   After installation, check the master cylinder fluid level and add fluid as necessary. Bleed the brake system as outlined in the next Section and test the brakes carefully before driving the vehicle in traffic.

10   Brake hydraulic system – bleeding

Refer to illustration 10.8
Warning: *Wear eye protection when bleeding the brake system. If the fluid comes in contact with your eyes, immediately rinse them with water and seek medical attention.*
Note: *Bleeding the hydraulic system is necessary to remove any air that manages to find its way into the system when it's been opened during removal and installation of a hose, line, caliper or master cylinder.*
1   It will probably be necessary to bleed the system at all four brakes if air has entered the system due to low fluid level, or if the brake lines have been disconnected at the master cylinder.
2   If a brake line was disconnected only at a wheel, then only that caliper or wheel cylinder must be bled.
3   If a brake line is disconnected at a fitting located between the master cylinder and any of the brakes, that part of the system served by the disconnected line must be bled.
4   Remove any residual vacuum from the brake power booster by applying the brake several times with the engine off.
5   Remove the master cylinder reservoir cover and fill the reservoir with brake fluid. Reinstall the cover. **Note:** *Check the fluid level often during the bleeding operation and add fluid as necessary to prevent the fluid level from falling low enough to allow air bubbles into the master cylinder.*
6   Have an assistant on hand, as well as a supply of new brake fluid, a clear container partially filled with clean brake fluid, a length of 3/16-inch plastic, rubber or vinyl tubing to fit over the bleeder valve and a wrench to open and close the bleeder valve.
7   Beginning at the right rear wheel, loosen the bleeder valve slightly, then tighten it to a point where it is snug but can still be loosened quickly and easily.

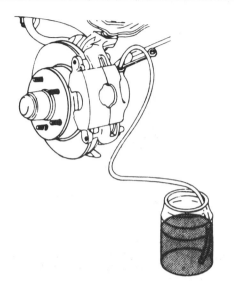

10.8 When bleeding the brakes, a piece of clear tubing is connected to the bleeder valve at the caliper or wheel cylinder and then submerged in brake fluid – air will be seen as bubbles in the tubing and container (all air must be expelled before moving to the next wheel)

8   Place one end of the tubing over the bleeder valve and submerge the other end in brake fluid in the container (see illustration).
9   Have the assistant pump the brakes slowly a few times to get pressure in the system, then hold the pedal firmly depressed.
10   While the pedal is held depressed, open the bleeder valve just enough to allow a flow of fluid to leave the valve. Watch for air bubbles to exit the submerged end of the tube. When the fluid flow slows after a couple of seconds, close the valve and have your assistant release the pedal.
11   Repeat Steps 9 and 10 until no more air is seen leaving the tube, then tighten the bleeder valve and proceed to the left front wheel, the left rear wheel and the right front wheel, in that order, and perform the same procedure. Be sure to check the fluid in the master cylinder reservoir frequently.

12   Never use old brake fluid. It contains moisture which will deteriorate the brake system components.
13   Refill the master cylinder with fluid at the end of the operation.
14   Check the operation of the brakes. The pedal should feel solid when depressed, with no sponginess. If necessary, repeat the entire process.
Warning: *Do not operate the vehicle if you are in doubt about the effectiveness of the brake system.*

---

11   Power brake booster – check, removal and installation

Refer to illustrations 11.7, 11.14a, 11.14b and 11.14c

Operating check

1   Depress the brake pedal several times with the engine off and make sure that there is no change in the pedal reserve distance.
2   Depress the pedal and start the engine. If the pedal goes down slightly, operation is normal.

Airtightness check

3   Start the engine and turn it off after one or two minutes.
Depress the brake pedal several times slowly. If the pedal goes down farther the first time but gradually rises after the second or third depression, the booster is air tight.
4   Depress the brake pedal while the engine is running, then stop the engine with the pedal depressed. If there is no change in the pedal reserve travel after holding the pedal for 30 seconds, the booster is airtight.

Removal

5   Power brake booster units should not be disassembled. They require special tools not normally found in most service stations or shops. They are fairly complex and because of their critical relationship to brake performance it is best to replace a defective booster unit with a new or rebuilt one.
6   To remove the booster, first remove the brake master cylinder as described in Section 8.
7   Locate the pushrod clevis connecting the booster to the brake pedal (see illustration). This is accessible from the interior in front of the driver's seat.

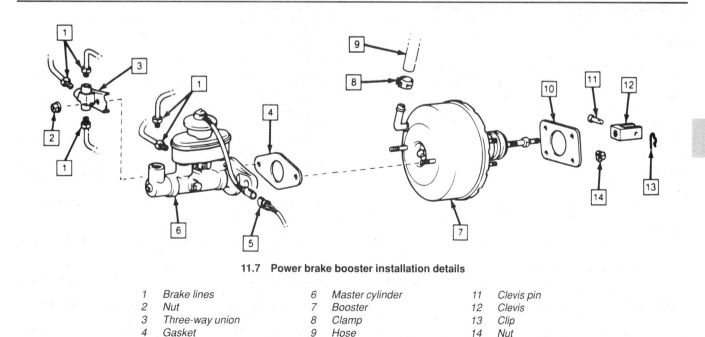

11.7   Power brake booster installation details

1	Brake lines	6	Master cylinder	11	Clevis pin
2	Nut	7	Booster	12	Clevis
3	Three-way union	8	Clamp	13	Clip
4	Gasket	9	Hose	14	Nut
5	Connector	10	Gasket		

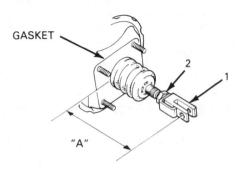

11.14a Be sure the pushrod clevis is set to the proper length

    1   Clevis
    2   Nut
    A   4-15/16 to 4-63/54 inches (125.5 to 126.5 mm)

**11.14c To change the length of the booster pushrod, hold the
serrated portion of the rod with a pair of pliers and turn the
adjusting screw in or out, as necessary**

8   Remove the clevis pin retaining clip with pliers and pull out the pin.
9   Holding the clevis with pliers, disconnect the clevis locknut with a wrench. The clevis is now loose.
10   Disconnect the hose leading from the engine to the booster. Be careful not to damage the hose when removing it from the booster fitting.
11   Remove the four nuts and washers holding the brake booster to the firewall. You may need a light to see these, as they are up under the dash area.
12   Slide the booster straight out from the firewall until the studs clear the holes and pull the booster, brackets and gaskets from the engine compartment area.

Installation

13   Installation procedures are basically the reverse of those for removal. Tighten the clevis locknut and booster mounting nuts.
14   If the power booster unit is being replaced, check the clevis rod length **(see illustration)**. Also the clearance between the master cylinder piston and the pushrod in the vacuum booster must be measured. Using a depth micrometer or vernier calipers, measure the distance from the seat (recessed area) in the master cylinder to the master cylinder mounting flange. With the engine running at idle, measure the distance from the end of the vacuum booster pushrod to the mounting face of the booster (including gasket) where the master cylinder mounting flange seats. Subtract the two measurements to get the clearance **(see illustration)**. If the clearance is more or less than specified, turn the adjusting screw on the end of the power booster pushrod until the clearance is within the specified limit **(see illustration)**.

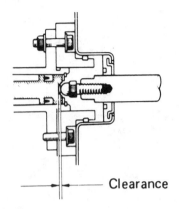

**11.14b The booster pushrod-to-master cylinder pushrod
clearance must be as specified – if there's interference
between the two, the brakes may drag; if there's too much
clearance, excessive brake pedal travel will result**

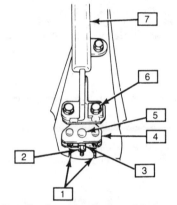

**12.3a Details of parking brake cable-to-passenger
compartment lever (Metro)**

1	*Parking brake cable*	*5*	*Pin*
2	*Brake cable locking nut*	*6*	*Parking brake lever bolt*
3	*Spacer*	*7*	*Parking brake lever assembly*
4	*Equalizer*		

---

12   Parking brake – adjustment

Refer to illustrations 12.3a and 12.3b
1   The parking brake lever, when properly adjusted, should travel four to nine clicks when a moderate pulling force is applied. If it travels less than four clicks, there's a chance the parking brake might not be releasing completely and might be dragging on the drum. If the lever can be pulled up more than nine clicks, the parking brake may not hold adequately on an incline, allowing the car to roll.
2   To adjust the cables, from inside the vehicle gain access to the lever base.
3   Use the proper nut(s) to loosen or tighten the cables **(see illustrations)**.

---

13   Parking brake cables – replacement

Refer to illustrations 13.4, 13.5a, 13,5b, 13.6, 13.7a and 13.7b
1   Block the front wheels of the vehicle.
2   Raise and securely support the rear of the vehicle.

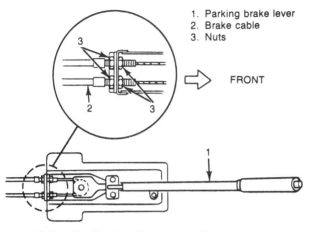

1. Parking brake lever
2. Brake cable
3. Nuts

FRONT

12.3b Details of parking brake cable-to-passenger compartment lever (Sprint)

13.4 Use needle-nose pliers to pull back the parking brake cable while detaching the lever from the cable

13.5a Squeeze the tangs (arrow) to separate the cable from the backing plate (Metro)

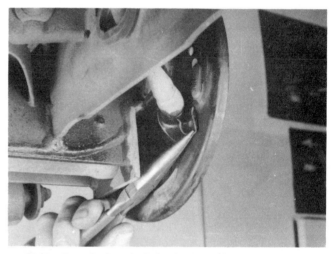

13.5b Remove the clip retaining the cable to the backing plate (Sprint)

6   On all models, detach the cable from under the vehicle at each body attaching point (see illustration).
7   Detach the cable from the parking brake lever in the passenger compartment (see illustrations).
8   Installation is the reverse of removal. Use some silicone sealer to seal the area were the cable meets the backing plate. Adjust the cable after installation (see Section 12).

14   Brake light switch – removal, installation and adjustment

Refer to illustration 14.6

Removal and installation

1   The brake light switch is located on a bracket at the top of the brake pedal. The switch activates the brake lights at the rear of the vehicle when the pedal is depressed.
2   Disconnect the negative battery cable from the battery.
3   Disconnect the wiring harness at the brake light switch.
4   Loosen the locknut and unscrew the switch from the pedal bracket.
5   Installation is the reverse of removal.

13.6 Typical cable-to-body attaching point

3   Remove the brake drum(s) and brake shoes (see Section 5).
4   Detach the parking brake cable from the brake shoe lever (see illustration).
5   On Metro models, use pliers to squeeze the tangs on the cable retainer and detach the cable from the backing plate (see illustration). On Sprint models, remove the cable retaining clip and detach the cable from the backing plate (see illustration).

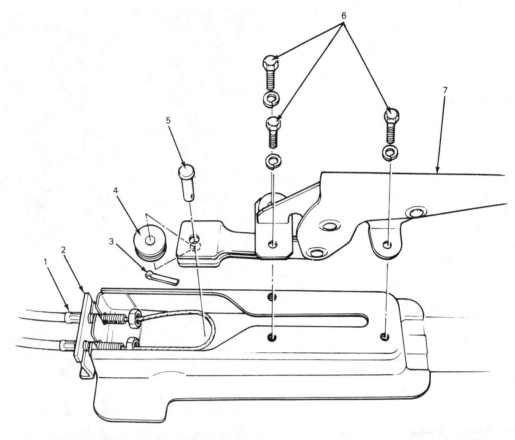

13.7a   Exploded view of the parking brake lever in the passenger compartment (Sprint)

1	Parking brake cable	4	Parking cable pulley	6	Parking brake lever bolts
2	Cable support	5	Clevis pin	7	Parking brake lever assembly
3	Cotter pin				

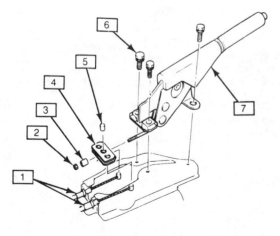

13.7b   Exploded view of the parking brake lever in the passenger compartment (Metro)

1	Parking brake cable	5	Pin
2	Brake cable locking nut	6	Parking brake lever bolt
3	Spacer	7	Parking brake lever
4	Equalizer		assembly

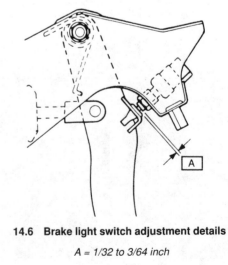

14.6   Brake light switch adjustment details

A = 1/32 to 3/64 inch

Adjustment

6   Loosen the locknut, adjust the switch so there is a gap of 1/32 to 3/64 inch between the threaded portion and the pedal stop **(see illustration)**, then tighten the locknut.

7   Connect the wires at the switch and the battery. Make sure the rear brake lights are functioning properly.

Chapter 10
Suspension and steering systems

Contents

Specifications

Torque specifications

Ft-lbs

Metro

Control arm bracket nuts	74
Control arm front bracket bolts	59
Control arm rear bracket bolt	32
Knuckle-to-control arm pinch bolt	44
Strut-to-knuckle bolts	59
Strut-to-tower nuts	20
Steering gear mounting bolts	18
Steering shaft joint bolts	18

Sprint

Control arm bolt	36 to 50
Knuckle-to-control arm pinch bolt	36 to 50
Stabilizer bar castle nut	29 to 65
Stabilizer bar mount bolt	22 to 39
Steering gear mounting bolts	14.5 to 21.5
Steering shaft joint bolts	14.5 to 21.5
Strut-to-knuckle bolts	50.5 to 65.0
Strut-to-tower nut	29 to 43

1   General information

The front suspension is a Macpherson strut design. The upper end of each strut is attached to the vehicle's body strut support. The lower end of the strut is connected to the upper end of the steering knuckle. The steering knuckle is attached to a balljoint mounted on the outer end of the suspension control arm.

On Sprint models, the front control arms are connected by a stabilizer bar, which also controls fore-and-aft movement of the control arms.

On Metro models, the rear suspension also utilizes struts. The upper end of each strut is attached to the vehicle body by a strut support. The lower end of the strut is attached to a knuckle. The knuckle is located by a pair of suspension arms on each side, and a transverse mounted control rod between the body and each knuckle **(see illustration)**. A coil spring is mounted between the body and each suspension arm.

On the rear suspension of Sprint models, a solid axle is used. In 1985 and 1986 leaf springs and shock absorbers are used to control the suspension. In 1987, coil springs, shock absorbers, trailing arms and a lateral rod is used to control the suspension.

On all models, the rack and pinion steering gear is located behind the engine/transaxle assembly on the firewall and actuates the tie rods, which are attached to the steering knuckles. The steering column is designed to collapse in the event of an accident.

Frequently, when working on the suspension or steering system components, you may come across fasteners which seem impossible to loosen. These fasteners on the underside of the vehicle are continually subjected to water, road grime, mud, etc., and can become rusted or frozen, making them extremely difficult to remove. In order to unscrew these stubborn fasteners without damaging them (or other components), be sure to use lots of penetrating oil and allow it to soak in for a while. Using a wire brush to clean exposed threads will also ease removal of the nut or bolt and prevent damage to the threads. Sometimes a sharp blow with a hammer and punch will break the bond between a nut and bolt threads, but care must be taken to prevent the punch from slipping off the fastener and ruining the threads. Heating the stuck fastener and surrounding area

with a torch sometimes helps too, but isn't recommended because of the obvious dangers associated with fire. Long breaker bars and extension, or "cheater", pipes will increase leverage, but never use an extension pipe on a ratchet – the ratcheting mechanism could be damaged. Sometimes tightening the nut or bolt first will help to break it loose. Fasteners that require drastic measures to remove should always be replaced with new ones.

Since most of the procedures dealt with in this Chapter involve jacking up the vehicle and working underneath it, a good pair of jackstands will be needed. A hydraulic floor jack is the preferred type of jack to lift the vehicle, and it can also be used to support certain components during various operations. **Warning:** *Never, under any circumstances, rely on a jack to support the vehicle while working on it. Whenever any of the suspension or steering fasteners are loosened or removed they must be inspected and, if necessary, replaced with new ones of the same part number or of original equipment quality and design. Torque specifications must be followed for proper reassembly and component retention. Never attempt to heat or straighten any suspension or steering components. Instead, replace any bent or damaged part with a new one.*

2   Stabilizer bar (front) – removal and installation

Refer to illustration 2.4

Note: *This procedure applies to Sprint models only.*

1   Block the rear wheels.
2   Raise the front of the vehicle and allow the control arms to hang.
3   Remove the front wheels.
4   Remove the stabilizer bracket bolts and brackets **(see illustration)**.
5   Detach the stabilizer bar from the front suspension arms.
6   Remove the stabilizer bar.
7   Installation is the reverse of removal.
8   When installing the stabilizer bar, loosely assemble all components while insuring that the stabilizer is centered before tightening components.

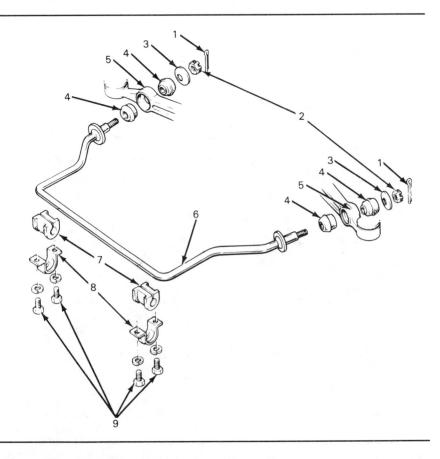

2.4   Mounting details of the Sprint stabilizer bar

1   Cotter pin
2   Castle nut
3   Stabilizer bar washer
4   Stabilizer bar bushing
5   Suspension control arm
6   Stabilizer bar
7   Mount bushing
8   Mounting bushing bracket
9   Mounting bracket bolt

3.3 A pair of needle nose pliers works well for removing the clip that retains the brake line to the strut bracket

3.4 Remove the nuts and bolts attaching the strut to the knuckle

3 Strut assembly (front) – removal, inspection and installation

Refer to illustrations 3.3, 3.4 and 3.5

1   Raise the front of the vehicle so the front suspension hangs free.
2   Remove the front wheels.
3   Remove the clip retaining the brake line to the strut bracket **(see illustration)**.
4   Remove the strut-to-knuckle nuts and bolts **(see illustration)**.
5   Working under the hood, remove the nuts retaining the strut to the strut tower **(see illustration)**.
6   Remove the strut assembly. Be careful not to damage the outer CV joint boot during strut removal. And don't over-extend the inner CV joint (one way to prevent this from happening is to wire the top of the steering knuckle to the body).
7   Check the strut body for leaking fluid, dents, cracks and other obvious damage which would warrant repair or replacement. Check the coil spring for chips and cracks in the spring coating (this will cause premature spring failure due to corrosion).
8   Inspect the spring seat for damage, hardness and general deterioration.
9   If any undesirable conditions exist, proceed to Section 4 for the strut disassembly procedure.
10   Installation is the reverse of removal.

4 Strut cartridge (front) – replacement

Refer to illustrations 4.4, 4.5, 4.6a, 4.6b, 4.6c and 4.10
Warning: *Whenever any of the suspension or steering fasteners are loosened or removed they must be inspected and, if necessary, replaced with new ones of the same part number or original equipment quality and design. Torque specifications must be followed for proper reassembly and component retention.*
Note: *You'll need a spring compressor for this procedure. Spring compressors are available on a daily rental basis at most auto parts stores or equipment yards.*

1   If the struts or coil springs exhibit the telltale signs of wear (leaking fluid, loss of damping capability, chipped, sagging or cracked coil springs) explore all options before beginning any work. The strut insert assemblies are not serviceable and must be replaced if a problem develops. However, strut assemblies complete with springs may be available on an exchange basis, which eliminates much time and work. Whichever route you choose to take, check on the cost and availability of parts before disassembling your vehicle. **Warning:** *Disassembling a strut assembly is a potentially dangerous undertaking and utmost attention must be directed to the job at hand, or serious bodily injury may result. Use only a high quality spring*

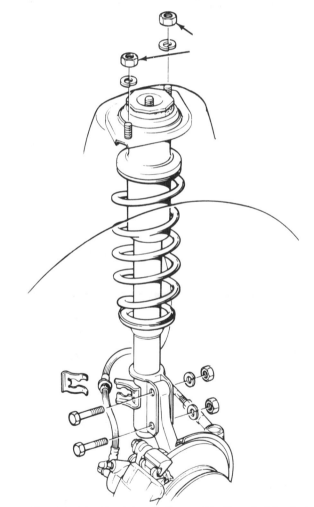

3.5 Mounting details of the strut assembly. Two strut-to-strut tower retaining nuts are used on this assembly (arrows)

compressor and carefully follow the manufacturer's instructions furnished with the tool. After removing the coil spring from the strut assembly, set it aside in a safe, isolated area (a steel cabinet is preferred).
2   Remove the strut and spring assembly (see Section 3).
3   Mount the strut assembly in a vise. Line the vise jaws with wood or rags to prevent damage to the unit and don't tighten the vise excessively.

10

4.4   Install the spring compressor according to the tool manufacturer's instructions and compress the spring until all pressure is relieved from the upper spring seat

4.5   Remove the damper shaft nut

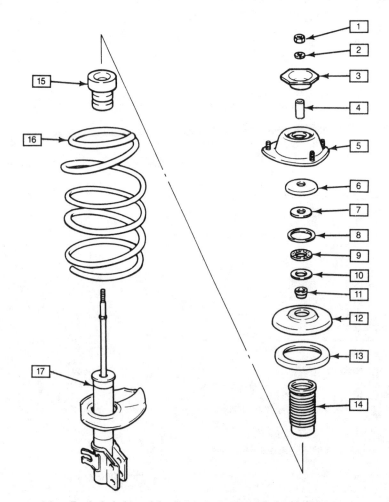

4.6a   Exploded view of the front strut assembly for the Metro

1	Nut	6	Bearing seat	10	Bearing lower washer	14	Strut cover
2	Washer	7	Bearing upper washer	11	Bearing spacer	15	Bump stopper
3	Stopper	8	Bearing seal	12	Coil spring upper seat	16	Coil spring
4	Inner spacer	9	Bearing	13	Coil spring seat	17	Strut
5	Support comp.						

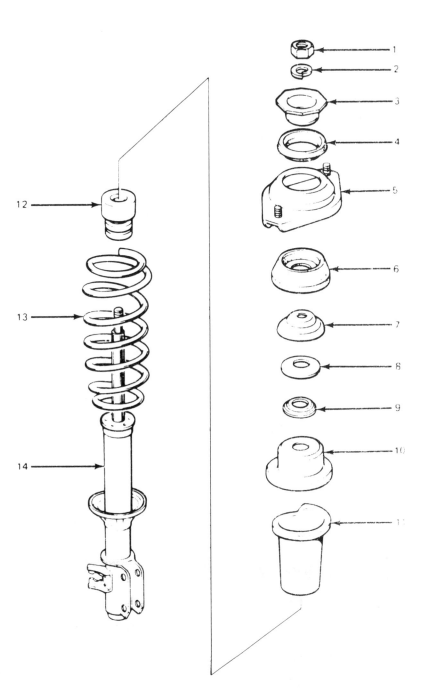

4.6b   Exploded view of the front strut assembly for the Sprint

1	Strut nut	5	Strut support
2	Strut lock washer	6	Strut mount
3	Strut inner support	7	Strut mount seat
4	Strut rebound stopper	8	Strut bearing seat

9	Strut bearing	12	Bump stopper
10	Spring upper seat	13	Coil spring
11	Strut spring seat	14	Strut assembly

10

4   Install the spring compressor in accordance with the manufacturer's instructions **(see illustration)**. Compress the spring until you can wiggle the strut (suspension) support.

5   Loosen the damper shaft nut with a socket wrench **(see illustration)**. **Note:** *If the shaft nut cannot be removed because the insert shaft rotates, use a pair of vise grips with a rag in the jaws for insulation clamped to the shaft to keep the shaft from rotating.*

6   Disassemble the strut assembly **(see illustrations)**. **Warning:** *When removing the compressed spring, it should be carefully lifted from the assembly **(see illustration)** and set it in a safe place, such as a steel cabinet. Never place your head near the end of the spring!*

7   Unscrew the retaining cap for the strut cartridge.

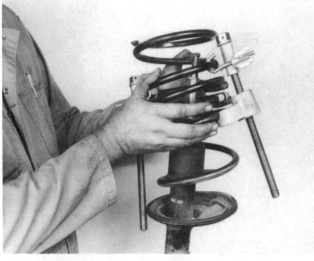

4.6c When removing the compressed spring assembly – keep the ends of the spring pointing away from your body!

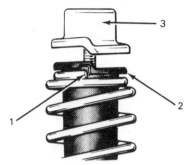

1. SPRING UPPER END
2. SPRING SEAT
3. SPRING UPPER SEAT

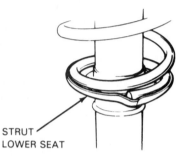

STRUT
LOWER SEAT

4.10 When assembling the strut, make sure the spring ends seat properly into the upper and lower seats

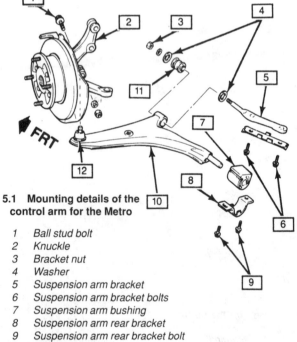

5.1 Mounting details of the control arm for the Metro

1 Ball stud bolt
2 Knuckle
3 Bracket nut
4 Washer
5 Suspension arm bracket
6 Suspension arm bracket bolts
7 Suspension arm bushing
8 Suspension arm rear bracket
9 Suspension arm rear bracket bolt
10 Suspension arm
11 Suspension arm front bushing
12 Ball stud

8   Pull out the cartridge from the strut housing.
9   Check the rubber parts for damage, cracking and hardness and re-place as necessary.
10 Reassembly is the reverse of disassembly. Be careful not to damage the damper shaft or the strut will leak. When installing the spring, be sure the spring ends mesh with the spring anti-rotation stops provided by the spring upper and lower seats (see illustration).

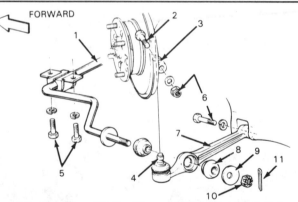

FORWARD

5.5 Mounting details of the control arm for the Sprint

1 Stabilizer bar
2 Ball stud bolt
3 Knuckle
4 Ball stud
5 Stabilizer bar
   mount bracket bolt
6 Control arm bolt
7 Suspension control arm
8 Stabilizer bar bushing
9 Washer
10 Castle nut
11 Split pin

5   Control arm (front) – removal, inspection and installation

Refer to illustrations 5.1 and 5.5

Removal
Metro
1   Remove the ball stud bolt (see illustration).
2   Remove the control arm rear bracket.
3   Remove the control arm front retaining nut.
4   Remove the control arm.

Sprint
5   Remove the ball stud bolt (see illustration).

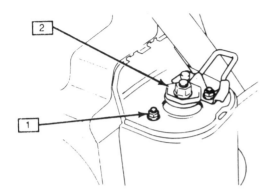

8.3   Remove the strut tower-to-strut retaining nuts

1   Support retaining nut   2   Strut

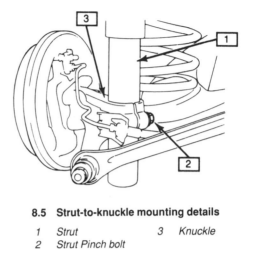

8.5   Strut-to-knuckle mounting details

1   Strut   3   Knuckle
2   Strut Pinch bolt

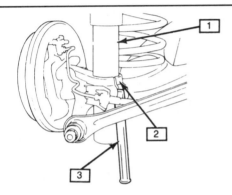

8.6   If necessary, use a chisel to spread open the slit of the knuckle a little

1   Strut   3   Wedge
2   Knuckle

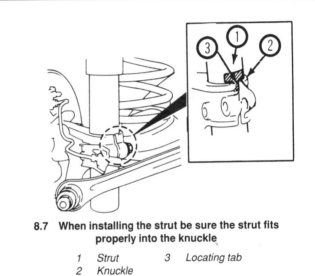

8.7   When installing the strut be sure the strut fits properly into the knuckle

1   Strut   3   Locating tab
2   Knuckle

6   Remove the control arm-to-body mounting bolt.
7   Remove the control arm from the sway bar.

Inspection
8   Check the control arm for distortion and the bushings for wear, damage and deterioration. Replace a distorted control arm with a new one. If the bushings are damaged, an arbor press is necessary to remove and install them.

Installation
9   Installation is the reverse of removal.
10   If the bushings are replaced, have the front wheel alignment checked and adjusted.

6   Balljoint (front) – replacement

On all models, the balljoint is replaced by replacing the control arm (see Section 5)

7   Steering knuckle – removal and installation

1   Raise and securely support the front of the vehicle so the front suspension hangs free.
2   Remove the front wheels.

3   Remove the brake caliper (see Chapter 9).
4   Remove the ball stud bolt **(see illustration 5.1 or 5.5)**.
5   Remove the clip retaining the brake line to the strut bracket **(see illustration 3.3)**.
6   Remove the strut-to-knuckle bolts **(see illustration 3.4)**.
7   Remove the knuckle.
8   Installation is the reverse of removal.

8   Rear strut assembly (Metro) – removal and installation

Refer to illustrations 8.3, 8.5, 8.6 and 8.7
1   Raise and securely support the rear of the vehicle.
2   Place a jack under the rear control arm.
3   Working at the strut tower, remove the nuts retaining the upper part of the strut to the tower **(see illustration)**.
4   Compress the strut.
5   Remove the pinch bolt from the knuckle **(see illustration)**.
6   By pulling up on the lower portion of the strut, detach the strut from the knuckle. If the strut is hard to remove, open the slit of the knuckle a little **(see illustration)**. **Caution:** *During strut removal, do not lower the jack more than necessary to prevent the coil spring from coming out, or brake hose from being damaged.*
7   Installation is the reverse of removal. Be sure the strut locating tab aligns properly with the rear knuckle **(see illustration)**.

10

9   Rear coil spring and suspension arms (Metro) – removal and installation

Refer to illustrations 9.3 and 9.4

1   Block the front wheels, raise and securely support the rear of the vehicle.
2   Remove the rear wheel(s).
3   Reference mark the position of the cam for rear toe adjustment **(see illustration)**.
4   Loosen the nuts mounting the suspension arm to the body **(see illustration)**.
5   Loosen the knuckle-to-suspension arm mounting nut.
6   Place a jack under the suspension arm to prevent it from lowering.
7   Remove the lower mount nut of the knuckle.
8   Raise the jack placed under the suspension arm enough to remove the knuckle-to-suspension arm mounting bolt.
9   Separate the knuckle from the suspension arm.
10   Lower the jack gradually and remove the coil spring.
11   Remove the body-to-suspension arm bolts.
12   Remove the suspension arm.
13   Installation is the reverse of removal. Be sure to place the rear toe adjustment cam in the same position as it was in before removal.

10   Rear leaf spring (1985 and 1986 Sprint) – removal and installation

Refer to illustration 10.4

1   Block the front wheels, raise and securely support the rear of the vehicle.
2   Remove the rear wheel(s).
3   Support the center of the axle with a floor jack.
4   Remove the U-bolt nuts **(see illustration)**.
5   Remove the bolt retaining the front of the leaf spring.
6   Remove the nuts and bracket retaining the rear of the leaf spring.

7   Remove the leaf spring from the shackle pin.
8   Installation is the reverse of removal.

11   Rear axle (Sprint) – removal and installation

Refer to illustrations 11.4a, 11.4b, 11.6, 11.8, 11.14, 11.18, 11.21, 11.24, 11.25a and 11.25b

1985 and 1986 (leaf spring equipped)

1   Raise the rear of the vehicle.
2   Remove the rear wheels.
3   Remove the brake drums.
4   Remove the clip retaining the brake line to the axle **(see illustration)**. Separate the steel brake line from the flexible hose **(see illustration)**.

9.3   Mark the relationship of the toe adjuster to the body on the inner end of the rear suspension arms

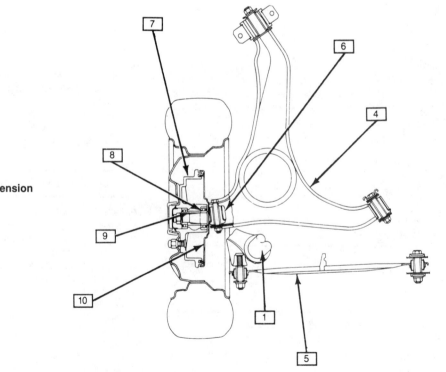

9.4   Overview of the rear suspension of the Metro

1   *Strut*
2   *Vehicle body*
3   *Coil spring*
4   *Suspension arm*
5   *Control rod*
6   *Rear knuckle*
7   *Brake drum*
8   *Wheel bearing*
9   *Bearing spacer*
10   *Brake back plate*

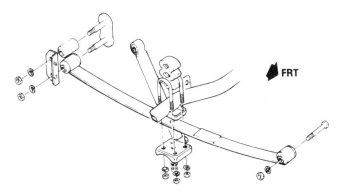

10.4   1985 and 1986 Sprint mounting details of the rear leaf spring

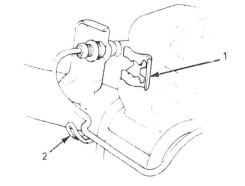

11.4a   Remove the clip retaining the brake line to the axle

1   Flex hose retainer   *2   Brake line retainer*

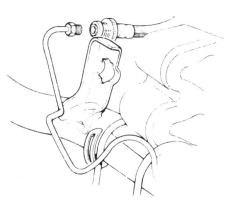

11.4b   Separate the steel brake line from the flexible hose

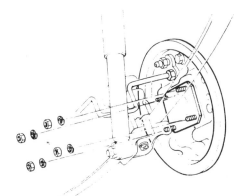

11.6   Four nuts retain the backing plate to the axle

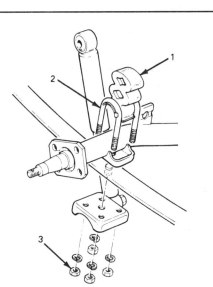

11.8   Remove the U-bolt nuts, the U-bolts and the jounce stops

1   Jounce stop   3   U-bolt nut
2   U-bolt

5   To prevent loss of brake fluid, plug the brake hose and line.
6   Remove the nuts retaining the backing plates to the axle **(see illustration)**.
7   Remove the backing plate from the axle.

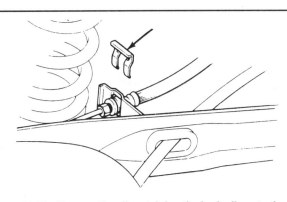

11.14   Remove the clip retaining the brake lines to the trailing arms

8   Remove the U-bolt nuts, the U-bolts and the jounce stops **(see illustration)**.
9   Remove the rear axle.
10   Installation is the reverse of removal. When installing the backing plate, apply sealant between the axle-to-backing plate surface. Be sure to bleed the brakes after installation (see Chapter 9).

1987 (coil spring equipped)

11   Block the front wheels, raise and support the rear of the vehicle by the body or frame.
12   Remove the rear wheels.
13   Remove the brake drums (see Chapter 9).
14   Remove the clip retaining the brake lines to the trailing arms **(see illustration)**.

10

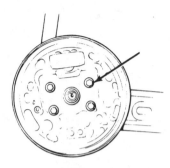

11.18   Remove the four bolts retaining the backing plate (arrow)

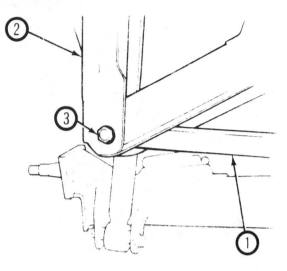

11.21   Remove the lateral rod-to-body bolt

1	Lateral rod	3	Lateral rod-to-body
2	Body		bolt

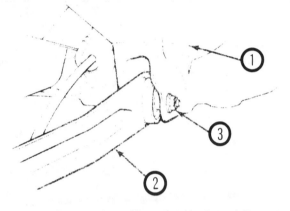

11.24   Remove the trailing arm-to-body retaining nut

1	Body	3	Trailing arm-to-body
2	Trailing arm		retaining nut

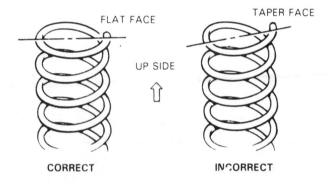

11.25a   When installing the spring, be sure the end of the spring with the flat face is up and . . .

21   Remove the bolt retaining the lateral rod-to-body **(see illustration)**.
22   Remove the lower retaining bolts for the shocks.
23   Lower the floor jack to release the spring tension.
24   Remove the trailing arm-to-body nuts and bolts and remove the axle **(see illustration)**.
25   Installation is the reverse of removal. When installing the springs be sure that the taper end of the spring faces down and meshes with the stepped part of the lower seat and the flat surface faces up **(see illustrations)**

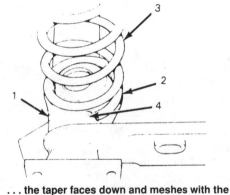

11.25b   . . . the taper faces down and meshes with the stepped part of the lower spring seat

1	Rear axle	3	Coil spring
2	Spring seat	4	Stepped part

12   Steering system – general information

Refer to illustration 12.1

All models are equipped with rack and pinion steering **(see illustration)**. The rack and pinion assembly is bolted to the firewall and operates the steering arms via tie rods. The inner ends of the tie rods are protected by rubber boots which should be inspected periodically for secure attachment, tears and leaking lubricant.

The steering wheel operates the steering shaft, which actuates the steering gear through universal joints. Looseness in the steering can be caused by wear in the steering shaft universal joints, the steering gear, the tie rod ends and loose retaining bolts.

15   Disconnect the brake lines from the wheel cylinders and plug the brake lines to prevent fluid leakage.
16   Remove the brake lines from the brackets on the trailing arm.
17   Remove the brake shoes and detach the parking brake cable from the shoe levers and backing plates (see Chapter 9).
18   Remove the bolts retaining the backing plate to the axle **(see illustration)**.
19   Remove the backing plates.
20   Using a floor jack, support the center of the axle.

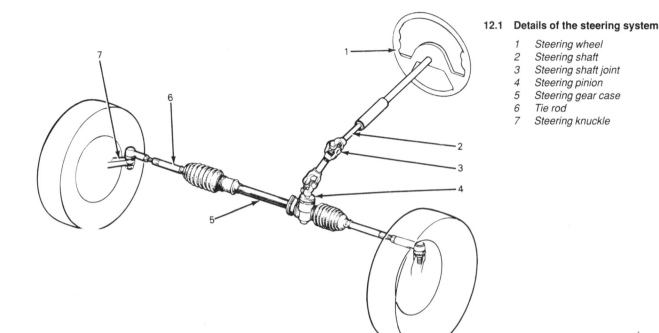

12.1   **Details of the steering system**

1   *Steering wheel*
2   *Steering shaft*
3   *Steering shaft joint*
4   *Steering pinion*
5   *Steering gear case*
6   *Tie rod*
7   *Steering knuckle*

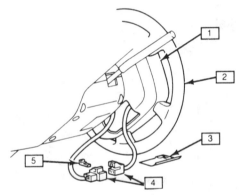

13.3   **Details of SIR wiring harness located in the steering wheel**

1   *Inflator module housing*
2   *Steering wheel*
3   *Rear plastic access cover*
4   *SIR harness connector*
5   *Connector Position Assurance (CPA)*

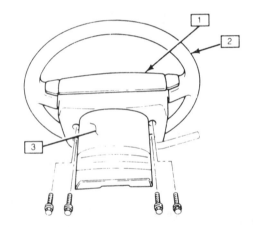

13.6a   **Mounting details of the SIR module**

1   *Inflator module*
2   *Steering wheel*
3   *Steering column upper trim cover*

---

13   Steering wheel – removal and installation

Refer to illustrations 13.3, 13.6a, 13.6b, 13.8, 13.9 and 13.14

1991 Metro with Supplemental Inflatable Restraint (SIR)

1   Turn the ignition switch to the Off position.
2   Remove the "SIR IG" fuse to the SIR fuse block.
3   Remove the plastic access cover at the rear of the inflator module housing **(see illustration)**.
4   Inside the inflator module housing, detach the yellow two-way connector and the position assurance connector.
5   Detach the negative battery cable.
6   Remove the four screws from the rear of the wheel and remove the inflator module **(see illustration)**. **Caution:** *When working around or car-*

ring an air bag module, keep the pad surface away from your face and body. When storing an air bag module, always place the padded area up and do not place anything on or near it **(see illustration)**.
7   Remove the steering wheel retaining nut.
8   Reference mark the position of the steering wheel-to-shaft **(see illustration)**.
9   While being very careful not to damage the SIR coil and turn signal/dimmer switch, use a steering wheel puller to remove the wheel **(see illustration)**.
10   Remove the horn switch screws and switches from the wheel.
11   Remove the screws retaining the rear steering wheel cover and remove the cover.
12   Using the reference marks made during removal and reversing the removal procedure, install the wheel.

All others

13   Detach the negative cable from the battery.

10

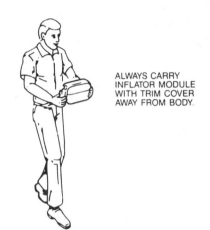

ALWAYS CARRY
INFLATOR MODULE
WITH TRIM COVER
AWAY FROM BODY.

13.8   Before removing the steering wheel, reference mark it's position (arrow)

ALWAYS PLACE
INFLATOR MODULE
ON WORKBENCH
WITH TRIM COVER
UP, AWAY FROM
LOOSE OBJECTS.

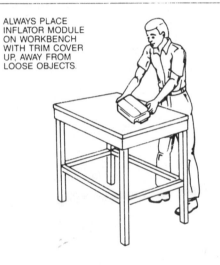

13.6b   Properly handle the SIR module

13.9   Use a steering wheel puller to remove the wheel

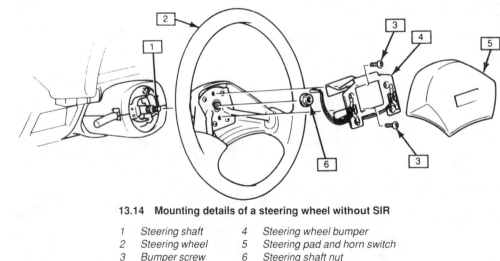

13.14   Mounting details of a steering wheel without SIR

1	*Steering shaft*	*4*	*Steering wheel bumper*
2	*Steering wheel*	*5*	*Steering pad and horn switch*
3	*Bumper screw*	*6*	*Steering shaft nut*

14   Pull up on the steering wheel pad and remove it **(see illustration)**.

15   Remove the nut retaining the steering wheel.

16   Reference mark the position of the steering wheel to the shaft **(see illustration 13.8)**.

17   Using a steering wheel puller, remove the wheel **(see illustration 13.8)**.

18   Using the reference marks made during removal and reversing the removal procedure, install the wheel.

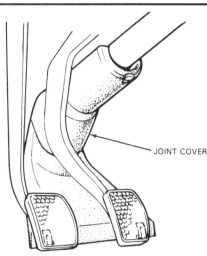

14.2 Remove the joint cover to expose the steering column-to-steering shaft

JOINT COVER

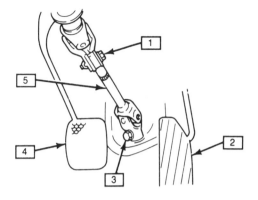

14.3 Details of the steering shaft joint

1 *Steering column-to-steering shaft joint*
2 *Accelerator pedal*
3 *Steering shaft joint lower mounting bolt*
4 *Brake pedal*
5 *Steering shaft joint*

---

14 Steering gear – removal and installation

Refer to illustrations 14.2, 14.3 and 14.8

1   Move the driver's seat as far back as possible.
2   Pull off the front part of the floor mat on the driver's side and remove the steering shaft joint cover **(see illustration)**.
3   Loosen the upper joint bolt for the steering shaft but don't remove it **(see illustration)**.
4   Remove the lower joint bolt for the steering shaft. Disconnect the lower joint from the pinion.
5   Raise the front of the vehicle and securely support it.
6   Remove both front wheels.
7   From both knuckles, remove the cotter pins and tie rod castle nuts.
8   Using a puller, detach the tie rod ends from the knuckles **(see illustration)**.
9   Remove the bolts mounting the steering gear to the body.
10   Installation is the reverse of removal. Be sure when connecting the steering lower joint into the steering pinion shaft, the brake discs and the steering wheel are in the straight ahead position.

---

15 Tie-rod ends – removal and installation

Refer to illustration 15.2

Removal

1   Loosen the wheel lug nuts. Raise the front of the vehicle, support it securely, block the rear wheels and set the parking brake. Remove the front wheel.
2   Loosen the jam nut enough to mark the position of the tie-rod end in relation to the threads **(see illustration)**.
3   Remove the cotter pin and loosen the nut on the tie-rod end stud.
4   Disconnect the tie-rod from the steering knuckle arm with a puller **(see illustration 14.8)**. Remove the nut and separate the tie-rod.
5   Unscrew the tie-rod end from the tie-rod.

Installation

6   Thread the tie-rod end on to the marked position and insert the tie-rod stud into the steering knuckle arm. Tighten the jam nut securely.
7   Install the castellated nut on the stud and tighten it. Install a new cotter pin.
8   Install the wheel and lug nuts. Lower the vehicle and tighten the lug nuts.
9   Have the alignment checked by a dealer service department or an alignment shop.

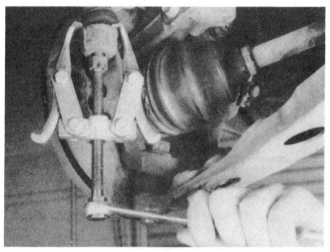

14.8 A two-jaw puller works well for separating the tie-rod end from the steering knuckle arm – note that the nut hasn't been removed (it will prevent the two components from separating violently)

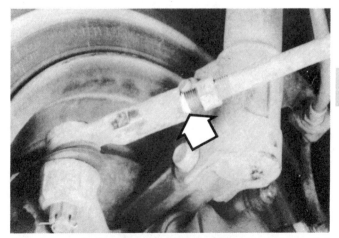

15.2 Loosen the jam nut and mark the relationship of the tie-rod end to the tie-rod with white paint

10

16   Steering gear boots – replacement

1   Loosen the lug nuts, raise the vehicle and support it securely on jackstands. Remove the wheel.
2   Remove the tie-rod end and jam nut (see Section 15).
3   Remove the steering gear boot clamps and slide the boot off.
4   Before installing the new boot, wrap the threads and serrations on the end of the steering rod with a layer of tape so the small end of the new boot isn't damaged.
5   Slide the new boot into position on the steering gear until it seats in the groove in the steering rod and install new clamps.
6   Remove the tape and install the tie-rod end (See Section 15).
7   Install the wheel and lug nuts. Lower the vehicle and tighten the lug nuts to the torque specified in Chapter 1.

17   Wheels and tires – general information

Refer to illustration 17.1

All vehicles covered by this manual are equipped with metric size fiberglass or steel belted radial tires **(see illustration)**. A label on the drivers door jamb indicates the size tire used. Use of other size or type of tires may affect the ride and handling of the vehicle. Don't mix different types of tires, such as radials and bias belted, on the same vehicle as handling may be seriously affected. It's recommended that tires be replaced in pairs on the same axle, but if only one tire is being replaced, be sure it's the same size, structure and tread design as the other.

Because tire pressure has a substantial effect on handling and wear, the pressure on all tires should be checked at least once a month or before any extended trips (see Chapter 1).

Wheels must be replaced if they are bent, dented, leak air, have elongated bolt holes, are heavily rusted, out of vertical symmetry or if the lug nuts won't stay tight. Wheel repairs that use welding or peening are not recommended.

Tire and wheel balance is important in the overall handling, braking and performance of the vehicle. Unbalanced wheels can adversely affect handling and ride characteristics as well as tire life. Whenever a tire is installed on a wheel, the tire and wheel should be balanced by a shop with the proper equipment.

18   Wheel alignment – general information

Refer to illustration 18.1

A wheel alignment refers to the adjustments made to the wheels so they are in proper angular relationship to the suspension and the ground. Wheels that are out of proper alignment not only affect vehicle control, but also increase tire wear. The wheel angles normally checked are camber, caster and toe-in **(see illustration)**, although the only adjustment possible is toe-in.

Getting the proper wheel alignment is a very exacting process, one in which complicated and expensive machines are necessary to perform the job properly. Because of this, you should have a technician with the proper equipment perform these tasks. We will, however, use this space to give you a basic idea of what is involved with wheel alignment so you can better understand the process and deal intelligently with the shop that does the work.

Toe-in is the turning in of the wheels. The purpose of a toe specification is to ensure parallel rolling of the wheels. In a vehicle with zero toe-in, the distance between the front edges of the wheels will be the same as the distance between the rear edges of the wheels. The actual amount of toe-in is normally only a fraction of an inch. On the front end, toe-in is controlled by the tie-rod end position on the tie-rod. On the rear end, it's controlled by a cam on the inner end of the suspension arm. Incorrect toe-in will cause the tires to wear improperly by making them scrub against the road surface.

Camber is the tilting of the wheels from the vertical when viewed from the end of the vehicle. When the wheels tilt out at the top, the camber is said to be positive (+). When the wheels tilt in at the top the camber is negative (-). The amount of tilt is measured in degrees from the vertical and this measurement is called the camber angle. This angle affects the amount of tire tread which contacts the road and compensates for changes in the suspension geometry when the vehicle is cornering or travelling over an undulating surface. Camber is not adjustable on the vehicles covered by this manual.

Caster is the tilting of the front steering axis from the vertical. A tilt toward the rear is positive caster and a tilt toward the front is negative caster. Caster is not adjustable on the vehicles covered by this manual.

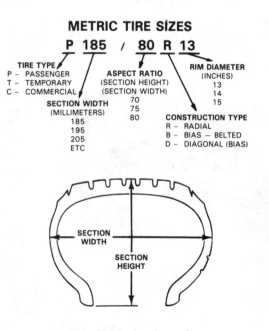

17.1   Metric tire size code

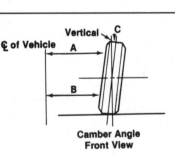

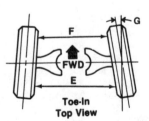

18.1   Wheel alignment details – camber (top) and toe-in (bottom) – the actual adjustment of these angles is beyond the scope of the home mechanic and must be preformed by an alignment shop or service station

A minus B = C (degrees camber)
E minus F = toe-in (measured in inches)
G = toe-in (expressed in degrees)

Chapter 11   Body

Contents

1   General information

These models feature a "unibody" layout, using a floor pan with front and rear frame side rails which support the body components, front and rear suspension systems and other mechanical components.

Certain components are particularly vulnerable to accident damage and can be unbolted and repaired or replaced. Among these parts are the body moldings, bumpers, hood and trunk lids and all glass.

Only general body maintenance practices and body panel repair procedures within the scope of the do-it-yourselfer are included in this Chapter.

2   Body – maintenance

1   The condition of your vehicle's body is very important, because the resale value depends a great deal on it. It's much more difficult to repair a neglected or damaged body than it is to repair mechanical components. The hidden areas of the body, such as the wheel wells, the frame and the engine compartment, are equally important, although they don't require as frequent attention as the rest of the body.
2   Once a year, or every 12,000 miles, it's a good idea to have the underside of the body steam cleaned. All traces of dirt and oil will be removed and the area can then be inspected carefully for rust, damaged brake lines, frayed electrical wires, damaged cables and other problems. The front suspension components should be greased after completion of this job.
3   At the same time, clean the engine and the engine compartment with a steam cleaner or water soluble degreaser.
4   The wheel wells should be given close attention, since undercoating can peel away and stones and dirt thrown up by the tires can cause the paint to chip and flake, allowing rust to set in. If rust is found, clean down to the bare metal and apply an anti-rust paint.
5   The body should be washed about once a week. Wet the vehicle thoroughly to soften the dirt, then wash it down with a soft sponge and plenty of clean soapy water. If the surplus dirt is not washed off very carefully, it can wear down the paint.
6   Spots of tar or asphalt thrown up from the road should be removed with a cloth soaked in solvent.
7   Once every six months, wax the body and chrome trim. If a chrome cleaner is used to remove rust from any of the vehicle's plated parts, remember that the cleaner also removes part of the chrome, so use it sparingly.

3   Vinyl trim – maintenance

Don't clean vinyl trim with detergents, caustic soap or petroleum-based cleaners. Plain soap and water works just fine, with a soft brush to clean dirt that may be ingrained. Wash the vinyl as frequently as the rest of the vehicle.

After cleaning, application of a high quality rubber and vinyl protectant will help prevent oxidation and cracks. The protectant can also be applied to weatherstripping, vacuum lines and rubber hoses, which often fail as a result of chemical degradation, and to the tires.

4   Upholstery and carpets – maintenance

1   Every three months remove the carpets or mats and clean the interior of the vehicle (more frequently if necessary). Vacuum the upholstery and carpets to remove loose dirt and dust.
2   Leather upholstery requires special care. Stains should be removed with warm water and a very mild soap solution. Use a clean, damp cloth to remove the soap, then wipe again with a dry cloth. Never use alcohol, gasoline, nail polish remover or thinner to clean leather upholstery.
3   After cleaning, regularly treat leather upholstery with a leather wax. Never use car wax on leather upholstery.
4   In areas where the interior of the vehicle is subject to bright sunlight, cover leather seats with a sheet if the vehicle is to be left out for any length of time.

This photo sequence illustrates the repair of a dent and damaged paintwork. The procedure for the repair of a hole is similar. Refer to the text for more complete instructions

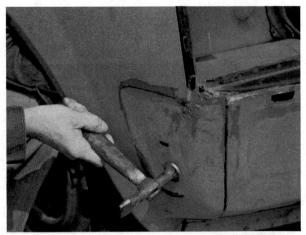

After removing any adjacent body trim, hammer the dent out. The damaged area should then be made slightly concave

Use coarse sandpaper or a sanding disc on a drill motor to remove all paint from the damaged area. Feather the sanded area into the edges of the surrounding paint, using progressively finer grades of sandpaper

The damaged area should be treated with rust remover prior to application of the body filler. In the case of a rust hole, all rusted sheet metal should be cut away

Carefully follow manufacturer's instructions when mixing the body filler so as to have the longest possible working time during application. Rust holes should be covered with fiberglass screen held in place with dabs of body filler prior to repair

Apply the filler with a flexible applicator in thin layers at 20 minute intervals. Use an applicator such as a wood spatula for confined areas. The filler should protrude slightly above the surrounding area

Shape the filler with a surform-type plane. Then, use water and progressively finer grades of sandpaper and a sanding block to wet-sand the area until it is smooth. Feather the edges of the repair area into the surrounding paint.

Use spray or brush applied primer to cover the entire repair area so that slight imperfections in the surface will be filled in. Prime at least one inch into the area surrounding the repair. Be careful of over-spray when using spray-type primer

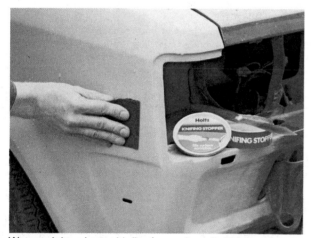

Wet-sand the primer with fine (approximately 400 grade) sandpaper until the area is smooth to the touch and blended into the surrounding paint. Use filler paste on minor imperfections

After the filler paste has dried, use rubbing compound to ensure that the surface of the primer is smooth. Prior to painting, the surface should be wiped down with a tack rag or lint-free cloth soaked in lacquer thinner

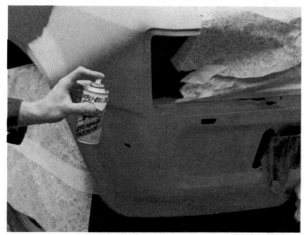

Choose a dry, warm, breeze-free area in which to paint and make sure that adjacent areas are protected from over-spray. Shake the spray paint can thoroughly and apply the top coat to the repair area, building it up by applying several coats, working from the center

After allowing at least two weeks for the paint to harden, use fine rubbing compound to blend the area into the original paint. Wax can now be applied

5 Body repair – minor damage

See color photo sequence

Repair of minor scratches

1   If the scratch is superficial and does not penetrate to the metal of the body, repair is very simple. Lightly rub the scratched area with a fine rubbing compound to remove loose paint and built-up wax. Rinse the area with clean water.

2   Apply touch-up paint to the scratch, using a small brush. Continue to apply thin layers of paint until the surface of the paint in the scratch is level with the surrounding paint. Allow the new paint at least two weeks to harden, then blend it into the surrounding paint by rubbing with a very fine rubbing compound. Finally, apply a coat of wax to the scratch area.

3   If the scratch has penetrated the paint and exposed the metal of the body, causing the metal to rust, a different repair technique is required. Remove all loose rust from the bottom of the scratch with a pocket knife, then apply rust inhibiting paint to prevent the formation of rust in the future. Using a rubber or nylon applicator, coat the scratched area with glaze-type filler. If required, the filler can be mixed with thinner to provide a very thin paste, which is ideal for filling narrow scratches. Before the glaze filler in the scratch hardens, wrap a piece of smooth cotton cloth around the tip of a finger. Dip the cloth in thinner and then quickly wipe it along the surface of the scratch. This will ensure that the surface of the filler is slightly hollow. The scratch can now be painted over as described earlier in this section.

Repair of dents

4   When repairing dents, the first job is to pull the dent out until the affected area is as close as possible to its original shape. There is no point in trying to restore the original shape completely, as the metal in the damaged area will have stretched on impact and cannot be restored to its original contours. It is better to bring the level of the dent up to a point which is about 1/8-inch below the level of the surrounding metal. In cases where the dent is very shallow, it is not worth trying to pull it out at all.

5   If the back side of the dent is accessible, it can be hammered out gently from behind using a soft-face hammer. While doing this, hold a block of wood firmly against the opposite side of the metal to absorb the hammer blows and prevent the metal from being stretched.

6   If the dent is in a section of the body which has double layers, or some other factor makes it inaccessible from behind, a different technique is required. Drill several small holes through the metal inside the damaged area, particularly in the deeper sections. Screw long, self-tapping screws into the holes just enough for them to get a good grip in the metal. Now the dent can be pulled out by pulling on the protruding heads of the screws with locking pliers.

7   The next stage of repair is the removal of paint from the damaged area and from an inch or so of the surrounding metal. This is done with a wire brush or sanding disk in a drill motor, although it can be done just as effectively by hand with sandpaper. To complete the preparation for filling, score the surface of the bare metal with a screwdriver or the tang of a file, or drill small holes in the affected area. This will provide a good grip for the filler material. To complete the repair, see the subsection on filling and painting later in this Section.

Repair of rust holes or gashes

8   Remove all paint from the affected area and from an inch or so of the surrounding metal using a sanding disk or wire brush mounted in a drill motor. If these are not available, a few sheets of sandpaper will do the job just as effectively.

9   With the paint removed, you will be able to determine the severity of the corrosion and decide whether to replace the whole panel, if possible, or repair the affected area. New body panels are not as expensive as most people think and it is often quicker to install a new panel than to repair large areas of rust.

10   Remove all trim pieces from the affected area except those which will act as a guide to the original shape of the damaged body, such as headlight shells, etc. Using metal snips or a hacksaw blade, remove all loose metal and any other metal that is badly affected by rust. Hammer the edges of the hole inward to create a slight depression for the filler material.

11   Wire brush the affected area to remove the powdery rust from the surface of the metal. If the back of the rusted area is accessible, treat it with rust inhibiting paint.

12   Before filling is done, block the hole in some way. This can be done with sheet metal riveted or screwed into place, or by stuffing the hole with wire mesh.

13   Once the hole is blocked off, the affected area can be filled and painted. See the following subsection on filling and painting.

Filling and painting

14   Many types of body fillers are available, but generally speaking, body repair kits which contain filler paste and a tube of resin hardener are best for this type of repair work. A wide, flexible plastic or nylon applicator will be necessary for imparting a smooth and contoured finish to the surface of the filler material. Mix up a small amount of filler on a clean piece of wood or cardboard (use the hardener sparingly). Follow the manufacturer's instructions on the package, otherwise the filler will set incorrectly.

15   Using the applicator, apply the filler paste to the prepared area. Draw the applicator across the surface of the filler to achieve the desired contour and to level the filler surface. As soon as a contour that approximates the original one is achieved, stop working the paste. If you continue, the paste will begin to stick to the applicator. Continue to add thin layers of paste at 20-minute intervals until the level of the filler is just above the surrounding metal.

16   Once the filler has hardened, the excess can be removed with a body file. From then on, progressively finer grades of sandpaper should be used, starting with a 180-grit paper and finishing with 600-grit wet or-dry paper. Always wrap the sandpaper around a flat rubber or wooden block, otherwise the surface of the filler will not be completely flat. During the sanding of the filler surface, the wet-or-dry paper should be periodically rinsed in water. This will ensure that a very smooth finish is produced in the final stage.

17   At this point, the repair area should be surrounded by a ring of bare metal, which in turn should be encircled by the finely feathered edge of good paint. Rinse the repair area with clean water until all of the dust produced by the sanding operation is gone.

18   Spray the entire area with a light coat of primer. This will reveal any imperfections in the surface of the filler. Repair the imperfections with fresh filler paste or glaze filler and once more smooth the surface with sandpaper. Repeat this spray-and-repair procedure until you are satisfied that the surface of the filler and the feathered edge of the paint are perfect. Rinse the area with clean water and allow it to dry completely.

19   The repair area is now ready for painting. Spray painting must be carried out in a warm, dry, windless and dust free atmosphere. These conditions can be created if you have access to a large indoor work area, but if you are forced to work in the open, you will have to pick the day very carefully. If you are working indoors, dousing the floor in the work area with water will help settle the dust which would otherwise be in the air. If the repair area is confined to one body panel, mask off the surrounding panels. This will help minimize the effects of a slight mismatch in paint color. Trim pieces such as chrome strips, door handles, etc., will also need to be masked off or removed. Use masking tape and several thicknesses of newspaper for the masking operations.

20   Before spraying, shake the paint can thoroughly, then spray a test area until the spray painting technique is mastered. Cover the repair area with a thick coat of primer. The thickness should be built up using several thin layers of primer rather than one thick one. Using 600-grit wet-or-dry sandpaper, rub down the surface of the primer until it is very smooth. While doing this, the work area should be thoroughly rinsed with water and the wet-or-dry sandpaper periodically rinsed as well. Allow the primer to dry before spraying additional coats.

21   Spray on the top coat, again building up the thickness by using several thin layers of paint. Begin spraying in the center of the repair area and then, using a circular motion, work out until the whole repair area and about two inches of the surrounding original paint is covered. Remove all masking material 10 to 15 minutes after spraying on the final coat of paint. Allow the new paint at least two weeks to harden, then use a very fine rubbing compound to blend the edges of the new paint into the existing paint. Finally, apply a coat of wax.

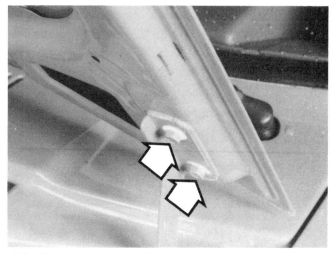

9.2   Use a permanent felt-tip pen or a scribe to mark the hood bolt locations (arrows)

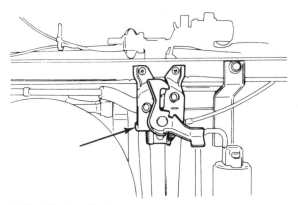

9.10b   The hood latch (arrow) is located on the radiator support on Geo Metro models – scribe around it, loosen the screws and adjust it's position (tighten the screws before checking hood alignment)

9.10a   On Sprint models, scribe around the latch located on the hood itself, loosen the screws, then adjust the position – the hood closed height can be adjusted by using a screwdriver to turn the locking adjustment screw (arrow)

8   Windshield and fixed glass – replacement

Replacement of the windshield and fixed glass requires the use of special fast-setting adhesive/caulk materials and some specialized tools. It is recommended that these operations be left to a dealer or a shop specializing in glass work.

9   Hood – removal, installation and adjustment

Refer to illustrations 9.2, 9.10a, 9.10b and 9.11
Note: *The hood is heavy and somewhat awkward to remove and install – at least two people should perform this procedure.*

Removal and installation
1   Use blankets or pads to cover the cowl area of the body and fenders. This will protect the body and paint as the hood is lifted off.
2   Draw around the bolt heads with a marking pen to ensure proper alignment during installation **(see illustration)**.
3   Disconnect any cables or wires that will interfere with removal.
4   Have an assistant support the hood. Remove the hinge-to-hood screws or bolts.
5   Lift off the hood.
6   Installation is the reverse of removal.

Adjustment
7   Fore-and-aft and side-to-side adjustment of the hood is done by moving the hinge plate slot after loosening the bolts or nuts.
8   Scribe a line around the entire hinge plate so you can judge the amount of movement **(see illustration 9.2)**.
9   Loosen the bolts or nuts and move the hood into correct alignment. Move it only a little at a time. Tighten the hinge bolts or nuts and carefully lower the hood to check the position.
10   If necessary after installation, the entire hood latch assembly can be adjusted up-and-down as well as from side-to-side on the hood or radiator support so the hood closes securely, flush with the fenders. To make the adjustment, scribe a line around the hood latch mounting bolts to provide a reference point, then loosen them and reposition the latch assembly, as necessary **(see illustrations)**. Following adjustment, retighten the mounting bolts.

6   Body repair – major damage

1   Major damage must be repaired by an auto body shop specifically equipped to perform unibody repairs. These shops have the specialized equipment required to do the job properly.
2   If the damage is extensive, the body must be checked for proper alignment or the vehicle's handling characteristics may be adversely affected and other components may wear at an accelerated rate.
3   Due to the fact that all of the major body components (hood, fenders, etc.) are separate and replaceable units, any seriously damaged components should be replaced rather than repaired. Sometimes the components can be found in a wrecking yard that specializes in used vehicle components, often at considerable savings over the cost of new parts.

7   Hinges and locks – maintenance

Once every 3000 miles, or every three months, the hinges and latch assemblies on the doors, hood and trunk should be given a few drops of light oil or lock lubricant. The door latch strikers should also be lubricated with a thin coat of grease to reduce wear and ensure free movement. Lubricate the door and trunk locks with spray-on graphite lubricant.

11

9.11   Turn the hood bumpers (arrow) to adjust the hood so it's flush with the fenders when closed

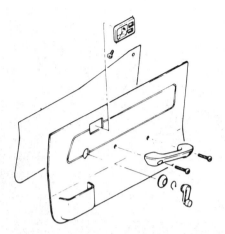

10.2   Armrest and door handle details

10.3   Work a cloth up behind the regulator handle and move it back-and-forth until the clip is pushed up so you can remove it

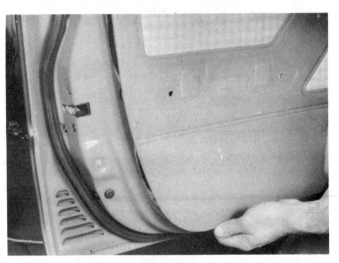

10.5   Pry under the retaining tabs until you can insert your fingers behind the panel to detach it

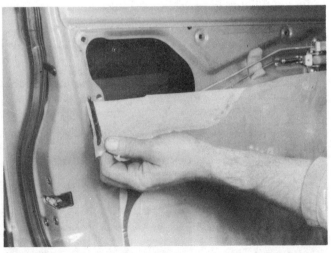

10.6   Be very careful when pulling the plastic water deflector off – don't tear it

11   Finally, adjust the hood bumpers on the radiator support so the hood, when closed, is flush with the fenders **(see illustration)**.

12   The hood latch assembly, as well as the hinges, should be periodically lubricated with white, lithium-base grease to prevent binding and wear.

10   Door trim panel – removal and installation

Refer to illustrations 10.2, 10.3, 10.5 and 10.6

1   Disconnect the negative cable from the battery.

2   Remove the door handle bezel and the door pull/armrest assembly **(see illustration)**.

3   Remove the window crank by working a cloth back-and-forth behind the handle to dislodge the retainer **(see illustration)**. With the retainer removed, pull off the handle.

4   Insert a wide putty knife or a thin pry bar between the trim panel and door to disengage the retaining clips. Work around the outer edge until the panel is free.

5   Once all of the clips are disengaged, detach the trim panel, unplug any electrical connectors and remove the trim panel from the vehicle **(see illustration)**.

6   For access to the inner door, peel back the plastic water deflector, taking care not to tear it **(see illustration)**. To install the trim panel, first press the water deflector into place.

7   Prior to installation of the door panel, be sure to reinstall any clips in the panel which may have come out during the removal procedure and stayed in the door.

8   Plug in any electrical connectors and place the panel in position. Press it into place until the clips are seated and install any retaining screws and armrest/door pulls. Install the manual regulator window crank or power switch assembly.

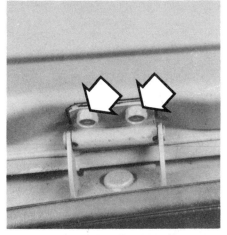

11.3 Mark around the hinge bolts (arrows) so you can return the liftgate to the same position when you install it

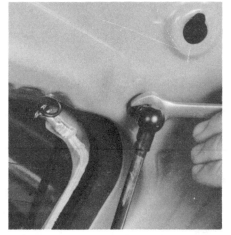

11.4 Use an open-end wrench to detach the support strut end

11.5 Unscrew the hinge-to-liftgate bolts

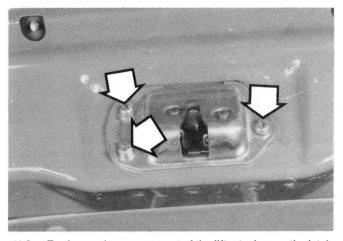

11.8a To change the engagement of the liftgate, loosen the latch mounting screws (arrows)

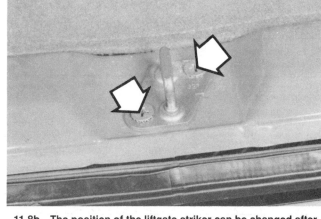

11.8b The position of the liftgate striker can be changed after loosening the retaining screws (arrows)

11 Liftgate – removal, installation and adjustment

Refer to illustrations 11.3, 11.4, 11.5, 11.8a, 11.8b and 11.9

1 Open the liftgate and cover the edges of the trunk compartment with pads or cloths to protect the painted surfaces when the lid is removed.

2 Disconnect any cables or electrical connectors attached to the liftgate that would interfere with removal.

3 Make alignment marks around the hinge bolt mounting flanges **(see illustration)**.

4 Have an assistant support the liftgate and detach the support struts **(see illustration)**.

5 While an assistant supports the liftgate, remove the lid-to-hinge bolts on both sides and lift it off **(see illustration)**.

6 Installation is the reverse of removal. **Note:** *When reinstalling the lift-gate, align the liftgate-to-hinge bolts with the marks made during removal.*

7 After installation, close the liftgate and make sure it's in proper alignment with the surrounding panels. Fore-and-aft and side-to-side adjustments of the lid are controlled by the position of the hinge bolts in the slots. To make an adjustment, loosen the hinge bolts, reposition the lid and re-tighten the bolts.

8 The height of the lid in relation to the surrounding body panels when closed can be changed by loosening the lock and/or striker bolts, repositioning the striker and tightening the bolts **(see illustrations)**.

9 Finally, adjust the bumpers on the liftgate or body so the liftgate, when closed, is flush with the body **(see illustration)**.

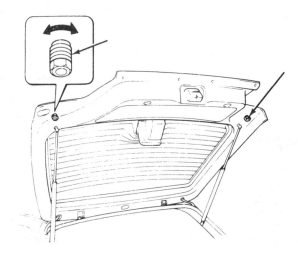

11.9 Turn the bumpers to adjust the liftgate so it's flush with the body when closed

11

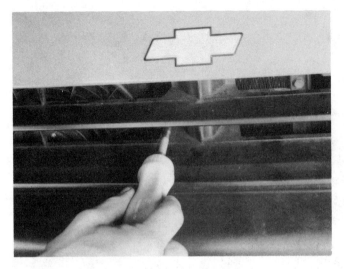

**12.2   Remove the screw hidden by the grille slats, using a
Phillips screwdriver**

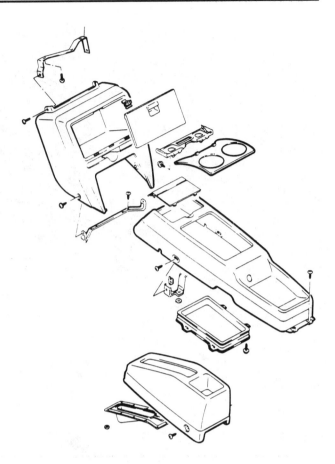

12   Radiator grille (Sprint models only) – removal
and installation

Refer to illustration 12.2

1   Remove the four screws along the top of the grille.
2   Remove the single hidden screw from the grille support **(see illustration)**
3   Once all of the retaining screws are removed, pull the grille out and
remove it.
4   Press the grille into place and install the screws.

13.2   Console details (Geo Metro shown)

13   Center console – removal and installation

Refer to illustration 13.2

1   Disconnect the negative cable from the battery.
2   Remove the screws, detach the console and lift it out **(see illustration)**.
3   Installation is the reverse of removal.

14   Instrument cluster bezel – removal and installation

Refer to illustrations 14.2a, 14.2b and 14.3

1   Disconnect the negative cable from the battery.
2   Remove the screws and detach the bezel **(see illustrations)**.
3   Pull the bezel out, disconnect the electrical connectors and remove
the bezel and switches as an assembly **(see illustration)**.
4   Installation is the reverse of removal.

**14.2a   Remove the screws along the
bezel lower . . .**

14.2b   . . . and upper edge

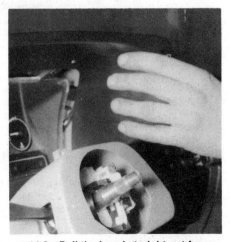

**14.3   Pull the bezel straight out for
access to the electrical connectors**

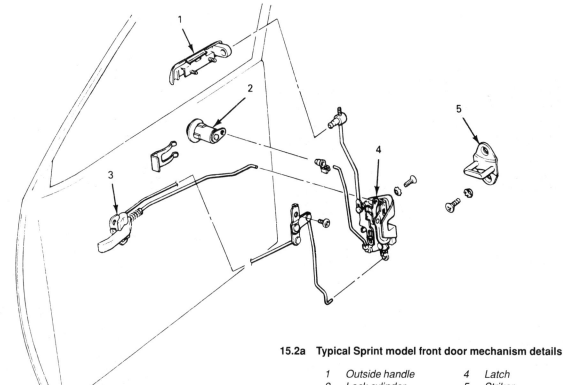

15.2a   Typical Sprint model front door mechanism details

1	Outside handle	4	Latch
2	Lock cylinder	5	Striker
3	Inside handle		

15   Door latch, lock cylinder and handle – removal and installation

1   Remove the door trim panel and water deflector (see Section 10).

Door latch

Refer to illustrations 15.2a, 15.2b, 15.3, 15.4a, 15.4b, 15.4c and 15.4d

2   Reach in through the door service hole and disconnect the control links from the latch **(see illustrations)**.

3   Remove the three door lock retaining screws from the end of the door **(see illustration)**.

4   Installation is the reverse of removal. When installing the front door operating rod to the outside handle, turn the joint to adjust the specified distance (A) to 5/64 in (2 mm) **(see illustrations)**. When placing the inside handle in position, adjust the control links to achieve the clearance between the latch inside opening lever rod and the outside opening rod of 5/64 in (2 mm) **(see illustrations)**.

Lock cylinder

5   Disconnect the control link from the lock cylinder.

6   Use pliers to slide the retaining clip off and remove the lock cylinder from the door **(see illustrations 15.2a and 15.2b)**.

7   Installation is the reverse of removal.

Inside handle

8   Remove the retaining screws **(see illustrations 15.2a and 15.2b)**.

9   Rotate the handle away and detach it from the door.

10   Installation is the reverse of removal.

Outside handle

Refer to illustration 15.11

11   Disconnect the control link from the handle **(see illustration)**.

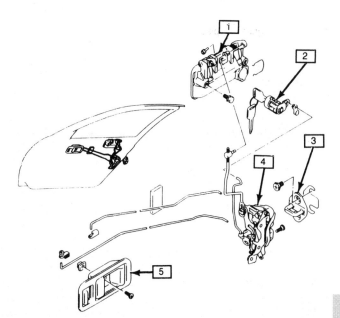

15.2b   Geo Metro door latch, lock cylinder and handle details

1	Outside handle	4	Latch
2	Lock cylinder	5	Inside handle
3	Striker		and bezel

12   Remove the nuts or bolts and detach the handle from the door **(see illustrations 15.2a and 15.2b)**.

13   Installation is the reverse of removal.

11

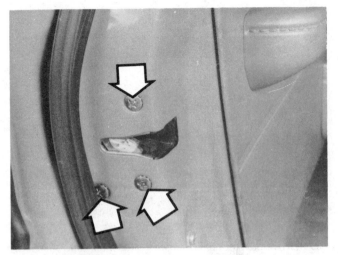

15.3 The door latch screws are located in the end of the door (arrows)

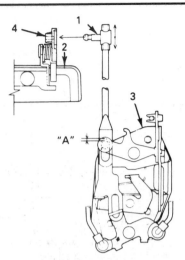

15.4a Sprint model front door outside handle adjustment details

1	Operating rod	4	Plate
2	Outside handle	A	5/64 in (2 mm)
3	Adjusting joint		

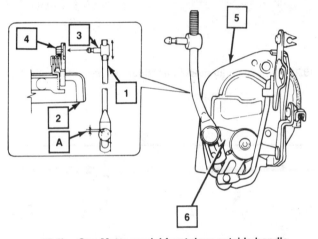

15.4b Geo Metro model front door outside handle adjustment details

1	Inside operating rod	5	Door latch
2	Outside handle	6	Outside handle
3	Adjusting joint		opening lever
4	Snap fitting	A	5/64 in (2 mm)

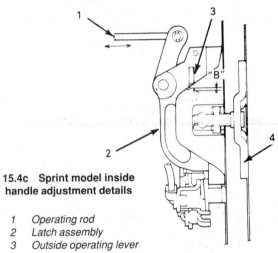

15.4c Sprint model inside handle adjustment details

1	Operating rod
2	Latch assembly
3	Outside operating lever
4	Door latch striker
B	5/64 in (2 mm)

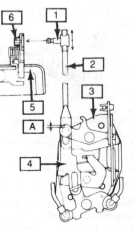

15.4d Geo Metro inside handle adjustment details

1	Adjusting joint
2	Operating rod
3	Latch assembly
4	Opening link
5	Outside handle
6	Snap joint
1A	5/64 in (2 mm)

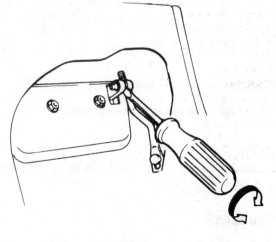

15.11 Use a screwdriver to detach the latch rod

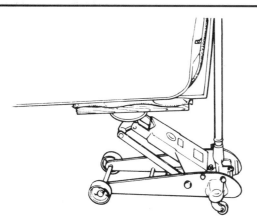

16.2   Use a jack (padded with rags to protect the paint) or jackstands to support the door during the removal and installation procedures

16.3   Remove the door check pin by tapping it out with a hammer

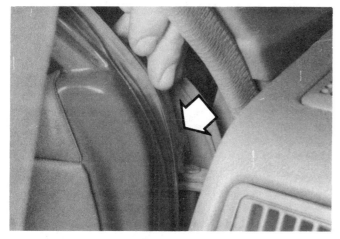

16.4a   On front doors, a thin wrench will be needed to remove the hard-to-reach hinge-to-body bolts

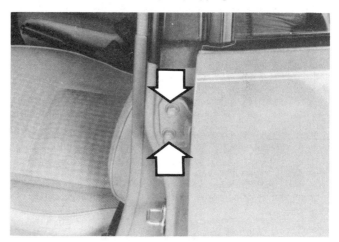

16.4b   With the front door open, the rear door bolts are easily accessible (arrows)

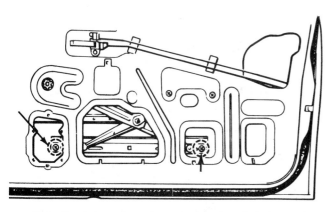

17.3   Front door glass channel screw locations (arrows)

16   Door – removal, installation and adjustment

Refer to illustrations 16.2, 16.3, 16.4a and 16.4b

1   Remove the door trim panel. Disconnect any electrical connectors and push them through the door opening so they won't interfere with removal.

2   Position a jack or jackstand under the door or have an assistant on hand to support it when the hinge bolts are removed **(see illustration)**.

Note: *If a jack or stand is used, place a rag between it and the door to protect the door's paint.*

3   Scribe around the door bolts. Remove the door check pin **(see illustration)**.

4   Remove the hinge-to-door bolts and carefully detach the door **(see illustrations)**. Installation is the reverse of removal.

5   Following installation, make sure it's aligned properly. Adjust it if necessary as follows:

a) Up-and-down and forward-and-backward adjustments are made by loosening the hinge-to-body bolts and moving the door, as necessary. A special offset tool may be required to reach some of the bolts.

b) The door lock striker can also be adjusted both up-and-down and sideways to provide a positive engagement with the locking mechanism. This is done by loosening the screws and moving the striker, as necessary.

17   Door window glass – removal and installation

1   Remove the door trim panel and water deflector (Section 10).

2   Lower the window glass.

Front door

Refer to illustrations 17.3, 17.5a and 17.5b

3   Remove outer weatherstrip, then remove the glass bolts **(see illustration)**.

11

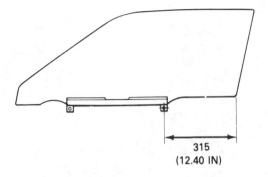

**17.5a   Sprint model front door glass-to-channel
installation details**

315
(12.40 IN)

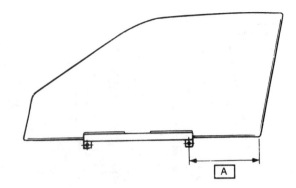

17.5b   Geo Metro front door glass-to-channel details

A   *Three-door models – 11.95 in (303.5 mm)*
A   *Five-door models – 9.69 in (253 mm)*

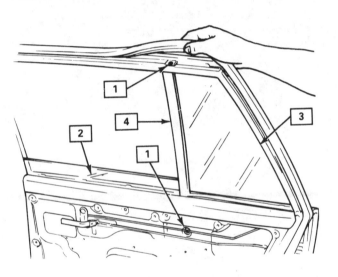

17.7   Rear door fixed glass removal details

1	*Screw*	3	*Stationary glass*
2	*Door window glass*	4	*Center guide channel*

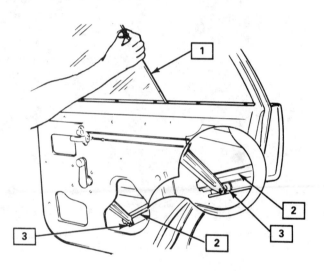

17.8   Sprint model rear door glass removal details

1	*Door glass*	3	*Regulator arm roller*
2	*Bottom channel*		

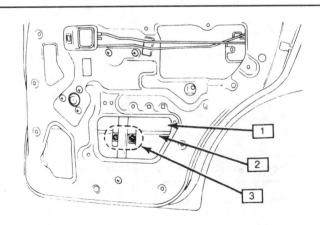

17.9   Geo Metro rear door glass bolt locations

1	*Door glass*	3	*Bolts*
2	*Bottom channel*		

4   Remove the window glass by sliding it up and out of the door complete with the bottom channel.
5   If it's necessary to remove the glass, detach it from the channel. Lubricate the channel with soapy water and tap the new glass into place with a plastic hammer, positioning it as shown in the accompanying illustrations.
6   Installation is the reverse of removal.

Rear door
Refer to illustrations 17.7, 17.8, 17.9, 17.10a and 17.10b

7   Remove the center guide channel and pull the stationary glass out of the door **(see illustration)**.
8   On Sprint models, pull the regulator arm roller out of the bottom channel and remove the glass and bottom channel as a unit **(see illustration)**.
9   On Geo Metro models, remove the glass bolts, then remove the glass and channel as a unit **(see illustration)**.
10   If it's necessary to remove the glass, detach it from the channel. Lubricate the channel with soapy water and tap the new glass into place with a plastic hammer, positioning it as shown in the accompanying illustrations.
11   Installation is the reverse of removal.

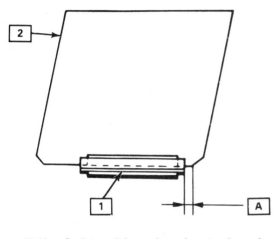

17.10a   Sprint model rear door glass-to-channel installation details

| 1 | Channel | A | 0.89 in (22.5 mm) |
| 2 | Glass | | |

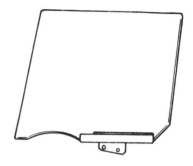

17.10b   On Geo Metro models, the rear door glass must be installed on the channel as shown

---

18   Door glass regulator – removal and installation

1   Remove the door trim panel and water deflector (see Section 10).
2   Remove the window assembly (see Section 17).
3   Remove the mounting bolts and detach the regulator from the door.
4   Installation is the reverse of removal.

---

19   Outside mirror – removal and installation

Refer to illustrations 19.1a and 19.1b

1   Remove the screw and adjusting lever and lift off the mirror trim cover **(see illustrations)**.
2   Remove the three retaining nuts and detach the mirror. On driver side mirrors, remove the set screw, separate the cable and withdraw it along with the mirror.
3   Installation is the reverse of removal. Align the break line with the "J" line on the mirror before tightening the nuts **(see illustrations 19.1a and 19.1b)**.

19.1a   Driver side mirror details

1	Mirror
2	Gasket
3	Reinforcement plate
4	Nut
5	Screw
6	Bezel
7	Set screw

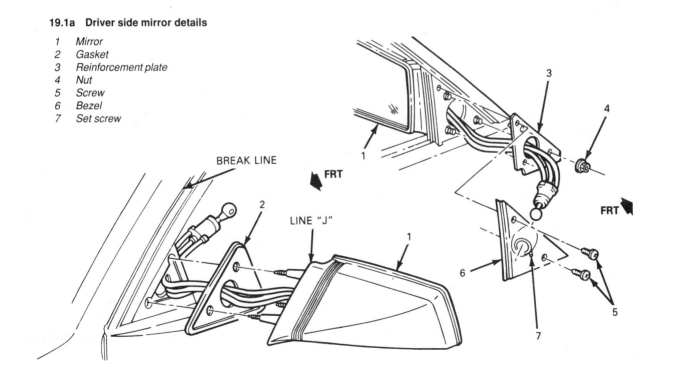

11

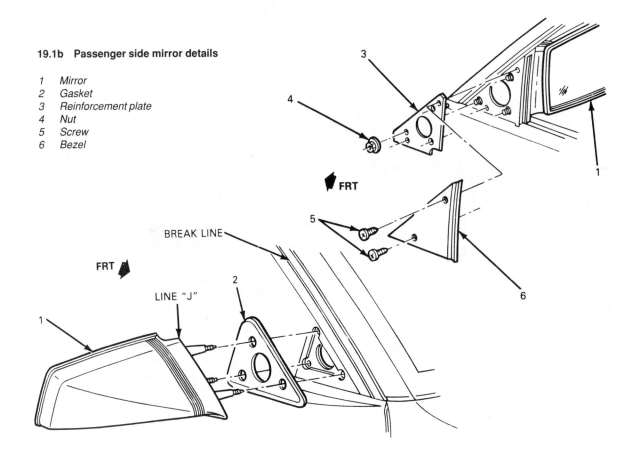

19.1b   Passenger side mirror details

1   *Mirror*
2   *Gasket*
3   *Reinforcement plate*
4   *Nut*
5   *Screw*
6   *Bezel*

FRT

BREAK LINE

FRT

LINE "J"

20   Bumpers – removal and installation

Refer to illustrations 20.1a, 20.1b, 20.1c and 20.1d

Warning: *Some models are equipped with an air bag or Supplemental Inflatable Restraint (SIR) system. When working in the vicinity of the bumpers on these models, the SIR system must first be disarmed (see Chapter 10).*

1   Detach the bumper cover **(see illustrations)**.

2   Disconnect any wiring or other components that would interfere with bumper removal. **Note:** *If the vehicle is equipped with the SIR system (see Warning), care must be taken not to damage the system sensors. If the sensors are removed, the SIR system must first be disarmed. When the sensors are installed, the mounting bolts must be tightened to the specified torques before they are plugged in and the system is reactivated.*

3   Support the bumper with a jack or jackstand. Alternatively, have an assistant support the bumper as the bolts are removed.

4   Remove the retaining bolts and detach the bumper.

5   Installation is the reverse of removal.

6   Tighten the retaining bolts securely.

7   Install the bumper cover and any other components that were removed.

21   Seats – removal and installation

Refer to illustrations 21.1a and 21.1b

1   Remove the retaining bolts, unplug any electrical connectors and lift the seats from the vehicle **(see illustrations)**.

2   Installation is the reverse of removal.

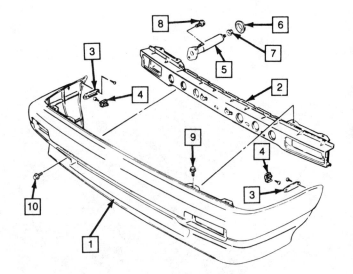

20.1a   Sprint front bumper details

1	*Cover*	6	*Absorber mount*
2	*Reinforcement*	7	*Nut*
3	*Side attachment*	8	*Bolt*
4	*Side support*	9	*Upper bumper bolt*
5	*Absorber*	10	*Lower bumper bolt*

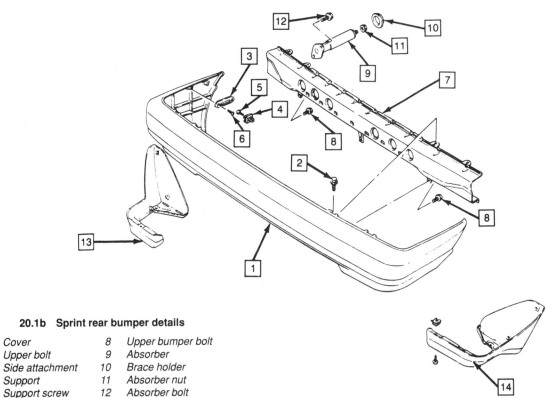

20.1b   Sprint rear bumper details

1	Cover	8	Upper bumper bolt
2	Upper bolt	9	Absorber
3	Side attachment	10	Brace holder
4	Support	11	Absorber nut
5	Support screw	12	Absorber bolt
6	Attachment screw	13	Splash pad extension
7	Reinforcement	14	Splash pad extension

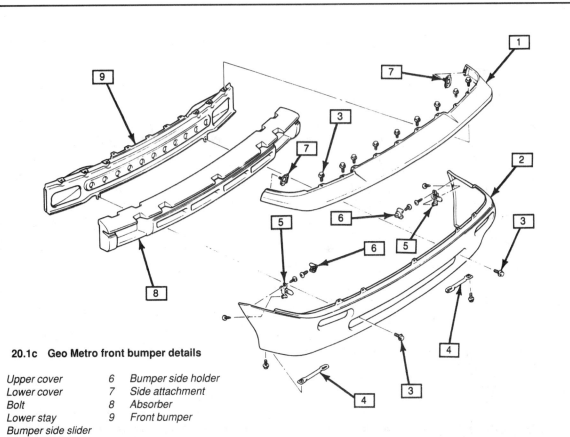

20.1c   Geo Metro front bumper details

1	Upper cover	6	Bumper side holder
2	Lower cover	7	Side attachment
3	Bolt	8	Absorber
4	Lower stay	9	Front bumper
5	Bumper side slider		

11

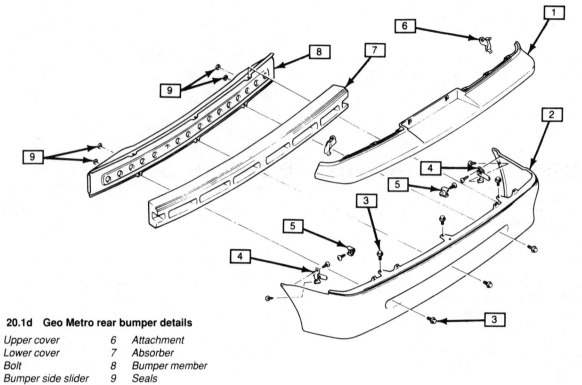

20.1d   Geo Metro rear bumper details

1	Upper cover	6	Attachment
2	Lower cover	7	Absorber
3	Bolt	8	Bumper member
4	Bumper side slider	9	Seals
5	Bumper holder		

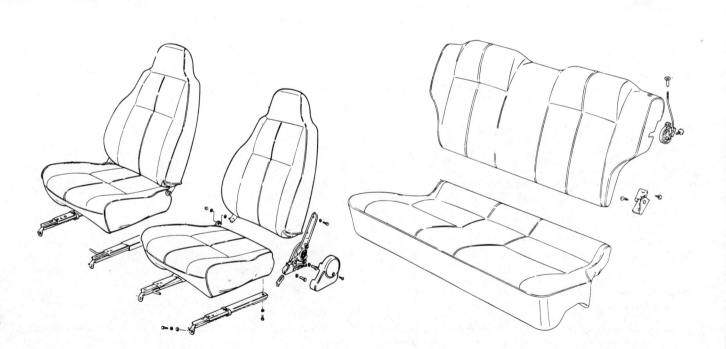

20.1a   Typical front seat installation details   **20.1b   Typical rear seat installation details (sedan models)**

Chapter 12   Chassis electrical system

Contents

1   General information

The electrical system is a 12-volt, negative ground type. Power for the lights and all electrical accessories is supplied by a lead/acid-type battery which is charged by the alternator.

This Chapter covers repair and service procedures for the various electrical components not associated with the engine. Information on the battery, alternator, distributor and starter motor can be found in Chapter 5.

It should be noted that when portions of the electrical system are serviced, the cable should be disconnected from the negative battery terminal to prevent electrical shorts and/or fires.

2   Electrical troubleshooting – general information

A typical electrical circuit consists of an electrical component, any switches, relays, motors, fuses, fusible links or circuit breakers related to that component and the wiring and electrical connectors that link the component to both the battery and the chassis. To help you pinpoint an electrical circuit problem, wiring diagrams are included at the end of this book.

Before tackling any troublesome electrical circuit, first study the appropriate wiring diagrams to get a complete understanding of what makes up that individual circuit. Trouble spots, for instance, can often be narrowed down by noting if other components related to the circuit are operating properly. If several components or circuits fail at one time, chances are the problem is in a fuse or ground connection, because several circuits are often routed through the same fuse and ground connections.

Electrical problems usually stem from simple causes, such as loose or corroded connections, a blown fuse, a melted fusible link or a bad relay. Visually inspect the condition of all fuses, wires and connections in a problem circuit before troubleshooting it.

If testing instruments are going to be utilized, use the diagrams to plan ahead of time where you will make the necessary connections in order to accurately pinpoint the trouble spot.

The basic tools needed for electrical troubleshooting include a circuit tester or voltmeter (a 12-volt bulb with a set of test leads can also be used), a continuity tester, which includes a bulb, battery and set of test leads, and a jumper wire, preferably with a circuit breaker incorporated, which can be used to bypass electrical components. Before attempting to locate a problem with test instruments, use the wiring diagram(s) to decide where to make the connections.

Voltage checks

Voltage checks should be performed if a circuit is not functioning properly. Connect one lead of a circuit tester to either the negative battery terminal or a known good ground. Connect the other lead to a connector in the circuit being tested, preferably nearest to the battery or fuse. If the bulb of the tester lights, voltage is present, which means that the part of the circuit between the connector and the battery is problem free. Continue checking the rest of the circuit in the same fashion. When you reach a point at which no voltage is present, the problem lies between that point and the last test point with voltage. Most of the time the problem can be traced to a loose connection. **Note:** *Keep in mind that some circuits receive voltage only when the ignition key is in the Accessory or Run position.*

Finding a short

One method of finding shorts in a circuit is to remove the fuse and connect a test light or voltmeter in its place to the fuse terminals. There should be no voltage present in the circuit. Move the wiring harness from side to side while watching the test light. If the bulb goes on, there is a short to ground somewhere in that area, probably where the insulation has rubbed through. The same test can be performed on each component in the circuit, even a switch.

3.1   The fuse block is located at the lower left corner of the dashboard

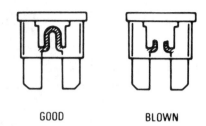

GOOD   BLOWN

3.3   The fuses used on these models can be checked visually to determine if they're blown

Ground check

Perform a ground test to check whether a component is properly grounded. Disconnect the battery and connect one lead of a selfpowered test light, known as a continuity tester, to a known good ground. Connect the other lead to the wire or ground connection being tested. If the bulb goes on, the ground is good. If the bulb does not go on, the ground is not good.

Continuity check

A continuity check is done to determine if there are any breaks in a circuit – if it is passing electricity properly. With the circuit off (no power in the circuit), a self-powered continuity tester can be used to check the circuit. Connect the test leads to both ends of the circuit (or to the "power" end and a good ground), and if the test light comes on the circuit is passing current properly. If the light doesn't come on, there is a break somewhere in the circuit. The same procedure can be used to test a switch, by connecting the continuity tester to the power in and power out sides of the switch. With the switch turned On, the test light should come on.

Finding an open circuit

When diagnosing for possible open circuits, it is often difficult to locate them by sight because oxidation or terminal misalignment are hidden by the connectors. Merely wiggling a connector on a sensor or in the wiring harness may correct the open circuit condition. Remember this when an open circuit is indicated when troubleshooting a circuit. Intermittent problems may also be caused by oxidized or loose connections.

Electrical troubleshooting is simple if you keep in mind that all electrical circuits are basically electricity running from the battery, through the wires, switches, relays, fuses and fusible links to each electrical component (light bulb, motor, etc.) and to ground, from which it is passed back to the battery. Any electrical problem is an interruption in the flow of electricity to and from the battery.

3   Fuses – general information

Refer to illustrations 3.1 and 3.3

The electrical circuits of the vehicle are protected by a combination of fuses, circuit breakers and fusible links. The fuse blocks are located under the instrument panel on the left side of the dashboard and on Geo Metro models next to the battery in the engine compartment **(see illustration)**.

Each of the fuses is designed to protect a specific circuit, and the various circuits are identified on the fuse panel itself.

Miniaturized fuses are employed in the fuse block. These compact fuses, with blade terminal design, allow fingertip removal and replacement. If an electrical component fails, always check the fuse first. A blown fuse is easily identified through the clear plastic body. Visually inspect the element for evidence of damage **(see illustration)**. If a continuity check is called for, the blade terminal tips are exposed in the fuse body.

Be sure to replace blown fuses with the correct type. Fuses of different ratings are physically interchangeable, but only fuses of the proper rating should be used. Replacing a fuse with one of a higher or lower value than specified is not recommended. Each electrical circuit needs a specific amount of protection. The amperage value of each fuse is molded into the fuse body.

If the replacement fuse immediately fails, don't replace it again until the cause of the problem is isolated and corrected. In most cases, this will be a short circuit in the wiring caused by a broken or deteriorated wire.

4   Fusible links – general information

Some circuits are protected by fusible links. The links are used in circuits which are not ordinarily fused, such as the ignition circuit. They look like large fuses, and are located in the engine compartment fuse box.

The fusible links on these models are similar to fuses in that they can be visually checked to determine if they are melted.

To replace a fusible link, first disconnect the negative cable from the battery. Unplug the burned out link and replace it with a new one (available from your dealer). Always determine the cause for the overload which melted the fusible link before installing a new one.

5   Circuit breakers – general information

Circuit breakers protect some components. Some circuit breakers are located in the fuse box. On some models the circuit breaker resets itself automatically, so an electrical overload in a circuit breaker protected system will cause the circuit to fail momentarily, then come back on. If the circuit does not come back on, check it immediately. Once the condition is corrected, the circuit breaker will resume its normal function.

6   Relays – general information

Several electrical accessories in the vehicle use relays to transmit the electrical signal to the component. If the relay is defective, that component will not operate properly.

The various relays are located in several locations throughout the vehicle.

If a faulty relay is suspected, it can be removed and tested by a dealer or other qualified shop. Defective relays must be replaced as a unit.

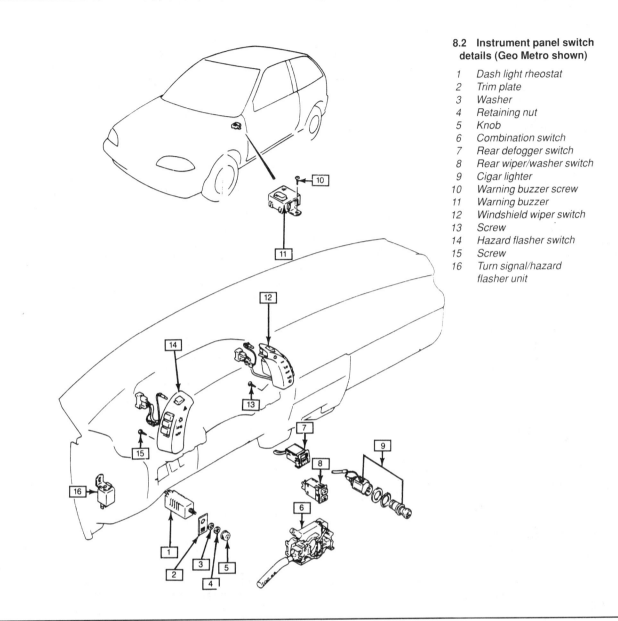

8.2 Instrument panel switch details (Geo Metro shown)

1   Dash light rheostat
2   Trim plate
3   Washer
4   Retaining nut
5   Knob
6   Combination switch
7   Rear defogger switch
8   Rear wiper/washer switch
9   Cigar lighter
10 Warning buzzer screw
11 Warning buzzer
12 Windshield wiper switch
13 Screw
14 Hazard flasher switch
15 Screw
16 Turn signal/hazard flasher unit

7   Turn signal/hazard flashers – check and replacement

Caution: *Some models are equipped with an air bag or Supplemental Inflatable Restraint (SIR) system. When working in the vicinity of the SIR system components, the system must first be disarmed (see Chapter 10).*

1   The turn signal/hazard flasher, a small rectangular canister shaped unit located in the wiring harness behind the fuse block under the dash, flashes the turn signals.

2   When the flasher unit is functioning properly, and audible click can be heard during its operation. If the turn signals fail on one side or the other and the flasher unit does not make its characteristic clicking sound, a faulty turn signal bulb is indicated.

3   If both turn signals fail to blink, the problem may be due to a blown fuse, a faulty flasher unit, a broken switch or a loose or open connection. If a quick check of the fuse box indicates that the turn signal fuse has blown, check the wiring for a short before installing a new fuse.

4   To replace the flasher, simply pull it out of the wiring harness **(see illustration 8.2)**.

5   Make sure that the replacement unit is identical to the original. Compare the old one to the new one before installing it.

6   Installation is the reverse of removal.

8   Instrument panel switches – check and replacement

Caution: *Some models are equipped with an air bag or Supplemental Inflatable Restraint (SIR) system. When working in the vicinity of the SIR system components, the system must first be disarmed (see Chapter 10).*

1   Disconnect the negative cable at the battery.

Headlight and windshield wiper/washer switches

Refer to illustrations 8.2, 8.3a, 8.3b, 8.3c, 8.3d and 8.3e

2   On these models headlight and wiper/washer switches are located in the instrument cluster bezel **(see illustration)**. Remove the instrument cluster bezel (Chapter 11) and unplug the electrical connectors. Remove the screws and separate the switches from the cluster.

12

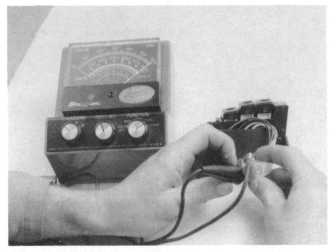

8.3a   Use an ohmmeter to check the switch continuity between the connector terminals

R/G	G/B	W/Y
B	O	R/Y

R/G: Red/Green	G/B: Green/Black
W/Y: White/Yellow	B: Black
O: Orange	R/Y: Red/Yellow

CONTINUITY BETWEEN TERMINALS

Switch Position	Terminal-to-terminal continuity
≡Ɔ	W/Y – O, G/B – B
≡Ɔ ƆΞ	W/Y – O
OFF	

8.3b   Sprint headlight switch continuity check details

LIGHT AND HAZARD SWITCH CONNECTOR

B/G	W			W/G	G/Y	G
B	R/Y	R/G	Y/R	Y	G/R	✕

B/G : BLACK/GREEN	R/Y : RED/YELLOW
W : WHITE	R/G : RED/GREEN
W/G : WHITE/GREEN	Y/R : YELLOW/RED
G/Y : GREEN/YELLOW	Y : YELLOW
G : GREEN	G/R : GREEN/RED
B : BLACK	

CONTINUITY BETWEEN TERMINALS

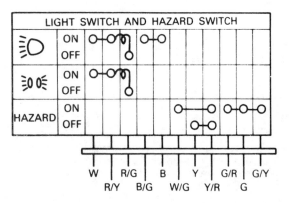

8.3c   Geo Metro headlight switch continuity check details

WIPER/WASHER SWITCH CONNECTOR

R/Y	Bl/W	Bl	Y/BL
B	B/Bl	Bl/R	R/G

R/Y: Red/Yellow	Bl/W: Blue/White
Bl: Blue	Y/BL Yellow/Blue
B: Black	B/Bl: Black/Blue
Bl/R: Blue/Red	R/G: Red/Green

CONTINUITY BETWEEN TERMINALS

Switch Position		Terminal-to-terminal continuity
⌒	(WASHER)	B/Bl — Y/Bl
HI	(WIPER)	Y/Bl — Bl/R
LO	(WIPER)	Bl — Y/Bl
INT.	(WIPER)	B — Y/Bl, Bl — Bl/W
OFF		Bl — Bl/W
R/G, an illumination lamp lead wire of the lighting switch, produces constant R/G — R/Y continuity.		

8.3d   Sprint windshield wiper/washer switch continuity check details

3   Use an ommeter to check continuity between the terminals **(see illustrations)**. The continuity should be as shown in the appropriate illustration; if it isn't, replace the switch.

Dash light rheostat

Refer to illustrations 8.4 and 8.5

4   Pull off the knob, remove the retaining nut and trim plate and push the rheostat back through the opening and remove it under the dash **(see illustration)**. Unplug the electrical connector.

5   Use a test lamp check the operation of the rheostat **(see illustration)**. The test lamp should brighten as the knob is turned clockwise and dim when it is turned counterclockwise. If it doesn't, replace the rheostat.

Rear defogger switch

Refer to illustration 8.7

6   Reach up behind the dashboard and unplug the switch electrical connector. Squeeze the clips on the sides of the switch together, push the switch out of the dashboard and withdraw it **(see illustration 8.2)**.

7   Use an ommeter to check continuity between the terminals **(see illustration)**. If the continuity does not check out properly, replace the switch.

8.4 Pull off the knob, remove the nut (arrow) and push the rheostat back through the hole in the dash to remove it

R/Y			BL/R	B
R/G	BL/Y	BL	Y/BL	BL/W

R/Y : RED/YELLOW   BL/R : BLUE/RED
B   : BLACK   R/G : RED/GREEN
BL/Y : BLUE/YELLOW   BL   : BLUE
Y/BL : YELLOW/BLUE   BL/W : BLUE/WHITE

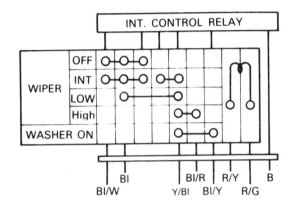

8.3e Geo Metro windshield wiper/washer switch continuity check details

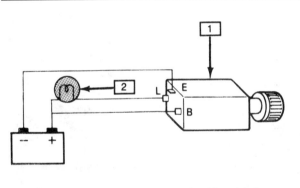

8.5 Dash light rheostat checking details

1   Rheostat   2   Test light (12 V, 3.4 W)

	Yellow/Green	Red/White	Black	Red/Green	Red/Yellow
OFF					
ON					

8.7 Rear defogger switch continuity check details

Rear wiper/washer switch

Refer to illustration 8.9

8   Reach up behind the dashboard, unplug the switch electrical connector, then squeeze the clips on the sides of the switch together. Remove it by pushing it out of the dashboard (see illustration 8.2).

9   Use an ommeter to check continuity between the terminals (see illustration). If continuity is not correct, replace the switch.

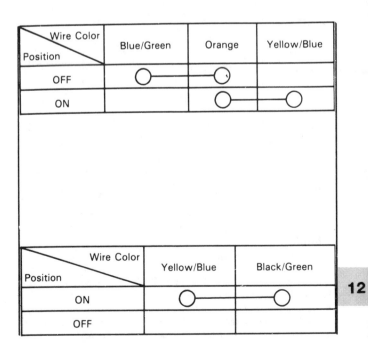

Wire Color / Position	Blue/Green	Orange	Yellow/Blue
OFF			
ON			

Wire Color / Position	Yellow/Blue	Black/Green
ON		
OFF		

8.9 Rear wiper/washer switch continuity check details

9   Combination switch – check and replacement

Refer to illustrations 9.2, 9.5a, 9.5b and 9.7

Warning: *Some models are equipped with an air bag or Supplemental Inflatable Restraint (SIR) system. When working in the vicinity of the SIR system components, the system must first be disarmed (see Chapter 10).*

1   Disconnect the negative cable at the battery.

12

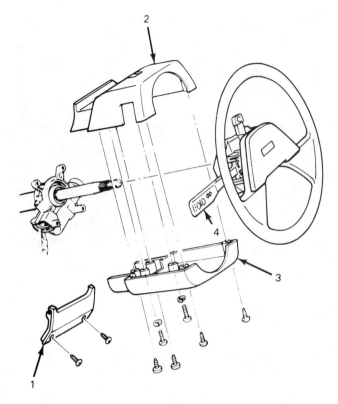

9.2   Steering column cover details

1	*Lower finish panel*	3	*Lower column cover*
2	*Upper column cover*	4	*Combination switch*

Switch Position	Terminal-to-terminal continuity
RH Turn Signal & Lane Change	G — G/Y
LH Turn Signal & Lane Change	G — G/R
Neutral	Y — Y/Bl
Hazard	G/Y — G — G/R
(RH-N-LH)	Y/Bl — W/G
Low Beam	R/W — G/B
High Beam	R — G/B
Passing	R — B

G:	Green	G/Y:	Green/Yellow
G/R:	Green/Red	Y:	Yellow
Y/Bl:	Yellow/Blue	W/G:	White/Green
R/W:	Red/White	G/B:	Green/Black
R:	Red		
B:	Black		

Bl/G, a horn lead wire, produces no continuity inside the turn signal/dimmer switch.

9.5a   Sprint combination switch continuity check details

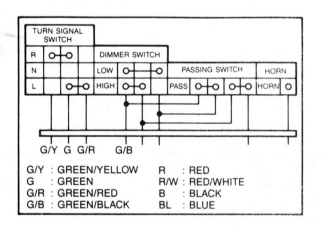

9.5b   Geo Metro combination switch continuity check details

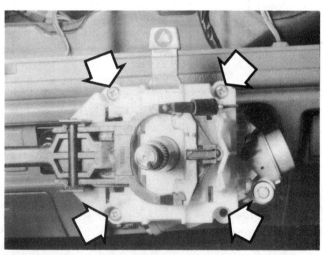

9.7   Remove the screws (arrows) and slide the combination switch off the steering shaft

7   Remove the combination switch retaining screws and slide the switch up and off the steering column (**see illustration**).
8   Installation is the reverse of removal.

---

10   Ignition switch – check and replacement

Refer to illustrations 10.3a, 10.3b, 10.6 and 10.7
Warning: *Some models are equipped with an air bag or Supplemental Inflatable Restraint (SIR) system. When working in the vicinity of the SIR system components, the system must first be disarmed (see Chapter 10).*

1   Disconnect the negative cable at the battery.
2   Remove the lower finish panel and the steering column cover (**see illustration 9.2**).

Check

2   Remove the lower finish panel and steering column cover (**see illustration**).
3   Trace the wiring harness down the steering column to the connector. Release the wiring retainer clamp (if equipped) and unplug the connector.
4   Use an ohmmeter or self-powered test light to check for continuity between the switch terminals at each switch position (**see illustrations**).
5   Replace the switch if the continuity is not as shown.

Replacement

6   Remove the steering wheel (see Chapter 10).

3   Trace the wiring harness from the switch to the connector under the dash and unplug it. Use an ohmmeter or self-powered test light to check for continuity at each key position **(see illustrations)**.
4   If there is no continuity at any position, replace the switch.
5   Remove the steering wheel (see Chapter 10).
6   Remove the screw and detach the ignition switch **(see illustration)**.
7   Installation is the reverse of removal, making sure to align the slot in the switch with the tab on the lock cylinder **(see illustration)**.

11   Radio – removal and installation

Warning: *Some models are equipped with an air bag or Supplemental In-flatable Restraint (SIR) system. When working in the vicinity of the SIR system components, the system must first be disarmed (see Chapter 10).*
1   Disconnect the negative cable from the battery.

Wire Color / Position	W/G	Bl	B/Bl	B/R	W	Bl/B
LOCK	○					
ACC	○—	—○			○—	—○
ON	○—	—○—	—○			
START	○		○—	—○		

ACC: Accessory   W/G   White/Green   Bl: Blue
B/Bl: Black/Blue   W :   White   Bl/B: Blue/Black

10.3a   Sprint ignition switch continuity details

Key	Position	W/G	BL	B/BL	Y/B		B	B	G	G
OUT	LOCK	○								
IN	ACC	○—	—○							
IN	ON	○—	—○—	—○—	—○				○—	—○
IN	START	○—		—○—	—○		○—	—○		

ACC : ACCESSORY   B : BLACK
B/BL : BLACK/BLUE   BL : BLUE
W/G : WHITE/GREEN   B/Y : BLACK/YELLOW
Y/B : YELLOW/BLACK   G : GREEN

10.3b   Geo Metro ignition switch continuity details

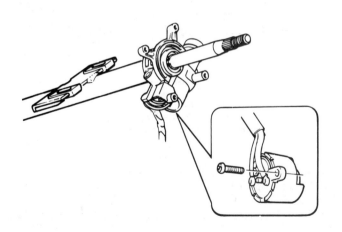

10.6   Remove the screw and detach the ignition switch from the key lock cylinder

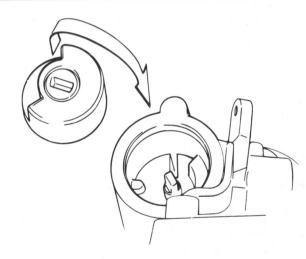

10.7   Insert the lock cylinder tab in the ignition switch notch

12

11.2a   Pull off the knobs, remove the retaining nuts . . .

11.2b   . . . then lift off the radio face plate

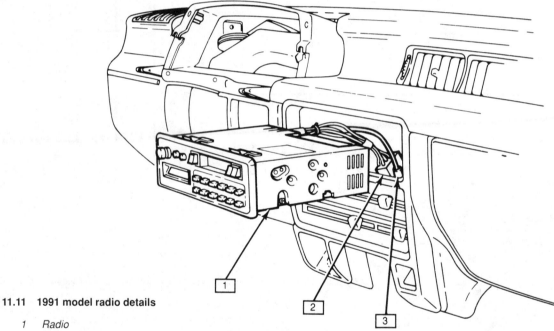

11.11   1991 model radio details

1   *Radio*
2   *Electrical connector*
3   *Antenna lead*

Sprint

Refer to illustrations 11.2a and 11.2b

2   Pull off the control knobs, then remove the nuts and radio face plate **(see illustrations)**.
3   Remove the ashtray
4   Pull the radio out, reach behind it and unplug the electrical connector and antenna lead, then remove the radio.
5   Installation is the reverse of removal.

Geo Metro

1990 and earlier models

6   Removal of the radio on these models requires the use of removal fork tools, available at your dealer.
7   Reach up behind the radio and remove the retaining bolt and unplug the electrical connector and antenna lead.
8   Insert the fork tools into the holes at each side of the face plate, release the radio and pull it straight out to remove it.
9   Installation is the reverse of removal. The fork tools aren't required for installation.

Later models

Refer to illustration 11.11

10   Open the glove box for access and remove the radio-to-mounting bracket attaching screw and the glove box retaining screw. Remove the glove box.
11   Working through the glove box, push the radio out of the dashboard and unplug the electrical connector and antenna lead **(see illustration)**. Remove the radio.
12   Installation is the reverse of removal.

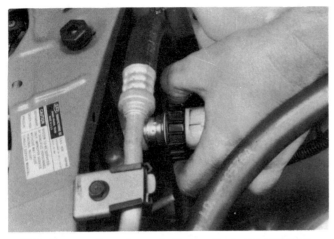

12.9   Unscrew the collar and withdraw the bulb holder from the housing

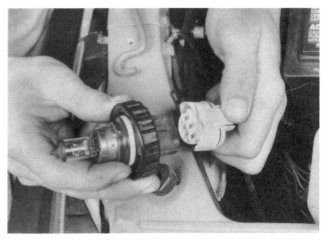

12.10   Hold the clip down and unplug the connector from the bulb holder

12   Headlights – removal and installation

1   Disconnect the negative cable from the battery

Sealed beam type

2   Remove the radiator grille (see Chapter 11).
3   Remove the headlight retainer screws, taking care not to disturb the adjustment screws.
4   Remove the retainer and pull the headlight out for access and unplug the connector.
5   Remove the headlight.
6   Plug in the connector securely, place headlight in position and install the retainer and screws. Tighten the screws securely.
7   Install the radiator grille.

Halogen bulb-type

Refer to illustrations 12.9 and 12.10.

Warning: *Halogen gas filled bulbs are under pressure and may shatter if the surface is scratched or the bulb is dropped. Wear eye protection and handle the bulbs carefully, grasping only the base whenever possible. Do not touch the surface of the bulb with your fingers because the oil from your skin could cause it to overheat and fail prematurely. If you do touch the bulb surface, clean it with rubbing alcohol.*

8   Open the hood.
9   Reach behind the headlight assembly, grasp the bulb holder and turn it counterclockwise to remove it. Lift the holder assembly out for access to the bulb **(see illustration)**.
10   Press the release clip in and pull the bulb assembly out of the connector **(see illustration)**.
11   Insert the new bulb into the holder and seat it in the holder.
12   Install the bulb holder in the headlight assembly.

13   Headlights – adjustment

Refer to illustration 13.6

Note: *It is important that the headlights be aimed correctly. If adjusted incorrectly they could blind the driver of an oncoming vehicle and cause a serious accident or seriously reduce your ability to see the road. The headlights should be checked for proper aim every 12 months and any time a new headlight is installed or front end body work is performed. It should be emphasized that the following procedure is only an interim step which will provide temporary adjustment until the headlights can be adjusted by a properly equipped shop.*

13.6   Use a phillips head screwdriver to turn the horizontal adjusting screw located on the side of the housing to aim the headlight

1   Headlights have two adjusting screws, one on the top controlling up and down movement and one on the side controlling left and right movement.
2   There are several methods of adjusting the headlights. The simplest method requires a blank wall 25 feet in front of the vehicle and a level floor.
3   Position masking tape vertically on the wall in reference to the vehicle centerline and the centerlines of both headlights.
4   Position a horizontal tape line in reference to the centerline of all the headlights. **Note:** *It may be easier to position the tape on the wall with the vehicle parked only a few inches away.*
5   Adjustment should be made with the vehicle sitting level, the gas tank half-full and no unusually heavy load in the vehicle.
6   Starting with the low beam adjustment, position the high intensity zone so it is two inches below the horizontal line and two inches to the right of the headlight vertical line. Adjustment is made by turning the bottom adjusting screw clockwise to raise the beam and counterclockwise to lower the beam. The adjusting screw on the side should be used in the same manner to move the beam left or right **(see illustration)**.
7   With the high beams on, the high intensity zone should be vertically centered with the exact center just below the horizontal line. **Note:** *It may not be possible to position the headlight aim exactly for both high and low beams. If a compromise must be made, keep in mind that the low beams are the most used and have the greatest effect on driver safety.*
8   Have the headlights adjusted by a dealer service department or other repair shop at the earliest opportunity.

12

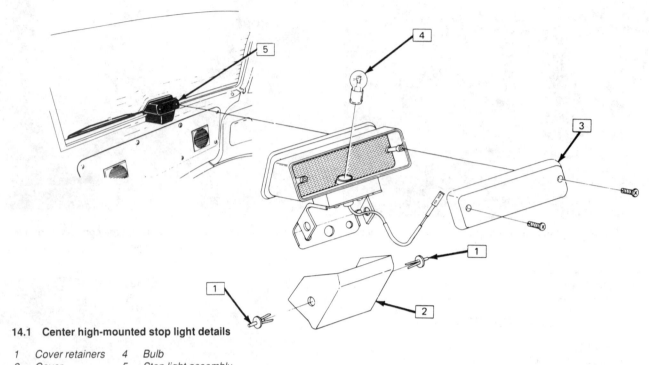

14.1   **Center high-mounted stop light details**

1	Cover retainers	4	Bulb
2	Cover	5	Stop light assembly
3	Lens		

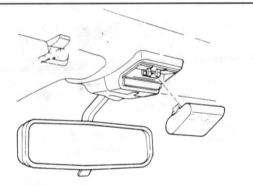

14.2   **The dome light bulb can be replaced after prying off the lens**

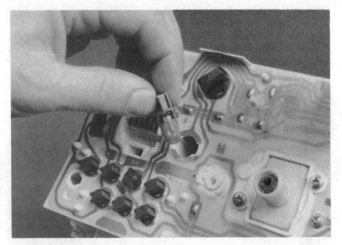

14.4   **After removing the instrument cluster, turn it over and replace the bulbs by rotating them and pulling them out**

14   Bulb replacement

Refer to illustrations 14.1, 14.2 and 14.4

1   The lenses of many lights are held in place by screws, which makes it a simple procedure to gain access to the bulbs **(see illustration)**.

2   On some lights the lenses are held in place by clips. The lenses can be removed either by unsnapping them or by using a small screwdriver to pry them off **(see illustration)**.

3   Several types of bulbs are used. Some, like the tail light bulbs, are removed by pushing in and turning them counterclockwise. Others can simply be unclipped from the terminals or pulled straight out of the socket.

4   To gain access to the instrument panel lights, the instrument cluster will have to be removed first **(see illustration)**.

15   Windshield wiper motor – check and replacement

Check

Refer to illustration 15.3

1   If the wiper motor does not run at all, first check the fuse block for a blown fuse (see Section 3).

2   Check the wiper/washer switch (see Section 8).

3   Unplug the connector from the motor and connect the battery positive terminal to the Blue (Bl) motor terminal and the battery negative terminal to the Black (B) motor terminal **(see illustration)**. The motor should run at slow speed. To check the high speed circuit, connect the positive battery lead to the motor's blue/red (Bl/R) terminal with the negative battery lead connected to the Black (B) terminal. The motor should now run at it's higher speed. If the motor fails either test, replace it.

Replacement

Refer to illustrations 15.5, 15.6 and 15.7

4   Disconnect the cable from the negative terminal of the battery.

5   Unplug the electrical connector, remove the mounting bolts and pull the motor and mount away from the firewall **(see illustration)**.

6   Remove the nut and disconnect the wiper linkage from the motor **(see illustration)**.

15.5 Unplug the wiper motor connector (A) and remove the mounting bolts (B)

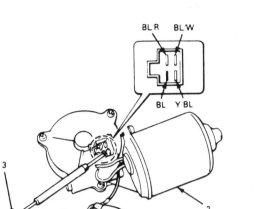

15.3 Windshield wiper motor test details

1	*Battery*	*3*	*Positive lead*
2	*Wiper motor*	*4*	*Negative lead*

15.7 Lift the wiper motor and mount off the firewall

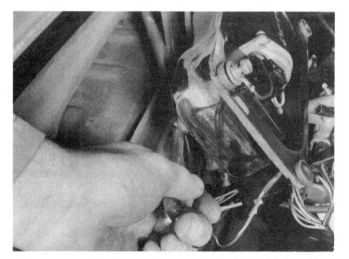

15.6 Reach behind the motor and use a wrench to remove the nut from the shaft, then detach the wiper linkage

7   Remove the wiper motor and mount as an assembly **(see illustration)**.
8   Installation is the reverse of removal.

---

16   Instrument cluster – removal and installation

Refer to illustrations 16.3, 16.5a and 16.5b
1   Detach the cable from the negative battery terminal.
2   Remove the cluster bezel (see Chapter 11).
3   Remove the instrument cluster screws **(see illustration)**.
4   Detach the speedometer cable from the transaxle and pull it up to provide enough slack for cluster removal.

16.3 Instrument cluster screw locations

12

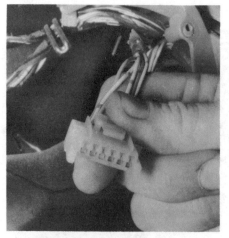

16.5a   Press the release clip before unplugging the electrical connector

16.5b   Press the speedometer cable clip in to release the cable from the cluster

17.2   Pull the speedometer cable out of the transaxle

17.3   Withdraw the drive cable from the speedometer cable housing

5   Pull the cluster out from the dash, unplug the electrical connectors **(see illustration)** and detach the speedometer cable **(see illustration)**.
6   Installation is the reverse of removal.

17   Speedometer cable replacement

Refer to illustrations 17.2 and 17.3
1   Disconnect the negative cable from the battery.
2   Disconnect the speedometer cable from the transaxle. On Sprint models, this is accomplished by removing a bolt in the transaxle and then withdrawing the cable end **(see illustration)**. On Geo Metro models, remove the bolt and detach the speedometer drive gear housing from the transaxle.
3   Pull the drive cable out of the speedometer cable housing **(see illustration)**. If you're also replacing the housing, disconnect the housing at the instrument cluster (see the previous Section).
4   Insert the new drive cable into the housing, making sure it seats securely in the instrument cluster, then connect the cable to the transaxle.

18   Cruise control system – description and check

The cruise control system maintains vehicle speed by means of a vacuum actuated servo motor located in the engine compartment which is connected to the throttle linkage by a cable. The system consists of the servo motor, clutch switch, stoplight switch, control switches, a relay and associated vacuum hoses.

Because of the complexity of the cruise control system and the special tools and techniques required for diagnosis and repair, this should be left to a dealer or properly equipped shop. However, it is possible for the home mechanic to make simple checks of the wiring and vacuum connections for minor faults which can be easily repaired. These include:

a) Inspecting the cruise control actuating switches and wiring for broken wires or loose connections.
b) Checking the cruise control fuse.
c) Checking the hoses in the engine compartment for tight connections, cracked hoses and obvious vacuum leaks. The cruise control system is operated by a vacuum so it is critical that all vacuum switches, hoses and connections be secure.

19   Wiring diagrams – general information

Refer to illustration 19.4
Since it isn't possible to include all wiring diagrams for every year covered by this manual, the following diagrams are those that are typical and most commonly needed.

Prior to troubleshooting any circuits, check the fuse and circuit breakers (if equipped) to make sure they are in good condition. Make sure the battery is properly charged and has clean, tight cable connections (see Chapter 1).

When checking the wiring system, make sure that all connectors are clean, with no broken or loose pins. When unplugging a connector, do not pull on the wires, only on the connector housings themselves.

Refer to the accompanying illustration for the wire color codes applicable to your vehicle.

B	=	Black	O	=	Orange
BR	=	Brown	P	=	Pink
G	=	Green	R	=	Red
GR	=	Gray	V	=	Violet
L	=	Light Blue	W	=	White
LG	=	Light Green	Y	=	Yellow

The first letter indicates the basic wire color
Second letter indicates the color of the stripe

19.4   Wiring diagram color codes

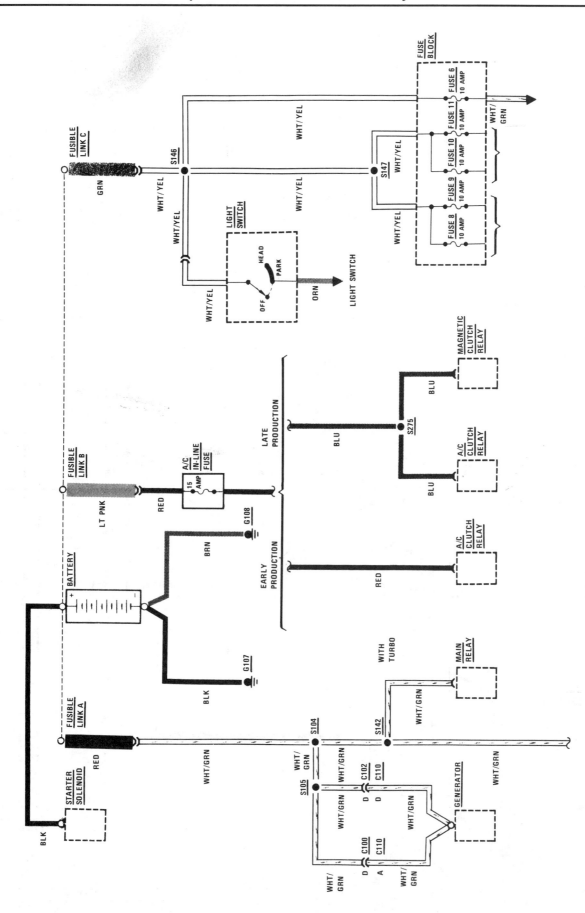

Power distribution circuits (Sprint) (1 of 2)

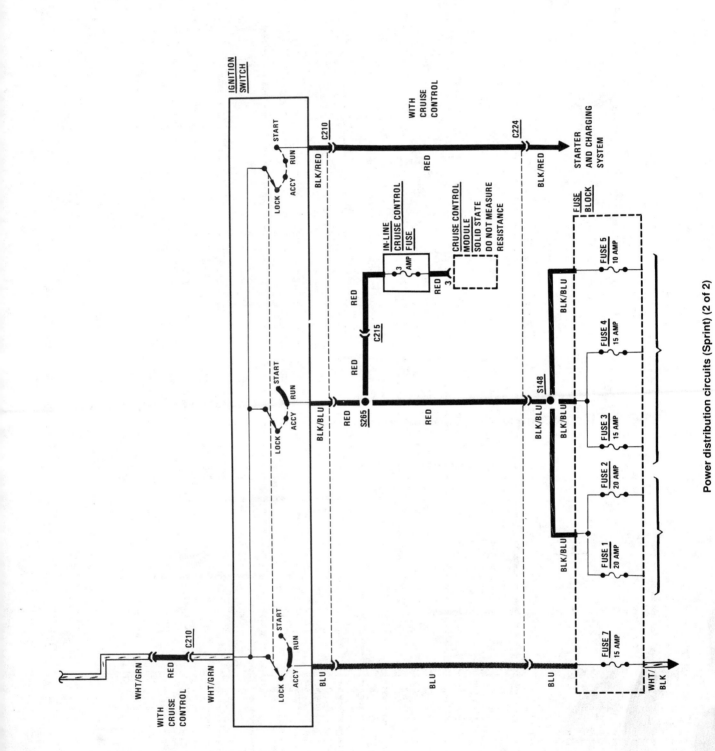

Power distribution circuits (Sprint) (2 of 2)

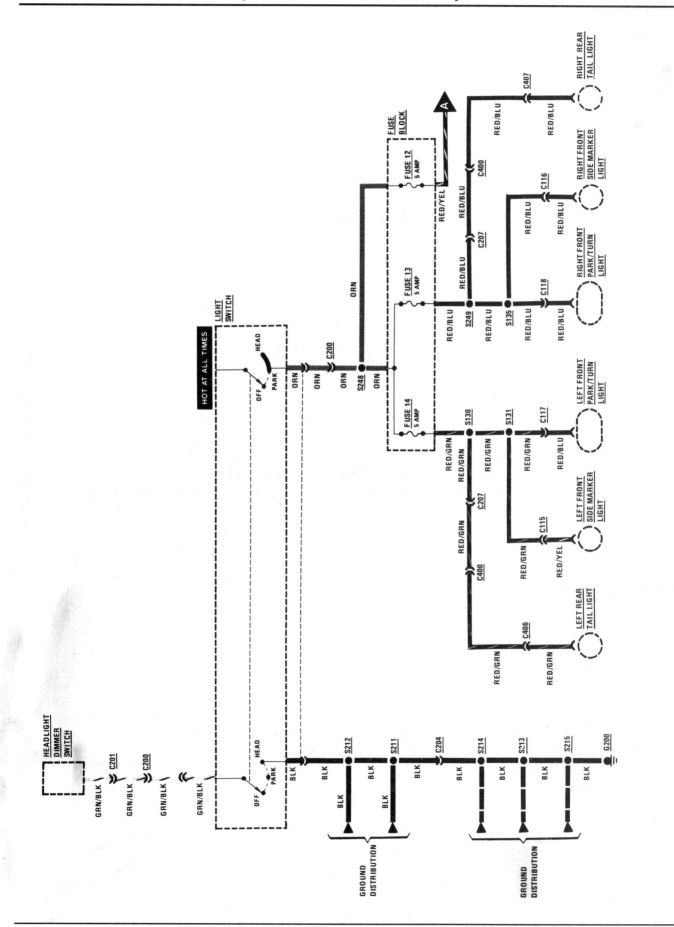

Light switch circuits (Sprint) (1 of 2)

12

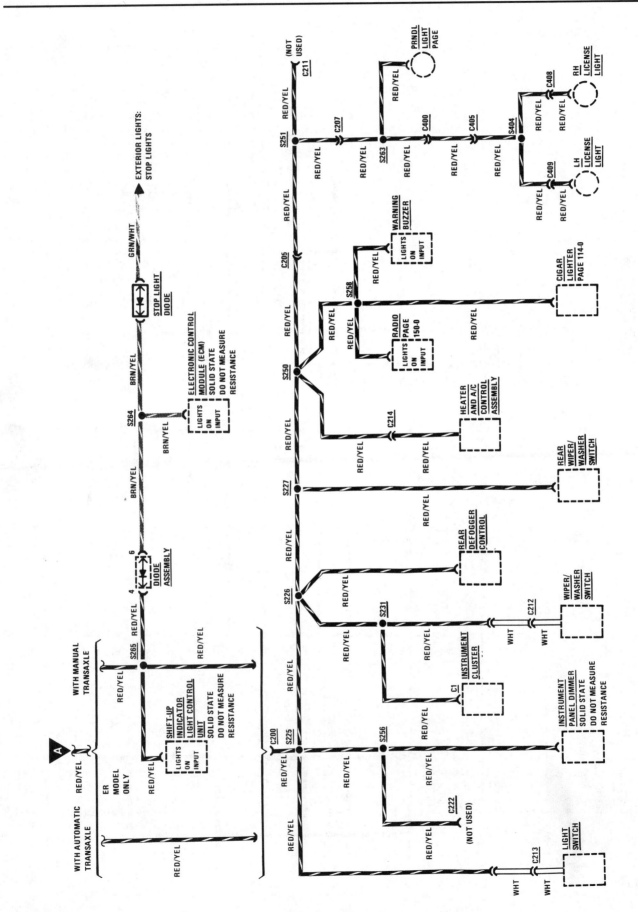

Light switch circuits (Sprint) (2 of 2)

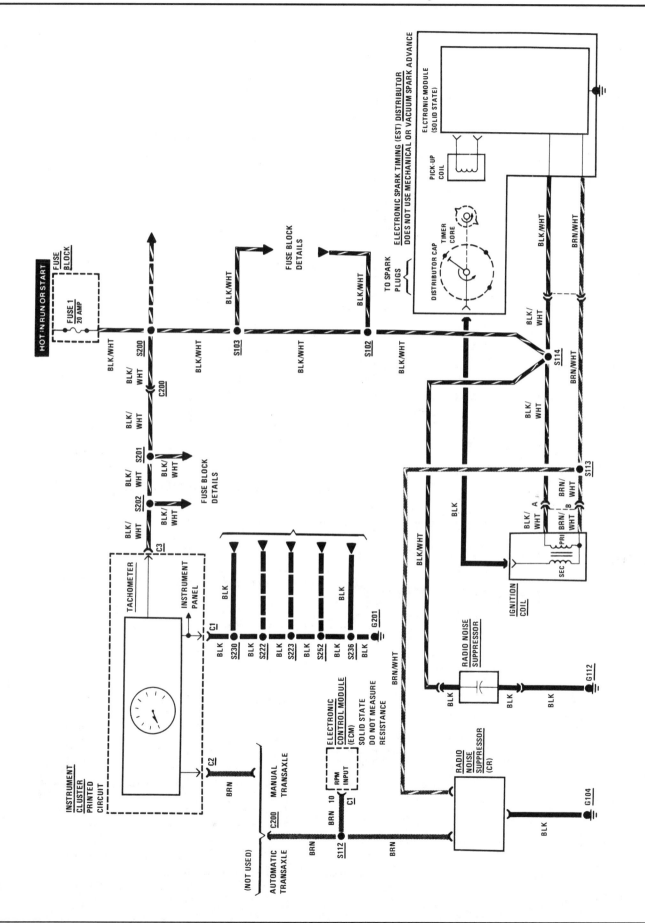

Ignition system circuits (Sprint)

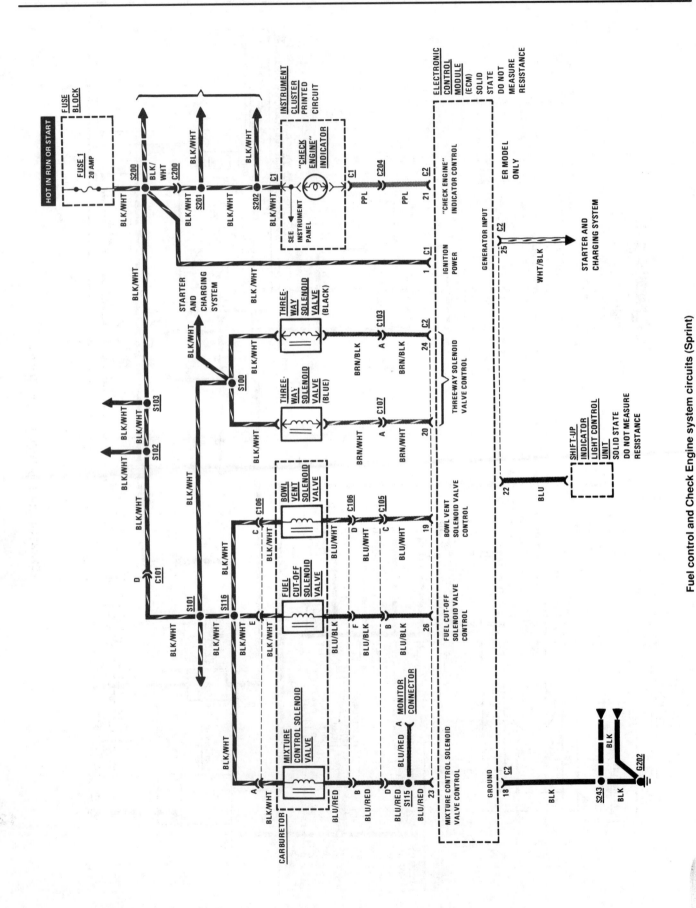

Fuel control and Check Engine system circuits (Sprint)

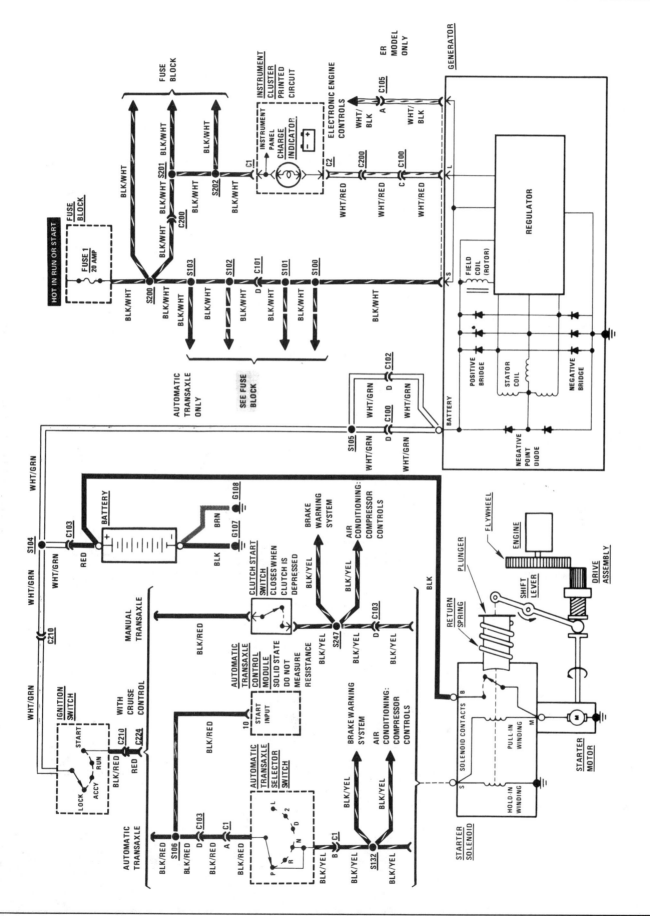

Starter and charging system circuits (Sprint)

12

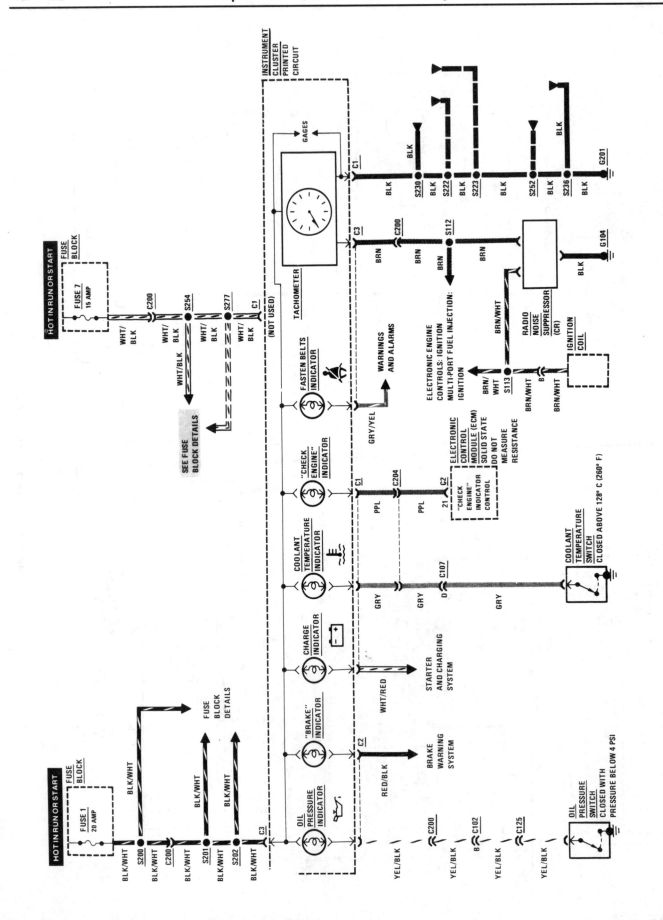

Instrument cluster circuits (Sprint)

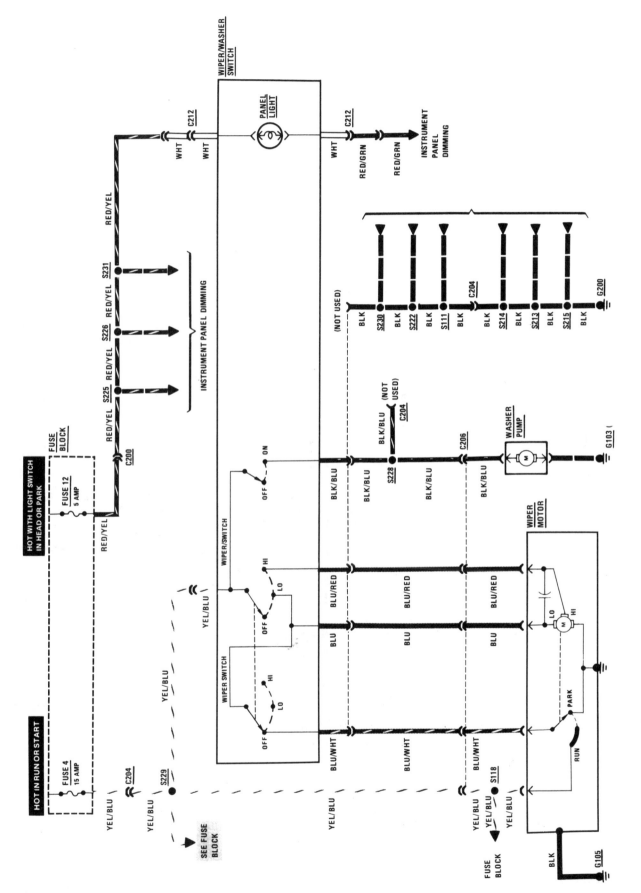

Wiper/washer circuits (Sprint)

12

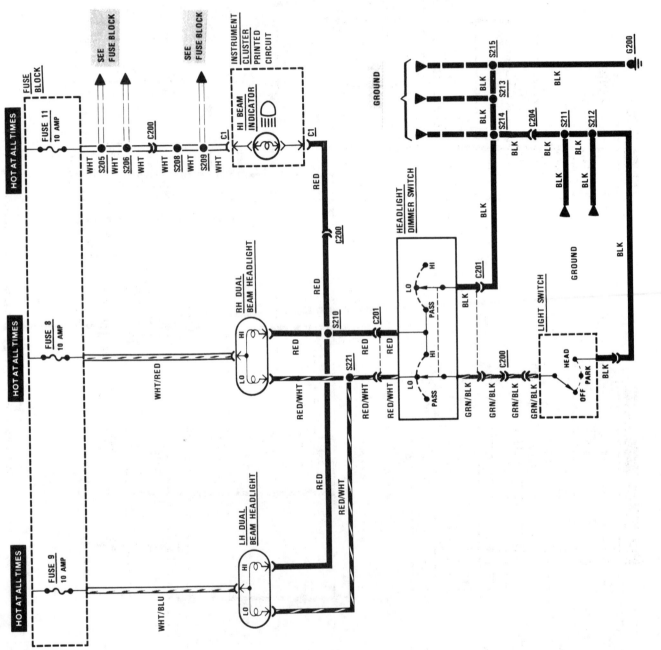

Headlight circuits (Sprint)

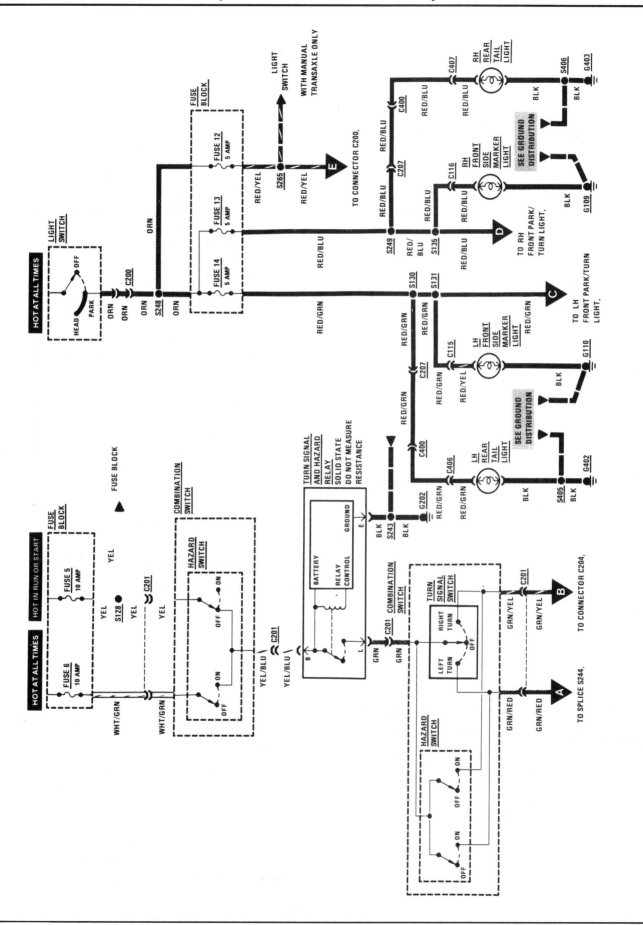

Turn/hazard/tail/marker and license light circuits (Sprint) (1 of 2)

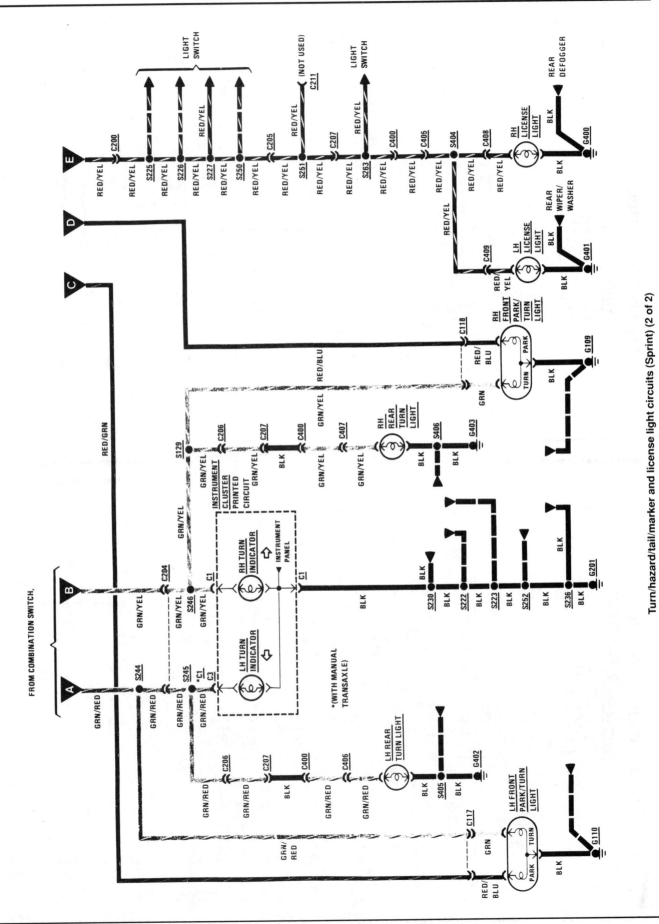

Turn/hazard/tail/marker and license light circuits (Sprint) (2 of 2)

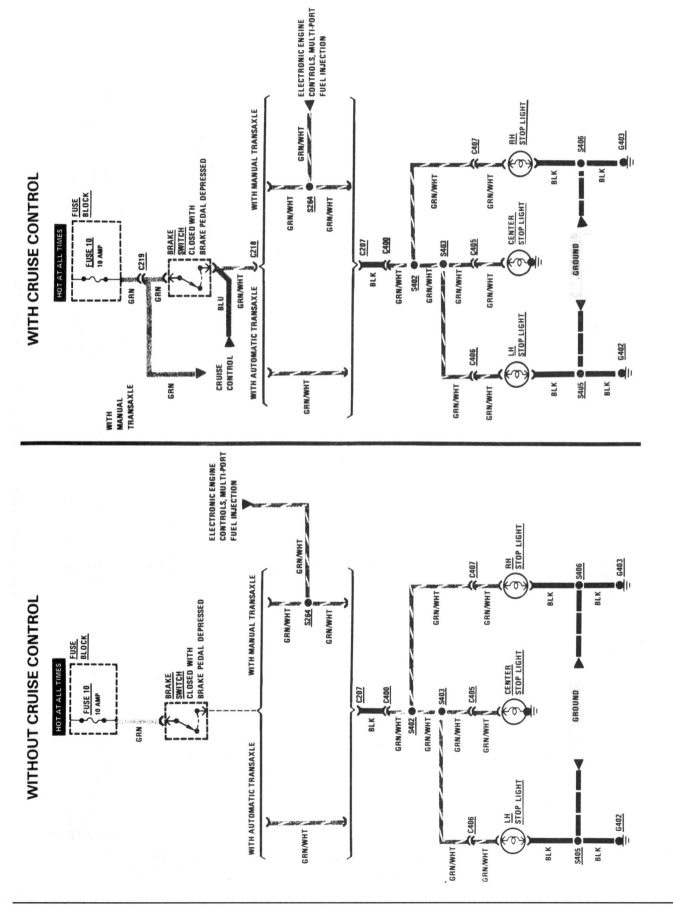

Stop light circuits (Sprint)

12

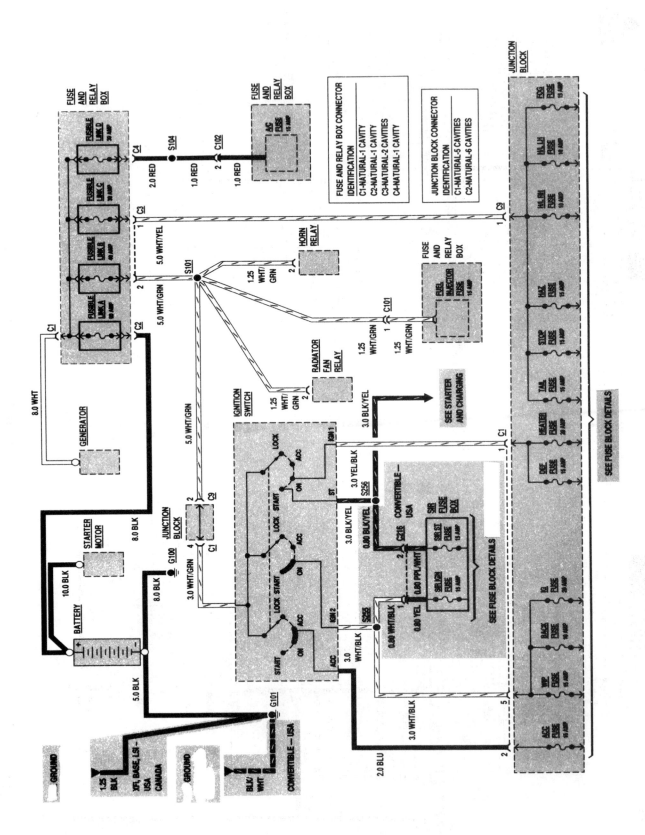

Power distribution circuits (Geo Metro)

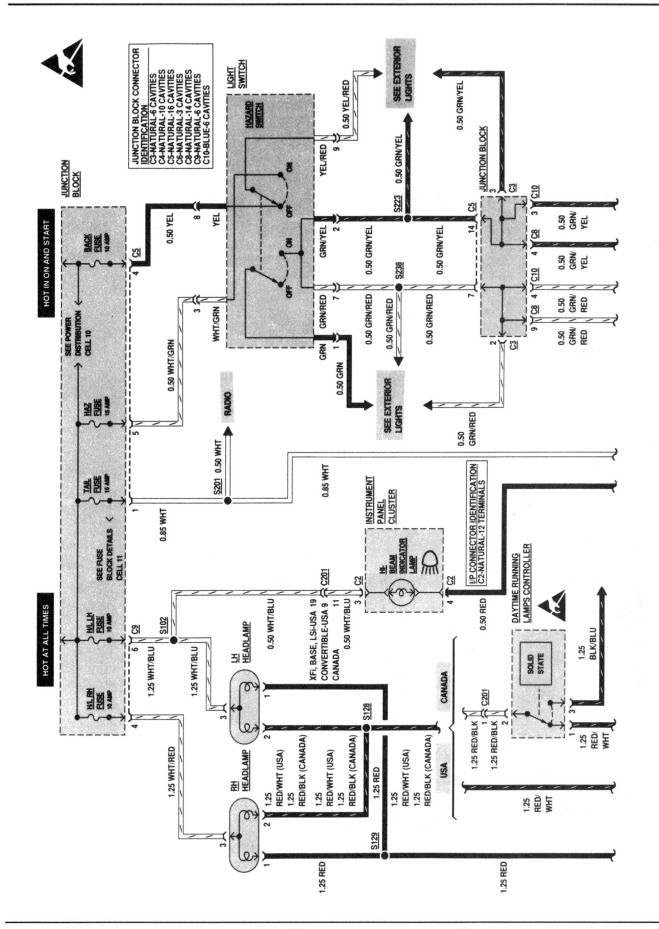

Light switch circuits (Geo Metro) (1 of 3)

12

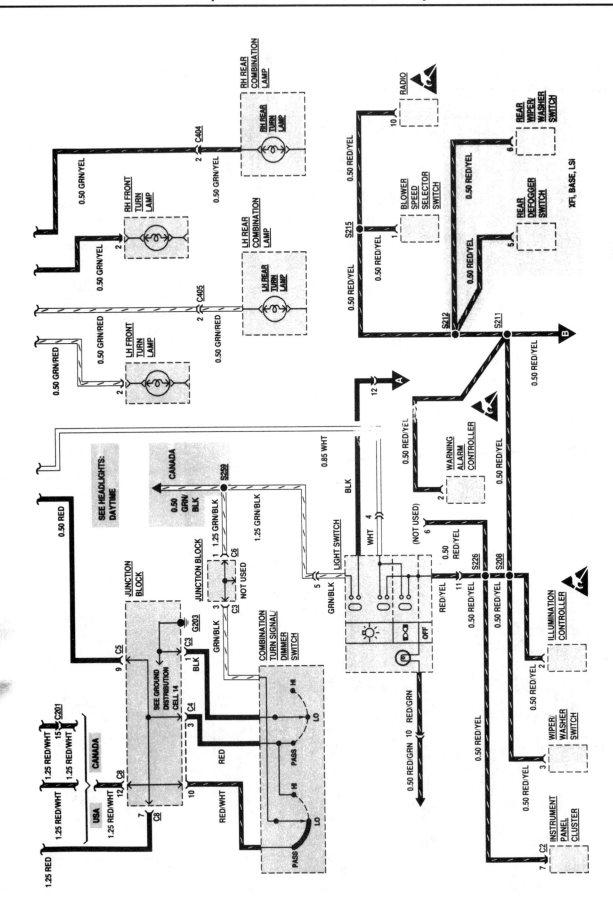

Light switch circuits (Geo Metro) (2 of 3)

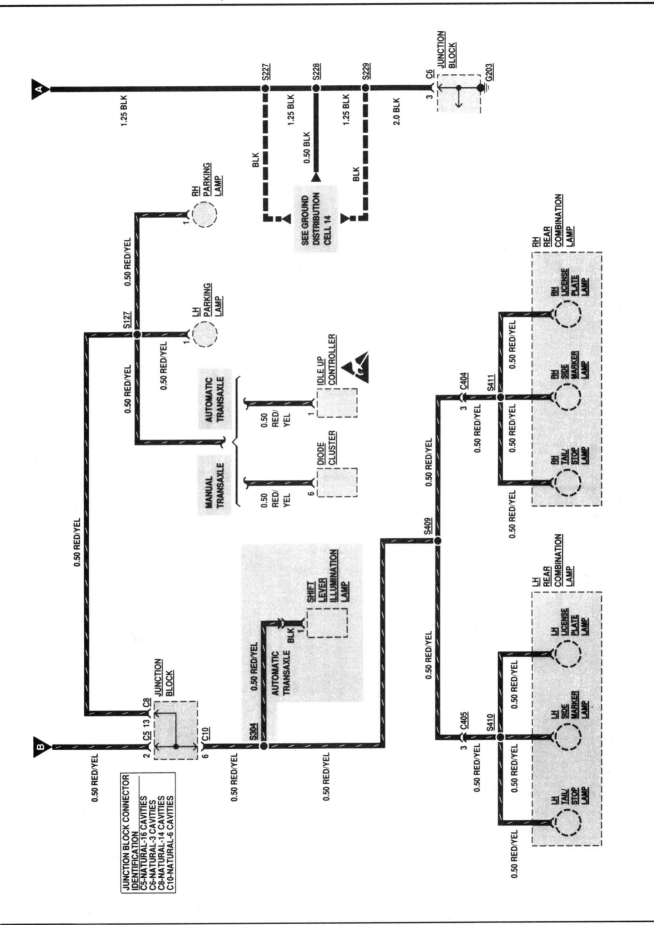

Light switch circuits (Geo Metro) (3 of 3)

12

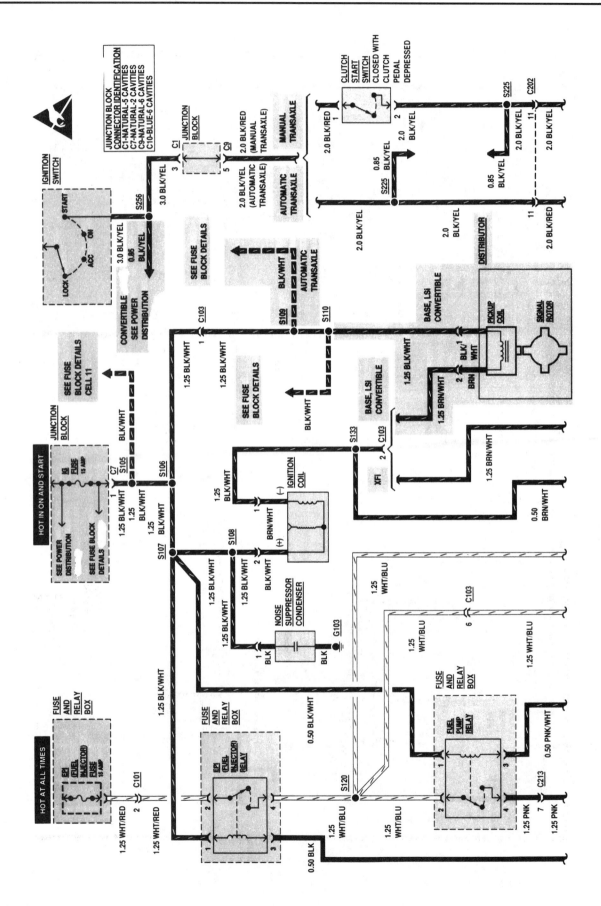

Fuel pump and ignition system circuits (Geo Metro)

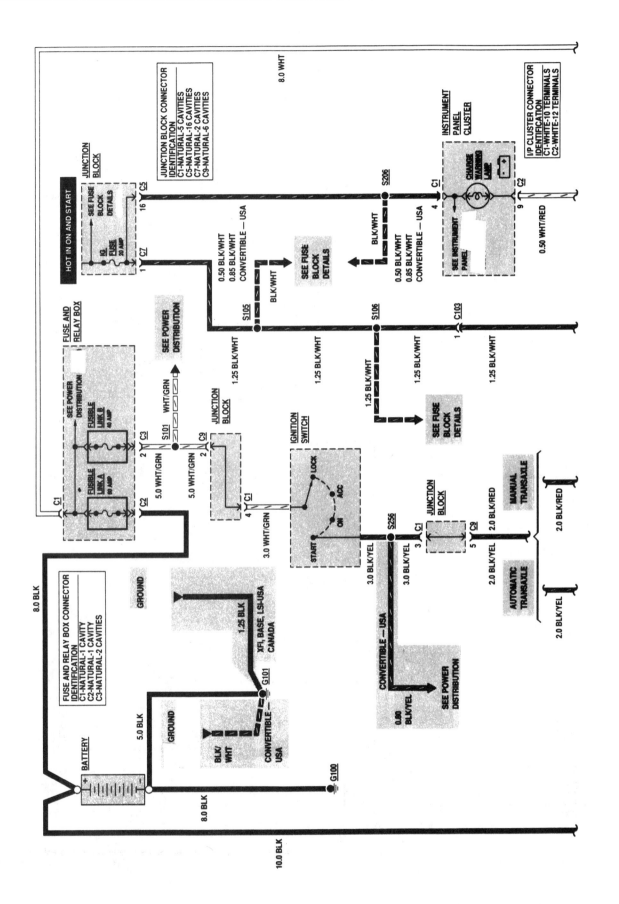

Starting and charging circuits wiring diagram (Geo Metro) (1 of 2)

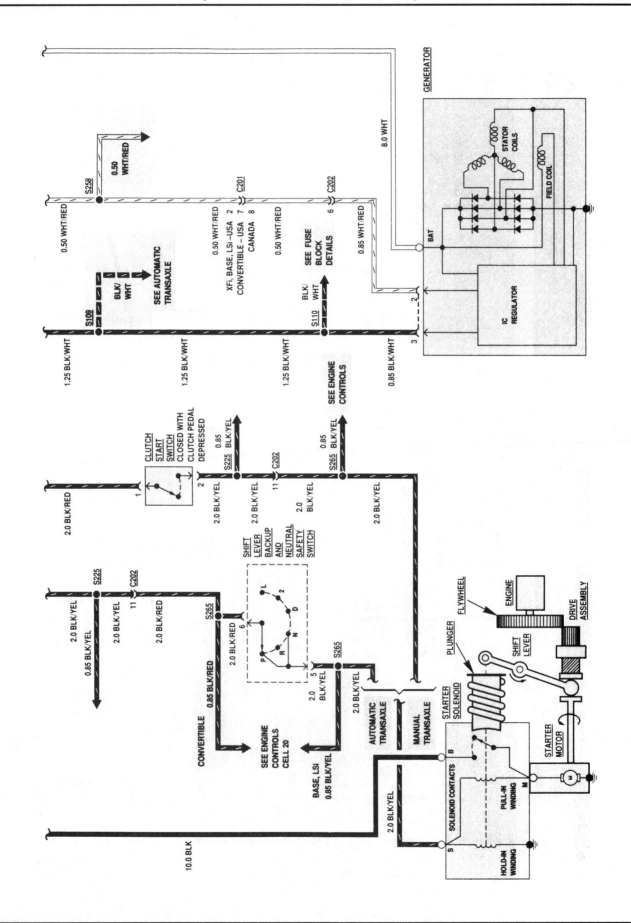

Starting and charging circuits wiring diagram (Geo Metro) (2 of 2)

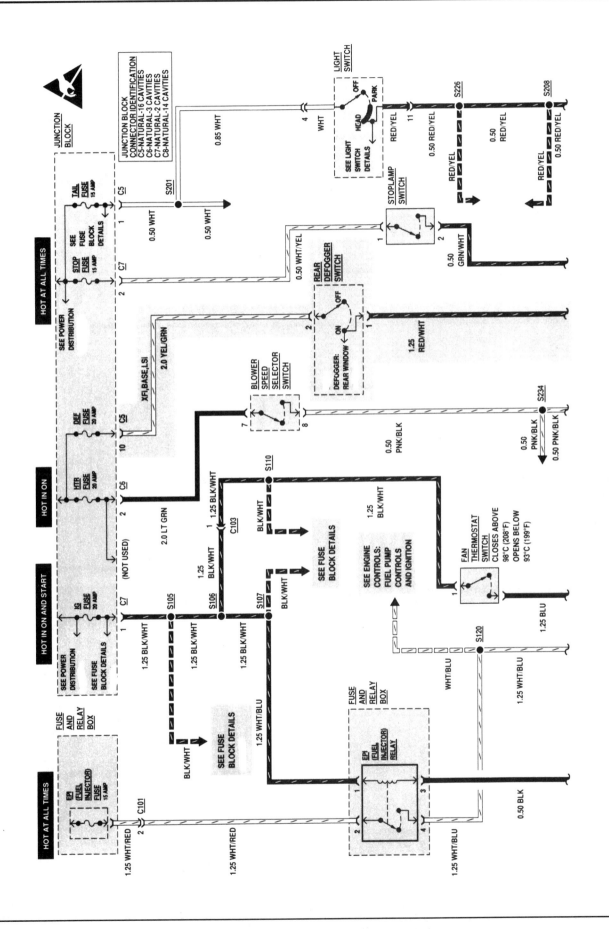

Engine idle speed control circuits (Geo Metro)

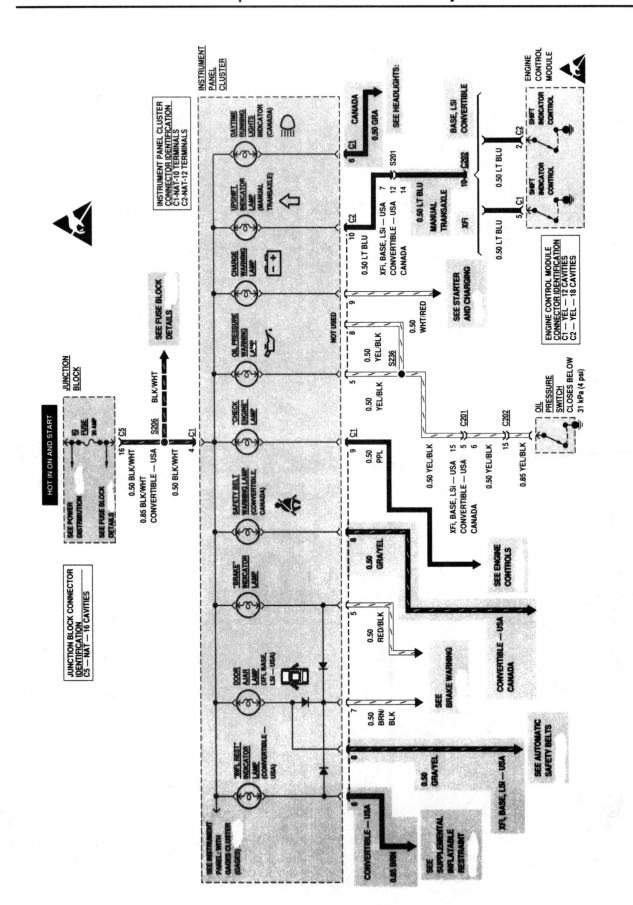

Instrument cluster circuits (Geo Metro)

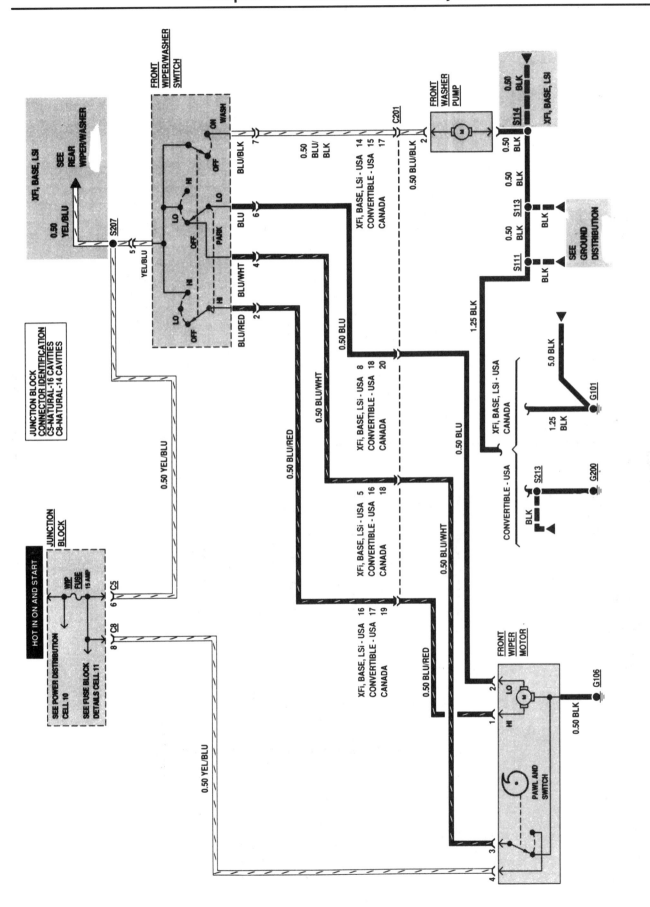

Wiper/washer circuits (Geo Metro)

12

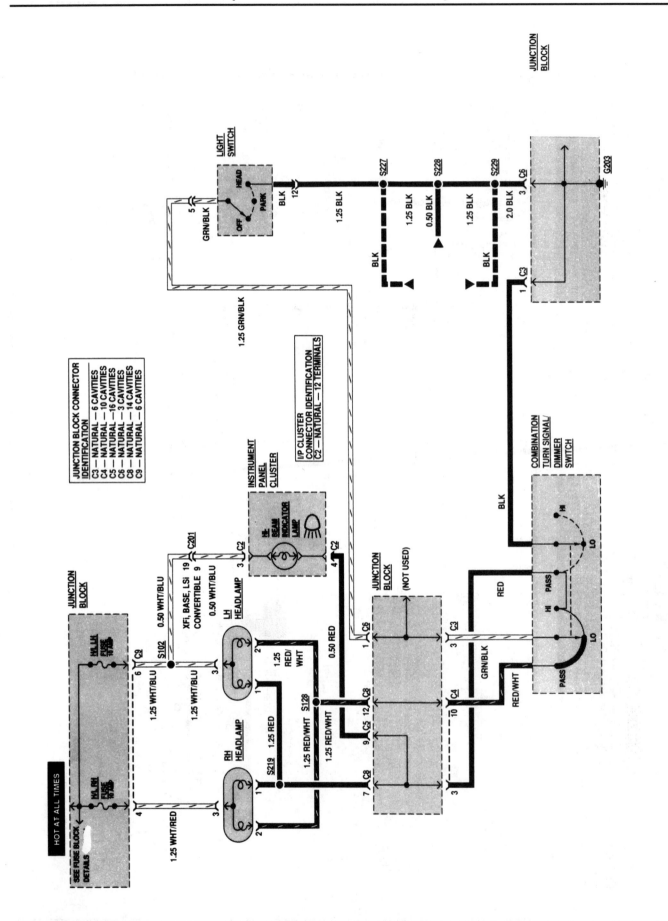

Headlight circuits (Geo Metro)

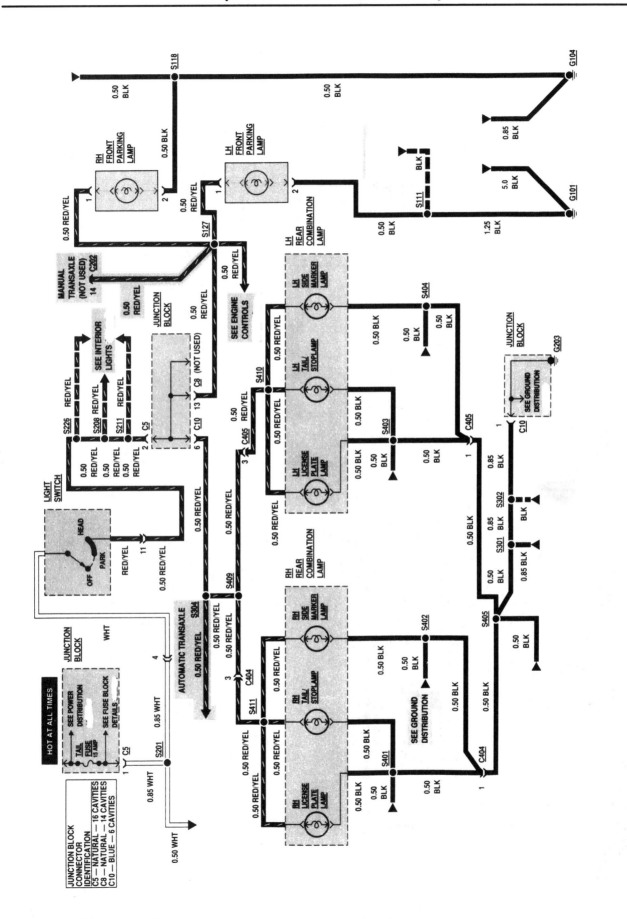

Park/turn/front marker/rear marker/license light circuits (Geo Metro)

12

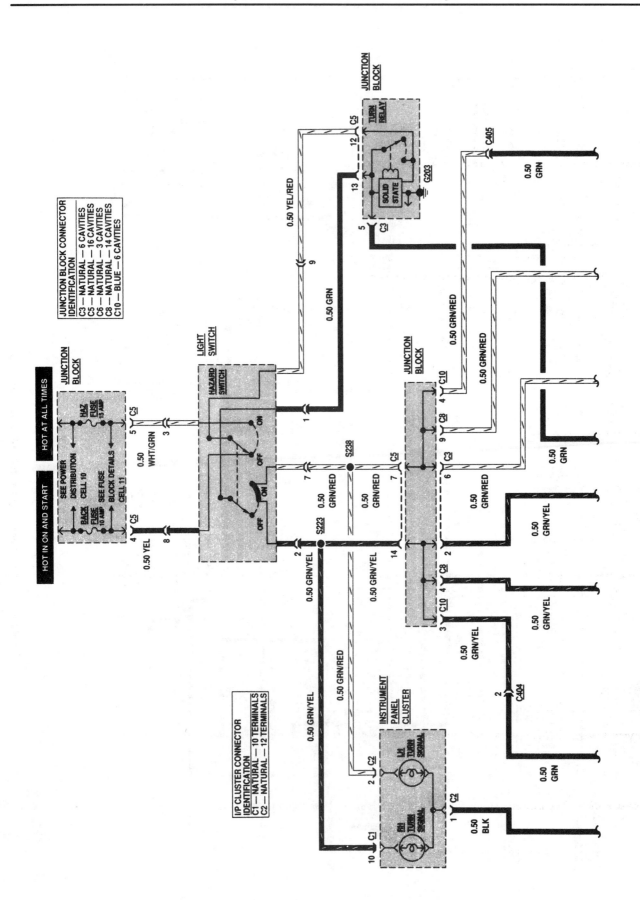

Turn/hazard light circuits (Geo Metro) (1 of 2)

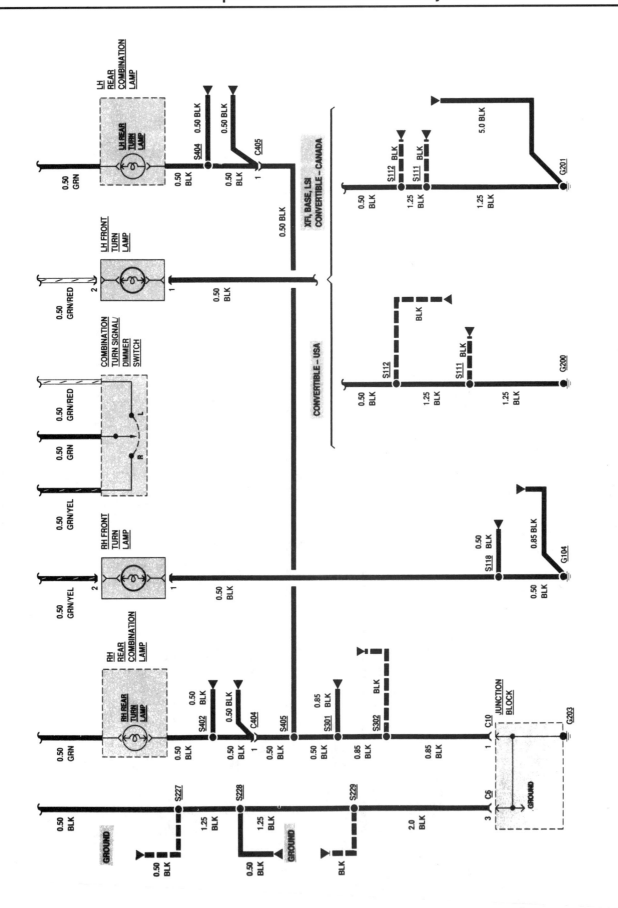

Turn/hazard light circuits (Geo Metro) (2 of 2)

12

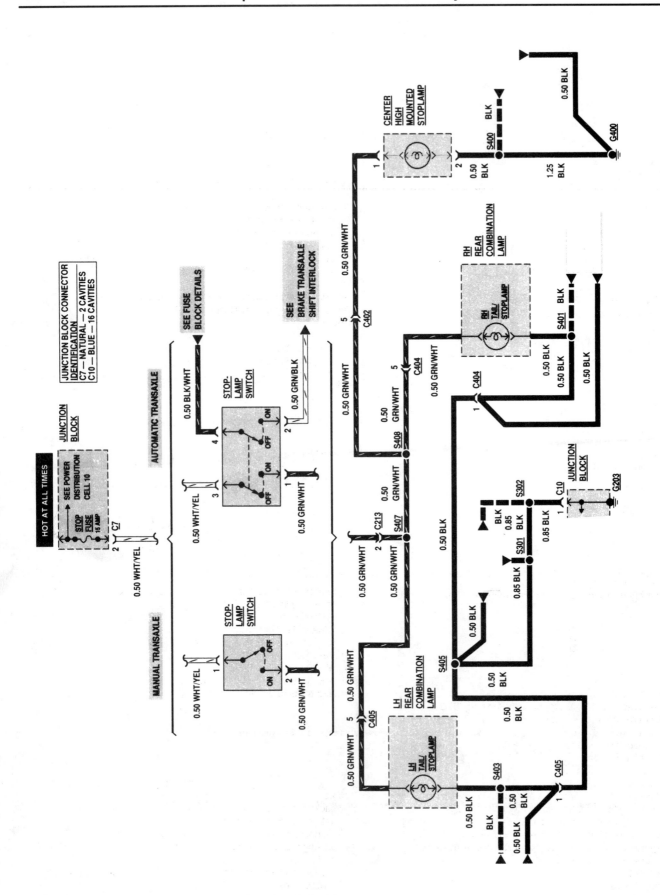

Stop light circuits (Geo Metro)

Index